LEARNING AND TEACHING COMMUNITY-BASED RESEARCH

Linking Pedagogy to Practice

Edited by Catherine Etmanski, Budd L. Hall, and Teresa Dawson

Community-based research, or CBR, is a mix of innovative, participatory approaches that put the community at the heart of the research process. *Learning and Teaching Community-Based Research* shows that CBR can also operate as a creative pedagogical practice, one that engages students, community members, and research experts alike.

This collection of original essays is an unmatched source of information on CBR theory and its use in a variety of university- and community-based educational settings. Based on research developed at the University of Victoria and its surrounding community, the volume includes numerous examples of Indigenous-led and Indigenous-focused approaches to CBR. *Learning and Teaching Community-Based Research* will be of interest to those involved in community outreach, experiential learning, and research in non-university settings, as well as those interested in the study of teaching and learning.

CATHERINE ETMANSKI is an assistant professor in the School of Leadership Studies and first-year program head for the Master of Arts in Leadership program at Royal Roads University.

BUDD L. HALL is co-chair of the UNESCO Chair in Community Based Research and Social Responsibility in Higher Education and a professor of community development in the School of Public Administration at the University of Victoria.

TERESA DAWSON is Director of the Learning and Teaching Centre and an assistant teaching professor in the Department of Geography at the University of Victoria.

Learning and Teaching Community-Based Research

Linking Pedagogy to Practice

EDITED BY CATHERINE ETMANSKI,
BUDD L. HALL, AND TERESA DAWSON

UNIVERSITY OF TORONTO PRESS
Toronto Buffalo London

ISBN 978-1-4426-4418-2 (cloth)
ISBN 978-1-4426-1257-0 (paper)

♾

Library and Archives Canada Cataloguing in Publication

Learning and teaching community-based research: linking pedagogy to practice/edited by Catherine Etmanski, Budd L. Hall, and Teresa Dawson.

Includes bibliographical references and index.
ISBN 978-1-4426-4418-2 (bound)   ISBN 978-1-4426-1257-0 (pbk.)

1. Research–Citizen participation.   2. Group work in research.   I. Hall, Budd L., editor of compilation   II. Etmanski, Catherine, 1976–, editor of compilation   III. Dawson, Teresa, 1965–, editor of compilation

Q180.55.C54L42 2014   001.4   C2013-907137-7

This book has been published with the help of a grant from the Canadian Federation for the Humanities and Social Sciences, through the Awards to Scholarly Publications Program, using funds provided by the Social Sciences and Humanities Research Council of Canada.

University of Toronto Press acknowledges the financial assistance to its publishing program of the Canada Council for the Arts and the Ontario Arts Council.

Canada Council
for the Arts

Conseil des Arts
du Canada

ONTARIO ARTS COUNCIL
CONSEIL DES ARTS DE L'ONTARIO
50 YEARS OF ONTARIO GOVERNMENT SUPPORT OF THE ARTS
50 ANS DE SOUTIEN DU GOUVERNEMENT DE L'ONTARIO AUX ARTS

University of Toronto Press acknowledges the financial support of the Government of Canada through the Canada Book Fund for its publishing activities.

*This book is dedicated to the people who sustain us:
our families and friends and members of many
different kinds of community around the globe.
We hope this book will be a useful resource
for the people who have taught us the lessons
we share here.*

Contents

Illustrations

Foreword

S. MARTIN TAYLOR

Soon after arriving at McMaster University in 1974 as a neophyte researcher and faculty member in the Department of Geography, I teamed up with one of my new colleagues to begin what became a decade of research on the community impacts of transportation noise. Our focus was on the effects of road traffic and aircraft noise on people living in residential neighbourhoods in southern Ontario located close to major highways and airports. In this context, the term community was used frequently in our research papers, but with little initial thought as to its significance beyond defining a population meeting certain spatial and noise exposure parameters for purposes of modelling the relationship between noise levels and annoyance, speech interference, sleep disturbance, and other measures of personal well-being (or lack thereof). As the work evolved, and as our results were increasingly drawn upon for residential planning and zoning purposes to delineate areas experiencing acceptable or unacceptable noise levels, it became clear that community characteristics and context mattered in ways that our simplistic spatial container approach made little allowance for.

My understanding of and appreciation for community in a more fulsome sense encompassing its socio-cultural, political-economic, and other dimensions was subsequently enlarged as my research program diversified engaging such issues as community-based mental health care, primary health care for maternal and child health, community-based health promotion, and the community impacts of noxious facilities, including waste-disposal sites and petrochemical refineries. While this list may leave the impression of a research dilettante, there is a coherent underlying theme which has the social geography of communities as a core element.

Moving away from autobiography to my discipline of Geography, I see my experience as a microcosm of what is central to geographical inquiry – the investigation of how complex interacting processes manifest themselves spatially in particular places defined at scales ranging from the neighbourhood to the global. In human geography, this translates to drawing on social theory and methodology to understand how social processes, broadly defined, interact with environmental factors to produce spatial dynamics and outcomes that are the warp and woof of our communities whether defined at the local, regional, or larger scales.

Geography of course by no means commands a monopoly on the study of communities; it is a research project shared with its sister social sciences and beyond. What is in common is the grounding of social process and events in places, and arguably the ground-truthing of abstract concepts and theories in the realities of the social geography (lower case) of everyday life. Implicit in this grounding is knowledge translation, the two-way exchange of ideas, information, and findings between the academy and practitioners, whether in government, the private sector, community agencies, or the public at large. Also implicit is the interdependence of research and learning and the ways in which community-based research can and should find expression in curricula. These implications for both knowledge translation and for the practice of teaching and learning are themes which loom large in this volume, and this is perhaps where its primary contribution lies.

The book chapters also point to a hallmark of community-based research – that its strength is its diversity but so too is perhaps its weakness. So varied are the preconceptions, predispositions, goals, and projects of its advocates and adopters that the ensuing landscape of the research may seem to some quite confused and confusing. Suffice to comment here that the tensions which still characterize the field, and are to some degree echoed in this volume, are largely healthy and indicative of vibrancy and bodies of theory and method which continue to evolve. Perhaps somewhat simplistically, and again reflective of my own experience, the history of community-based research shows that the preposition matters: while research practice still covers the spectrum from studies on, with, and for communities, the strength of evidence of our research is advanced by recognizing and incorporating the insights derived from the diverse perspectives signalled by the prepositional referents.

This volume is based on work conducted by faculty and students at the University of Victoria which naturally raises the question of why this has been a particularly fertile academy for community-based research (CBR). This is arguably ground for a CBR study in itself – what have been the factors and alignments conducive to the leadership position that UVic has shown? The introductory chapter explores some of the relevant history and the determinants and so repetition here is not required. Yet a few additional comments are warranted from my perspective as one who had the privilege of serving as UVic's Vice-President Research during a period (1998–2007) when the latent potential for CBR evolved into forms and fora that became more blatant.

It is presumptuous to claim leadership in the national academy in any area of research or education, but, while recognizing the risk, there was a long and strong history of community engagement in UVic's programs across a broad range of faculties and departments, which led to the formation of the Office of Community Based Research as a strategic and structural initiative in 2006. Prior validation of UVic's position nationally had come in 2005 when then SSHRC President, Marc Renaud, commended UVic on its proven CBR leadership in his keynote address at a Community Based Research Forum. The precursors of the Office, and its subsequent success in catalysing programs and projects, bear testimony to the vision and leadership of some early and then continuing champions, several of whom have been instrumental in fashioning this book. It is also important to recognize that the leadership and commitment were shared with partners and agencies beyond the campus, reinforcing a cardinal quality of CBR, that it is born and nurtured through relationships at the individual and organizational levels. UVic has been fortunate indeed to have had such a fertile and supportive receptor community in which to participate and contribute to mutually beneficial CBR initiatives. The interaction between "town" and "gown" in this regard has bred authenticity, trust, and shared learning which should be at the heart of CBR.

I want to turn now to the intrinsic benefits of promoting CBR approaches in the academy by again drawing principally on the UVic experience, although I believe these comments are generalizable well beyond our campus.

The first is profiling the university as an intellectual milieu which, far from being an ivory tower, is proactive in engaging issues of importance and relevance for the host city and region. This is not to suggest that the university depends on formalizing CBR per se to achieve this kind of engagement and knowledge translation. There have been and are a broad range of program initiatives and activities through which this can be accomplished and which encompass the full spectrum from science and engineering to fine arts. That said, CBR has particular strengths and advantages for addressing social issues and challenges in areas of community health, well-being, sustainability, and development, and these are well represented in the case examples in the following chapters.

Closely linked is the benefit of enriching the research and teaching programs of the university. Long gone is the naïve concept that knowledge translation from university research is a one-way channel from the experts to the receptors. In short, the university has much to gain from listening to community voices whether it be in the formulation of research questions, the engagement of relevant and responsible individuals and agencies in the research, or in the application of findings to inform policies, programs, and practices. Likewise, the two-way interaction is mutually advantageous in enriching the teaching curricula, where there are manifold opportunities, for example, in identifying case studies for problem-based learning, creating placements for co-op students, and, more generally, by grounding more abstract ideas and theories in real-world situations.

Another related benefit is fostering interdisciplinarity in research and teaching. For UVic, and most universities, this is now a proclaimed priority, recognizing the inherent complexity of most of the processes and events we investigate in our research and share with our students in our teaching. Here again, the case studies presented in this volume effectively demonstrate the strength of bringing together interdisciplinary teams of faculty, students, and research partners. Similarly, our students gain a much fuller appreciation of how the various disciplinary strands of their degree programs interconnect through exposure to CBR examples where disciplinary linkages are tangible.

Central to this book is the added benefit of CBR as a conduit for integrating research and teaching, which is enshrined as a priority of the UVic Strategic Plan, and is now echoed in the plans of most universities. Indeed, a strength and significant contribution of the book lies in its communication of examples of research-teaching integration and by so doing it provides models for how others might adapt their curricula to enrich learning outcomes. The concept of integration is a good one, and almost a truism for the academy, but the danger is that it can default to a taken-for-granted if not consciously built into the design of curricula and thereby implemented in explicit ways that enrich the teaching experience of the faculty and the learning experience of the students.

As an autobiographical aside, I would note that my personal route of entry to CBR as pedagogy came quite early in my career at McMaster University. The pathway was somewhat indirect, emanating from the opportunity in the early 1980s to participate as a preceptor in a population health course in the Faculty of Health Sciences. The course was required for all first year MD students as part of what was a very progressive (and at the time radical) medical program based on problem-based learning (PBL), in which understanding the social determinants of health was given significant prominence. As an immediate convert, I subsequently based my Geography of Health course on PBL and developed CBR modules as the problem case studies, which, drawing in part on my own research program, were as wide-ranging as explaining spatial variations in esophageal cancer in China and understanding community responses to noxious facilities in southern Ontario. The positive feedback from the students and their success in grasping quite complex epidemiological concepts and social processes strongly reinforced the value of the pedagogy. Moreover, it certainly required me as the instructor to be all the better prepared both in developing the modules and for engaging in the group problem-solving. As a result, I believe it was a rewarding and satisfying learning experience for all concerned, and one that continues to shape my approach to teaching today.

Community engagement takes particular form and force in relation to Indigenous research, a field in which UVic researchers have been very active given the importance of Indigenous peoples and communities in British Colombia. Moreover, the university has been proactive in supporting research and teaching initiatives designed to promote post-secondary educational opportunities for Indigenous students and, in parallel, to address social, cultural, and political-economic questions through its research programs. Several chapters in this volume echo this theme and effectively demonstrate ways of developing and implementing Indigenous-led or Indigenous-focused approaches to learning and teaching CBR.

Cultural distancing and the attendant challenges of conducting sensitive, appropriate, and meaningful research can also apply to studies undertaken in an international context where language and other divides often have to be addressed in defining, designing and conducting the research. Here again, CBR approaches can serve as routes of entry and engagement whereby purposeful studies can be completed and useful results shared and applied. This argument is reinforced by the fact that core elements of CBR, such as participatory research, have their roots in an international context, not least in the social movements of the developing world, including in South America, Africa, and India. This is again a theme recognized and reflected in the book chapters, and one that has served to connect UVic CBR researchers with their counterparts internationally, for example with the Society for Participatory Research (PRIA) in India.

Taken together, these benefits translate into a very substantial return on investment in CBR at UVic, and well beyond, as faculty and students connect and collaborate with their colleagues nationally and internationally, and at the same time build a network of powerful partnerships with community agencies and organizations. The net result is the advance of theory, method, knowledge, and application through CBR scholarship which enriches the research, inspires new teaching and learning opportunities, and enables evidence-based development of social policies, programs, and practices at all scales from the local to global. This is an ambitious project and one to which this book makes a very valuable contribution.

S. Martin Taylor
President and CEO Emeritus
Ocean Networks Canada
University of Victoria
Victoria, BC

Preface

This book took its editors by surprise. One day, the three of us (one from the Office of Community Based Research, one from the Learning and Teaching Centre, and one with a foot in both) mused that there was an extraordinary intersection occurring at the University of Victoria (UVic) around the teaching and learning of community-based research. "Maybe," we thought, "some colleagues would like to get together and share their experiences, brainstorm on challenges, and exchange ideas about learning and teaching community-based research?" We offered coffee, tea, and cookies, and a welcoming space in which to come together. What has happened since then surprised us. The voices that came together were so thoughtful, so powerful, so inspiring, so diverse that they simply could not stay hidden away in that room. We wondered if perhaps those who had been involved might like to bring their thoughts together in a book. And they did. After witnessing the dialogue, debate, and reflection on issues related to the learning, teaching, and practice of community-based research (CBR) throughout a lunchtime speaker series, we thought these conversations could contribute to a national dialogue on the topic. We are grateful that the University of Toronto Press agreed with us so the stories can come to you. We hope they will inspire and challenge you as they have us.

– The Editors

Acknowledgments

We acknowledge that we are visitors to the unceded territories of the Coast and Straits Salish peoples.

We would also like to recognize:

- The people in the Learning and Teaching Centre and the Office of Community Based Research at the University of Victoria, who created the space for us to come together.
- All the contributors, whose joyful and unyielding dedication to co-creating a more compassionate and just world inspired us throughout the writing of this book.
- The acquisition editors and staff at the University of Toronto Press, whose support for and commitment to this work help to ensure that communities become stronger through research.
- Marge Reitsma-Street, whose spark for teaching action-oriented approaches to research ignited mine. (CE)
- Paulo Freire (Brazil), Orlando Fals Borda (Columbia), and Phyllis Cunningham (USA) – very special teachers and friends, who are no longer with us, but to whom I owe so much. (BH)
- My parents, who were my first teachers and my son Julian, who will be a part of the future we hope for with these words. I wish for you a world that is more gentle and kind than it is today. (TD)

LEARNING AND TEACHING
COMMUNITY-BASED RESEARCH

Linking Pedagogy to Practice

Introduction

CATHERINE ETMANSKI, TERESA DAWSON,
AND BUDD L. HALL

As in many other parts of Canada and around the world, engaged scholars on Vancouver Island are endeavouring to address the seemingly intractable global challenges of our times. These challenges are related to
the rights of Indigenous peoples, sustainable community economic development, food and water security, poverty, health, housing, disability,
violence, addictions, aging, systemic racism, education, democratic participation, global citizenship, the impacts of climate change, and more.
The complexity and interconnectedness of these issues is demanding an
increasingly holistic, multisectoral, and multidisciplinary approach to
action, and, correspondingly, to scholarship. Although it is certainly not
a panacea, the methodology of community-based research (CBR) provides a feasible and long-standing framework for generating the kind
of boundary-crossing knowledge and community organizing strategies
necessary for addressing multifaceted issues in the real world. And as
the practice of CBR gains momentum, so too do strategies for teaching
CBR – in community settings and in institutions of higher learning.

This is not a book *just* about the practice of CBR, although of course it
is that too. What we are exploring here are the challenges that lie at the
intersection of teaching and learning community-based research. For,
while practising CBR itself has many challenges, teaching and learning
it are rich with even more complex dilemmas and opportunities. It is
this particular intersection that we wanted to explore and that we found
had not yet been treated in a substantial way. With this book we are
bridging the gap between teaching, learning, and practice as we explore
how researchers and practitioners engaged in CBR undertake the practical, theoretical, emotional, and spiritual guidance of new researchers –
how they and we engage the hands, heads, hearts, and spirits of learners

of all ages. In our effort to link pedagogy to practice, we propose that just as the *practice of CBR* advances respectful, ethically sound working relationships, the co-construction of new, useful knowledge, and socially just, action-oriented outcomes, so too does its *pedagogy*. What is more, the ethical challenges and dimensions of power encountered in research processes or community-university partnerships are often reflected in the microcosm of teaching and learning spaces, faculty meetings, project teams, and so on, turning each of these into sites in which to deepen the scholarship and practice of CBR. More generally, this book speaks to the mutually beneficial sharing, mentoring, knowledge co-creation, and expansion of ontological possibility that occur between and among community members, students, staff, and faculty in diverse educational settings.

This book has emerged from a 2-year lunchtime seminar series initiated by the three editors and supported by many of our colleagues. The first year of the series was entitled, "Challenges of Teaching Community-Based Research at the University of Victoria" and the second year, "Engaging Scholars: Best Practices in Community-Engaged Scholarship." The series showcased the scholarship of over 60 faculty members and graduate students across the full disciplinary range of the university: from better known CBR approaches in Education, Indigenous Governance, Health, Social Policy, and Social Work, to emergent, participatory, interdisciplinary, and community-oriented practices in Law, Business, and Engineering.

In this introductory chapter, we set the tone for the chapters that follow. We open by explaining the central conundrum we face as scholars, that is, the at times arbitrary divisions between learning, teaching, and research. We then provide an overview of what we really mean when we use the phrase "community-based research" and go into some depth about the traditions and approaches that inform this work. From there we present the context of an increasing emphasis on CBR in universities, including how these approaches help to fulfil universities' long-standing mandate of service to community, and the particular ways in which CBR has been emphasized at the University of Victoria.

Following a review of literature related to *teaching* CBR, we suggest the ways in which this book makes a unique contribution to the field: by privileging more emancipatory approaches to CBR, as well as non-dominant epistemological standpoints, by providing concrete examples of curriculum and pedagogy, and by demonstrating how this work is grounded in a sense of place. We wrap up this introduction with an overview of each of the chapters and some thoughts on the audiences for whom we hope this book will be useful. With the road ahead clearly described, let us now embark on the journey.

A Crucial and Holistic Intersection of Teaching and Research

Teaching and learning has historically had a narrow definition in institutions of higher education. There has been a clear direction and relation of power from teacher to learner. "Learning" has occurred in a confined environment usually assumed to be synonymous with "the classroom" (a concrete space inside a building, commonly with educational technology installed and positioned so as to assist in the conveyance of knowledge). Although there have been many years of attempts to change this model and some advances have undoubtedly been made, this is still a common experience for both "student" and "teacher," and at very least is the norm against which we measure change. By contrast, the act of teaching and learning community-based research offers us an opportunity to redefine what we mean by teaching and learning, to deconstruct false dichotomies, and to upend rigid power relations that constrain our possibilities for learning. One of the key aims of this work is to disturb current assumptions about what is meant by teaching and learning and, through this powerful intersection of scholarship and teaching, to show what might be possible.

There is, on one hand, no defining signature pedagogy for (methodology for the teaching of) community-based research. Rather, we hope the opposite: that the possibilities for teaching and learning are endless and emancipatory. On the other hand, some clear characteristics emerge as one reads. What stands out, perhaps, is the ability to start with the learners and to see and understand them in context. We see this repeatedly in the chapters as they unfold. In the following section we outline some of the traditions that inform this work.

What Do We Really Mean by Community-Based Research?

The names *community-based research* (CBR) and *community-based participatory research* (CBPR) are often used as catch-all or umbrella terms for various action-oriented and participatory approaches to research. *Community-led research* is another term often used by researchers not associated with universities, suggesting that the very idea of research being *based* in community is laden with university-centric assumptions. Specific labels notwithstanding, Strand, Marullo, Cutforth, Stoeker, and Donohue (2003) suggest that the history of community-based research draws from traditions ranging from popular education (e.g., Freire, 1970; Horton, 1989), to participatory research (PR) (e.g., Hall, 2005; 2001; Tandon, 2002), and to action research (AR) (e.g., Lewin, 1948; Reason & Bradbury, 2001; Stringer, 2007). CBR practitioners also draw from participatory action research (PAR), Indigenous research, feminist PAR, youth PAR, community-university partnerships, engaged scholarship, and more (see Table 1.1). The term *community-based participatory research* (CBPR) is predominantly, but not exclusively used in the health sector (see, e.g., the edited collection by Minkler & Wallerstein, 2003).

Although the traditions of PR and PAR are often associated with scholars in the Majority World (i.e., in the Global South; see, e.g., Fals Borda, 2001; Tandon; 2002) or with marginalized communities, AR is frequently associated with organizational change or action learning within organizations. AR is sometimes perceived as less overtly politicized than PR in that the action can take place no matter the nature of the organization. However, there is no agreement on one single usage of the term AR and it too is sometimes perceived as an umbrella term. Kinsler (2010), for example, subcategorized AR according to technical, practical, and emancipatory goals, while Chandler and Torbert (2003) generated a typology of "27 flavours" of AR. The AR manifesto advanced by the *Action Research Journal* offers a statement of what AR entails that has been endorsed by many key scholars in this field (see "Action Research: Transforming the Generation and Application of Knowledge," by Bradbury Huang et al., n.d.). Interested readers could see Brown and Tandon (1983) for further insight into the historical and ideological differences between AR and PR.

While the editors of this book draw primarily from the participatory research tradition, we suggest that the following concepts, approaches, terminology, and traditions contribute important dimensions to the overall practice of CBR. Moreover, we recognize that there is much overlap among some of the scholarly domains listed in the table below. At the risk of offending some readers with *either* our inclusiveness *or* our accidental omissions, we offer the list in Table 1.1 as a point of reference.

The list in Table I.1 is not meant to be exhaustive; rather, it is intended to give a general overview of the terrain we cover in the chapters that follow. Note that various approaches to applied research that may or

Table I.1 Terminology and Traditions Associated with CBR

Action learning (research)	Coghlan & Coughlan, 2010; Zuber-Skerritt, 2002
Action research	Lewin, 1948; Reason & Bradbury, 2001; Stringer, 2007
Arts-based research	Eisner, 1981, 1997; McNiff, 1998
Arts-informed research	Knowles & Cole, 2008
Community action research	Brown & Reitsma-Street, 2003; Reitsma-Street, 2002
Community-based participatory research	Israel, Schultz, Parker, Becker, Allen, & Guzman, 2003; Minkler & Wallerstein, 2003
Community empowerment research	Ristock & Pennell, 1996
Community service learning	Marullo, 1996; Mooney & Edwards, 2001; Strand, 2000
Community-university partnerships	Ball & Janyst, 2008; Jansson, Benoit, Casey, Phillips, & Burns, 2010
Collaborative inquiry	Bray, Lee, Smith, & Yorks, 2000
Co-operative inquiry	Heron, 1996
Decolonizing methodology	Tuhiwai Smith, 1999
Engaged scholarship	Fitzgerald, Burack, & Seifer, 2010
Feminist action research	Maguire, 2001
Feminist community research	Creese & Frisby, 2011
Indigenous methodology	Kovach, 2009
Knowledge democracy	Santos, 2012, 2007
Knowledge mobilization	Dobbins, Robeson, Ciliska, et al., 2009; Levin, 2008; Sá, Li, & Faubert, 2011
Knowledge translation	Banister, Leadbeater, & Marshall, 2010; Jansson, Benoit, Casey, Phillips, & Burns, 2010
Organizational action research	Burke, Lake, & Paine 2009; Coghlan & Brannick, 2010
Participatory action research	Fals Borda 2001; Fals Borda & Rahman, 1991; Kemmis & McTaggart, 2000; Selener, 1997
Participatory development	Campbell, 2002; Hayward, Simpson, & Wood, 2004; Kothari, 2001; Oakley, 1991
Participatory evaluation	Brunner & Guzman, 1989; Chambers, Wedel, & Rodwell, 1992; Jackson & Kassam, 1998; Wallerstein, 1999
Participatory research	Hall, 2005, 2001; Park, Brydon-Miller, Hall, & Jackson, 1993; Tandon, 2002
Participatory rural appraisal	Chambers, 1994; 1997; Chambers & Blackburn, 1996
Research as ceremony	Wilson, 2008
Scholarship of engagement	Boyer, 1990, 1996
Science shops	Living Knowledge: The International Science Shop Network, n.d.

may not have a social change agenda are often included under this umbrella, as are emerging systems and complexity approaches to social change, including Social Innovation Laboratories, Change Labs, and Design Labs (see Westley, Geobay, & Robinson, 2012, for example).[1]

Terminologies aside, suffice it to say that there are two defining characteristics of this body of research: it is action-oriented and it is participatory. An orientation to action means that the researchers, whether as members of the community or outsiders, commit to supporting the community in improving conditions in some way. What, exactly, constitutes meaningful action is an ongoing debate and will vary under different circumstances. Moreover, as discussed in the conclusion, the idea of community itself is a contested concept: communities are not homogenous entities where members always speak with unified voices. Rather, as some authors in this compilation suggest, relations of power within communities influence the process of teaching and ultimately practising CBR (see in particular, chapter 4, by Mukwa Musayett et al.). Nevertheless, this orientation to action is essential – however the community may be defined.

The notion of participation also tends to have specific connotations within these traditions (see Etmanski & Pant, 2007). Here, the word participatory means that the intended beneficiaries of the research (i.e., community members) have significant control over some if not all parts of the research process: from problem definition, to research design, data collection, representation, and dissemination of findings. Yet, even the idea of participation can be somewhat fluid: as Israel et al. (2003) suggested, not everyone can be involved in all parts of the research at all times.

Although the term *community-based research* is sometimes seen to encompass a broad range of activity, not all of this activity is explicitly aligned with and informed by the theory and practice of CBR. At times, practitioners who do not self-identify as community-based researchers are nevertheless included under the umbrella because they somehow "engage" members of the community, however meaningfully or superficially (see Arnstein's 1969 ladder of participation as a point of reference). As a result, some proponents of CBR take issue when the term is used to describe shorter-term, or more technical or transactional approaches to research. For such scholars, claiming that there is indeed something importantly different about the work they and we are doing is essential. This is especially so in an academic context where short-term projects tend to be celebrated and valued equally as CBR alongside, for example, 4-year projects where members of a research team have struggled together to overcome differences and create a meaningful, long-term relationships based on mutual accountability and trust. Indeed, a lifetime's commitment to one's community or to a program of research must be understood as a different kind of CBR than a short-term project.

Conversely, other scholars feel more comfortable having their work aligned with the term *engaged scholarship* rather than CBR. Often, the purpose of this alignment is to differentiate their work from approaches to research perceived as partisan or activist – approaches we celebrate in this collection while also recognizing that they continue to be misunderstood in the academy. Here we suggest that no research can be entirely neutral, because our values and biases are expressed in the very questions we choose to pursue and the resulting methodological approaches we choose to explore. Regardless, the scholarship of engagement (Boyer, 1990, 1996) informs much of the current momentum around CBR.

As editors we wondered about the implications of inclusivity for building a movement that promotes socio-economic and ecological justice through research. If our intention is to encourage greater understanding of the range of CBR practices, and foster a warmer climate for this kind of work inside the academy, then certainly there is merit in employing CBR as an inclusive umbrella term for all the approaches listed above. If, however, our intention is to refine the practice and scholarship of CBR, then setting higher standards of excellence for relationship-building or concrete social impact may become more important. Contributors to this book raised further questions around the kinds of CBR that *do* find fertile ground in the academy; namely, ones that do not destabilize the status quo too drastically, or that integrate better into pre-existing institutional structures, for example, time frames for courses or project funding.

We do not have concrete answers to these questions, but we have seen that no matter the theoretical positioning of the authors, or the context in which they carry out their work, each of the settings discussed in the following chapters provide insight into learning *about* CBR. In compiling this work, our intention was to not only document how activists, scholars, and practitioners are teaching hands-on skills and theories related to CBR, but also how they and we are teaching the values of participation, cooperation, and respectful relationships, as well as non-dominant ways of thinking, being, doing, and knowing. One course may not fully equip a person to undertake CBR, and a project or paper completed within a typical one-semester timeframe does not normally entail CBR; however, such learning experiences, whether in classrooms or communities, online or face-to-face, in internships, field schools, work-study placements, direct actions, or social movements can put learners on a trajectory for continuing to deepen their understanding of CBR.

The Emergence of CBR

Practitioners and scholars at the University of Victoria are, of course, not alone in the desire to promote and enhance engagement with community. We recognize that this kind of scholarship has deep roots in Canada and around the world. For example, in 1912, the Extension Unit of the University of Alberta was established with a mandate for outreach and engagement (Hall, 2009a). Father Jimmy Tomkins and his cousin Moses Coady created what became known as the Antigonish Movement during the 1930s and 1940s. This movement linked research, adult education, community economic development, and social action to support the economically depressed people living in Atlantic Canada's fishing communities (Welton, 2001). When the first participatory research group was established in Canada in the mid-1970s, most of the members were students in the Adult Education Department at the University of Toronto (Hall, 2005). Elsewhere, Hall (2005) has documented how the tradition of PR took shape around the world.

As the result of an extraordinary groundswell of this kind of work over the past three decades, universities have demonstrated an increasing interest in community-engaged scholarship (Boyer, 1990; 1996; Fitzgerald, Burack, & Seifer, 2010; Gibson, 2006; Hall, 2009a). Vogelgesang, Denson, and Jayakumar (2010) described how the 1999 US-based Kellogg Commission "challenged institutions to renew their commitment to address the pressing issues of the day" (p. 438). Sandmann, Thornton, and Jaeger (2009) suggested that universities' current turn toward community engagement is "a natural evolution of their traditional missions of service ... along with their commitments to the social contract between society and higher education" (p. 1). At the Univeristy of Victoria, we are deeply connected to these various historical and contemporary movements promoting community-university engagement. We also believe that we are living in a unique historical moment where there is a convergence of and synergy between community-oriented scholars at this university, scholars who see CBR not as research *on* community, but research *with* community.

CBR and the University of Victoria

The University of Victoria (UVic) has had a long history in CBR through a legacy of scholars working in Indigenous studies, health promotion, history, geography, policy studies, environmental studies, water quality studies, technology adaptation for people with disabilities, community law, adult education, and community development. In 2006, then President David Turpin, with support from Martin Taylor, the vice-president for research at that time, established UVic's Office of Community-Based Research (OCBR) to support students and faculty members who were already working in these ways, and those who would like to learn more. UVic was among the first universities in Canada to include specific references to CBR in its strategic plan (University of Victoria, 2007). In addition, in 2008, UVic was host to the third annual Community-University Expo, which brought over 600 community and university scholars from across Canada and elsewhere in the world to the campus. UVic is currently the institutional home of Community-Based Research Canada (CBRC), the Global Alliance for Community-Engaged Research (GACER), and one of the UNESCO co-chairs in Community-Based Research and Social Responsibility in Higher Education. At the time of writing, acitivities originally supported by the OCBR are now shared between the Research Partnerships and Knowledge Mobilization (RPKM) unit and a new, inter-faculty research centre, the Institute for Studies and Innovation in Community-University Engagement. All of these initiatives contribute to a thriving culture in support of CBR and related methodologies.

On the teaching and learning side, UVic's Learning and Teaching Centre (established in 1981) has had a long history of supporting under-recognized teachers, learners, and pedagogies. By focusing on scholarly approaches to teaching and learning, the Centre has resisted the dichotomy of teaching and research in very concrete ways. Recent developments have involved increasing the flexibility of competitive grants for the scholarship of teaching and learning to a broader range of scholars' needs. For example, feedback from Indigenous scholars suggested that the annual grant cycle was too short to allow for the kind of community engagement and mentoring of students that was required to achieve important teaching, learning, and research goals. Simple changes to the terms of the grants allowed for more realistic project implementation and stronger outcomes for all involved.

Through the drafting of Teaching Assessment Guidelines, the Centre has also been heavily involved in advocacy regarding the way that teaching is defined and assessed in teaching dossiers for promotion and tenure (see Mateer & Dawson, 2009). Initially, this advocacy involved carefully modelling what is possible within the confines of existing university structures. More recently, however, this has evolved into a conversation about how those structures might themselves bend to accommodate new ways of knowing – the ways of knowing outlined in the chapters of this book. We are fortunate to have worked with visionary leaders who have been prepared to listen to possibilities for valuing and rewarding innovative approaches to teaching and learning.

As a result of these efforts, at UVic we are beginning to see broader definitions of what teaching and learning mean: what kinds of teaching and learning scholarship "count" and – perhaps most importantly – given that the university is open to these broader definitions, how this assessment of teaching can be achieved in practice. In the university teaching guidelines, a table of illustrative activities for the teaching dossier clearly points to examples of teaching and learning community-based research. Activities like mentoring, for instance, are also illustrated, although we recognize that what mentoring might mean in a community context is very different from mentoring in a lecture class of 300 students. We still have a long way to go, but some inroads have been made and boundaries have been pushed in a visible way. (See chapter 14 by Antone and Dawson in this volume for more information on preparing and assessing teaching dossiers.)

As editors we also understand that not all CBR is conducted by academic scholars or even in association with universities and other institutions of higher learning. As one of us has explained elsewhere, "much of the energy and impulse for deepening the understanding of [participatory research] came from the social movement contexts in Latin America, Africa, Asia, the Caribbean and elsewhere" (Hall, 2005, p. 22). Action-oriented, community-centred, and participatory approaches to research have been characterized as natural ways that people organize and work together to solve pressing issues affecting their communities. Many practitioners would agree with Patricia Maguire's statement, "I am not a social scientist interested in more participatory research, but an educator and activist exploring alternative paradigm research as one tool in the multifaceted struggles for a more just, loving world" (cited in Reason & Bradbury, 2001, p. 1).

This book does not, nor does it intend to, represent the full range of activity undertaken by activist-scholar-practitioners in the Greater Victoria area, whether associated with UVic or otherwise. Nor does it solely focus on work that will be counted as CBR by institutions of higher education. Indeed, it is the courageous focus on what did not count, but arguably should have, that has led to so much positive change in what is even possible for activist scholars today. We are mindful that change is and should be possible in institutions that value learning and we hope that this book will act as a catalyst in this regard, allowing for the greater valuing of what we know is important work. In the meantime, for those already working in the field, this book features a range of concrete educational strategies put forward by people who may self-identify as educators and activists first, or as scientists, scholars, administrators, and learners in pursuit of "a more just, loving world" (Patricia Maguire, cited in Reason & Bradbury, 2001, p. 1).

The chapters in this compilation are all linked to UVic in some way, yet the contributors are nationally and globally connected and our professional affiliations have shifted over time. In the chapters that follow, some of us have featured work we completed elsewhere and some of us are connected to UVic through relationships with other members of our writing teams. We are each scholars, activists, administrators, facilitators, learners, and teachers in our own capacity, and we hope readers will find points of connection with the multiple positions from which we, the collection of authors, write.

Our Contribution to the Literature

While literature related to the *practice* of CBR abounds, literature documenting *how* the values, skills, and knowledges associated with CBR are communicated to and fostered among the next generation of researchers is harder to come by. Over the years, we have witnessed some of the most transformative work in the teaching and learning of CBR being done by Indigenous colleagues such as Eileen Antone (1997, 2000, 2003a). Many Indigenous scholars have challenged the traditional dichotomies of teaching and learning; teaching and research; teaching and scholarship; and learners and teachers. These colleagues have provided direction on where and how learning could happen (often not in the classroom) and invited us to learn, respectfully, from their traditions (see, e.g., Antone, 1997; Calliou, 1995; Graveline, 1998, 2002; Corbiere, 2000; Antone, Gamlin, & Provost-Turchetti, 2003).

The dominant teaching literature on CBR often reflects case studies of face-to-face or online courses or programs of study. To provide a few examples: Walsh, Rutherford, and Sears (2010) documented an undergraduate CBR course on poverty and homelessness with Social Work and Nursing students at the University of Calgary. Rosenthal et al. (2009) related experiences of implementing community-based participatory research (CBPR) curricula into the training of physician researchers in an effort to "improve health and reduce inequities through health service research" (p. 478), training that involved community members affected by those very inequities. Kur, DePorres, and Westrup (2008) told of their experience teaching action research in a graduate program in Organizational Development in Mexico, and how this process holds the possibility of becoming emancipatory for students. Finally, colleagues from the Action Research Center at the University of Cincinnati are, like us, in the process of documenting the various ways in which they are working to embed action research into their teaching, as well as their institutional and community change practices.

A few journals have published special editions on learning and teaching practices related to CBR. Levin and Martin (2007) made an important contribution through their special edition of the *Action Research Journal* on the topic of "Educating Action Researchers." Contributors to this edition took up some of the themes we continue to grapple with today, such as the need to transform institutions of higher education themselves to create more hospitable conditions for CBR (Barazangi, 2006; Greenwood, 2007) and the importance of integrating systemic reflection into the learning process (Etmanski & Pant, 2007; Grant, 2007; Peters & Gray, 2007). Several case studies of courses and programs from around the world were included in this compilation as well.

A separate compilation, published in the *Journal of Geography in Higher Education*, likewise grappled with the issue of linking PAR with university teaching. One of the contributors (Pain, 2009) suggested that this reflects a "recent resurgence of activism and participatory modes of research engagement in human geography" (p. 82) or what Kindon and Elwood (2009) referred to as a "participatory turn" in geography. In their introduction to this geography symposium, Kindon and Elwood provided a useful, although not intended to be exhaustive, list of ideal soft skills for learning and teaching PAR. These are (p. 25):

- Facilitation – concepts and practice/methods, group dynamics, facilitation techniques
- Interactive training/teaching – concepts and methods/techniques
- Interdisciplinarity – a conceptual and team perspective
- Lateral and systems thinking – with a view to changing perspectives
- Management of change – processes, leadership, roles, and functions
- Organizational development
- Process management, planning, and quality assurance
- Knowledge management – concepts and practice
- Solution-oriented and appreciative approaches and models – theory and practice
- Facilitation of learning processes among multiple stakeholders and groups
- "Emotional intelligence" in personal development – self-awareness, empathy, critical self-reflection, and social skills
- Process consultation and coaching skills
- Team skills, team management, team building, feedback culture, learning culture
- Negotiation and conflict management – concepts and practice/skills
- Self-soothing and self-care skills, and
- Creative skills – drama, storytelling, art, music, digital design.

Kindon and Elwood further suggested that teaching such skills requires innovations in assessment practices, as well as modelling appropriate strategies for mitigating equity issues and power dynamics in research and teaching contexts.

Strand's (2000) work supported this conversation by drawing attention to how teaching CBR, particularly community service learning approaches to CBR, promotes more effective teaching in the classroom. She suggested that not only can students learn particular skill-sets, methods, and strategies as suggested above, but they can also grapple with epistemological issues in methodology. For example, including CBR in traditional research methods courses can help students to better understand contemporary debates stemming from diverse research paradigms (constructivist, critical, and so on; see, e.g., Creswell & Miller, 2000, or Lincoln, Lynham, & Guba, 2011) and begin to question their "fundamental assumptions about knowledge production in the social sciences" (Strand, 2000, p. 87). She also emphasized the importance of the opportunities for connected and experiential knowing that teaching

CBR provides, in that learners can begin to understand the challenges of applying theory in action and learn how to work collaboratively to problem-solve in real-life contexts.

In a later publication, Strand, Marullo, Cutforth, Stoecker, and Donohue (2003) went on to propose

> Another and related appeal of CBR is that its core features – collaboration, democratization of knowledge, and a social change/social justice agenda – dovetail well with the goals of what is often called "critical pedagogy." Varieties of critical pedagogy, including feminist pedagogy, have made their way into classes at every educational level and inspire the work of teachers committed to teaching and learning in ways that fundamentally challenge and transform – rather than reproduce and legitimate – existing social arrangements, including what are considered some of conventional education's most oppressive features. (p. 11)

This is achieved, they argued, through (1) increased focus on collaboration and less emphasis on hierarchy and the authority of teachers or other so-called experts; (2) validation of experience as a source of knowledge, thereby deconstructing the belief that knowledge is neutral and objective; and (3) social change as a primary focus in teaching.

Our book picks up at this pivotal crossing of epistemology, critical pedagogy, and methodology. While we have built on the contributions above, we believe this work is unique in four important ways. First, we are deliberate and unapologetic in privileging the more emancipatory approaches to teaching and research (see Kinsler, 2010). The majority of the contributors to this volume are working for social change and community renewal, both inside the university and out, and this is evident in their pedagogical approaches.

Linked to this focus on emancipatory CBR, the second key area where this book makes a contribution is in our intentional effort to bring to the forefront ways of knowing and being that are not conventionally understood as science. Santos (2007) drew a clear link between social injustice and epistemological injustice. That is, the dominance of positivist research paradigms that emphasize Western notions of logic and reason leaves little room for other, or othered, ways of knowing that are equally valid, equally rigorous, equally rich in their contributions to knowledge, and equally alive despite their ongoing marginalization. Proponents of CBR and its methodological cousins have slowly been carving out a space in the academy, and in so doing, many of these same scholars are simultaneously endeavouring to break the epistemological dominance and "monopoly" that universities hold over processes of knowledge production (Hall, 2005, 2001, 1992). In highlighting the ways in which Indigenous knowledges, arts-based knowledges, interdisciplinary knowledges, and knowledges grounded in social action are taught and learned, through the writing of this book we are venturing to move a few steps closer to cognitive justice within the academy.

Third, we specifically asked our authors to contribute concrete curricular or pedagogical examples as part of their reflections. Because many of these strategies diverge from typical classroom activities, we found that providing examples from the teaching and learning context was more powerful than almost any other approach in illustrating the scholarship of learning, teaching, and practising CBR. Without such concrete examples, we have found there can be a tendency to "talk past one another" as though we were speaking different languages, which we wanted to avoid. In sharing these examples, we hope to build more understanding of CBR scholarship in the academy and to invite colleagues who have not experienced these ways of learning, teaching, and researching to engage in the critical intersections explored here.

Fourth, and finally, this work is grounded in a sense of place. According to local Songhees resident Cheryl Bryce, UVic is geographically located on the land of the Chekonen (Lekwungen) family group and it was commonly known as Sungayka (snow patches). Turner, Bryce, and Beckwith (2002) reported that this permanent winter village existed, "until the establishment of Fort Victoria by the Hudson's Bay Company in 1843" (para. 2). We recognize that this book is grounded in a particular time and a particular place, and that our work has been deeply influenced by local peoples, local protocols, and the surrounding natural landscape – including our position on an island on the Western-most coast of what is now called Canada. This influence is particularly evidenced in contributions to this book on Indigenous-led or Indigenous-focused approaches to learning and teaching CBR (see, in particular, chapters 1, 4, 8, 10, 11, and 14).

Although the writing teams do not consist exclusively of UVic scholars, each writing team is linked to this institution in some way. In documenting the local, our desire is for readers to take what is useful from our experiences and selectively adapt and apply these lessons in their own contexts. As we have already described, we know that the scholarship of CBR is not unique to UVic, although readers may find that that we approach it in a way that is unique to this context. Just as Kur,

DePorres, and Westrup (2008) explained, in terms of teaching action research, "rather than decontextualization, as can occur in widely generalized research, faculty explain that the particular context the student finds himself or herself in is actually celebrated as the vessel wherein knowledge is formed" (p. 329). In this sense, this book is not prescriptive; it is not a "How-To manual" for teaching CBR. Rather, it is a descriptive account and a celebration of some of the work we have collectively accomplished in the particular institutional "vessel" in which our knowledge has been formed.

Having provided the background context and literature that frames the accounts of teaching CBR you will find throughout this book, we turn now to an overview of the specific content.

Overview of the Chapters

We asked contributors to identify the epistemological sites they have encountered, the sites where knowledge around CBR is co-constructed. The short answer was that the learning and teaching of CBR occurs everywhere – at all levels of the university, in classrooms and communities, among different members of communities in face-to-face trainings and online settings. Administrators learn better ways to support community-campus collaborations, just as community members learn the particular rituals associated with academe and better ways to partner with academics. This book is organized around those various epistemological sites.

Part I focuses on learning by doing: how various people learn CBR in the process of practising CBR. The opening chapter by Jessica Ball outlines many of the challenges facing faculty, community collaborators, and graduate student researchers as they endeavour to work together in the context of university-community partnerships. She also discusses how memoranda of understanding agreed on at the outset can help to mitigate some of those challenges. The subsequent two chapters, written by former and current graduate students (and some of their community collaborators) provide examples of how students and activists have successfully worked around some of the challenges Ball outlines – or how the challenges look from their perspective.

Chapter 2 by Elicia Loiselle, Ruth Taylor, and Elizabeth Donald is an example of learning by doing critical girl-centred participatory action research in the context of Elicia's Master's research, which was co-designed with nine girls at Artemis Place, including Ruth and Lizz. The chapter documents how the girls and Elicia became researchers and collectively navigated power dynamics and learning moments throughout a process of creating a documentary film "talking back" to some of the negative stereotypes associated with girls who have been alienated by the mainstream education system.

In chapter 3, Tamara Herman and Mark Willson document lessons from learning CBR through a harm reduction strategy organized through the Vancouver Island Public Interest Research Group (VIPIRG). The authors suggest that this site provides a unique opportunity for students to get involved in grassroots action and "on the fly" community organizing that is not often available in a classroom setting. Taken together, this cluster of three chapters provides diverse definitions of what it means to learn CBR through practising it, and addresses many of the uncertainties and long-term struggles intrinsic to research in changing community contexts.

Part II is organized around the theme of teaching CBR in community settings. Chapter 4, by Mukwa Musayett (Shelly Johnson), Sandrina de Finney, Kundouqk (Jacquie Green), Leslie Brown, and Shanne McCaffrey, relates stories of how the Siem Smun'eem Indigenous Child Welfare Research Network draws on Indigenous and Métis communities' complex knowledge systems to co-design culturally appropriate community-based trainings throughout British Columbia.

Chapter 5, by Jon Corbett and Maeve Lydon, describes various community mapping projects they have facilitated through the Common Ground mapping initiative and in collaboration with universities. They describe how teaching community mapping can help people to see and deconstruct the unnamed values embedded in maps, and connect more deeply to their home places.

Darlene Clover discusses issues stemming from facilitating and teaching feminist visual arts–based methodologies in chapter 6. Through various examples, she demonstrates how she supports women in naming and re-envisioning their worlds through creative media. She also reflects on the ethics and purpose of arts-based methodologies, as well as strategies for data analysis.

In chapter 7, Budd Hall documents his formative experiences of learning and practising participatory research in Tanzania in the 1970s. He highlights the importance of knowing who we are, and who we are not, as we learn to listen and learn to work in solidarity with communities. The four chapters in Part II share a range of concrete research strategies the authors employ, from weaving baskets to mapping; from photography, quilts, and poetry to reflections on power and privilege. Chapters 5, 6, and 7 all provide examples of how the authors have transformed and applied the teaching methods refined in communities in their classroom settings.

Part III moves us into programming areas built around ethical community relationships and engaged practice. Jeff Corntassel and Adam Gaudry's chapter 8 explains the principles and pedagogy of insurgent education with examples drawn from the Indigenous Governance Program at UVic. They describe how pedagogies of discomfort serve to disrupt colonial assumptions, while place-based experiential learning that follows Indigenous protocols can promote community resurgence and the return of stolen homelands and waterways.

In chapter 9, Catherine Worthington, Francisco Ibáñez-Carrasco, Sean Rourke, and Jean Bacon share experiences from Universities Without Walls (UWW), a national, interdisciplinary HIV health research training program. Theirs is the only chapter in this collection that demonstrates how the spirit of collaboration and values of CBR can be generated in a blended, but primarily online learning environment.

Chapter 10, by Anne Marshall, Ruby Peterson, Jennifer Coverdale, Samantha Etzel, and Nancy McFarland tells student and instructor stories from the Aboriginal Communities Counselling Program (ACCP) at UVic. The chapter documents how students and instructors come to learn and develop respectful professional practices while "walking in the two worlds" of Indigenous and Western research and counselling traditions. The three chapters in this section tell of holistic areas of research and education both inside and beyond classroom walls.

Part IV takes us into the classrooms where CBR is being taught. Although it is taught for course credit, these classrooms have porous walls in that they often take students into community settings, or invite members of the community to the campus. Lorna Williams, Michele Tanaka, Vivian Leik, and Ted Riecken provide an account of a class designed to bring Indigenous ways of learning and teaching into the university environment in chapter 11. In two iterations of this class, community, student, and faculty learners and teachers worked together to carve a welcoming pole and produce a fabric mural, both of which are now on display at UVic.

Chapter 12, by Joaquin Trapero and Agata Stypka, shares an innovative multidisciplinary design for a course offered through the Office of VP Research and Faculty of Graduate Studies at UVic. Through partnering with community and government agencies, graduate students are able to work with community mentors to gain hands-on skills and experience addressing research problems identified by the community. Students also have a unique opportunity to learn from each other in an intentionally interdisciplinary context.

In chapter 13, Catherine Etmanski shares experiences from teaching participatory and action-oriented research, learning, and community organizing strategies through the arts. She highlights the importance of creating a space conducive to learning through the arts, and demonstrates how an in-class workshop designed by participants serves to build skills through experiential learning.

The authors in these chapters highlight innovative course designs and clearly demonstrate how the lines between learners and teachers and researchers and participants are blurred in classrooms where CBR is taught.

Part V provides insight into the future of teaching CBR in universities, by summarizing the unresolved tensions in this work. In chapter 14, Eileen Antone and Teresa Dawson share the way in which Eileen's scholarship was presented for the purpose of tenure and promotion. In articulating their reflections on this particular case, these authors provide a useful example for others to follow, while simultaneously challenging dominant ideas about what constitutes effective teaching and research. In so doing, they present a critique of standard tenure and promotion processes.

We close with a thematic overview of some of the challenges CBR educators and practitioners continue to face as we work both inside the academy and out. We reflect on these challenges with a sense of humility, knowing that simply because we have made some progress does not mean our work is complete. The productive tensions we present in this closing chapter represent the lingering conversations that are drawn not only from themes generated during the lunchtime series that was the inspiration for this book, but also from conversations between authors throughout the writing process. Each chapter provides insight into how these tensions play out in practice.

Intended Audiences

This book is designed to support a broad sector of pedagogical approaches related to teaching and learning within the CBR family. It is for people who already teach CBR, or want to, and also for people who are not inherently drawn to CBR, but will still find useful pedagogical strategies and methodological debates in the range of examples we provide. It is for people in all levels of their institutions who are seeking to create a more hospitable climate for CBR. It is for community social change advocates who may wish to use this scholarship to support their work. It is for people associated with Public Interest Research Groups (PIRGs), Community Research Councils, Learning and Teaching Centres, and other networks that support critical, action-oriented, participatory, community-led approaches to teaching, learning, and scholarship. It can be used as a resource in general methods courses on campuses, or CBR trainings in communities. In short, we hope this book will be useful for researchers, educators, activists, artists, community developers, administrators, and learners of all ages. More importantly, though, we hope this work will help to create more compassion, more justice, and more peace in this world where suffering abounds. After all, the purpose of community-based research is not simply to document the world's injustices, but to transform them. Please contact us to continue the conversation.

PART I

Learning by Doing: Learning CBR through the Practice of CBR

1 On Thin Ice: Managing Risks in Community-University Research Partnerships

JESSICA BALL

During a community-university research partnership some years ago, my Indigenous research partners insisted we conduct a meeting on their turf, away from the university, in a locale in which they felt more at home. They suggested we meet in an ice fishing hut on Poplar Lake in the middle of Nipissing Game Reserve. Although the setting was within their traditional territory, our expedition took us all into unexplored terrain, breaking trails with our snowmobile through the snow in the northern Ontario wilderness. For me, a city-dwelling, non-Indigenous woman living in the temperate climate of Vancouver Island, stepping out onto an expanse of ice deep in a forest reserve was deeply unsettling: What if the ice could not support our activity? The partners were aware of uncertainties as well. We were entering a space that no one owned, and no one knew for sure what could, or would, happen. With a sense that our lives depended on focusing only on what was important, we fished successfully – and our conversation about our research work together was equally productive. We were fortunate, in this shared space, that the ice was thick and strong enough to support our endeavours. Our community-university engagement yielded a good catch.

In the new geographies of community-university engagements, such is not always the case. Although community-engaged scholarship has become a buzzword in many research disciplines within Canadian universities, the enthusiasm and emerging ethics associated with it create certain challenges on both the university and the community sides of the partnership equation, and for teaching and mentoring students in this approach through community-based research projects. This chapter addresses some of these tensions. In my experience, gained through a wide range of community-university research partnerships over three decades and spanning three continents, the indeterminate processes and outcomes of these engagements, and a lack of familiarity with the contexts and conditions for research carried out in communities, can evoke, for all parties, a sense of venturing onto thin ice.

Many of the projects I have been involved in have been conducted with Indigenous community partners.[1] The projects have been intended, in part, to demonstrate the implementation of emerging frameworks for ethical research conducted within a broader social agenda of restorative justice and self-determination of Indigenous peoples (Ball, 2005). Guiding principles have included community relevance, community participation, mutual capacity building, and benefit to Indigenous communities. In two recent projects, each carried out over 5 years, testimonials obtained from community representatives before and after the research projects indicated that both projects had benefited the communities in the form of substantive knowledge; strengthened capacities to engage in collaborative research through community-campus partnerships were an additional benefit (Ball & Janyst, 2008). Although they were successful in terms of research productivity and contributions to community goals, these projects were tremendously challenging for all parties. They yielded a number of insights, learning points, and unresolved dilemmas, and underscored some of the tensions between the aims and needs of university-based investigators[2] and students and those of their community partners.

The act of situating research conceived, conducted, and communicated by university-based investigators and independent scholars in the community is not new. For example, education faculty members have often tested pedagogical theorems and program designs in kindergartens, schools, and community programs. Mechanical engineers routinely test innovations in factories and dockyards. Biochemists use hospitals and clinics to recruit participants for clinical trials. Anthropologists and sociologists have been conspicuous in their zeal to conduct research in "the field." And community-engaged research is the sine qua non for the field of community psychology. Student involvement in "service learning" projects (Kahne & Westheimer, 1996) emanating from virtually every corner of a university campus is another well-established tradition, with proven effects on student retention (Thomas, 2002), on developing students' social and civic consciousness (Boyte & Kari, 2000), and on their confidence and competence for work outside the shelter of the campus (Astin, 1999; Eyler & Giles, 1999). Indeed, basing research in communities has been so common across many academic disciplines that drawing attention to it now seems almost redundant. For the past half-century, almost without exception, universities have sought ways to remediate their reputation as bastions of intellectual elitism and become more integrated, both physically and through outreach activities, with the communities in which they are embedded.

Yet, while community-based research is not new, it has recently generated fervour to such an extent that many universities are adjusting their strategic plans and realigning budgetary commitments to motivate and enable faculty and students to engage in it, thereby bolstering the university's central role and credibility in contributing to solving social problems and responding to social goals. In many institutions in Canada and the United States, in-service training and workshops aim to motivate faculty members to consider ways to engage communities and students in their research programs and to expand course content to prepare students to undertake course assignments and thesis research in communities. Across Canada, several universities are holding discussions to consider whether or how faculty evaluation policies should be adjusted to reward faculty members who engage successfully in research with communities and innovate strategies for involving students in such research.

This chapter explores the significance of the new expectations and enthusiasms for community-engaged research with reference to the mission of the university, the goals of faculty, the trajectories of university students, and the goals and needs of communities. Many advocates of civic engagement in research envision a blurring of differences – including those of institution, role, status, and authority – between communities and academic institutions, between professors and students, and between "expert" knowledge in the academy and local knowledge in the community (Barber, 1992; Shefner & Cobb, 2002; Strand, 2000). Efforts to elevate the status afforded to community-based knowledge and the knowledge students can bring to and take from a project are extremely important, but I suggest that it is perilous to deny that differences exist between communities and universities in the ways that knowledge and resources are organized, managed, and distributed, because these differences have implications for students' learning and for project outcomes. Both opportunities and challenges are likely to be overlooked, while students, faculty, and community members may be surprised at every turn. While acknowledging that universities and communities are highly differentiated and complex social spaces, and that there is tremendous heterogeneity within and across constituencies that comprise them, the view taken in this chapter is that a unifying and distinctive feature of most universities in Canada is their commitment to generating new knowledge through various forms of research. This chapter foregrounds the need for faculty, students, and community members to appraise realistically the distinctive locations of universities and communities in terms of mission, scope, strategic priorities, accountability, stakeholders, resources, needs, and goals. I hold as an ideal the potential for concepts such as ethical space (Ermine, 1995; Poole, 1972) to help transcend community-university binaries in the process of knowledge creation and to mobilize towards a holistic understanding of universities and communities as integral contributors to knowledge and praxis in a learning society. Like the chapter's opening scenario illustrating the creation of new geographies for community-university collaboration, Ermine elaborates the concept of ethical space as recognizing parties' distinctive positionalities – perspectives, world views, knowledge repositories, and epistemologies – as they come together to engage in mutual learning and collaborative action in a space that no one owns or controls.

A Brand New Day?

Given that community engagement has actually been a feature of university activity for over 50 years, the question arises as to whether there is anything new about how university faculty and students understand their mission, the nature of community engagement, and their own locations, and whether we might expect new yields from research that engages communities. Certainly, the rhetoric used to elevate the significance and nature of community-engaged research has changed. Where communities once were viewed as data plantations (Ladson-Billings, 2000), with knowledge to be harvested and consumed by universities, today protestations of sincerity, the centrality of authentic relationship building, mutual respect, and benefits for communities dominate many discussions in workshops and courses for students and faculty on community-involving research. Approaches to community-engaged research have evolved in recent years beyond asking community members to host and participate in research to engaging communities as full partners at every stage. Although far from being the beginning of a brand new day for communities interested in partnering with universities (Boyer, 1990), recognition is dawning in some university quarters of communities' rights to control and regulate access to knowledge, methods of categorizing and creating knowledge, and strategies for disseminating knowledge products.

A Part or Apart?

A foundational argument for community-university research partnerships, variously defined, insists that, after all, the university is a *part* of the community, and therefore it is not a big step for community members, students, and faculty to work together to resolve mutually concerning social problems and pursue mutually beneficial goals. This viewpoint aims to dismantle the image of the university as a distinct and bounded entity in a community-university binary. There is undeniable appeal in disrupting the anachronistic vision of separate worlds in which emissaries from each must reach across a great divide to engage with each other. This image is often reinforced in university media depictions and academic conference reports of unforeseen positive returns from innovative projects that compelled university faculty and students to venture "beyond the borders" of university campuses and communities to "breach the walls" of the universities.

Universities and communities are distinct social entities, however, with very different mandates, missions, modi operandi, capacities, distributions of power in relation to different constituencies, and abilities to respond to emerging challenges and opportunities. In my experience, attempts to bridge the chasm between universities and communities can be fraught with bureaucratic barriers, interpersonal hurdles often involving cross-cultural differences, and seemingly incommensurable needs, senses of time, ways of doing things, and superordinate agendas.

From this standpoint, a naïve view of the distinctive natures of universities and communities and how they operate can result in gross underinvestments in the time and consultation processes needed to consider and formally negotiate community-university research engagements, including the roles of students, faculty, and community members in a project. Rather than venturing into communities with idealism, good intentions, and a linear research plan, it is important to identify some of the structural difficulties and tensions in terms of the missions and functions of the university and the community group or organization, with consideration of how these tensions will be reduced or managed. These preliminary clarifications and negotiations provide the foundation for productive working relationships, ethical conduct, procedural integrity, and responsiveness to the changing circumstances that invariably occur over the course of a community-university research project.

"You'll Never Believe What Happened ..."

Cherokee author Thomas King (2003) suggests a phrase that is "always a good way to start ... You'll never believe what happened" (p. 5). Over the course of many community-university research partnerships that have very often been characterized by ambiguities, sudden changes in direction, team members, circumstances, expectations, and anticipated outputs, I have found it helpful to rely on this phrase as a motto. Every partnership project yields surprises, sometimes from beginning to end, that often create monumental challenges to the project's feasibility or plausibility. Just as often, a windfall of opportunities allows the partners to explore new questions and data sources. King's motto alerts those who take up partnered research to be ready for the unexpected. Universities have elaborate self-regulating structures, and they tend to be slow to change, making them relatively stable partners. In contrast, a community's dynamic and emergent nature means that its circumstances, needs, and goals, even its boundaries, composition, and leadership can significantly change in a short period of time – one short enough to drastically affect a research engagement. The implications of this inherent instability for those involved are serious, particularly for students, who are invariably engaged for a prescribed period and with predetermined expectations for completing a piece of work.

The current fervour in certain university circles about engaging students and faculty members with communities for research about "real world problems" tends to focus on establishing trusting relationships as the biggest hurdle and the many benefits that will accrue to students and community participants as the biggest boon of community-engaged research (Strand et al., 2003). Although these are important considerations, they represent only a fraction of the many complexities, obstacles, and potential risks and benefits that frequently face university-based investigators and students who embark on community-university research partnerships. Some of these complexities and a strategy for coping with them – the negotiated Memorandum of Agreement – are explored in the following sections.

University-Based Investigators on Thin Ice

Indeterminate Processes. In funded, university-based research, the *findings* of research projects are indeterminate, but the *fact* of conducting a research project with a predetermined beginning, middle, and end is taken as a given, especially by granting agencies. It is assumed that a project will be done more or less as specified in a proposal, without major shifts in topic, methodology, timelines, budgets, or anticipated products. In partnered research, however, many events, often on the community side of a partnership, can derail a project, for better or worse. For example, a project in which I was involved was delayed for 6 months after three community members drowned in a boating accident. According to cultural protocol, the community could not carry on the research until the spring, when the water was warm enough for the bodies to surface and be properly buried. Another project was shut down when the chief and council of a First Nation, who were signatories to a Memorandum of Agreement governing the research, were voted out in an election and the new leadership did not wish to support a project initiated by the outgoing leaders. Several other projects have shifted significantly in topic focus as more urgent or more apt questions have emerged, or new data sources have been uncovered, or a better methodology has been hammered out. University-based investigators can often accommodate these changes through ongoing communications with granting agencies and ethics committees. Students, however, are more vulnerable to having their own needs going unmet when a project they were counting on for a course or thesis is significantly delayed or altered.

Indeterminate Outcomes. One of the most frequently expressed principles of community-engaged research is that some benefit must accrue to the community as a result of partnering in the research. But how far can university-based researchers go to promise benefit when research is inherently a journey of discovery with unknown outcomes? Research is not a contract that carries with it pre-commitments to particular outcomes. This in itself can be news to a community that may have experience contracting independent consultants to undertake projects going by the names of "research" or "program evaluation" and in which a specific outcome is expected. Common examples in my field of study are requests for "research projects" to document a program's success or to demonstrate the extent of an unmet service need. In one such case, when a community leader approached me about a possible research partnership, he said he thought that community members would be favourably inclined to participate, "mainly because I think the project will make us look good! We'd like other communities to see what can be done and to learn from us some really good ways to go about it." Understandably, many community partners anticipate that participating in a project will yield findings that benefit them, often in tangible ways, such as providing evidence of service needs or effective practices that can be used to advocate for more financial resources from government or other sources. University investigators need to introduce the possibility that a community-university research project could yield findings that are counterintuitive or surprising to the community – and may even run counter to the community's objectives. The discursive process that provides preliminary clarification about the nature, goals, and possible outcomes of a research project can help a prospective community partner to understand that a defining feature of serious research is that particular results cannot be guaranteed. All partners in these engagements need to be prepared for their own "you'll never believe what happened" moments and potentially surprising outcomes. These understandings can be formalized in a Memorandum of Agreement.

In the end, the collaborating community may decide that the findings are not beneficial because they do not support its agenda. This possibility needs to be taken into account when a team aims to ensure that a community will benefit from participating in a project. A puzzling aspect of much of the discourse about community-based research (e.g., Strand et al., 2003), and earlier literature about participatory action research (e.g., Hall, 1992), is the presumed pre-commitment of campus-based collaborators to research that not only will address a community-identified need but will contribute to positive change towards social justice. However, without being biased from the start, how can researchers be certain that their findings will point in the direction of positive social change or support a social justice agenda? For example, in my program of research, a study was undertaken because several First Nations were concerned that mainstream tools for screening children's development were culturally biased and should probably not be used with Indigenous children, especially those living on reserves. Among other components of the research project, parents and Elders were interviewed about their perceptions of these screening tools. The results showed that the younger the parents, the more positively they perceived the mainstream screening tools and the more they disagreed with Elders who asserted that the tools should not be used. Overall, the study did not support the collaborating communities' initial goal, which was to gather evidence to advocate for government investment in creating a new First Nations–specific screening tool.

Further, defining community engagement in research in terms of social change and justice seems unnecessarily limiting; community-university collaborations can also be useful for basic research that generates new knowledge without immediate tangible benefits. For the past decade, for example, I have been active in research documenting English language and speech patterns of First Nations children to determine the extent and nature of First Nations English dialects, the developmental emergence and situational conditions for linguistic code switching, and the patterning of First Nations children's storytelling (e.g., Ball & Bernhardt, 2008). Many communities and individuals have participated in this research, with a clear understanding that it will not tangibly benefit them or First Nations in general for many years, when enough data have been obtained and the range and determinants of language differences are well understood. All of the collaborators in this research have agreed that if it takes 30 years to consolidate understandings, it will still have been a benefit. Much of the fervour about community-university research collaborations seems to be fuelled by a motivation – easy to harness among youthful students – to contribute to immediate social change. Yet, one of the most important messages for students to hear is that significant, sustainable social change often takes time and can be served by painstakingly careful, time-consuming research whereby evidence accrues and is replicated and refined over time and across locations.

Indeterminate Dissemination. As with all research, community partners and individual participants have the right to exercise control over the information they have contributed, including the right to restrict access to it or to withdraw part or all of the information from the research findings. Memoranda of Agreement typically include agreements to protect not only individuals but also community partners from negative impacts that might result from the project findings being made public. These measures may include placing a moratorium on the research material for an agreed period of time or keeping certain material confidential. For example, in my experience with a study of youth risk behaviours conducted in partnership with public schools in Singapore

(Ball & Moselle, 1999), the Singaporean government indicated that if the findings were not helpful to its overall mission with regard to youth development policies and services, they would not allow them to be published. In another community-university partnership project initiated at the request of the staff of a program that was hard won and heavily used by families, the program evaluation research failed to confirm that program participation resulted in improved outcomes compared to no program participation. In the Memorandum of Agreement, the community had specified that it had the right to suppress findings that could threaten the program's funding base. If investigators or students want to ensure the right to disseminate findings – or any other areas of control – this needs to be specified during the partnership negotiation stage and, ideally, codified in a Memorandum of Agreement. However, agreement by faculty, students, or community members to unilateral decision making on any important matters in a collaborative research effort seems both unlikely and unwise, and raises concerns about ethics. Nevertheless, a question must be asked about where this kind of ambiguity leaves a university-based investigator who is committed to advancing knowledge in a given field or a student whose course assignment, thesis, or research scholarship may rest on being able to report research findings.

Students on Thin Ice

The momentous – and less momentous – shifts that can occur in a community-university research project can provoke a great deal of anxiety for students on the project team. Students may learn a great deal from being participant observers of the process of iterative change in a community-engaged project, but they may also feel helpless as they watch their course assignment or thesis research going ineluctably off course or becoming unfeasible, especially within their time, financial, and other practical constraints. Large shifts in a project call for a re-engagement with one or more research ethics review committees (e.g., with the university, a public institution, civic organization, or Indigenous community). Students can be effectively timed out of a project because reviews of proposed changes to research can be lengthy processes. Students and their supervisors need to be able to provide an unvarnished characterization of how student engagement in a prospective project fits into the student's course of studies, assignment deadlines and grading criteria, funding for student engagement with the community, and other realities.

The foregoing discussion implies that community-university partnered research is best suited to investigators who can tolerate a high degree of ambiguity and are willing to shift gears in a research project to accommodate emerging constraints and opportunities. This flexibility is a virtue for seasoned researchers who may be able to keep their eye on epistemological and methodological integrity and the potential validity and reliability of findings. However, when students are involved, what impact do such demonstrations of flexibility have on their learning, as novice researchers? It is often a challenge for students to see the links between particular epistemological positions, ontological viewpoints, and methodological approaches, so that their theoretical frameworks and research designs are coherent and cohesive. When students are immersed in a project that necessarily shifts to accommodate often-inchoate preferences or emerging needs or constraints within a community, the quality of their learning experience can be compromised. While it is good for students to understand the need to be nimble, is it optimal for a student's inaugural foray into research to involve the kinds of emergent, often catch-as-catch-can and nick-of-time accommodations that can perplex and tax even more experienced researchers?

Community-Based Collaborators on Thin Ice

A specific set of challenges frequently arises for community-based partners in a research project. Most universities are bureaucratic institutions that are relatively inhospitable to community members with no formal (e.g., salaried, tuition-paying, or revenue-generating) affiliation with the institution, for example, in terms of providing services, sharing facilities, opening access to library resources, or creating easy pathways for the flow of funds to community-based team members. Significant involvement by community partners in a research project occasions a number of practical negotiations involving finances, among other things. Financial transactions often signify trust and recognition of contributions. Yet, in the bureaucracy of a postsecondary institution, the policies, procedures, and timing that govern matters such as travel advances, expense claim reimbursements, payroll time sheets, cheque disbursements, and food purchases can seem labyrinthine and protracted, even to the most conditioned employees.

Procedural ambiguities and the slow pace of resolving some practical matters – described by a community collaborator in one project as "straddling two worlds that are often in collision" – can be almost overwhelming and, in fact, created so much ill feeling in one of my research collaborations that it led to the resignation of two community-based research collaborators, who were subsequently replaced by individuals with previous employment experience in postsecondary institutions.

As mentioned, my program of research involves partnerships with Indigenous communities and organizations. It is beyond the scope of this chapter to address the many challenging situations that invariably arise in cross-cultural research, but one point must be mentioned here: The long histories of catastrophic interventions by colonial governments that devastated Indigenous lives and of researchers exploiting knowledge in Indigenous communities and using community members as unpaid, uncredited knowledge providers have led many Indigenous community partners and individual team members and participants to be understandably sceptical about trusting university-based investigators and students.

With any community-university research partnership, university-based investigators and students need to devote time to establishing some basis for community partners to trust them enough to collaborate in the research project. They must be prepared to observe cultural protocols and to define who they are, the scope and nature of their authority over knowledge sources and methodologies, and their purposes, plans, and expectations in relation to the project.

Some of the challenges of partnered research may not be apparent to prospective community partners because of their lack of experience in university-partnered research or with university and research funding bureaucracies. Yet, just as a university researcher would expect to be shown around a prospective partner community or given an orientation to the way a partnering community-based institution operates, one of the roles of university investigators is to provide prospective partners with a look at the inside workings of the university. Community partners need to understand what the university can and cannot (or will and will not) do and how the bureaucracy works, with regard, for example, to research ethics review, the flow of funds and reimbursement procedures, library and facility resources, and so on.

These tensions need to be understood within the context of community partners casting their lot with a mainstream institution, in some cases for the first time. In my experience, addressing these challenges requires (1) recognition of historical and ongoing unilateralism be-tween public institutions and community groups that can shape how expectations, performance criteria, and mundane procedural matters can be interpreted by community members; (2) frank discussion be-tween community and university partners as issues arise; (3) good-faith efforts to learn about one another's work ecologies and to measure responses based on these understandings; and (4) humour. Across all critical and quotidian events, a Memorandum of Agreement can be an invaluable tool.

Memorandum of Agreement: Efforts to Control Indeterminacy

Increasingly, prospective partners for a research engagement are ne-gotiating agreements between the leading members of the university- and community-based teams (see, e.g., Minkler & Wallerstein, 2003). These agreements typically specify most of the activities to be under-taken, including: (1) the purpose and plans for an investigation; (2) the conduct of the research; (3) accountability of all members of an investi-gative team; (4) the nature of data to be obtained from specific sources; (5) the nature of data and data sources that must specifically be exclud-ed; (6) jurisdiction over data regarding ownership, possession, storage, and access; and (7) primary decision making over research outputs, including dissemination of the knowledge yielded by the study.

In my experience, formally written and co-signed Memoranda of Agreement have been invaluable for establishing understandings and embodying key principles for the conduct of research involving Indige-nous community partners (Ball & Janyst, 2008). Community partners and university-based team members often refer to the Memorandum of Agreement to recall or reinforce agreements. The Memorandum is also a record that can be used to introduce new team members to the prin-ciples and procedures agreed on with each community partner. This is especially helpful for students who may cycle through a project at vari-ous points. Memoranda of Agreement are critical when projects are em-bedded within larger collaborative or networked investigations that may involve large numbers of faculty and students from various insti-tutions and community members who have no relationships with one another, discussed subsequently.

Significant changes are possible in any research project, but this probability is greatly magnified in community-university partnered re-search. Sometimes changes can improve a project, while at other times they can result in a project being aborted or significantly compromised (e.g., overdue, over budget, or underperforming). As surprises happen (e.g., if conditions change or opportunities or needs emerge) over the course of a project, the Memorandum of Agreement can be a critical document for partners to review together, to revisit where the project started and who committed to what, and to negotiate changes relating to the research plan or the people involved. As an administrator in one partner community stated, "our MoA was a mast to cling to in stormy weather."

Yet, even with a fully developed Memorandum of Agreement, community-university research partnerships typically are not contracts, and all parties have the right to withdraw from the project or to change the nature or extent of their commitments at any time. My most daunting experience with this potentiality occurred in a project on Indigenous young children's development involving five rural community partners that had signed Memoranda of Agreement after a full year of discussion, negotiation, and communitywide information-sharing events. The Indigenous project coordinator employed as part of the university-based research team encountered innumerable challenges. As someone familiar only with working in Indigenous community organizations, the coordinator was understandably mystified and frustrated by various university policies surrounding such practical arrangements as travel advances and reimbursements, disbursement of funds for honoraria for Elders, and the seeming authority of the research ethics committee over research processes about which the communities had already expressed their preferences. Adding to these tensions, the project was one component of a networked study that involved nine other components based at other universities. The coordinator was often the only Indigenous person in meetings populated by investigators and a changing cast of graduate students who were unfamiliar yet entitled to peer through the windows, as it were, of the vehicle that was carrying the community-university research team conducting the Indigenous child development project component of the larger study.[3] When tensions became too great, the coordinator resigned precipitately and asked the community partners to reconsider their collaboration in the project. Without prompting, each partner reviewed the Memorandum of Agreement they had cosigned with me. One community chose to discontinue their partnership, while the other four elected to continue, stating that their review of the Memorandum reassured them that, despite the problems experienced by the coordinator, the project was proceeding as had been agreed on and there was no need to rethink their commitment. This necessary process took several months and two graduate student team members had to move on to other, more expeditious, projects.

Optimizing the Benefits of Community-University Research Partnerships

Researchers who work successfully with communities tend to have an open-ended, flexible program of research that can shift in focus to accommodate communities' requests and emerging needs and take advantage of emerging opportunities to pursue a question through knowledge sources and methods that reside in communities. The greatest challenge within these negotiated partnerships is remaining open to emergent opportunities, needs, and concerns while establishing a structure sufficiently clear and stable that community partners and research participants know what they are agreeing to and do not feel blindsided by unexpected objectives or demands. Strong relationships, nurtured from a project's inception, are the backbone for ongoing negotiation of ethical, productive practice in partnership research. Open communication about project details and points that remain ambiguous or subject to change helps to establish trust between the university- and community-based team members. Open communication also generates insights on both sides of the partnerships about what the partners need, want, and can bring to the work.

Although community-university partnerships are not a panacea for research, they do hold the potential to benefit partners and the learning society in a number of ways, as explored in the following sections.

Redistribution of Power

One of the rationales often given for community-university partnership research is that it "levels the playing field" and redistributes power over the legitimation of truth claims and access to knowledge-mediated resources. As pressure has mounted for university-based investigators to demonstrate the social relevance of their research, the pendulum has swung towards a focus on communities' knowledge needs and the primacy of deploying university-based expertise to assist communities with resolving social problems and pursuing social goals. A growing repository of case studies illustrates the benefits that have accrued to communities as a result of university engagements (e.g., Banister, 2005; Institute for Community Research, 2007). Many of these projects answer questions posed by communities using data sources – and sometimes ways of knowing – that reside in communities. While these instances are to be celebrated, it is important not to overlook universities' distinctive role to refine methodologies for generating knowledge and communities' distinctive role to respond to their constituents' immediate needs. Knowledge generation and problem solving characterize the work of both universities and communities, but resources to undertake these tasks are distributed unevenly, a point that is usefully addressed by Flicker (2008). University faculty members and many students have expertise in research design and data collection and analysis that allows them to make unique contributions to the quality of research outcomes. In a case study described by Williams, Labonte, Randall, and Muhajarine (2005), "maintaining 'buy-in' from diverse constituencies, while drawing limits around the research terrain itself, was partly managed by gradual acceptance by community partners that university researchers needed somewhat more authority over research design and methodology" (p. 295).

Both faculty and students need to acknowledge that as members of mainstream social institutions – typically with funding and university positions – they have certain kinds of power. The potential to oppress and exploit community partners must be a matter of concern, and deliberate efforts are needed to level the playing field in negotiated research relationships.

Institutional Change

Considerable enthusiasm in the literature on community-engaged research focuses on the contributions that faculty and student involvement in community-university research can make to advancing community agendas for change, as if the academy is not also susceptible to and in need of reform. Yet, when students and faculty engage as partners with communities, the possibility exists to stimulate critical engagement within the institution about principles, policies, and procedures that create barriers for university-based partners to be responsive and productive with community-based partners. Examples of some of the spheres where I have found it necessary to become active include policies and procedures for research ethics review; the conditions governing access to university resources, such as meeting rooms, online and physical libraries, and equipment; and procedures for disbursement of funds. As well, engagement with research funding bodies is critically needed to stimulate changes that enable more community involvement during proposal development, more funding flowing directly to partner communities to enable their collaboration on an equal financial footing, more funded time for negotiating Memoranda of Agreement during a project's inaugural year, and so on; see Williams, Labonte, Randall, and Muhajarine (2005), for a good discussion of issues pertaining to funders. The processes of mutual engagement and multilateral learning that often occur through community-university research have the potential to shift how the university sees itself and its primary mission as an institution embedded within the broad context of society.

Mutual Learning in Ethical Space

Capacity building is a top priority for Indigenous people across Canada: Indigenous researchers are urgently needed to take the lead on a range of projects in all fields that will contribute to the development of Indigenous people. Partnership in research can be an opportunity to learn new skills, explore topics of interest, and network with other individuals and organizations. This learning is not unidirectional, however. Research that is premised on principles of social justice involves commitments to strengthening capacity on both sides of a partnership. This principle exemplifies the concept of ethical space: a space between two knowledge systems, where engagement involves openness and mutual learning (Poole, 1972). As expressed by Ermine (2006), "it's a gift to walk in two worlds, but also a responsibility. Ethical space does not exist unless you look at it, affirm it" (para. 9). Through partnerships, there is much that students, faculty, and community partners can learn about themselves and about ways of knowing, living, and communicating, in addition to the primary products of a research project: generating and testing the application of knowledge. This learning can expand ideas about research, about the topic under study, and about the roles of communities and universities in a knowledge society.

Engagement in Applied and Basic Research

As noted above, defining community engagement in research in terms of social change and justice is unnecessarily limiting. Community-university partnerships can be useful not only in research oriented primarily towards social action or social change, as in participatory action research (Park, Brydon-Miller, Hall, & Jackson, 1993), but also in programs of basic and applied research (Flicker et al., 2010). For example, in my research on multilingual language acquisition in childhood, community partners worked tirelessly with me on a series of case studies to identify instances of bilingual code-mixing to examine their grammatical properties. It would be a long way from this basic research to any practical recommendations regarding language socialization practices or early learning programs. Yet, both the community and university partners were keen to explore this aspect of some Indigenous children's early language experience, and neither could have undertaken this research effectively without the other.

Although the literature is dominated by examples of community-involved research that draws on qualitative data sources (Hall, 1992; Leadbeater, 2006; Tuhiwai Smith, 1999; Wilson, 2008), community-university engagement, including projects with Indigenous partners, does not prescribe any particular methodology. In my research with Indigenous communities on the topic of fathers' involvement, the community-based collaborators were emphatic about their preference for a survey tool with largely closed-ended questions rather than a storytelling or narrative approach (Ball & George, 2007). The collaborators explained that they wanted to impose some limits on the scope and depths of fathers' self-disclosures during this first study in Canada to examine Indigenous fatherhood. They anticipated that many fathers had experienced trauma or secondary trauma associated with Indian Residential Schools, and the community members who were collecting the data might be unprepared to deal with the psychological impact for fathers of telling their whole story.

Following this study, the community partners wanted to expand the research nationally, and they collaborated with me on a proposal to the Social Sciences and Humanities Research Council of Canada for a study using an original, population-based survey tool that would be administered electronically, by telephone, and by mail. The proposal received feedback that the grant request was denied because it did not use a narrative or storytelling approach, which the Council deemed more appropriate for an Indigenous topic focus. The community-university team was also informed that the proposed research should use a community-based research approach, which the Council defined as involving relationship building with one community. This response reflects an unnecessarily constricting vision of the nature, potential scope and focus of community engagement with university faculty and students to do research that addresses a community-identified social issue.

Overcoming Binaries of Local and Expert Knowledge

Just as scholars have begun to write about new geographies for Indigenous-academic engagements (Tipa et al., 2009), my journey with my community partners to the mutually unfamiliar territory of the Nipissing Game Reserve allowed us to engage in a space that none of us owned, where hierarchies of authority and status and contested notions of who knows what were blurred. Within this space, we were able to more easily recognize that we possessed expertise that transcended boundaries of expert and local. The community partners, for example, possessed a lot of (academic) knowledge about linguistic features of Indigenous and English languages. I, for example, had (applied) knowledge of a school-based initiative called "English as a Second Dialect." I knew how to make bannock over a fire (Indigenous knowledge); they possessed (Western technical) knowledge about snowmobiles and augers. This easing of knowledge boundaries provided the conditions for creative, constructive discourse and project planning with the solid foundation of understandings articulated in our Memorandum of Agreement to stand on.

Conclusions

Relationships don't always end when a project concludes. I am still involved in some way with nearly every community that has been a partner in a research project. Many projects have sparked other projects within the same community or in ones nearby. Dissemination and mobilization of findings from research have been given more wheels because community- and university-based collaborators, including students, have different forms and avenues for communicating findings, and they respond to requests from different audiences and end-users.

In the expanding terrain of community-university engagement, risks are real and must therefore be carefully assessed. Before university-based and community partners venture onto the ice, they must be reasonably certain it is strong enough to withstand having holes drilled in it without risking lives. A negotiated, carefully crafted Memorandum of Agreement provides partners with a measure of insurance, but this insurance must be coupled with a brutally realistic appraisal of the short- and long-term risks and benefits to the community, the students involved, the university, and society as a whole. Within clearly structured and mutually agreed on project parameters, however, community-university research engagements hold significant potential for communities and universities to generate and mobilize knowledge in partnership, and for students to develop insight and skill in deploying research in meaningful ways.

ACKNOWLEDGMENTS

This chapter reflects experiences in research funded by the Social Sciences and Humanities Research Council of Canada, the British Columbia Ministry of Children and Family Development, Health Canada, and Human Resources Development Canada. The author thanks the Indigenous individuals who have offered their guidance about engagement with Indigenous communities for research, especially Kim Anderson, Ron Tsaskiy George, Pauline Janyst, Christine Leo, Onowa McIvor, Sharla Peltier, and Audrey Wilson.

2 When Girls Talk Back: Learning through Doing Critical, Girl-Centred Participatory Action Research

ELICIA LOISELLE, RUTH TAYLOR,
AND ELIZABETH DONALD

I don't think that people really take girls like us seriously. They see it like it's our fault and we just have to conform to society. It hurts and it's really not accurate. It's stuck in people's heads that you change for society, society doesn't change for you. In Project Artemis we were talking back to that and I feel like we made people take us seriously. It was like being in a room full of people and standing up in our seat, shouting out "shut up we want to talk." It wasn't disrespectful though. It was as if we've been interrupted our whole lives and we're finally being listened to. We made that opportunity for ourselves and it was really brave of us because we're not "supposed to" share our opinions, especially being young women in a patriarchal society.

– Lizz

Project Artemis is a critical, girl-centred participatory action research project that served as a participatory evaluation of Artemis Place Secondary School, an alternative integrated education and counselling program for marginalized girls in Victoria, British Columbia (see www .artemisplace.org). As a participatory evaluation, Project Artemis was designed as an opportunity for girls to guide the direction of the education and counselling programming by identifying what was working and what was not working for them and to investigate if/how they had experienced change and/or transformation in their lives during their time in the program. Our research simultaneously explored girls' schooling experiences more broadly and the intersecting structural inequities they negotiate across the multiple contexts of their lives. Ultimately, our research served to challenge and create alternatives to the constructions of "risk" that download responsibility for social problems onto marginalized girls. As Lizz exemplifies in the quotation above, our critical, girl-centred PAR framework was fundamentally concerned with why girls have such limited access to the means of research and which girls are excluded to a greater extent from legitimatized knowledge production. As Griffin (2004) states, "if girls and young women have been and remain relatively invisible in most youth research, then some girls have been more invisible than others" (p. 30). Our critical PAR process and practices were, therefore, deliberately designed to interrogate and account for the structural barriers that have historically marginalized the critical knowledge and experience of the girls in Project Artemis and girls more broadly. Many of the salient findings of our research can be accessed in our documentary film, *The Artemis Effect: When Girls Talk Back*,[1] as well as in Elicia Loiselle's (2011) Master's thesis.

The primary goal of this chapter is to delineate how our process of *learning* PAR through *doing* this critical research was an important piece of transformative social action. Grounded in social justice, our process was about simultaneously interrogating systems of exclusion experienced by girls and figuring out how to see/think/do things differently, which included the collective authoring of this chapter. We describe how we worked collaboratively, through many challenges, to: position ourselves as researchers and knowledge producers; critically analyse the "at-risk" labels we get stamped with; generate alternatives; share our experiences and perspectives on our own terms; and call community stakeholders to action to create change. As McClelland and Fine (2008) articulate, "while the challenges of youth participatory action research (PAR) can be substantial, the contribution of critical research to social theory, social policy, and social movements can be exhilarating in terms of challenging dominant scripts and reimagining new conceptions for social justice" (p. 253). It is in this spirit that we write about the challenges and possibilities that emerged as important moments of collective transformation and social action in our process of learning by doing PAR.

Writing Collectively: Contesting Individual Claims to Knowledge

We, the authors, are three co-researchers from the Project Artemis research team writing together to reflect on and share our experiences of doing critical, girl-centred participatory action research (PAR). Ruth, Elizabeth (Lizz), Sarah, Leah, Jordanna, Ashley, Beckie, Starr, and Taylor (ages 15 to 18) were all co-researchers in Project Artemis alongside Elicia who, at the time of this inquiry, was a graduate student at the

University of Victoria. Our research explored our experiences as girls who have been alienated by and/or pushed out of the mainstream education system and labelled "drop outs," "at-risk," "high risk," and / or "problematic." As Fine and Rosenberg (1983) state, "critical perspectives on social institutions are often best obtained from exiles, that is, persons who leave those institutions. This is perhaps why exiles' views are frequently disparaged as deviant and in some cases, conspicuously silenced" (p. 257). Our critical, girl-centred PAR process took shape out of our desire to speak back to and disrupt the constraining and oppressive categories of "risk" that place us and our complex experiences under erasure.

Throughout this chapter we wrote in a "we" voice in some sections, while in other sections our individual voices are distinguishable. The "we" voice is at once problematic and foundational to what we aim to do through our writing process. The first issue that must be addressed is that "we" is most often interpreted to stand in as representative of all voices – as consensus. First, because only three of us were able to engage in this collaborative writing process together, we cannot claim that our perspectives and reflections are representative of the six other co-researchers in Project Artemis. Second, although we wrote as "we" to talk about ourselves as girls with very particular experiences of marginalization, one co-author, Elicia, is an adult academic researcher and does not necessarily share the same social location(s) and experiences as the girls. However, it is important to us to acknowledge through "we" that our knowledge and analyses have been co-constructed throughout our research process and in the writing of this chapter. As a process note, the "we" sections in this chapter were conceptualized by the three of us collectively in discussion, written up by Elicia, and then discussed and revised by the three of us together. We have also written pieces from our own perspectives with our names appearing before those sections. We share these reflections and caveats on writing collectively in hopes that it will inspire other researchers to critically assess whose voices are being represented through the narratives in their own texts and to consider the simultaneous value and limitations of any particular voice(s) and/or analysis when sharing the process and/or findings of collective research.

We wrote this chapter using the same model we used throughout our PAR process – although this time across geographical distance. Together we generated broad questions about and reflections on our research. We then worked collectively to refine which important learnings we wanted to share. Then we engaged in multiple rounds of writing and discussion to articulate our ideas in a way that made sense to all of us. What we aim to do is explore some of the most critical aspects of our research process (which was undertaken as a deliberate praxis of social justice) as an offering to other community-based researchers undertaking this kind of work. We cannot offer a template for PAR, because this type of research is necessarily highly contextual and emergent. We hope, however, that our writing is meaningful and useful in its consideration of some of the foundational ethics, opportunities, and challenges involved in learning and doing this kind of collective research.

Notes on the Non-linear Structure of This Chapter

Our reflections move in a non-linear fashion (like our research process) through the conceptual, theoretical, political, and applied knowledge and learning that guided and constituted our research. We resisted imposing a linear structure on this chapter because we felt it would constrict us in accurately capturing how our learning happened. We chose instead to offer this non-linear account through narratives and analysis that, when woven together, create a picture that feels more true to what we went through together. We also hope our approach to telling this story better enables different readers to engage with this text in different ways that are most useful and powerful for their own contexts. We recognize that this method of presenting research can be disorienting to readers who are used to more traditional argumentation typically representative of the linear rationality of Western thought. For us, this is part of interrupting normative structures. That is, we believe that any discomfort this text may elicit for some readers accustomed to (and more comfortable with) more linear writing is an important part of the process of promoting knowledge democracy and decentring the privileged ways of knowing, being, and doing that have contributed to the inequities and social exclusion we have experienced. With this in mind, we now move on to unpack some of the salient and transformative learning and action we undertook through doing critical PAR.

Context

Our research took place at Artemis Place during program hours over 5 months from February to June 2009. We used arts- and discussion-based methods to cycle multiple times through the iterative phases of PAR: exploration/data collection, critical reflection/analysis, and action. We initially worked with Photovoice[2] and graffiti walls[3] to explore research questions and begin to refine themes before deciding, 5 weeks into our process, to use video documentary as our primary arts-based research method and dissemination tool. We partnered with local film-maker Monique Cartesan, who mentored us throughout the production of our film. We also partnered with local non-profit film organization MediaNet, which provided low-cost equipment rental, editing suites, and technical training and support. For the first 12 weeks, we met for a 2-hour research session each week. From there, we continued our weekly sessions, along with additional blocks of time throughout the week for film production.

Some of the Contexts of Our (the Girl Co-researchers') Lives

In our first research sessions, we began with the broad questions: How have things changed for us since coming to Artemis Place? How and why did we (in this case, "we" being the girls in particular) come to Artemis Place (or "end up" there)? Many of us had been to multiple schools and alternative education programs before Artemis Place. A few of us were living independently for months or years at the time our research began. Several of us were working jobs after school and on weekends to support ourselves. Some of us were either in government care (foster care, group homes, kinship care) at the time of the research or had had different forms of involvement with the Ministry of Child and Family Development over the course of our lifetimes. We were all living in contexts of relative poverty. Six of us identified as White (of these six, one of us also identified as a Romanian Jew), one of us identified as part White and part Métis, one of us identified as Indigenous, and one of us did not identify her race/ethnicity. As we stated earlier, Elicia was located quite differently than the girls in our research.

Being the Adult Researcher: On My Multiple (Privileged) Locations

Elicia: I am a White, queer, feminist activist. I am an adult, a youth worker, and, at the time of this research, I was a graduate student. My own critical consciousness about girlhood has been shaped by my academic grounding in feminist, anti-racist, anti-colonial, and queer scholarship, as well as my extensive experience in youth and feminist grassroots organizing. As a co-researcher positioned very differently than the rest of the research team, a significant part of my contribution was to introduce analytical tools that could help us deepen our understandings of the structural inequities girls were negotiating. These theoretical lenses also informed the ways in which I attended to power in our research space. Throughout this chapter, I explore some of the tensions I experienced in naming, unpacking, and working through / with how dominant power structures position me in relation to the girls and in relation to this thing called "research." This is important for researchers because good intentions do not mediate power. That is, if we choose to remain unaware of how we benefit from dominant systems, our actions can easily reproduce (rather than challenge) the very systems that are causing harm to the communities with whom we are doing research.

My complex motivations for engaging in this collaborative project were primarily grounded in my personal investment in advocating for social justice with and for girls. This commitment was and is incited by my personal girlhood experiences of sexism, sexualization, and classism, as well as from my experience as an adult and youth worker watching girls' experiences, knowledges, and strategies of resistance ignored or pathologized by many of the adults and systems with which they must interact.

These motivations were in the forefront for me, but I also had particular requirements to meet for, and significant benefits to gain from, my Master of Arts degree. At times I was resentful of being bound to the institution of academia; at other times I was glad to be working within the institution both to learn the critical discourses of PAR and to simultaneously challenge academia's hegemonic structures through critical PAR; and, most of the time I wondered about our ability to effectively do the latter when our work is still marginalized by the tight discursive grip "traditional" research has on academic legitimacy.

Although it was important for me to communicate to the team how I was making meaning of our research, it was difficult for me to articulate to them reflections that were at once intellectual, embodied, past, present, and future. The only way I was able to express this in a tangible way was to put it into a spoken word piece that I wrote and shared with the girls. I offer this piece, woven throughout this chapter, as encouragement to (PAR) researchers to experiment with multiple and creative forms of engaging their complex selves in and through the research process (see Clover; Hall; or Etmanski, this volume for more information on arts-based process).

Question 1: Why me?

As if to remind me of the path I travelled here
to this place
where curiosity is a privilege I enact
within the walls of stale buildings
that house the ideas of too few
obscure the realities of too many
as if to remind me of the path I traveled here
to this place
I feel an unrelenting clawing in my gut
And
I picture the dirty fingernails on the small hands of my girl self
Scratching at my insides as though across a chalk board
producing the penetrating sound of pain I cannot seem to close my ears to
Nails tear unapologetically through the tidy lessons of girlhood etched
    in white
Making messy and illegible
that which was taught with so unquestionable a claim to truth
that it seemed incontestable
And
when the dust settles around that chalk outline of the "good" girl
There appear silenced herstories
scrawled in a cadence of strength and desperation between the lines of
sugar and spice and everything/nice girls keep their knees together and
    never speak out of /turn that frown upside down
Herstories trying to rid themselves of the shame of living in the shadow
    of the good – white – girl,
trying to write into existence a girl who does not have define herself
    through damaging dichotomies:
tease or whore? smart or pretty? spit or swallow?
Swallow
Swallow words too often, swallow pride too often, swallow desire
    too often
But not always
Never always
And eventually not often
and that's this path
the beginning, the middle, still moving

Learnings about PAR

Why Critical, Girl-Centred PAR Matters

Youth participatory action research (YPAR) is designed to place young people's perspectives at the centre of decision making in service-provision, research, and policy that directly affects them. Such participatory methodological frameworks create opportunities for young people to identify and study social problems affecting their lives and create recommendations for organizational, institutional, and social change (Cammarota & Fine, 2008; Sabo Flores, 2008). Because the Artemis Place program is designed to "successfully support the most at-risk girls in our community as they transform their lives" (Artemis Place, n.d.), our inquiry into how we got or ended up there opened a space to critically explore the systemic and/or systematic processes through which we have been marked "at-risk" or "high risk" and the structural inequities and/or barriers that are rendered invisible by these individualized "risk" labels. This allowed us to look at how we are positioned as "in need of help," and how our own understandings of our experiences contest this positioning and challenge these labels.

Lizz: I knew the other girls and I were being judged just by saying we go to an alternative school and I wanted to help change that.

Ruth: The title of our documentary, *The Artemis Effect: When Girls Talk Back*, was representative of the girls talking back to the stereotypes and separating themselves from these definitions and becoming self-advocates and not victims. We used a quotation in the film, and I think part of it speaks to how we felt within the process: "girls are being labelled victims of society and, by implication, passive dupes – whether or not they themselves actually feel this way" (Baumgardner & Richards, 2000, p. 185). There was an article that came out in the newspaper about Artemis Place a week or so before Project Artemis's first session. Many of the girls, including myself, were angry at how we were depicted in the article, which was explained to us as a way to get fundraising. It generalized and stereotyped the girls and their experiences. I felt the article made us seem like helpless victims that wouldn't stand a chance in mainstream society.[4] We reflected a lot on these stereotypes and in the final action phase of the PAR cycle we wanted to talk back to some of these stereotypes and generalizations. We wanted to show the community who we were in our own words. We wanted to advocate for ourselves.

Key Tenets of Critical PAR

In order to create a girl-led research process, through which girls guided what was important in our inquiry and decided how they wanted to engage in action and advocacy, we drew on underlying tenets of YPAR that have been clearly articulated by Tuck et al. (2008):

- There is transparency on all matters of the research.
- The research questions are co-constructed.
- The project design and design of research methods are collaboratively negotiated and constructed.
- The analysis is co-constructed.
- The products of the research are dynamic, interactive, and are prepared and disseminated in collaboration.

In some ways, we can say we achieved all of these tenets. In other ways we can also say these are tenets towards which we aspired, but in different moments felt ourselves coming up short. For instance, we placed a strong emphasis on co-construction as an ethical grounding for our work. However, we were always negotiating the challenges of accessible participation. As we discuss later, not all co-researchers could be equally involved throughout the process, so our co-construction relied on creative ways to bring girls' perspectives forward from previous sessions to account for the multiplicity in our group when not everyone was present.

Although YPAR is taken up in many different ways (some of which co-opt participation in the service of reproducing dominant discourses and "norms"), Torre, Fine, Stoudt, and Fox (2012, p. 2) outline the distinctions of *critical* PAR:

> Rooted in notions of democracy and social justice and drawing on critical theory (feminist, critical race, queer, disability, neo-Marxist, indigenous, and/or post-structural) critical PAR is an epistemology that engages research design, methods, analyses, and products through a lens of democratic participation. Joining social movements and public science, critical PAR projects document the grossly uneven structural distributions of opportunities, resources and dignity; trouble ideological categories projected onto communities (delinquent, at risk, damaged, innocent, victim) and contest how "science" has been recruited to legitimate dominant policies and practices.

Elicia: Critical approaches to YPAR are deeply invested in "analyz[ing] power relations through multiple axes. Thus, race intersects with gender, class, and sexuality within typical PAR inquiries" (Cammarota & Fine, 2008, p. 6). Intersectional analyses work to expose the complex power relations of difference. They challenge existing discourses of difference (read: acceptance, tolerance, multicultural mosaic), which "work to erase power ... [and] threaten to reduce all forms of difference to the same," effectively de-contextualizing, essentializing, pathologizing, and marginalizing the *other* (Burman, 2003, p. 296). An intersectional approach works to name the complex, deeply intertwined roots of oppression that are obscured by these dominant discourses, unsettling power and rendering it contestable. This is the approach we endeavoured to use throughout Project Artemis in order to analyse and talk back to stereotypes of "at risk" girls.

Critical PAR Requires Ongoing Critical Reflection and Action

An important learning in our process – and one we would like to highlight for readers – is that having a grounding in critical theoretical frameworks, as an academic researcher and/or as a research team, does not guarantee ease in practising critical PAR. It is difficult work, precisely because the research and all of us as co-researchers were and are embedded in dominant systems of white, capitalist, hetero-patriarchy, which are powerful forces that produce(d) multiple and ongoing contradictions in our lives and in our critical research process. Tuck (2009b) frames these contradictions as "a thirding of the dichotomized categories of reproduction and resistance" (p. 419), which she explains as an important way to understand the complexity of people's lives,

> because it more closely matches the experiences of people who, at different points in a single day, reproduce, resist, are complicit in, rage against, celebrate, throw up hands/fists/towels, and withdraw and participate in uneven social structures – that is, everybody. (p. 420)

As an example, during one research session we analysed gendered double standards of sex and beauty (i.e., different standards for "appropriate" appearance, expression, and sexual behaviour applied to girls / women and boys/men). Then, the following week, a few of us came into the next session all abuzz about what happened the night before on the television show, *America's Next Top Model* – who is more beautiful and who should be kicked off because she's a bitch. Importantly, we ended up discussing and joking about how our fascination with this gendered reality show survival-of-the-prettiest/bitchiest discourse juxtaposed with our analyses of sexism, sexualization, meritocracy, and social exclusion – all factors that shaped girls' experiences in the mainstream school system and, subsequently, at Artemis Place. It was important to us not to see PAR as a linear, purely counter-hegemonic, transformative space or process; to do this would be to undermine the multiplicity of peoples' lives as they negotiate complex, unequal social structures (Guishard, 2009; Tuck, 2009b). That is, our process of doing PAR was non-linear and contradictory, just like our lives.

Staying Critical of Gender-Specific Research while Doing Girl-Centred PAR

Through Project Artemis, we sought to engage with the nuances, complexities, and contradictions of our multiple subjectivities as we explored and theorized our realities to speak back to the dominant discourses and structural inequalities that marginalize us as girls, in education systems and beyond. By working in this way, we embodied and enacted a critical PAR framework that allowed us to centre our experiences of being girls across the multiple contexts of our lives, while we simultaneously tried to unpack "girl" as a complex, constructed, tenuous, and contestable category. For us, this meant asking questions not only about how and why we have been labelled as "drop-outs," "at-risk," "vulnerable," and so on, but also about how these discourses that construct us through and as "problems" intersect with discourses of gender (of what it means to be a "girl" – how our bodies are labelled, regulated, objectified, and sexualized in very specific, gendered ways) and how gender is simultaneously shaped by experiences of classism and racism.[5]

At the same time, a significant tension in doing gender-specific inquiry (within a gender-specific program such as Artemis Place) is the implicit risk of reifying the gender binary. Driver (2007) notes that "even feminist academic researchers have learned to translate the intensities of flesh-and-blood teen worlds into safely packaged knowledges. The very categories of 'girl' and 'boy' remain distinct and clear, erasing those who identify as both/and or neither" (p. 305). Our approach to critical, girl-centred PAR was not intended to essentialize "girl." Rather, it was intended to explore and politicize how "girl" is discursively constructed through multiple, shifting, and uneven structural forces that shape the disparate material conditions of "at-risk" girlhoods. We centre "girl" for the purpose of calling it into question, even as the repetition of "girl" in our research and writing reproduces the erasure of, for instance, transgender, gender queer, and gender non-conforming subjectivities. This tension is not easily resolved, even as the project of challenging girl as a naturalized, fixed category aligns with the project of disrupting dichotomous constructions of gender.

Becoming "Researchers"

Our sense of relative cohesiveness as a research team happened quickly because we had all known each other for weeks, months, or years and had been in numerous group discussions together in the program. Elicia had been working with the girls as a youth work practicum student at Artemis Place for 4 months before we began our research together and she had been invited by the executive director to facilitate a participatory evaluation with the girls in addition to her practicum. As part of her Master of Arts thesis, Elicia developed a loose structure to engage girls in such an evaluation and held two information and recruitment sessions during program hours to invite girls to participate as co-researchers. Our understanding of participatory action research was initially framed by Elicia, who explained the cycles of PAR (exploration/data collection, critical reflection/analysis, and action) and why critical PAR is considered important for social justice. Elicia had been doing social justice work with youth for 10 years as a youth herself and as an adult ally. She also took courses in feminist PAR and community-based research in graduate school, and had read a lot of the current literature on critical youth participatory action research (YPAR) (e.g. Cahill et al., 2008; Cammarota & Fine, 2008; Evans et al., 2010; Fine & Torre, 2004; Fine, 2009; Torre, Fine, Stoudt, & Fox, 2008; Torre, 2009; Tuck, 2009a, 2009b; Tuck et al., 2008). Some of the girls also had a bit of experience with research. A couple of girls had vague memories of doing an interview with a researcher or filling out a survey and not really knowing what happened as a result, which was exactly the opposite of the kind of research we were aiming to do through Project Artemis. Ruth had experience in youth-led activism and had previously co-facilitated a couple of focus groups, including one on resiliency at Artemis Place in which some of our co-researchers had participated. Lizz had prior experience sharing her story at a youth conference. Many of the girl co-researchers, however, had not had these kinds of opportunities. Still, as early as the research recruitment sessions, girls were already hyped about it, wanting to do something to refute the ways they were positioned in the newspaper article about Artemis Place mentioned above and in society more broadly.

Elicia emphasized from the beginning that this type of research is necessarily collaborative and it would be extremely important for the project to be guided by all of us. In our first session, Elicia asked the questions for all of us to answer and discuss: Why are we here? What are our hopes for the project? What does each of us need from the group to feel comfortable participating as fully as we would like as a co-researcher? Some of the girls were initially concerned about girls coming only for the honoraria (a symbolic $5 per 2-hour session), so we discussed why that would be a valid reason to come and how people could show up because they get paid and still make a really valuable contribution to the team. One way Elicia framed this was that a lot of adults can only do work they're passionate about because they get paid to do it. She gave herself as an example, with the benefits she was getting from using Project Artemis for her degree. She also noted that youth often aren't compensated properly for their time, knowledge, and stories in research and elsewhere because of unequal power relations between youth and adults in society. That's why Project Artemis research sessions were held during program time, and girls were also able to learn useful research skills and use the project for credit in their courses. (And having food at every session was super important too.) The girls expressed an impassioned desire to use the project to change the perceptions of them (and girls like them) in society, create awareness in the community about why Artemis Place is an important program, and have a say in what was working and what could be improved in the program.

Co-constructing Our Critical Research Framework

Elicia: Having worked with the girls as a youth work practicum student at Artemis Place, I had already learned so much from them through the critical, analytical lenses I witnessed many of them bringing to group discussions, life skills groups, course assignments, and day-to-day conversations. So, although I framed the philosophical underpinnings and outlined the cycles of PAR for the girls at the outset of our research, our critical framework and approach was very much collectively developed over the months we researched together through the way we teased out and named the structural inequalities shaping their experiences. I asked many of the critical probing questions in our first couple of discussions, but a few of the girls also came into the project with a critical lens on social justice issues and provoked other co-researchers to notice and ask questions about why things seemed unfair and why girls (who are poor, in care, alienated from mainstream schools, etc.) were positioned in certain ways.

Ruth: Our process of research was realizing our individual problems as greater social problems. There always seemed to be a "theme," like a string leading back to these greater issues. We're so used to being blamed for things we can't control that we start blaming ourselves. Instead of looking out, we internalize. A lot of the anger that many girls admitted to feeling, in the critical reflection stages of PAR, came from a feeling of powerlessness and social limitations. Once we started analysing the "cause and effect" we came to the conclusions that the effects were not random and the causes were systemically rooted. The point in this is not to take the blame from ourselves and place it elsewhere; it is to come to a greater self- and social awareness and to use this awareness, understanding, and often pain as a motivation for social change.

What Does a Researcher Look Like?

Elicia: I felt it was important that we created a research space in which we could understand ourselves as *already* knowledgeable, *already* exploring and theorizing our own realities, *already* becoming critical, and by extension, as *already* researchers. Although this was my hope for our research space, my hope did not mitigate the dominant discourses that position research as the territory of "objective experts" in academic institutions.

The dominant image of the researcher that girls articulated in our research sessions was one of a highly educated, white-haired, White man in a lab coat (see also Mukwa Musayett et al., chapter 4 in this volume). We framed our research to contest this limited understanding of who can be a researcher. Still, given these dominant ideas and the ways in which girls had been alienated from mainstream educational institutions where their knowledge and experiences were ignored and/or devalued, not all of the girls would have readily identified with the label "researcher." It was not necessary for everyone on the team to self-identify in this way. However, we always called our work together "research," emphasizing the importance of each of our particular contributions in the process, and creating space to reflect on how our multiple cycles of data collection, critical analysis, and action were moving us forward and deepening our understandings. A key opportunity for sharing own own understandings of our processes and our findings came less than halfway through our process, when our presentation proposal (submitted by Elicia) was accepted into a graduate student conference at UVic. To collectively prepare our presentation, we discussed where we had come and where we were going in our process and why our findings were guiding us in that direction. We then drew out key aspects of our work to highlight for the particular audience at the conference. This work provided a useful space for reflection on our process.

Researcher/Participant: Navigating Dual Roles

As we moved through our process, becoming researchers through researching our own experiences produced particular challenges and vulnerabilities for the girls that we worked through together, as Ruth explains:

Ruth: I use the words researcher and participant almost interchangeably because we were doing the research about ourselves; we were researchers and participants. It was hard to play these two roles sometimes because we would say something brilliant on film and as researchers go "that's great, it totally speaks to what we're trying to show" and as a participant say "well I don't know if I'm comfortable sharing that now that I think about it." As researchers we had to push ourselves as participants, which required reassurance from other group members. A lot of girls had trouble seeing themselves on camera, and even though they were saying something important all they would notice is how bad their hair was that day and they would need someone to remind them of the value of their voice. When being interviewed many of the girls would ask: "Did that sound stupid?" "Is that relevant?" or "Did it make sense?" Because we're used to having our voices silenced, we don't know how valuable, relevant, and intelligent they are. That is something we had to work on collectively by reassuring and encouraging each other. We also revisited conversations often to recheck with girls if they were comfortable sharing what they had said in the last week's discussions or if they would prefer using an alias or "code name." You need that safe environment where people feel free to share but also to look out for people and leave it open for them to decide what is shared and what isn't so you're not exploiting their experiences.

Choosing and Using Methods

Throughout our process we used focused discussion, thorough flip chart notes, Photovoice, graffiti walls, mind mapping, video, and journaling as methods of data collection. Elicia offered a general question to discuss for our first session ("What has changed for you, good or bad or whatever, since coming to Artemis Place?"), but later topics for discussion were determined by girls' photos and stories and our collective analysis of the themes emerging in this data. Photovoice was chosen by Elicia for the second session to introduce the group to a creative method, and girls were encouraged to provide honest feedback about how the method worked for them. Only some girls remembered or chose to take photos over the couple of weeks we used Photovoice, although these few photos still produced important discussions and salient themes for our research. However, around the fourth week of our process, the girls established a consensus that they wanted to produce a documentary film about the experiences they were researching.

The process of learning to use video as a research method and dissemination tool was dynamic and created numerous opportunities for sharing leadership in the team. In partnership with filmmaker Monique Cartesan and the local non-profit film organization MediaNet, girls learned about and took on different roles in the process: facilitating storyboarding, designing interview questions for other girls in the program and for street interviews, helping each other practise interviewing, conducting interviews, filming, doing sound and lighting, editing, and engaging in a community dialogue at the premiere screening and in multiple presentations thereafter. We analysed our Photovoice, graffiti wall, and discussion data (the latter captured in thorough flip chart notes) for emerging themes to explore in greater depth through film. Interview questions were constructed to explore these themes with other girls in the program who would be interviewed on camera and also offered the possibility of doing an audio recording instead. Girl co-researchers led the recruitment session to invite other girls at Artemis Place to participate in the interviews. The opportunity to participate was presented during each weekly check-out and check-in session over the 3 weeks of filming, so that girls could choose to participate at any point. We would review footage in research sessions and in the editing suite to do deeper level analysis of our themes and choose what we wanted to show in the public documentary film. The process of producing a documentary film was also intensely time consuming. Because of this, two editing positions were created for girl co-researchers, who would be provided with extra honoraria for the time they spent outside of the program editing the film. The two girls chosen by the group had been the most consistent in their attendance at research sessions. In addition, our budget would not have allowed us to do this project had it not been for many hours donated by Monique and substantially reduced rates offered by MediaNet.

Constructing a Girl-Led Process

Ruth: The process was girl-led, in that our motivation and ideas were never forced, there was always open dialogue, and it was never one person deciding on behalf of the group what was important or what we would do next. And even though Elicia was the facilitator she did a very good job of always making sure the researchers' voices were the main focus of the project. She let the girls lead the discussions and decide on the topics we would focus on. She never assumed that her views, opinions, or education were more important than ours. I think she truly was learning from us and not just using our experiences for her work. She understood her role was to facilitate us in our own process and not to guide the project away from that.

Elicia: It's cool for me to read Ruth's perspective of our girl-led process, and it reminds me how difficult it was for me to attend to power and equitable collaboration in our process, given the broader systemic inequities within which we were operating. We talked a lot about power as a research team. How power functioned at Artemis Place between and among staff and girls, how power operates at broader systemic levels to privilege some people/experiences/knowledge and marginalize others, as well as how we understood power in our process. For instance, I acknowledged from the beginning that I had more power coming into the room as an adult, youth worker, and academic researcher, and we discussed what that would mean for us – how, as a co-researcher with different and particular accountability to the rest of the research team, I would position myself as an ally and advocate in our research and activism, how I would access resources at the university and in the community to support our research and make sure that we would have venues to reach our intended audiences in the dissemination phase. Within the trusting relationships we built, we relied on each other to identify if any of us perceived our process to be straying away from our commitment to our collective ethic of PAR as co-constructed. At the same time, I was aware that our relationships with each other were all different, with power operating and shifting differently between and across our experiences with and positions in relation to each other, and it could not be taken for granted that trust would level power.

Even when Ruth says that I "let the girls lead the discussions," which could be taken (and was in many ways intended) as a power-mediating practice, I am brought to the heightened awareness that dominant social structures position me as the one with the power to "let" the girls lead the process. I felt a steady discomfort about that, echoing Eve Tuck's (2009a) similar experience that "it was difficult at first ... not to become preoccupied with equal distributions of knowledge, power, responsibility, and vision" (p. 60). At the same time, my co-researchers were clear that it was important for them that I provided consistency and structure that would allow them to engage deeply in the research without having responsibilities downloaded onto them that were unrealistic and inappropriate, given the kinds of responsibilities they were already shouldering in their daily lives.

Some of the most difficult work of critical PAR is getting comfortable with discomfort – the uncertainty of and tensions within the process – in order to really engage with what is emerging. I found that after a while I began to count on the messiness as an indication that we were digging into the complexity of deep, collective work, and/or as a reminder that we were doing research within complex and often unpredictable lives and within powerful structural forces. These things needed to be honoured for their importance, even if they did produce a perpetual knot in my belly.

Question 2: Why them?

They would not be contained
Their bodies and minds wanted to resist it
even if they couldn't quite put their finger on what *it* was
Why were they so *fucking* angry?
Didn't matter
no one seemed to care
because education is a well oiled machine that stops for nothing and no one
Not for poverty, not for sexism, not for racism, and certainly not for girls
who want to learn

Not for girls whose minds and mouths are too big, too loud, too open, too
   demanding, too much of a disturbance
So they were – they are – bound involuntarily to labels that mark them
   liabilities,
Make them disposable:
"at-risk," "high risk," "disordered," "delinquent," "uncontrollable"
They are pushed out of the machine
but it's their own damn fault right?
For being girls who rebel, refuse, resist – dissenters, disturbers,
   disillusioned

Reproducing Structural Inequities through the Structure of PAR

Elicia: Even as we were committed to investigating girls' intersecting, complex realities, our process in Project Artemis cannot be roman-
ticized and was not innocent of reproducing problematic erasures.
One of the most difficult admissions for me as a social justice researcher
and activist is our inadequate exploration and analysis of racism and
whiteness/neo-colonialism across girls' experiences and within our
research process. It is important to recognize that "whiteness" is not
merely a description of skin colour; rather, it is a paradigm with "profound power and exclusionary privilege" (Skott-Myhre, 2008, p. 168)
that (re)produces the supremacy of white, patriarchal institutions and
systems of thought, marking racialized (classed, sexed, gendered, etc.)
"others" as "abnormal," worth/less, and in need of help. Whiteness is
invisible because "it is not seen as whiteness, but as normal" (Dyer,
2002, p. 12), particularly to White people who are not marked as
"Other."

Although they were inconsistent and infrequent, there were a couple
of research sessions in which we unpacked racism and neo-colonialism
via the personal experiences shared by the Indigenous co-researcher on
our team, who was the only visibly non-White co-researcher. These conversations, however, only happened in the sessions when this young
woman was present, and only through analyses of particular moments
she experienced or particular labels that targeted her as a racialized
"Other." This practice was and is contrary to what I know: that it is inadequate and also unethical to rely on racialized members of the research
community to bring their experiences forward in order to undertake
these analyses – particularly in spaces like ours, which was dominated
by White co-researchers.

As discussed earlier, critical YPAR is designed to make visible the marginalizing erasures within dominant, traditional forms of academic research. It is designed to deliberately investigate and theorize race and racism in intersection with the multiple, mutually constituting processes of subject formation within and across marginalized communities of youth. Fine et al. (2000) write,

> "Race" is a place in which poststructuralism and lived realities need to talk. "Race" is a social construction, indeed. But "race" in a racist society bears profound consequences for daily life, identity and social movements and for the ways in which most groups "other." (p. 112)

Because we did not consistently interrogate whiteness across all of our experiences and within our research process, we reinscribed "othering" discourses by interrogating racism only as attached to the experiences and the body of one co-researcher, and we reproduced the hegemonic invisibility of whiteness by not exploring our own complicity in reproducing (and, for most of us, benefitting from) racist, white power structures. Disrupting whiteness (alongside other dominant structures) should be an integrated part of the critical lens researchers bring to PAR, and ours was only partial at best. It is not easy and has to be deliberate precisely because whiteness is so ubiquitous – always present and being reinforced through our PAR practices. Girls, unsurprisingly, were not choosing to inquire about what many of them perceived to be outside of their personal experience – for example, racism – even though all of our gendered and classed subjectivities are constituted through structures of dominant whiteness (e.g., although being poor marks White girls as outside of normative girlhood, being White does work to mediate violence in how they are marked and targeted). Our research into the structural inequities that girls negotiate focused only on unpacking their experiences of and their responses and/or resistance to marginalization. Within such a framework, it can become difficult to interrogate sites of privilege that interlock in complex ways with oppressive structures. This is not a new dilemma; it has been well analysed, for instance, in critiques of Western feminism (e.g., Mohanty, 2003; Moraga & Anzaldua, 1983) that developed as a White, middle-class, women's movement seeking gender equality and an end to (some/privileged) women's oppression.

I chose to write this section from my own perspective, because, as a research facilitator equipped with a critical framework from which to interrogate whiteness in our process, I must take responsibility for what I withheld and ask myself why. My own preoccupation with creating space for the girls to make decisions about what we inquired about, and not to impose my own agenda, allowed us to remain easily embedded in whiteness. In an attempt to disrupt hegemonic power relations within our research team I focused on a girl-led PAR praxis, neglecting my responsibility to share a particular and necessary critical lens with our team. In so doing I neglected to attend to the macro forces of power constituting and constituted by our practices. I see this as a leakage of dominant (white) research discourses, in that I slipped into seeing myself as an outsider who should be objective and not taint the girls' voices and experience. This is highly problematic because, contrary to our commitment to critical consciousness, it assumes that girls have a pure, unmediated voice or perspective that is outside of complex power structures. That I thought of exploring and analysing whiteness as my own agenda is a force and function of whiteness that reduces analyses of race to a special interest, allowing white power structures to remain hidden from view. As Frankenberg (1997) notes, whiteness works to "cover the tracks of its constructedness, specificity, and localness, even as they appear" (p. 16). These tensions in our process cannot be resolved; rather I offer this critical lens now to hold myself and all critical PAR researchers accountable to the foundational ethics of this approach, even as I struggle with my lack of accountability in the moment(s) of our research.

Question 3: Why us?

It was serendipitous
The kind of serendipity turned synergy
that emerges
in the space between one herstorical, present, ever-shaping moment
and the next
A space bridged by relationship
A convergence of paths that mark the beginning
of a road too seldom traveled
When I connects with Them
and fumbling toward
Some ever shifting version of
We
Threaded together through
some common understanding of pain

common belief in love
common desire for change
We
move in and out of unison through cycles of knowledge production
bound to circles of lives
of girls' lives
We
endeavour to speak our individual and collective selves
into existence
through a critical language of resistance
that will give this moment the power
to revise the next
We
use our bodies, not to fulfill the requirements
of our good girl assignments
but to resist, demand, act
acting out a new performance of girl
a nuanced performance of girl
that demands
a nuanced understanding of and from the world

Strategizing to Talk Back – What to Tell and What Not to Tell

The title of our video documentary, *The Artemis Effect: When Girls Talk Back*, reflects our desire to reappropriate "back talk" as a politicized tool for mobilizing resistance. As such, talking back requires strategic deliberation about which stories to tell and how. It requires: thinking through the entanglements of representation, audience, and the presentation of research especially as we hoped to speak to a broad audience with diverse political commitments. What is safe to share and what isn't? Who is made vulnerable by the research? ... These decisions are at the heart of the ethical commitment of PAR and point to our responsibility, and a process, to consider the political ramifications of making the invisible visible. (Cahill, 2007, p. 367)

Our documentary film was strategically produced for public consumption, omitting some of our more complex analyses, the nuances of which we felt might be misinterpreted via dominant "girl-in-crisis" scripts (de Finney, Loiselle, & Dean, 2011). This process of determining the audience and anticipating the interpretation of the findings is an imperative part of the dissemination of social justice research. The girls knew this because they had been on the receiving end of misrepresentation. Through the back and forth of discussing the politics of representation and what we wanted to show, we developed a deep understanding of the function of silence in decentring powerful, oppressive discourses. What we do not say or show cannot be misinterpreted and used against us. At the same time, we were able to use the complex analyses we generated collectively throughout our research process to speak our critical knowledge, to advocate for ourselves and girls like us, and to articulate our strengths, skills, and hopes. By using film as our dissemination tool, we were also able to show the humour, satire, and laughter that emerged in our research. This is one way we resisted damage-centred research, "the danger ... [in which is] that it is a pathologizing approach in which the oppression singularly defines a community" (Tuck, 2009b, p. 413).

Elicia: I remember Sarah, Ruthie, and I were in my car driving to MediaNet. It was crunch time – a couple of days before the premiere with lots of editing left to do. We were going over the priority order for the editing we'd be doing that day. I think it was Sarah who excitedly added, "and we're doing the blooper reel today, too." I was wrought with anxiety at the amount of work we had to get done in such a short amount of time, so I said, "How about if we plan to do that once we've got a handle on the content of the film itself? I know you really want to have the bloopers in there, and if we don't get to it for the premiere we could still put that reel in after for future dissemination, no?" Ruth wasn't having it. She said, "No, I think it's really important for it to be in there for the screening. It helps show the audience more of who we are." Later, at the first screening of the film, I could feel my heart expand, witnessing laughter fill the theatre as the bloopers played on the screen. It was so cool. It really brought home for me how privileged I was to be part of those generative moments of levity that breathed a different kind of energy into our work.

Elicia: Postscript on Being the Academic Researcher

Question 4: Why me?

Through this process
I cycle back to myself

And my girlhood becomes entwined with theirs
With ours
I am there
AND I am here
and how I cross the space and time in between
is marked on
this body which travels
this path
And so I feel an unrelenting clawing at my gut
reminding me how I got here
to this place
Where serendipity
is a privilege that takes me outside these stale walls
Where multiple ideas and realities (e)merge
unauthored and unauthorized
Where the boundary between I and Them
goes in and out of focus
and
We
Become
Are
always becoming
change

Conclusion

Bringing this chapter to a conclusion seems as challenging as bringing
our PAR process to an end, which has not really happened in the years
since our initial project wrapped up in 2009. The learning goes on in
iterative cycles, and different combinations of our research team members have continued to present, workshop, and write about our process
and findings. When research is deeply entwined with and grounded in
"lived lives" (Tuck, 2009a), it can become embodied and mobilized into
indeterminable present and future possibilities, as each of us takes it
with us and enacts it in different ways. Even with our intention towards
a relatively loose and nonlinear writing structure, the inherent linear-
ity of the written word has still come into tension with the nonlinearity
of our learning, practice, and reflections. However, we hope we have
succeeded in articulating some of the messy complexity and richness

of what PAR is and has been for us as a collective of researchers. And we hope it will be taken up in the spirit in which it is offered – as enticement towards the challenging, unsettling, empowering, personal, political, and ethical commitment to deeply participatory and collaborative research that is grounded in social justice and action for change.

Lizz: We stopped letting society define us and started to define and create ourselves. I think we really surprised a lot of people in that process because "problematic" girls like us are and were considered lazy / crazy/stupid. I believe we changed that by telling our stories and sharing how we feel about how we're being treated and looked at, and doing so in a responsible and respectful manner. I think that people were surprised at how capable we proved to be.

3 Learning CBR through Community Organizing: Reflections on Struggles for Essential Health Services for People Who Use Drugs

TAMARA HERMAN AND MARK WILLSON

> Community organizing at its best has created sites for the practice of opposition.
> – Schragge (2003)

As Victoria's only fixed-site needle exchange prepared to close its doors in May 2008, a group of concerned city residents met to strategize. The needle exchange, which had been evicted from the building where it had been housed, was a lifeline for one of Victoria's most marginalized communities: people who live in extreme poverty and use illicit drugs. The small group of city residents who vowed to fight for a needle exchange knew that they would face tremendous obstacles. Yet, the group never imagined that the city would still be without a needle exchange 4 years later. It was, after all, armed with a plethora of research and policy reports calling for health services for people who use illicit drugs in Victoria. It was in this context of contradictions and paradoxes that Harm Reduction Victoria (HRV) carried forward a campaign that included – among its community organizing tools – community-based research (CBR).

Students at the University of Victoria (UVic) have been deeply involved in HRV, often learning about CBR and its role in community organizing by taking on tasks outside the protective buffer of a classroom. This chapter is an honest look at engaging in CBR in a social struggle marked by conflict, and through the institutional structures of a contemporary university. We draw on our experiences working with (and as) students at the Vancouver Island Public Interest Research Group (VIPIRG), a campus-based non-profit organization, and HRV, a community group that spearheaded the campaign for a needle exchange.

Our work in harm reduction has exposed, at times, a disjuncture between the interests and availabilities of students – which tend to be organized around the learning requirements of academic institutions – and the needs of the community groups who collaborate with student researchers. In this chapter, we take a closer look at the apparent discords between students' learning needs and HRV's community organizing needs. We first highlight instances where HRV's advocacy context required a different approach to research than those offered in standard descriptions of CBR research design. Our experiences suggest that a pedagogy conducive to learning, practising, and teaching key CBR principles must embrace eclectic mixes of skill-sets that are not part of the traditional repertoire of "how to do research" lesson plans. We then discuss successes and challenges in our teaching work, primarily in sharing community organizing skills between students and community members, and the difficulties of reconciling these commitments with the time and funding constraints students face within the university.

We see that our difficulties reflect deeper challenges in taking action on social justice issues in a reactionary social and economic context, which shape the skills, capacities, and assumptions researchers bring to their community work, and which influence the organizational capacities and structures of the communities and institutions researchers work with. Here, we highlight community-based social justice struggles as praxis-oriented spaces that offer students opportunities to engage directly with CBR principles, albeit in ways that contribute to and, at best, alter or challenge our understandings of the practical work we do and the theoretical models we use to guide our work. We conclude with a reflection on ways these forms of learning community organizing have encouraged us in investigating and reimagining the relationship between research and social change in a period of continued neo-liberal social and economic ascendance.

Locating Ourselves

Both authors of this chapter are reflecting on our work on harm-reduction issues from various vantage points within a broad spectrum of learning and teaching CBR. Our experiences as university students – at the time of writing, Mark is a doctoral student at UVic and Tamara recently completed a Master's degree – provide us with insight into the workings of academia. Although we are not formal "teachers," we facilitate student involvement in HRV through our work at VIPIRG. We have both been very active with HRV since 2008: Tamara, as VIPIRG's former research coordinator, where her work facilitating community research projects included mentoring students seeking experience in CBR; Mark, as a former member of VIPIRG's Coordinating Collective, which assumes the same responsibilities as a Board of Directors, and as outgoing research coordinator. In terms of community organizing, Tamara has worked on a variety of social justice issues both locally and internationally over the past 16 years, and Mark has been working on local poverty-related issues for the past 6 years. The critiques and ideas that we share come from our roles in learning and guiding CBR, as student researchers and as community organizers, and through our work in linking these realms.

VIPIRG is part of a network of Public Interest Research Groups (PIRGs), which are non-profit organizations based on university campuses across Canada and the United States that conduct research in the public interest. Initiated in the 1970s by Ralph Nader, PIRGs play a central role in connecting student researchers to community organizations working on environmental and social justice issues. VIPIRG, which was established at UVic in 1983, has been active on a variety of fronts over the years. Our emphasis is on collaborative action-research, which we see as an ongoing collective process of systematically gathering, analysing, and communicating information in the interest of inciting and/or contributing to social and environmental change. Research, then, includes analysing social and environmental issues, devising strategies to counter injustices and oppressions, evaluating the most effective means to publicize the data and information that we gather, and adopting tactics for action. Since 2007, VIPIRG's focus has been on local poverty, and we work closely with several local collectives and organizations. Most of these groups do not receive government funding of any type, and therefore their visions, strategies, and tactics are not constrained by the requirements of donor institutions.

VIPIRG's unique location as an on-campus organization that takes action on issues implicating the broader community enables it to facilitate student involvement in local social justice groups. Students participate in various community campaigns through work-study positions, practicum placements, and co-op jobs. Many others devote their time and energy on an unpaid basis.

In general, students begin their experiences by approaching VIPIRG to apply for the work-study jobs, request practicum supervision, or simply to get involved with research and community organizing. VIPIRG staff members meet with the students to discuss their interests and skills while briefing them on the relevant issues and groups. In most cases, staff members invite students to the group's next organizing meeting and follow-up afterwards. Students receive ongoing support and mentorship over the course of their involvement in the form of one-on-one meetings and informal check-ins. That said, VIPIRG's limited budget means that all staff members work part-time, balancing many obligations and commitments. The students who work with us must take responsibility for their own involvement, work fairly autonomously, and feel confident asking for support when needed.

The arrangement can be very beneficial to many students and community groups. Students learn from their involvement by engaging in many facets of CBR and community organizing while gaining hands-on experience in the non-profit sector. They do so within a framework of mentorship and support, but in a context where they are able to act autonomously. The grassroots, primarily volunteer-driven organizations with which VIPIRG collaborates, benefit, in turn, from the many hours students contribute to their campaigns and initiatives. One of VIPIRG's most significant contributions is to offer a grassroots model for skill and resource sharing between the university and community. We do so by working with community groups that, because of limited time and financial resources, and also informal organizational structures, use of confrontational tactics, and radical analyses, lack access to more formal community-university partnership models. Working with these grassroots organizations facilitates student engagement in community work that is free of the constraints facing larger NGOs, such as federal restrictions on advocacy work (Bridge, 2009) and "stringent approval and reporting requirements" that require resources be targeted towards research in the form of justifying and auditing project deliverables (Phillips & Levasseur, 2004, p. 452), allowing an opening for students to take part in a particularly broad range of organizing tactics.

Context: Confronting a Health Care Crisis

Among the groups that VIPIRG works closely with is Harm Reduction Victoria, a local collective committed to taking action in support of adequate and comprehensive health and social services for people who use illicit drugs and who live in conditions of relative poverty. As mentioned, HRV was formed in 2008, when Victoria's only fixed-site needle exchange was forced to close. The needle exchange, which had operated for 23 years, was serving upwards of 2,000 clients at the time of its closure. Yet, the site had been plagued by underfunding and understaffing in the years leading up to its eviction. As the only evening drop-in service for people who use illicit drugs in the city, the needle exchange was overburdened and unable to respond to the needs of its many clients, who often gathered on the block. The closure was the result of pressure from neighbourhood home and business owners following complaints of noise, crimes, garbage, and human waste in the area.

When the eviction of the needle exchange appeared imminent in 2008, the Vancouver Island Health Authority (VIHA) positioned itself to relocate the services to a building that it had purchased.[1] The building, which would also house adjacent support services, was located next to "Our Place," one of Victoria's major service providers for homeless and street-involved people. It was located a block away from an elementary school and the Victoria Conservatory of Music, both of which opposed the relocation. The school and the Victoria Conservatory confronted VIHA and the City Council, who promptly announced a moratorium on plans for the new needle exchange site. With no fixed site, the needle exchange service was reduced to a mobile exchange. The staff began performing their duties on foot and out of a van. Notably, needle exchange workers were also restricted from distributing clean syringes in an area surrounding the school through an informal and controversial agreement on a "no service zone" (VIHA, 2010). Because the school was one block away from Our Place, the no service zone essentially barred the needle exchange staff from attending to clients in the very neighbourhood where most street-involved people who used illicit drugs were located.

As will be further discussed, HRV has advocated not only for a new fixed-site needle exchange, but for broader policies, programs and services that address the discrimination, criminalization, stigmatization, and isolation experienced by people who use illicit drugs. This entails articulating demands for housing, supports, and more comprehensive health services for drug users, including supervised consumption services (HRV, 2011; Wallace & Willson, 2008/2010). It must be emphasized that these demands are neither unheard of nor untested. In Vancouver, the city and the regional health authority opted to improve and create comprehensive harm-reduction services rather than scale them back when confronted with many of the same issues. Following a courageous and effective campaign waged by drug user groups, their allies, and service providers, the regional health authority worked closely with local government and neighbourhood associations to raise awareness of the systemic issues underlying harm reduction and the need for improved harm reduction. A collaborative effort underpinned by both a far-reaching public awareness campaign and a firm commitment to the principles of harm reduction has crystallized in the establishment of two comprehensive supervised consumption services in Vancouver. Neither has been subject to mass opposition in the neighbourhoods where they are located.

Unlike most agencies providing health services to people who use illicit drugs, HRV does not receive any funding from VIHA, the City of Victoria, or the Province of British Columbia. HRV's autonomy and independence has allowed the organization to put forward very critical viewpoints while adopting a range of tactics. These include organizing forums, a guerrilla needle exchange, demonstrations, and city hall speak-outs.

As a result, the students who approach HRV to become involved often find themselves in a charged environment. HRV is a relatively small collective of people. Yet, the group confronts government and public health agencies that respond to the concerns, fears, and legal threats expressed by housed residents at the expense of the community of illicit drug users whose lives are at stake. Most students who are interested in HRV are deeply committed to the issue, and the experience of working on such a controversial campaign can be trying and heart-wrenching.

As students, researchers, community organizers, and people facilitating student involvement, we have had to reconcile a number of chasms, unmet expectations, assumptions, and difficulties in our work. On reflection, we see these challenges as emerging – in part – from a disjuncture between the models of CBR that students learn, the way in which academic requirements organize student interests and availabilities, and the specific research requirements that emerge from HRV's work. We offer some examples of these discords and mismatches in the sections that follow, beginning with our observations on how research design is taught in the classroom and how it evolves in the context of community organizing and advocacy.

Research Design in a Protracted Policy Context

CBR Research Design and Service Learning

The constant flow of students who approach VIPIRG to learn about CBR is a testament to its growing importance in several academic fields. CBR is located within a broader sphere of critical inquiry that recognizes research as a profoundly political activity, in terms of both the processes through which it is constituted and the data that it uncovers (Kirby, Greaves, & Reid, 2006). There is no singular definition of CBR, which traces its roots to a range of intellectual traditions (Wallerstein & Duran, 2008; Israel et al., 2005). Practitioners often describe CBR as a set of principles as opposed to a definitive set of methods. In their comprehensive and much-cited introductory text, Minkler and Wallerstein (2008, p. 9) highlight six core principles that unite varied strands of CBR:

1 It is participatory.
2 It is cooperative, engaging community members and researchers in a joint process in which both contribute equally.
3 It is a co-learning process.
4 It involves systems development and local community capacity building.
5 It is an empowering process through which participants can increase control over their lives.
6 It achieves a balance between research and action.

As seen in CBR core principles, all conceptions of CBR carry a commitment to research as part of broader processes of social change (Kirby, Greaves, & Reid, 2006; Israel et al., 2005, p. 4). CBR practitioners have noted, though, that social change does not necessarily occur as an automatic result or consequence of applied social scientific research (Stoecker, 1999, p. 845). Social change, rather, depends on some level of community organizing, or the process of mobilizing communities in pursuit of political action to defend their interests (Schragge, 2003; Stall & Stoecker, 1998). This mobilizing work is accomplished through collective action and collaborative learning (Schragge, 2003; Park, 1993; Hall, 2005). An important consideration here is how those working in the tradition of CBR conceive of the relationship between research and action: conceptions that are dependent on the multiple ways that research itself can be understood.

Although the principles of CBR can be read from multiple perspectives, including those of community mobilization and popular education, a challenge we have faced in teaching CBR through HRV can be traced to a relatively narrow conception of research offered to students in university curricula. Descriptions and discussions of research design in introductory texts offer insights into the ways CBR principles can be interpreted and weighted within the university setting. Strand et al. (2003), for instance, describe a research project as involving the following elements: identifying the problem, constructing the research question(s), developing research instruments, collecting and analysing data, interpreting results, producing the final report, issuing recommendations, and implementing initiatives (p. 6). Although CBR is often described as a cyclical, iterative process (Minkler &Wallerstein, 2008, p. 29), discussions of the research process often unfold in a linear manner, where problem-identification and data-collection lead to analysis and reporting. These phases are often followed by an expressed hope that the research will be used by community organizations to good effect. There are a number of assumptions about research here, particularly regarding the role of the researcher and the goal of CBR projects, which speak to some of the difficulties that come with teaching CBR from the perspective of the academic researcher.

As Stoecker (1999) points out, the way CBR is approached by academic researchers is not simply a matter of emphasis within the research project, but, rather, involves a particular perspective on what forms of knowledge and activity a CBR project might entail. Stoecker highlights substantive goals underlying CBR practice – pursuing relevant knowledge and skills, developing relations of solidarity, and engaging in action that wins victories and builds self-sufficiency – as a way of identifying gaps between narrow academic conceptions of research and broader commitments of CBR projects:

> The problem ... is not with the approaches but with a conception that PR is a research project. It is not. It is a community organizing and/or development project of which the research is only one piece. As such, it has three goals: – learning knowledge and skills relevant to the task at hand – developing relationships of solidarity, and – engaging in action that wins victories and builds self-sufficiency. Doing research is not, in itself, a goal. Research is only a method to achieve these broader goals. (p. 845)

As researchers grounded in the academy ourselves, we see a need for self-reflection on the meaning and practice of core CBR principles. We recognize that these meanings are shaped by CBR's "coming in from the cold," as principles and practices that emerged in the context of social movement struggles are taken up, interpreted, and accorded meaning within the particular epistemological and institutional contexts of the contemporary university (Hall, 2005).[2]

Like Hall, we see a number of possibilities and a number of risks that come with the way CBR has been taken up within the university. The academic emphasis on traditional conceptions of social scientific rigour of the research project, for instance, makes sense from the perspective of promoting "service learning," where students supplement classroom learning by applying these social scientific research methods in practical research contexts. The idea here is that students have the opportunity to gain both a more nuanced understanding of social scientific research (Strand, 2000, pp. 87–92), and a sense of their own capacities to engage in struggles for social change (Strand et al., 2003, p. 11). In our experience, though, the emphasis on learning and developing social scientific research skills also serves to shape student expectations and capacities in ways that are not always compatible with the types of skills and forms of assistance that are most valuable for community groups, or with broader CBR commitments to co-learning and social change, such as those highlighted above.

This incompatibility has been particularly evident in our work with HRV, where, as we describe in the following sections, the context has required an emphasis on policy implementation and community organizing and advocacy skills that often remain undeveloped in university-based introductions to CBR.

HRV: CBR as Community Organizing

Harm Reduction Victoria uses community-based research as a tool for its broader community organizing process, which seeks tangible outcomes for a particularly vulnerable and marginalized group of people. In this particular case, however, HRV has steered away from conducting further research on the group of people in question. In fact, HRV's research work has been guided by the fact that the withdrawal of needle exchange services in Victoria has occurred *despite* numerous research reports and policy papers recommending more services for people who use illicit drugs.

The Vancouver Island Health Authority, which is mandated by the BC Ministry of Health to deliver and manage health care services on the island, commissioned and/or endorsed 10 studies over the course of a 7-year period. These studies brought together not only researchers from the health authority, but also university researchers, the police, local service providers, and the City of Victoria, all of whom were unanimous in recommending more harm-reduction services (City of Victoria, VIHA &

Victoria Police Department, 2003; Stajduhar, Poffenroth & Wong, 2000; Wallace & Willson, 2008/2010).[3] Many were written before the fixed site was evicted, and their existence is stark evidence that the crisis in harm reduction predates the closure of the needle exchange. In response to the recommendations drawn from research, a document articulating VIHA's strategic focus (VIHA, 2006) outlined its commitment to providing comprehensive needle-exchange services. By 2007, the situation was critical enough to merit the establishment of a Mayor's Task Force on Breaking the Cycle of Mental Illness, Addictions and Homelessness (City of Victoria, 2007). The Task Force recommended expanding the needle exchange to include more comprehensive support services from doctors, nurses, and social workers. That the fixed-site needle exchange was identified as insufficient before its closure renders the failure to open an improved site even more puzzling.

Research has also been carried out in Victoria in the wake of the closure of the needle exchange. A study conducted by a team of UVic researchers shows that the lack of a fixed site has presented additional challenges for people who use drugs in accessing clean needles, disposing of used syringes, and accessing other health services that the needle exchange provided (MacNeil & Pauly, 2008; MacNeil & Pauly, 2011). Ivsins, Chow, Marsh, Macdonald, Stockwell & Vallance (2010), in their comprehensive study of drug use trends, noted an increase in "unsafe injecting practices" in the years since the needle exchange closed its doors, and calculated a decrease of over 15,000 in clean needles distributed per month (p. 1). A student affiliated with VIPIRG surveyed needle-exchange workers about the change from the fixed site to the mobile service. They reported encountering several barriers in their work, including a lack of privacy for clients, time restrictions, and a reduced ability to build relationships (Zangger, 2011). A policy framework for Greater Victoria on Housing and Harm Reduction specifically lists the closure of the fixed-site needle exchange as a challenge to addressing homelessness and the health needs of drug users (Pauly et al., 2011).

Because of the sheer quantity of existing research on the benefits of harm-reduction services for the health of people who use drugs, a central part of HRV's initial strategy involved publicizing and circulating these reports, with the aim of encouraging informed decision making on health services in Victoria. Immediately following VIHA's decision not to open the new needle exchange, HRV held public forums where experts in the field explained report findings and offered overviews of recommendations. A letter-writing campaign in local publications was organized to encourage public scrutiny of the health authority's action. HRV collaborated with organizations led by people who use drugs in writing letters to VIHA outlining the various ways that its actions were at odds with the research findings and recommendations of its own reports.[4] Popular education has been an important component of this work, as HRV engages with community members in an effort to build a collaborative campaign for harm-reduction services in Victoria. A key principle underlying this work is that people who use drugs are members of, and not an external threat to, local communities. A difficulty that HRV has faced in its collaborative popular-education project is challenging the discrimination and stigma faced by people who use drugs that fuel objections to establishing harm-reduction services in neighbourhoods.

During 3 years of unsuccessful attempts at ensuring that policies regarding services for people who use drugs are implemented, students and community members have had to reassess the strategies and activities required to hold the health authority accountable to its public health mandate. There have been no experts in this process of reassessment, as people who use illicit drugs, community organizers, front-line social workers, parents whose children have suffered unnecessarily from the criminalization of drug use, students, and instructors from fields as diverse as nursing, law, and political science have struggled to identify barriers to policy implementation that have often eluded us. As students and organizers, these experiences have led us to reflect on the highly contingent and uncertain relationship between research and social change: an uncertainty due, in part, to the messy internal workings of the institutions responsible for undertaking policy reforms.

Student Expectations vs. Research Design "On the Fly"

From the perspective of research design, the Harm Reduction Victoria project involved many of the methodological components that students would expect to find given their introductory training to CBR. One nuance is that the HRV context has involved a highly recursive, nonlinear application of these components, where the immediate issue of policy implementation guided a relatively extensive process of problem-definition and construction of research questions and tools. Over time, and through experimentation, what began with a hypothesis regarding the need for education and a degree of pressure for the implementation of policy became a more focused research question concerning the local institutions we were dealing with: "what conditions – institutional and / or otherwise – are preventing public health recommendations from being implemented?" For ourselves and for students we work with, at issue is a research focus that is sometimes overlooked in methods training: that of "researching up" (Desmond, 2004). Here, research aimed at explicating power relations and the internal workings of local institutions has outweighed the need for further research of the marginalized and powerless persons who are often the objects of social scientific research.

In our research on institutions, we have found that the failure of medical knowledge and unanimous recommendations to instigate the provision of essential health services for people who use drugs is not unique to Victoria. In fact, inconsistencies between research, policy, and practice are so common that the term "evidence-based" decision making has become a topic of discussion in advocacy and literature on harm reduction (e.g., Ball, 2008). The term "evidence-based" emerges from the medical and health fields, where using evidence drawn from research to inform policy and practice is generally regarded as standard practice (Kemm, 2006). Yet, the history of harm-reduction services indicates that evidence does not necessarily lead to the provision of health services for drug users (e.g., Buchanan et al., 2003; Rosenstock & Jackson Lee, 2002).

Among the reasons that evidence in support of harm reduction is often overlooked are public opposition and political will. Buchanan et al. (2003), for example, conducted a study in Massachusetts to explore why needle exchange programs were considered controversial by both government and the public despite eight major reports attesting to their benefits. They found that "advocates of needle exchange tend to define the issue strictly as an empirical, scientific matter, whereas opponents define the question primarily as a normative, ethical one" (Buchanan et al., 2003, p. 430). The same may be said of the controversy surrounding the needle exchange in Victoria, where public opposition to harm reduction appears to have shaped service provision more than research-based evidence.

It has become clear to us that we need knowledge geared at understanding, addressing, and countering institutional and community resistance to health services for drug users. Yet, the institutions that govern provision of health services and communities are not two separate realms. The issues of stigma and discrimination that underpin community resistance to harm-reduction services are deeply embedded in institutional discourses (Smith, 2005; Smith, 2006), and, as such, the ways in which institutions charged with regulating and administering harm-reduction services operate (Tempalski et al., 2007). The failure of VIHA to implement its own recommendations – as paradoxical as it may appear – is indicative of the scope of the challenge faced by HRV and its allies.

HRV, then, has been confronted by a situation where exploring the "problem" leads us into a complex, multifaceted web instead of pre-senting clear "solutions." The transition from textbooks to terrain has at times amounted to a reality shock for students learning CBR. For some, initial expectations that publicizing existing recommendations would result in the reopening of fixed-site needle exchange services in Victoria led to feelings of disappointment when all venues for pressuring VIHA appeared to be exhausted. After holding numerous demonstrations, waging successful media campaigns, bringing over a hundred residents to testify in support of harm reduction at City Hall, operating a "guer-rilla needle exchange," and pursuing legal recourses, even the most te-nacious organizers began running out of ideas. Research skills that we bring with us from the university have been insufficient for under-standing, let alone gaining the feeling of productively engaging with, the political terrain that sets the contours of the project.

Working through this disorientation highlighted for us some of the obstacles presented by thinking of social scientific research as, in itself, contributing to processes of social change. In particular, we found that the idea of social change as driven by well-reasoned findings and rec-ommendations relies on an assumption that institutions themselves are guided by rational planning processes (Nutley, Walter, & Davies, 2007, p. 36; O'Connor, 2001, p. 165; Smith, 2010, p. 177). Yet, looking critically at institutions reveals complexes of social relations (Smith, 2005; Smith, 2006) and the chasms between their policies and actions expose how power operates in the issues – and lives – at stake. As Nutley, Walter, and Davies (2007) point out, it may be more helpful to think of policy as being "evidence-influenced" (p. 14), where research does not lead to direct policy implementation so much as it contributes conceptual tools for use in broader political struggles over how particular social issues are interpreted and defined as problems (p. 36). Such an understanding of the role of research in policy change offers a constructive way of thinking through the relationship between research and action. In our work with HRV, this has played out in an awareness of the ways an initial selection of research focus can inadvertently constrain or direct the action components of a project, and a heightened awareness of the range of skills required to do the political work of challenging discriminatory attitudes towards people who use illicit drugs in local institutions and in the broader community.

Regardless of our actual background beliefs about the nature of institutions and political struggles for social change, for instance, we found that our research choices put us in the position of acting as if VIHA's actions were simply dictated by the strategic plans and policy recommendations that we downloaded and read from its website. This assumption oriented our expectations regarding the project in a number of ways, from the skills required to do the project, to the pace at which we expected to see changes implemented, to where and how we identified and assessed successes in our work.

When VIHA did not respond as a rational policy-driven actor that implemented its own recommendations, we found ourselves back at the drawing board, re-envisioning our research needs and reassessing the analytical and practical skills that we required. For Tamara, who brought years of community organizing experience to the project, there was a need for institutional knowledge to understand the intransigence of a health authority that was beyond the scope of any single participant's training or experience. For Mark, whose primary contributions had been through writing projects, such as research briefings, Ombudsperson's complaints, and Freedom of Information requests, there was a need to engage in organizing and mobilizing work that were outside the scope of his formal training or practical research experience.

Perhaps more importantly, students working with the project through single-term work-study or co-op positions did not always leave the project with a clear sense of how their contributions added to or furthered this ongoing struggle. On reflection, part of this has to do with the type of work students took on, which was often guided by the research skills they brought from their respective academic fields. As we outline above, these skills were not the most relevant to HRV's research context. Here, our emphasis on achieving a policy goal through engaging an institutional actor made it more difficult for us to highlight the importance of the ongoing mobilizing work we had been engaged in with students, and to recognize many of the smaller (and less obvious) successes that had been brought about in the course of our project. Some of our greatest challenges and greatest gains were flip sides of the same coin: we found we required a diverse mix of skill-sets to challenge the deeply held biases against drug use that shape public and institutional responses to the issue of harm reduction. This led to a number of questions regarding what skills to share and how to create spaces for learning and mentorship.

Skill-Sharing within the Constraints of University Funding and Timelines

What type of knowledge was necessary for the community organizing work undertaken by HRV? Which skills did we need to learn to take action? How did we ensure that time and space for skills sharing and mentorship were integrated into our work? On the one hand, our work compelled us to develop an understanding of the ways in which a complex of institutions governing the provision of health services for marginalized groups operates in a specific, timely, and local setting. At an analytical level, students and organizers alike were drawn into an ongoing process of assessing the intricate workings of VIHA, the City of Victoria, and other relevant institutions, while developing strategies accordingly. On the other hand, the closure of the fixed-site needle exchange spoke to broader ideas about who is entitled to what health service and on which terms. Like that of other groups addressing the intersections of health, poverty, and illicit drug use, our analytical work involved developing strategies that addressed both the local issue we struggled with and the broader discursive context (Tempalski et al., 2007).

HRV's work emphasizes skills in an area that are not often foregrounded in approaches to teaching CBR: applying the knowledge we gathered through the practice of community organizing. Although it has been difficult at times, our approach to teaching CBR in the HRV advocacy context has aimed at addressing some of the limitations in our academic skill-sets, rather than redefining the project to match the skills that teachers and student researchers bring with them to the project.

Skills Sharing and "Grunt Work"

Regardless of how well-researched, discipline-traversing, or deeply thought-out it may be, for every action there is a "to do" list. This may appear simple enough, but the question of who takes on what tasks reflects some of the more fundamental challenges that our model of CBR poses to the realm of academic research. A wealth of material has been written on how relations of power permeate social justice research (e.g., Kirby et al., 2006; Tuhiwai Smith, 1999; Stoeker, 1999). In the field of CBR, in Canada specifically, Flicker et al. (2007) review the reflections of community-based researchers on what they would do differently. They note that "[underlying] many of these tensions and concerns are issues of power" because collaborative teams, "no matter how well intentioned, still operate in socially and politically inequitable environments that privilege certain knowledge systems over others" (p. 249). The manner in which privilege and power permeate academic-community relations merits significant attention and concern when research implicates marginalized and vulnerable people. As explained by bell hooks (1989): "When we write about the experiences of a group to which we do not belong, we should think about the ethics of our action, considering whether or not our work will be used to reinforce and perpetuate domination" (p. 43).

Although some HRV members have self-identified as people who at present use illicit drugs or have used them in the past, most consider themselves to be allies. HRV works closely with the Society of Living Illicit Drug Users (SOLID), an organization that is led by and for people who use or have used illicit drugs. Questions around power and privilege are most visible when planning or executing our strategies and actions, especially when we work with SOLID. Whose opinions count most and how the division of labour occurs are deeply political matters.

Researchers in Victoria have written about power and the division of labour between academia and community in CBR. Janet Rabinovitch (2004), for example, notes that research can fail to acknowledge the mobilization work required in struggles for social justice by encouraging a division of labour between professionally trained researchers and community members (p. 152). Marge Reitsma-Street (2002), in her reflections on an urban poverty research project, observed that the "risk is that the research in Community Action Research takes precedence over action and community, and the benefits of theorizing, writing, publishing go to the researchers while the other project partners are left with the same complex issue that they started with" (p. 82).

In Harm Reduction Victoria , we have attempted to be aware of the type of work that those of us who identify as allies take on within the broad spectrum of activities that we include in our research. The most visible manifestation of our analysis of working in social struggles with marginalized groups of people is who takes on the "grunt work." That said, an integral part of the mentoring work that we do at VIPIRG consists of providing students with resources on how to integrate analyses of power and privilege into practice, and most students understand the value of taking on grunt work. Students, in turn, have benefited from engaging in a collective process of learning and teaching diverse analytical and practical skills. The eclectic mix of HRV members includes people who share their skills in fields as varied as popular education, social work, media relations, law, and street actions. Students have found themselves acting as media spokespeople, standing behind SOLID members as they speak to the City Council, cooking community meals, petitioning grocery stores for donations, sending email callouts, designing posters, facilitating meetings using consensus decision-making, and learning about safer drug use while operating the "guerrilla needle exchange."

This form of education is inherently packed with troubleshooting, inventions, and taking on tasks outside of our areas of expertise or comfort. It is also a form of education in the full spectrum of community-based research that most students – even those who take practicum placements or research positions in more formal NGOs – cannot obtain anywhere else.

Institutional Constraints

While the learning conditions we describe above are developed through long-term relationship building, university supports and requirements have often constrained the capacity of students to fully engage in these processes. The most immediate constraints that students face in their engagements with HRV are work-study and co-op positions that support students for a single term of applied work with community groups. Although it is helpful for students to receive funding to learn community-based research skills, community-organizing projects rarely fit comfortably into a single 4-month term (Heaney, 1993, p. 45). It is difficult for students, given term schedules in which they are often balancing a range of other work obligations concurrent with class assignments, to become familiarized with a new project, find their place within it, and see a task completed before moving on to their next set of obligations in a new term. The limited nature of this involvement is such that it is often easier for students to take on specific writing or administrative tasks. Unfortunately, these are the tasks in which students are most likely to apply skills they already have, as opposed to being exposed to situations where they are able to pick up new skills and engage directly in the mobilizing work that has been a key aspect of the HRV project. For students, the difficulty in engaging in such skill-sharing processes has much less to do with willingness or interest than it does with the simple need for the time to develop relationships of trust with community members from differing backgrounds, and the time to work slowly in passing along knowledge and skills as these relationships develop.

These time and funding constraints fit into a broader picture of the life of a student within a university structure that is increasingly oriented towards market-based revenue streams and managerial models of productivity and efficiency (Slaughter & Rhoades, 2008; Conlon, 2000; Polster, 2003).[5] For students, the impacts of this trend can be seen in the growing number of students who work concurrent with full-time studies (Canadian Association of University Teachers, 2010, p. 40).[6] The impacts can also be seen in increasing economic pressures to complete studies within limited time frames, as students take on larger student loan debt.[7] In Victoria, these issues of economic limits to community engagement are particularly potent, as the city has among the highest rents in the country, in a province with the lowest minimum wage in the country.

Where students are encouraged to engage in a calculus regarding limited time and funds, it is most efficient for students to engage in community work that translates easily to course assignments and that makes use of already-existing skills, whether in the form of formal research studies or papers. Further, given the rush to complete and the need to work concurrent with studies, it is difficult for students to commit to staying with a community project once their funding has ended. In some instances, students are able to move from one community-based project to another through different funding supports. Unfortunately, it appears to be more difficult to secure funding to remain and develop skills within a single long-term project. As a result, student engagement in community organizing elements of the HRV project have tended to occur *despite* university supports and study commitments rather than *through* these supports and studies, as students continue their HRV work unpaid and concurrent with other work and study commitments.

A key issue we face as teachers and students of CBR, then, is a mismatch between structural conditions for student engagement that make short-term and conventional social scientific research most feasible for university-based researchers, and the need for long-term commitments, a varied skills set, and a range of curiosities more in line with substantive learning with regard to community organizing for social change.

Reflections on Mobilization and CBR Praxis

The nature of the dominant form of community action is connected to the broader political-economic context of any historical period.
— DeFilippis, Fisher, & Schragge (2010, p. 57)

Our successes in teaching CBR through sharing community organizing skills have encouraged us in reassessing our teaching and learning work with regard to the political role of CBR pedagogy when set against the broader social and political contexts that shape current community struggles. In doing so, we have been most struck by the challenge of ensuring that guiding assumptions and approaches of community-based research pedagogy and practice remain cognizant of, and faithful to, the changing (and often difficult to track) circumstances shaping community work.

In thinking through the role of teaching community organizing in CBR within community organizing practice, it has been helpful for us to consider what political work CBR is doing in particular advocacy contexts, and what broader social economic factors inform and shape our work.

How reliant, for instance, is community research on the existence of communities with already-existing capacities for mobilizing around research findings? If there has been a notable shift in the capacity of NGOs to support mobilizing work, where demands for corporate assessment and accountability practices orient community organizations towards professional representation and service-delivery (DeFilippis, Fisher, & Schragge, 2010, p. 3; Ilcan & Basok, 2004; Phillips & Levasseur, 2004), in what ways can teachers and students with roots in the university work to challenge rather than encourage these conditions?

Further, what struggles within our own institutions must students and teachers engage in to ensure we retain the space for continuing such forms of critical pedagogy? To what extent, for instance, can the current drive for university-community partnerships be interpreted as a means of providing labour and expertise to meet the reporting and auditing requirements that ultimately limit the scope and independence of advocacy by NGOs? And to what extent are these forms of governance through reporting and auditing increasingly mirrored in our own research conditions within the university (Smith, 2010)?

Our approach to these questions has been to work with grassroots organizations that, because of their lack of funding and associated reporting restrictions, offer a number of openings for experimentation with the role of research and its relationships to action for social change. Reflecting on our experiences, we see an opportunity here for teachers and students to engage in mobilizing work in a context where there remain few spaces for this type of community organizing, and for passing on and picking up a range of skills that may otherwise lack adequate forums for dissemination. Although such an approach attempts to cope with the immediate challenges we face in a reactionary social and economic context, it can learn from the struggles that led to the formation of past CBR traditions.

Questions about the role of the researcher, what it means to do community-based research, and goals of forging relations of solidarity and of engaging in action that brings about social change, have been addressed in various ways by CBR practitioners. These range from Hall's (2005) suggestion that the researcher must be a "militant rather than a detached observer" (p. 12), to descriptions by Fals Borda and Rahman (1991) of such projects as "social intervention" and "militant research" (p. 25). Such conceptions of the militant researcher are helpful, we suggest, in challenging assumptions that set research and social action, often understood as the distinctive purviews of academic research and community organizing work, apart from one another as distinctive forms of knowledge and activity. They are also useful in focusing on the collaborative work that needs to be done to maintain and create spaces for these forms of engaged social action.

Considering the challenges presented by these changing institutional arrangements and shrinking spaces for social action emphasizes a unique opportunity VIPIRG and HRV provides for students and mentors. Unlike term papers that earn a high grade or well-funded research, our accomplishments may be less tangible. There may still be no fixed-site needle exchange in Victoria, but there is a new set of lessons learned that we can contribute to our local and not-so-local heritage of using CBR for social justice organizing. The students who have worked with HRV and VIPIRG – as well as Mark and Tamara themselves – are now better-armed with a plethora of hard skills, analytical devices, and experiential insights that they can apply to the ongoing work in support of rights and dignity for drug users, as well as other social and environmental justice issues. We have learned, for example, more about how to read through an institutional policy document and define media talking points, build solidarity links across related struggles, work as allies supporting people who use illicit drugs as they prepare an art show or stage a public demonstration followed by a direct action. From mobilizing social media to researching "up" through institutions, our work on harm-reduction issues in Victoria has equipped us for a lifetime of continued social struggle. Many of the students who have worked on these campaigns are still active, in both Victoria and other locations. Importantly, the work of HRV has also marked the landscape of dialogue and discourse in Victoria, raising critical issues and questions related to poverty, health, and community accountability. If HRV had not joined people who use illicit drugs and undertaken the work it has, the closing of the fixed-site needle exchange would have been met with one less voice of opposition.

As social movement theorist Steven M. Buechler (2000) suggests, "dominant institutions in the contemporary world are inscribed with the imprints of past struggles and conflicts. Even when movements fail, they often leave institutional traces because of how the prevailing social order responded to the movement before its demise" (p. 70). We think that VIPIRG's model of CBR pedagogy offers one such trace, primarily through the community organizing skills that continue be shared and passed along in the small space we have managed to carve out within the university and community. Our hope is that this model can contribute to ongoing critical reflection about the current conditions and imperatives shaping research – and researchers – within the community and within the university, and about the possibilities of pursuing social justice work despite these restrictions.

Part II

Learning with Community:
Teaching CBR in Community Settings

4 Siem Smun'eem (Respected Children): A Community-Based Research Training Story

MUKWA MUSAYETT (SHELLY JOHNSON),
SANDRINA DE FINNEY, KUNDOUQK (JACQUIE GREEN),
LESLIE BROWN, AND SHANNE McCAFFREY

> Research is a ceremony for improving your relationship with an idea.
> – Shawn Wilson (2008)

This chapter tells the story of the Siem Smun'eem Indigenous Child Welfare Research Network[1] (the Network) and our experience of developing and delivering research training to, and with, Indigenous communities in British Columbia. We acknowledge that we live on the unceded traditional lands of Indigenous peoples, one of us on Secwepemc territory, one on Wsáneć territory, and three on Lekwungen territory. Out of respect for our physical location on the traditional lands of the Lekwungen, we consulted and asked for guidance from Elders and knowledgeable traditional language speakers, in our choice of a Coast Salish name, Siem Smun'eem (meaning "Respected Children"), to represent the Network. This name reflects our commitment to Indigenous reclaiming, restorying, and reimagining our Indigenous community-based research (ICBR) training, and remembering who we hope will be the beneficiaries of our work. This story is intended to illustrate how we understand and enact a community-based approach on the traditional territories of the communities we inhabit and engage protocols that ground our research and research training. We five authors form the executive of the Network, coordinating a provincewide initiative that aims to respond to the need for research that supports Indigenous approaches to caring for children and families.

The Network brings diverse Indigenous people and knowledges together to support Indigenous children and families. It emerged from a meeting of academics, social workers, child and youth workers, policy makers, Elders, and community members who recognized that most reformations of child welfare policy and practice intended to respond to the needs of Indigenous peoples were still grounded in Euro-Western ways of knowing and thinking. Rooted in a vision for healing and the inclusion of diverse voices, Network initiatives seek to reclaim Indigenous ways of knowing and doing and reposition them at the core of child and family wellness initiatives. The Network provides a space for critical dialogue about Indigenous research, as well as opportunities for research-related training, knowledge transmission, and resource sharing. Our hope is to work in partnership with communities to incorporate their traditional knowledge and teachings into services and policies for children, youth, and families. We see Indigenous research as an underused resource to help in this process.

The hub of the Network is made up of academics, and it is administered through the University of Victoria, as this is where most of the resources (researchers and funding) are located. In addition, one of the Network's researchers is based at Thompson Rivers University in the interior of British Columbia. It is an ongoing challenge for a university-run initiative to keep a commitment to be community based and focused at the same time as maintaining a provincial perspective. The Network's complex contribution to community-based and provincially focused work is a critical function that fills a gap for communities that must pay inward attention within available resources, yet can benefit from awareness of potential provincial connections.

One of the Network's initiatives is the development and delivery of research training for community members, professionals, and others with an interest in Indigenous child welfare. We want to demystify the very idea of research, making research processes transparent and more accessible to Indigenous communities. In the past 2 years, a number of 2-day training workshops, with an accompanying toolkit of resources, were provided in various BC regions. Each individual training workshop was developed and delivered in collaboration with local partners, including Elders, youth, service providers, and researchers, reflecting our commitment to a relational approach of ICBR.

Another Network initiative, in addition to working with communities to design and deliver Indigenous child welfare research training throughout British Columbia, is to provide research support, guidance, and resources via the Network website (Siem Smun'eem, n.d.). Indigenous faculty, community-based researchers, and child welfare agency personnel act as steering committee members and contribute to a wide range of information regarding Indigenous research methods available through our website and physical library resources. Their contributions guide the Network in the delivery of research training and support to students and communities.

The Network has an advisory committee that is situated throughout the province and represents various communities, agencies, and those who have a vested interest in caring for Indigenous children. Often, it is through our relationship with advisory committee members that we get invited to work with a particular community. For example, through our relationship with the Northwest Internation Community and Family Services Society, we hosted a training session in Prince Rupert, where we worked closely with Lax Kwa'alaams Elders and Youth. Similarly, our advisory suggested sessions in Coast Salish (Burnaby) and Secwepemc or Shuswap (Kamloops) territories. Other training delivery opportunities have come through other relationships, such as those established by the trainers with Network members, community members, or government sponsors. The Network's relationship with advisory members facilitates our offering of training sessions and ensures that we adhere respectfully to their specific protocols and ethics.

Indigenous Community-Based Research

In this chapter, we delve into how we conduct Indigenous community-based research (ICBR) training. The examples and stories that follow explicate how the Network conceptualizes issues of planning, facilitation, content, collaboration, protocol, and methods when delivering research training to and with diverse Indigenous communities. In the 2 years following the inception of the Network, we developed and delivered training sessions with a range of Indigenous communities and provincial government staffing groups. In British Columbia, the Network provided training in Burnaby (a city close to Vancouver on Coast Salish territory); Prince Rupert (Lax Kwa'alaams territory, which is pronounced phonetically as "*La-kwa-lahms*"); Port Hardy (Gwa'sala-Nakwaxda'xw territory, which is pronounced phonetically as "*Gwah-sah-la Nock-wock-doe*"); Métis Community Services (Coast Salish territory on Vancouver Island); Kamloops (Secwepemc/Shuswap territory, which can alternately be pronounced phonetically as "*Shi-HUEP-muh*" or "*She-KWE-pem*" and "*Shoo-swap*"); Duncan (Quw'utsun' territory, pronounced phonetically as "*Cow-ut-zun*") and to the provincial government Ministry of Children and Family Development (MCFD) staff (Coast Salish territory on Vancouver Island).

The Network research training embraces a community-based approach whereby university partners work with community members to develop and deliver the training. Such an approach includes the following key features:

- Respect for local protocols
- Engagement with local knowledge (Indigenous ways of knowing as well as experiential and research knowledge)
- Co-development of research training
- Co-presentation of research training
- Provision of resources that enable the community to partner, participate, and implement training
- Guiding assumptions that we, as individual academics, are in relationships with the people involved in the training and research forever (i.e., not project time-limited) and that these relationships are personal as well as professional
- Self-reflection and evaluation embedded in every aspect of the work
- Peer mentoring and leadership building: Training participants are invited to teach each other and past participants are invited to co-facilitate future sessions.

Our collaborative approach ensures community contribution to the content as well as to the process of the training. Prior to the development of a 2-day research training agenda, a Network representative meets with the community worker (usually a Network advisory member) to organize a meeting between the Network, community Elders, and youth. That the university academics partner with and travel to a community to develop the training collaboratively, and return at a later date to deliver the training increases our costs. However, this is a key step to build a collaborative curriculum. As part of the training, participants are also invited to share resources, skills, and strategies that address their specific community research needs. Contextualizing the training to the local communities in which the training is offered helps to avoid the externally defined, top-down approach often espoused by traditional university research designs, even ones claimed to be community-based. The training, both in its process of delivery and its content, reinforces the ethic that we as researchers and research trainers are accountable to the communities we work with. We provide an agenda template and begin a shared research planning process by listening to ancestral teachings from the traditional owners of the territory on which the training is scheduled. We work in partnership with local Elders and youth to discuss and plan what aspects of traditional teachings are important to enhance the lives of children and families in that territory. Based on their guidance and direction, we incorporate examples of Indigenous research methods that have been conducted on their territories since time immemorial. For example, in one training session, a local Indigenous basket weaver shared protocols and the process of gathering cedar to make baskets. In this session, we linked this basket-weaving process to the importance of respecting protocols and relationships in research. This process of learning from ancient methods has taught us, as researchers, about patience, respect for the natural evolution of knowledge sharing, and how to participate and engage in respectful relationships with co-creators of research and/or research participants.

Once the 2-day agenda is developed, the sessions are widely advertised and offered free of charge. They are targeted to community groups and agencies that provide services to Indigenous children, youth, and families as well as all other interested people. The majority of community-based participants are Indigenous; they include Elders, youth, service providers, agency managers, community representatives, researchers, students, policy makers, and non-Indigenous government and private sector employees. Participants receive a toolkit – a large binder filled with articles and multimedia resources related to Indigenous research, including sections on a range of Indigenous methodologies, protocols, and ethics, as well as examples of successful applied research from diverse Indigenous communities. Although some participants register "just to check it out" and have never considered conducting research, most bring research-related questions and goals. Many Indigenous agencies and communities have had negative experiences with dominant forms of research and are eager to learn more culturally congruent methodologies. They want information about how to conduct a range of community-based research projects, including graduate student research, agency evaluations and funding reports, action-centred projects, collaborative research, and larger studies with non-Aboriginal partners. They also want ethical guidelines for conducting community-engaged research in their agencies and communities. Most importantly, they want to reclaim knowledge that is already held in their communities and find ways of incorporating it more consistently into their services for children, youth, and families.

The training is participatory, delivered by a Network team that includes steering committee members and local co-facilitators. Elders guide us on the proper protocols for honouring local territories, conducting sessions, sharing stories, and thanking respected teachers and storytellers with appropriate gifts and words. Anonymous evaluations by participants are sought at the end of each day. The content usually follows this process: a review of Euro-Western research assumptions and their impact on the invisibility of Indigenous knowledge in academia; the need to reconceptualize Indigenous research as central to transforming services for children, youth, and families; examples of diverse community-based Indigenous research projects and methodologies; and interactive exercises designed to help participants explore their cultural teachings and values, and design their own research study. One analogy we use to train participants is to connect various research paradigms to movie genres. We discuss horror films in this paradigm and provide examples of positivist research that sought to measure the size of an Indigenous person's skull as "proof" of diminished capacity for intelligence. We link documentary film genres to research such as the Royal Commission on Aboriginal Peoples (Indian and Northern Affairs Canada, 1996), and stress that although many research projects are funded, many times no action is taken that results in meaningful improvement. We highlight the diverse Indigenous cultures of British Columbia by problematizing Canada's enforced notions of "Aboriginal," "on or off reserve," and "status or non-status." We acknowledge that many Indigenous peoples were forcefully removed from their families, places, and cultural teachings by child welfare, adoption, and residential school polices, colonial policies over which they had no control. We encourage participants to consider ways in which Indigenous peoples resisted these powers, and discuss the resurgence or "relearning" of Indigenous ways of knowing and being. As such we ensure that our research training is respectful of diverse and evolving Indigenous identities, places, and experiences.

Delivering ICBR Training in an Emergent, Contextualized Approach

I sense that I come from my strongest location when I come from that place of tribal grounding and epistemology that uniquely roots me to my ancestry and history. It signifies who I am within both my tribal and relational location to people, territory, and time.

– Kovach (2009)

As discussed in the previous sections, our training sessions are rooted in an emergent, localized approach. For this reason, the Network only conducts training when and where we are invited to do so, and our sessions are always designed in partnership with a local agency or community. Each training session is unique to each community, and the Network remains respectful of traditional teachings and ceremonies belonging to the specific territory on which the Network is a visitor. It is our assertion that Indigenous communities have always undertaken research and that Indigenous research cannot be extricated from teachings that are deeply intertwined with everyday life.

To support understanding of the ICBR training methods and practices, we offer three training stories from our work on the traditional territories of the Coast Salish, Secwepemc, and Gwa'sala-Nakwaxda'xw peoples. The stories highlight processes, skills, values, and knowledges we employ to contest the damaging legacy of child welfare by centring research models that are more congruent with Indigenous world views.

Story 1: Coast Salish Session – Basket Weaving

The Burnaby training session incorporated the Coast Salish cultural practice of basket weaving. In the morning of Day 1, we invited a basket weaver to share the process of weaving cedar baskets with ICBR training participants. In the afternoon we linked the various steps and processes of basket weaving to conducting research in an ethical, Indigenous way. The entire basket-weaving process shared by the basket weaver is complex and lengthy. For the purposes of this chapter, the preparation, weaving and usage process is condensed. For example, the basket weaver shared the important preparation process of readying oneself, physically, emotionally, mentally, and spiritually, to pick the cedar, and how traditional knowledge is used to know when the cedar picking time is "right." To ensure the sustainability of this sacred resource, the weaver must know where on the land to pick cedar, how to prepare it, rip it into pieces, soak it, and ready it for weaving. Once the preparations have been made, the weaver will weave unique patterns into a basket. When the cedar basket is complete, this beautiful piece has many uses: It can be used to collect berries while out berry picking, to store food or objects, to hold water, or as a gift to someone. Each basket may be made for different purposes and people in the same way that different research methodologies or processes produce different knowledge for different audiences and purposes. As researchers, we must also know the community that we enter when we conduct research or ICBR training. We must adhere to all the necessary steps and protocols prior to conducting the research by building and nurturing relationships with the people and communities in which the research or ICBR training occurs. Once we have gathered our data, the findings should have immediate and long-term uses such as supporting a community to develop programs, policies, and/or traditional teachings.

Story 2: Secwepemc (or Shuswap) Session – Dip Nets

A second example of ICBR training occurred in the Kamloops (Tk'emlups) session located on unceded traditional Secwepemc or Shuswap territory. Elders and youth brought a fishing dip net, materials to weave pine needle baskets, and creation and hunting stories as examples of their traditional Indigenous research practices. It was important to the Elders that Network members understood the history of the Secwepemc peoples: that their ancestors thrived in the interior region of what is now known as British Columbia for approximately 10,000 years prior to European contact. Their traditional economy was based on hunting, fishing, and trading until Secwepemc peoples experienced a severe smallpox epidemic in 1862 that devastated and drastically reduced their population. The assimilative threat to their children and families continued when two residential schools opened in 1890 and 1893 at the northern and central areas of their territory. Secwepemc children were forced to attend the institutions meant to "kill the Indian in the child" (Canada, 2008). In this training session, two Indigenous researchers, one university based and one health based, shared qualitative and quantitative research examples focused on Indigenous strategies to "put the Indian back in the child." The qualitative study focused on the unique educational and cultural needs of urban Indigenous children in BC's child protection system (Johnson, 2011) while the quantitative training focused on the significant health needs of Indigenous peoples.

The Elders and youth used a 16-foot dip net and pole as an example of an Indigenous research practice that sustained Secwepemc children, families, and communities for thousands of years. This was, and remains, a primary fishing technique used by the Secwepemc peoples to harvest salmon from traditional fishing sites still in use today. The dip net, time consuming to make, was traditionally made of inner cedar bark or spun nettle and attached to the end of a fir or cedar pole. The method meant that Secwepemc peoples were required to stand above dangerous river currents, tied to a rock, on a wooden platform or the shore, and dip (or sweep) the large net into the water. The fish were trapped in the net and hauled up, and then the net was emptied and the process repeated. We used this traditional dip netting practice to demonstrate the strength and resilience of Secwepemc peoples, who used the land and river resources to ensure the continued health of their children. It also provided a metaphor to demonstrate the risk that Secwepemc peoples believe is worth taking to reclaim their children from dangerous places, such as Canada's child protection systems, and return them to the safety of their families and communities.

Story 3: Gwa'sala-Nakwaxda'xw Session – Oolichan Fish and Oil as Metaphors for Vanishing Children

In Gwa'sala-Nakwaxda'xw territory located on the northern tip of Vancouver Island, the training session was sponsored by Legal Services Society of British Columbia in collaboration with the Gwa'sala-Nakwaxda'xw peoples. Our relationship building and learning included gaining a better understanding of the nation's history and child protection experiences. The Gwa'sala-Nakwaxda'xw peoples are actually two nations, the *Gwa'sala* and the *Nakwaxda'xw*. Their uprooting, disruption, and reconfiguration as one nation was enforced by the federal Department of Indian Affairs in 1964, when the communities were moved off their traditional territory to a region that was generally used as a temporary clam digging camp by many Kwakwaka'wakwk people (Gwa'sala 'Nakwaxda'xw, 2010). We recognize that, when working in community with a group that includes both Indigenous community members and a government organization, it is important for Indigenous practitioners, facilitators, and educators to walk on "both sides of the feather," that is, translating Euro-Western methodologies of knowledge, practice, and policy into an Indigenous approach that honours traditional knowledge, experiences, protocols, and culture. To walk on both sides of the feather with a group of learners that involves Elders, spiritual leaders, youth, and government requires a balanced, skilled, and sensitive approach in both the conceptual development and delivery of an ICBR practice framework.

In our first meeting with Elders, youth, and community members, a prayer was gifted to invite the Creator and good spirits in for our meeting. We listened as the participants began to talk about their experiences, memories, and visions for changing child welfare. Working with Elders, wisdom keepers, spiritual leaders, and youth requires a different, more organic process supported by trust and relationship in order to move learning to a good place. In our diverse collective indigenous traditions, we never "teach" Elders. They, as well as children and youth, connect with us to provide reciprocal learning and teachings, collecting and affirming until we reach a collective understanding. In our beginning conversations with this very unique group of participants, it became clear that we were being asked by Elders, youth, and community to come to listen and to bear witness to their stories and experiences around child welfare and the high rates of removal of children from within their communities by child protection authorities.

Growing out of the child removal or "vanishing" stories came parallel stories about the new reality that the oolichan (or candle fish as it is sometimes known) are also vanishing from their territory. The oolichan catch and the rendering of oolichan oil, "t'lintna," is in crisis; many Elders have run out of it and there is little left in community. T'lintna has been described by Elders as the "backbone" of their culture. They affirmed how sacred and treasured are both the little silver oolichan and the children of the Gwa'sala-Nakwaxda'xw people. Participants shared candid memories of children born and lost, and they linked good practices in traditional parenting to the process of making t'lintna:

> Making good relationships with children is life-long work; There is something to be learned at every stage; It is a skill and practice that improves with experience, reflection and time; It is a practice that is embedded in family, culture, and tradition and is part of the identity of Kwakwaka'wakw peoples.

With some of the historical context in view, this small and closely bonded community began to convey their profound concern about their children, youth and families using the metaphor of oolichan oil.

These three stories from Coast Salish, Secwepemc, and Gwa'sala-Nakwaxda'xw traditional territories are offered as ways to demonstrate the holistic nature that beats at the heart of our contextualized approach to ICBR training. They reaffirm our commitment to follow local Indigenous protocols and knowledges and to acknowledge the primacy of Indigenous experiences and teachings.

Lessons Learned

In this section we discuss challenges and successes we have encountered in the training process, as expressed in anonymous evaluation
feedback collected at various training sessions.[2] We have learned important lessons from challenges that arise in our partnership work, particularly in the area where available resources clash with the 4 Rs of
Indigenous research protocols advanced by Kirkness and Barnhardt
(1991) – respect, relevance, reciprocity, and responsibility:

> Respect is demonstrated toward Aboriginal Peoples' cultures and com-
> munities by valuing their diverse knowledge that contributes to Aboriginal
> community health and wellness. Relevance to culture and community is
> critical for the success of Aboriginal training and research. Reciprocity is
> accomplished through a two-way process of learning and research ex-
> change. Both community and university benefit from effective training
> and research relationships. Responsibility is empowerment and is fostered
> through active and rigorous engagement and participation. (p. xx)

Our commitment to partnerships requires adequate time and resources, a lesson the Network learned early. For instance, in an effort to cut
costs at our very first session, we provided only limited food options.
Participants, particularly Elders, made it clear to us that providing
enough food was a non-negotiable cultural expectation that is critical to
relationship building and values of reciprocity:

> In our culture we always feed our guests.
>   Elders needed fresh food; it is basic respect for our Elders.

Lessons like this have reinforced our commitment to not cut corners
and to invest only in processes to which we can fully commit. However,
we also recognize that as trainers coming in from the outside, we cannot fully understand or speak to the complex histories and needs of
each community or agency. Our training is offered free of charge and is
open to all who express an interest, but because communities are inherently diverse and each holds its own complex dynamics and tensions,
some potential partners and voices are inevitably excluded, as noted by
these participants:

> The Elders were nice; it would have been nice to see Elders from all the
> local communities. To have Elders present at every table.

More youth voice. The youth voice should be more present as presenters. There's a lot of practitioners but more government people should also attend this training to change services from the inside out.

Concerns about whose voices are included or excluded, and who gets to decide who is invited or not, extend to our roles as university partners. The Network includes Indigenous academics from throughout British Columbia, and collectively we have personal and professional connections with many Indigenous communities, but we do not always have pre-existing relationships with the communities in which we are invited. Tuhiwai Smith (1999) reflects on the challenges of being both insider and outsider when doing research in an Indigenous community. Even if one is from a particular community, and enjoys family and cultural connections in that community, the stance of "being a researcher from the university" has many different implications in how we negotiate partnerships and how we are perceived in community. Although our place on the continuum of insider-outsider shifts with the context, we always carry an aspect of being an outsider. Mitigating this are our relationships with peoples, places, and projects in a community. An Indigenous approach to research and practice embraces the building of relationships, and therefore much of the Network's work is the development and nurturing of new and existing relationships. Our research training is part of this strategy and echoes a relational approach; indeed, networking is a key outcome. The ethics of a relational approach, including accountability to community and participants and reciprocity of knowledge exchange, are necessarily embedded in the training. The Network's commitment to community-based planning and delivery ensures that the training's benefits continue to grow long after we have left the community and is critical to breaking down the stereotype that researchers and their research reside outside of Indigenous communities:

> This has been so inspirational because I never thought before that we could design and control our own research according to our own values.
> It's so nice to see youth present and to see them take a leadership role, how they can become researchers and bring a new future to our nations.

As we have discussed, although our training is shaped around a shared conceptual framework, the pace and content of each training session is determined by the local context and the participants' skills and needs.

What works in one context may not work in another; therefore, we consciously resist the desire to develop a prescriptive training model. Participants are encouraged to present their own teachings and research projects and to engage in peer teaching. In this way, local knowledge gains saliency and visibility, and connections among Network members are strengthened, as expressed by the following participants:

> [The training] models process with community. Hearing what others are doing in their own community agencies and their research.
>
> As someone new to research it was really great to see research from Indigenous perspective and to meet others who are doing great work. This was valuable in helping understanding how culture and research can work together.

A Commitment to Reclaiming Research

As Indigenous scholar Linda Tuhiwai Smith (1999, p. 1) observed, the word "research" itself "is probably one of the dirtiest words in the indigenous world's vocabulary. The ways in which research is implicated in the worst excesses of colonialism remains a powerful remembered history for many of the world's colonized peoples." Given this history, our training aims to decenter the hegemony of Euro-Western thought that is so entrenched in communities that many Indigenous participants find it difficult to imagine how research might be conducted in a different way:

> [This training] has enriched my research experience by deepening my understanding of Indigenous research methods and values which I intend to employ in my own work in community.
>
> I did not know there was Indigenous ways of doing research. I am delighted to learn how to do research, "in a good way."

To re-story research "in a good way," we share many examples of effective Indigenous research, including examples drawn from participatory action research, policy change, traditional storytelling, and youth-engaged studies. The common thread in these examples is their guidance of how to document and integrate traditional teachings and values into a re-visioning of child, youth, and family services and policies. We start from the foundational assertion that Indigenous communities have always possessed complex knowledge systems and have always conducted community-based research. We convey this message by framing research as something that is inextricably connected to every community's sacred laws and ways of life:

> The delivery model made it easy to realize that the basis of our lives is a journey of research and learning. So new, yet such an old methodology that has been steeped into our history for millennia past and a millennium to come. At the end of the day it is hoped that the following generations will reinforce and implement those values.

Despite the positive feedback we receive from participants, the journey of "reclaiming" Indigenous research can also be very difficult. One challenge we encounter relates to the familiar and important dilemma of how to conduct Indigenous research when community members are disconnected from the teachings and practices that would inform Indigenous epistemologies and methodologies. As a result of generations of dislocation from community caused by colonial practices including residential schooling, external adoptions, and high rates of Indigenous children in the child protection systems, it is a common experience for participants to express a deep sense of longing and grieving for cultural knowledge that might have informed their research process, and for limited access to Elders and teachers who might guide their work:

> Growing up not knowing my culture, now I wonder how I would do research using teachings I don't have, and I don't want to do it the white way either.
> [One benefit of the training is] to bridge traditional with people who were not raised in a traditional manner.

This loss of knowledge is a source of much discussion during training. We emphasize the importance of communities starting from where they are and drawing on their own expertise and needs, rather than holding themselves up to external ideals of what culturally centred ICBR "should look like." These complexities are particularly salient in urban contexts with many different cultural traditions. For instance, some participants have expressed concerns that as specific local teachings are lost, Indigenous research methods increasingly rely on a pan-Indigenous model. One of the most important lessons we have learned is the importance of engaging directly with these complexities, because they are critical to the negotiations that Indigenous agencies and communities must engage in to develop their own research models. We always acknowledge that many participants have conflicted feelings about the very notion of research as a result of their negative experiences in school and postsecondary educational systems that excluded their Indigenous perspectives. For many Indigenous people who have grown up thinking that research is something that white men in lab coats do (see also, Loiselle, Taylor, & Donald, this volume), and who think of research as a tool for appropriation and exploitation, a focus on Indigenous research is revolutionary:

> [The training] challenged my belief that research can only be done by experts.
>
> Give hope that Indigenous research can create meaningful, nurturing relationships and also create change and transformation for Indigenous people.
>
> It legitimated/validated the importance of our worldview and way of life.
>
> The training has given me confidence to use my teachings and values not just for my work with children and families but also in how we do research as an agency.
>
> You've given me hope!

We acknowledge that the image of the analytical, disconnected researcher is one that CBR practitioners, no matter what our background, struggle to challenge. When we engage in training, we locate ourselves not only as knowledge holders, but also as family members, activists, advocates, allies, community members, and participants in political and community movements. We try to adopt a very different epistemological stance, one rooted in humility and a collaborative spirit that is critical to building trust, a stance that participants appreciate:

> The cohesiveness of the facilitators was impressive. I have never attended a workshop that ran so smoothly with so much fun and valuable knowledge.
>
> It is so amazing – the ladies provided the information, shared experiences and maintaining your humility without elevating yourselves – often First Nations with credentials put themselves above others!! You did not!

In addition to a stance of humility and collaboration, we also have a political commitment to foregrounding Indigenous world views. As Indigenous women academics, we often find that it is our colleagues and institutions who cling tightest to colonial, patriarchal Euro-Western notions of what counts as valid research. Yet, some of the workshops included non-Indigenous peoples who expressed interest in learning Indigenous ways of conducting and participating in research processes. Their participation depended on the context and who they were. In the Ministry of Children and Family Development training session, for example, there was a significant number of non-Indigenous people, which shifted the way the workshop was done and how, then, people participated. We found some differences in participation: a non-Indigenous person working for and or otherwise steeped in Indigenous community might participate quite differently than a non-Indigenous person working for a government. What we found was that the context and constituency of the group is an indicator of differential impacts and may reflect how non-Indigenous people participate in the workshops.

To unsettle the impact of colonization on academia, we focus on the many examples of effective Indigenous research, the potential for partnerships with allied non-Indigenous researchers, and the possibilities offered by a re-storying approach. We aim to engage participants in a radical reimagining that generates excitement and commitment to reclaiming research. We do so by modelling an inclusive collaborative stance towards working together across disciplines, backgrounds, and experiences:

> I felt the workshop was very inclusive of everyone. I think it was respectful and brought forth examples that are useful to open ways to have success in a research project.
> Thank you so much for including me in the workshop!
> This training can be very helpful for both Indigenous and Non-Indigenous researchers in community. It challenges the traditional views of research and provides practical examples of how to do things differently.

As facilitators we commit to struggling together with our participants through the complex issues of protocols, representation, accountability, accessibility, political tensions, and ownership that inevitably arise in ICBR. In this journey, silence, humour, and visceral learning are powerful tools. We try to engage all senses and skills by using a variety of methods and tools, including exercises, frequent energizers, music, stories, art, theatre, multimedia presentations, large and small group discussions, and other interactive activities. In any given training session, we share laughter, hugs, food, stories, and tears; we take time to stop, stand together, and ponder those powerful moments when someone has shared a sacred teaching, a powerful theatre image, or a healing song. Our sessions are always filled with drumming, songs, and story-telling that we invite participants to share, which is important in help-ing people bring their whole selves into the process:

> Listening, networking, peer learning, thinking differently. Opportunity to listen and speak.
>
> Loved, loved, loved the games, like the stories, facilitators were person-able/knowledgeable and made a safe learning environment.

As we work through the training, participants engage in a series of exercises and discussions designed to help them consider such issues as making sure the research directly includes diverse community members across all phases; ethics, ownership, and cultural protocols; partnership agreements with non-Indigenous researchers and funders; how traditional knowledge will be respectfully collected, shared, and protected during the course of the study; and how the study will im-pact services for children, youth, and families. In Euro-Western re-search, budding researchers are often taught that studies should be grounded in a thorough review of the literature. In accordance with Indigenous methodologies identified and developed by Kovach (2009), Wilson (2008), and Tuhiwai Smith (1999), we teach that a research de-sign should be grounded in the community's values, ethics, and teach-ings – knowledge that the dominant literature too often ignores. Examples of Indigenous knowledge in which participants have chosen to root their research designs are as diverse as they are inspirational. Some participants from Cree and Blackfoot Nations designed their re-search study around the teachings of the tipi, wherein each aspect of the tipi represents an important value that guides research to inform a new program for youth at risk in their community. Members of a West Coast Nation used the eagle as the foundational symbol for conduct-ing research funded by their band that is rooted in their local teachings and protocols. Two Métis participants chose the Métis sash as their guiding metaphor, relaying how the threads of the sash represented different knowledge perspectives that had been kept alive for genera-tions by families and could now be celebrated and integrated into so-cial programming. In a rural northern community, participants chose the drum, representing a heartbeat that would protect and nurture children, as a framework for conducting community research to in-form their local child and family services. These traditional symbols

and practices help to honour community research knowledges to reduce the sense of isolation experienced by many communities engaged
in policy and service transformations:

> Yes, generous sharing of knowledge translation and institutional partner-
> ship with community.
>
> The training was invaluable and opened my eyes on how to incorporate
> Indigenous research in my day-to-day work/life. Also reaffirmed some of
> my beliefs about the ineffectiveness of mainstream research with Indig-
> enous Peoples.
>
> It was valuable to me to reinforce my teachings and demonstrate how to
> practice in research. It was very tangible, lots of examples, hands-on, and
> I like this kind of learning.

These words provide a powerful incentive for us to work to reach as
many agencies and communities as possible, to support a common vision for change that so many of our participants hold in their hearts and
spirits:

> At the end of the day, this is for our children and families; they need this
> urgently. We cannot afford to wait.
>
> Making and using our own laws and ways to protect and care for our
> children.
>
> Putting trauma behind us, knowing the trauma and impacts of residen-
> tial school, how it harmed parenting skills. Honouring our teachers and
> those who have taught us.
>
> Holding on to our children, bringing our children home.
>
> We are still here. We were here first. We know this territory. It is all.

Our Way Forward

Our training day ended in a resolute commitment that Indigenous children,
youth, and families were worth more than just supporting; they are worth
fighting for. Together, we are stronger and that certainly was the message that
emanated from our gathering.

– S. McCaffrey, personal communication, 24 February 2011

At every session the Network gathers suggestions for additions to the
current training content and toolkit. Usually, participants request more
of everything, including more policy and evaluation examples, more

time to connect with other participants, and more follow-up and consultation assistance with research projects after the training. They also ask for more advanced and hands-on training to enable communities to actually develop independent research proposals and conduct research in partnership with the Network or other bodies.

Other ongoing and important components of the ICBR training and Network capacity development are focused on "more" as well, including increasing the Network's training delivery sites, advisory committee membership, and connections to Indigenous community-based researchers. In addition the Network continually adds to its extensive website resources and improves outreach and collaborations with other educational institutions across British Columbia and Canada. The Network seeks to develop additional capacity through exploration of new funding relationships; presentations at international, national, provincial, and local conferences; and plans to develop a national Indigenous Child Welfare Research Network conference. The dissemination of helpful Indigenous research materials to more Indigenous communities, especially those that are northern or remote, remains a primary task.

The Network engages the oral storytelling ways of Indigenous knowing through listening and telling of all kinds of stories. When we engage with a community to provide research training, we learn from each other how to validate our knowing. Affirming for the grannies in Lax Kwa'alaams that they have a story to tell, and knowledge worthy of sharing, teaches us not only about caring for children, but about how to listen when we do research, how to work together and follow cultural protocols. We all learn how to weave traditional knowledge with contemporary experience, cultural values with research ethics. We witness each other learning, teaching, knowing, and researching. Through that act of witnessing, our Network – and each of us – continues along our healing journeys and grows stronger.

Through our ICBR training experiences, we have learned that when working with Indigenous communities, particularly in the area of child welfare, our learning can be intense, full of grief and loss, but also healing. In some training sessions, the facilitators witness, affirm, and record participant child welfare events and experiences on large pieces of chart paper. Often for the first time outside their own community, participants encounter public legitimacy and validation of their experiences, find a greater understanding of the intersectional colonizing factors at work in their lives, and begin to develop research strategies that promote healing and social justice.

We are profoundly moved by the generosity and spirit of so many participants who have survived to tell their stories of the colonizing legacy of residential schools, enforced community relocations and political identities, the "sixties scoop," and child welfare abductions. Their strength and determination are brought into our decolonizing research, work, practice, and teaching as well as into our thinking, our identities, and our hearts. It is healing to witness each member of the circle rip up the paper that tells of the colonizers' offences against Indigenous communities, and stand together to watch as it is scorched to ashes. The ICBR process practised by the Network represent the beginning of a new era; it reflects participants' determination to take control and respond in a new way to traumatic colonial experiences. This becomes our new shared experience, and energy, that we harvest from the smoke. It is these communal actions that inform our thinking and understanding and further develop healing and restorying in our ICBR practice. All these experiences help the Network members to grow as Indigenous learners, teachers, community members, and academics "from the University" – all our relations.

5 Community-Based Mapping: A Tool for Transformation

JON CORBETT AND MAEVE LYDON

Maps, like theories, have power in virtue of introducing modes of manipulation and control that are not possible without them. They become evidence of reality in themselves and can only be challenged through the production of other maps and theories.

– David Turnbull (1989, p. 54)

We are all mapmakers. Any community can make maps. Community mapping rests on such a claim and assumption. Maps are inspiring. They provide a unique language for humans to communicate with one another. Maps can enable and record great losses and discoveries, the changes of physical and political landscapes, great beauty and great destruction. They reflect our relationship to ourselves, to one another and to the environment. They reflect the history and geography of our lives and communities. Maps can be used as tools to reinforce the boundaries of colonization, but also as tools for emancipation.

Whether conscious or not, our cognitive or mental maps guide the paths and routes that make up our lives. Each of us has a different mental map, a different sense of place, and a distinct way of seeing and being in the world. We each have our own stories and geographies, as well as different physical, mental, and social landscapes that we experience and inhabit every day. How we spatially and visually represent such stories and geographies is, in effect, cartography. When we do this with other people we are "community mapping."

A community can be geographical (e.g., local, school, neighbourhood, regional, national, or global), socio-cultural (e.g., ethnic, women, men, gay, youth, or children), sectoral (e.g., education, recreation, government, police, or health), and ecological (e.g., bioregion, plant, animal, or biosphere). Community mapping is the process of creating collective representations of the geography, history, and shared experiences of these communities. Community mapping "lets people think together graphically, instead of verbally" (Wood, 1994, p. 24). It tells the stories of what is happening in our communities, and every community has stories, recent or long buried, in the lives and landscapes of our common ground.

There is increasing interest in interdisciplinary community-based research (CBR) frameworks and teaching methods that can bridge academic disciplines (the arts, sciences, fine arts, and humanities), more effectively address the complex issues of our times, and reflect the interplay among social, environmental, and economic forces. CBR requires creative pedagogical tools and methods that both engage students and community learners and make research socially relevant. Community mapping is an effective and holistic CBR pedagogic tool used in formal and informal classroom and community settings, where the participants and learners become the mapmakers and re-present their knowledge and experiences both as individuals and collectively. Community mapping is a powerful modality for learning, because it can expose and then deconstruct totalizing or essentializing claims to knowledge, power, and territory. Moreover, it places decision making, knowledge exchange, and production in the hands of the learners – the mapmakers – and, in the case of jointly produced maps or mapping projects, back into the hands of the broader community that the maps claim to represent. On a psychological level, community mapping employs theory and methods that emphasize collective learning and knowledge production based on the engagement and affirmation of the lived experience, gifts, world view, and connection to place that every human has. Community mapping can awaken the social and ecological self and a collective geographical and historical imagination that is often neglected or degraded in an individualized and commodified world.

This chapter has two objectives: First, we share the experience of community mapping as practised by the Common Ground Mapping project and the University of Victoria (UVic) in collaboration with the worldwide open-source mapping system called Green Map. Second, we use the experiences from the University of British Columbia (UBC) and UVic to examine the emerging role of community mapping as a teaching method that serves to link university students with relevant social issues, and in doing so we make the case that community mapping is a powerful pedagogic tool that can initiate, stimulate, and support community-based research, learning, and civic engagement.

The first section of the chapter lays the theoretical foundation for community mapping and discusses how it can become a transformative tool for knowledge production, reflexive learning, and empowering action that is grounded in real time and place. This begins with exploring the meaning of maps and mapmaking with reference to Indigenous and anti-colonial mapping. It then introduces the Green Map System, and provides some guidelines for facilitators who are working with beginning mappers. The second section focuses on the practice and pedagogy of community mapping as core CBR methodology. It describes a range of situations where community mapping could be employed, and then goes into some depth on two mapping projects.

The final section of the chapter focuses on the challenges and opportunities for the ongoing development of community mapping as a CBR teaching tool within and between the academy and community. This includes recognition of the tensions, power imbalances, and mediation between people and technology, between product and process, and between institutional knowledge and community-based knowledge. The chapter concludes that an academic context that favours interdisciplinarity and applied learning and creates mutually beneficial relationships and real-life projects generated with communities provides a solid foundation for the development of community mapping.

Community-Based Mapping Discourse

In teaching community mapping, an ideal starting point is the analysis of maps and the history of cartography. Maps are tools to represent knowledge claims and selective perceptions of reality. They are also tools of power, used to validate local and global scale planning, world views, and claims to territory. On a primary level they re-present the relationship of humanity to itself, to each other, and to the physical and metaphysical world that they believe exists or relate to. In his famous critique of scientific knowledge Korzybski (1941) reminds us that *the map is not the territory* and instead is paradigmatic of the *mapmakers'* situated knowledge and inevitable bias. Key questions emerge such as, who makes the maps and therefore whose knowledge and reality counts? The work by Haraway (1988) on situated knowledges helps explain the inherent bias in all knowledge claims, including maps, as each one of us occupies a different space and place in time and has different experiences.

The Origin and Power of Maps

Community mapping leads naturally to a discussion and debate about the origin, nature, and function of maps themselves. Questions arise such as, what is a map? Why do maps have power and how does this power manifest itself? And, why do we need maps? Harley and Woodward define maps in *The History of Cartography* as "graphic representations that facilitate a spatial understanding of things, concepts, conditions, processes or events in the human world" (in Turnbull, 1989, p. xvi). Such representations, according to Turnbull (1989), could be iconic (pictorial or visual portrayals) and/or symbolic (conventional signs and symbols like letters and numbers). However, all maps represent and reflect how individuals or societies name and project themselves onto nature, literally and symbolically. Mapmaking has thus both sociocultural (myth-making) and technical (utilitarian and economic) functions and traditions. The latter are more pronounced in the West, where cartography has been professionalized as a discipline.

In "The Origins of Cartography" (1987), Malcolm Lewis suggested that the development of language and spatial consciousness in early humans enabled the development of the first maps, cognitive (mental) ones. This involved the naming of symbols, place names, individuals, and actions and the sequencing of these symbols. Some humans expanded beyond oral language and wrote down these icons and symbols. They became written maps. Whether oral or written, however, the belief systems or myths of those making the maps are reflected on the maps themselves. Thomas Kuhn (1970), in his work on the philosophy of science, refers to this as the paradigm, meaning:

> The pattern of knowledge that determines which "entities" nature is said to contain and how they behave. The paradigm creates theories, a "map" whose details are elucidated by scientific research: And since nature is too complex and varied to be explored at random, the map is as essential as observation and experiment to science's continuing development ... paradigms provide scientists not only with a map but also with some of the directions essential for map-making. In learning a paradigm, the scientist acquires theory, methods and standards together, usually in an inextricable mixture. (p. 109)

Maps and Knowledge

Given this paradigmatic lens, mapmaking as a scientific or technical tradition can be seen as self-referencing; it is anchored in a knowledge system dependent always on the cultural paradigm and world view of the mapmaker. Barbara Bender (1996), in *Mapping Alternate Worlds*, believes that all maps are actually "indexical" in that they point to people's sense of history and relationships. Ronald Wright (1991) extends Kuhn's and Bender's explanation of mapping to the world of myth making. A passionate writer on the history of colonial and Indigenous relations in the Americas, Wright believes that to recover and reclaim power effectively, Indigenous and non-Indigenous peoples alike need to oppose and transform the discovery myth of the conqueror:

> Myth is an arrangement of the past, whether real or imagined, in patterns that resonate with a culture's deepest values and aspirations ... Myths are so fraught with meaning that we live and die by them. They are the maps through which cultures navigate through time ... while Western myths are triumphalist, those of the losers have to explain and overcome catastrophe. If the vanquished culture is to survive at all, its myths must provide a rugged terrain in which to resist the invader and do battle with his myths. (p. 5)

The myth of discovery has guided the colonial cartographic tradition. Since the advent of perspective geometry in the fifteenth century, followed by the rise of colonialism and the Scientific Revolution, maps became possessions and instruments of military, cultural, and economic power, and increasingly in the hands of those with colonial and commercial interests (Harley, 1989). Cartography soon became an indispensable tool of state and colonial power, while portraying the world with a European bias. Spaces and cultures were "indexed," and the geography and cultures of other spaces and places were subjugated, vanquished, or colonized in the process. Until this century, the Mercator Projection, named after the Flemish cartographer, was the standard classroom wall map depicting the entire world. However, it was argued that this projection disproportionately represented a larger-than-reality Northern Hemisphere. In doing so it was argued that maps such as this were used as tools to accompany a hegemonic world view and manipulated the reader's understanding of territory and the relative importance of different states.

Colonial maps and mapping were thus graphic representations of the myth of discovery and became key symbols and tools of formalizing and maintaining power relations. However, marginal people and places, mostly Indigenous peoples worldwide, have increasingly used maps as a mechanism to resist control and attempt to recover their land and culture. These examples have provided a foundation and inspiration to community mapmakers worldwide. The myth of discovery is challenged by a vision for cultural survival and sustainability.

Historical and contemporary Indigenous maps and mapping inspire non-Indigenous community mappers to re-examine their own values and relationship to their local places. In Canada, for example, partnerships have been formed between First Nations and non-Indigenous community mappers. Gitxsan mappers from British Columbia have shared their mapping stories and work with groups throughout Canada and the United States, as well as with Indonesian community and Indigenous groups and activists. They also inspired and acted as mentors for the Victoria urban-based mapping project Common Ground. The Gitxsan gave workshops in Victoria (which is on the traditional territory of the Coast and Straits Salish Nations) and on their own traditional territory, sharing practices, principles, and their overall vision of community mapping. The Gitxsan emphasized to the city dwellers that the key elements of community mapping included: the recovery of local history and stories from young and old; developing an inventory of local economic, social, and environmental assets; and the importance of getting out and walking one's home territory. This partnership and the identification of common goals between a First Nations and Victoria residents illustrate that Canadians from all communities have much in common. In this case, a rural First Nation taught and inspired an urban non-Indigenous project to begin the process of rediscovering their sense of place and community. This provides an ironic turning of the mapping table and directly bucks the trend of the colonial Canadian mapmaking tradition.

The Green Map System

The Green Map System (2009) was started in 1997 by the New York–based eco-designer and community educator Wendy Brawer. She created an iconic language that can be presented using a cartographic map to be shared by global citizens wanting to re-present and protect their environment and communities (see www.greenmap.org/ for details). The system has now spread worldwide and has resulted in over

700 different Green Map projects. There are organizing "hubs" in North America, Europe, and Asia, and in countries such as Japan and Cuba, there are extensive national green map networks. Green Map provides comprehensive teaching and engagement tools for community, schools, and campus use. Their website includes tools created by universities and school-based educators for course- and community-based research projects. Wendy Brawer and the universities who have engaged with Green Map have applied the mapping and mapmaking processes to a wide range of university courses including architecture, art and design, community development and social issues, and environmental and global education.

Wendy Brawer acknowledges academic pioneers and bioregionalists such as Doug Aberley and Briony Penn (see, e.g., Aberley & Harrington, 1999; *Giving the Land a Voice: Mapping Our Home Places*) as having a big pedagogical influence on the Green Map System's early development. She now regards Victoria as a centre for community mapping experience and expertise. Brawer met Maeve Lydon from Common Ground in 1998. Common Ground is a Victoria community-based mapping and planning project that provides mapping and learning resources for schools, neighbourhoods, and communities wishing to undertake sustainable community development and planning projects. In coming together, they connected the Green Map System and its global networks (especially among educators) with the participatory learning and planning processes for inclusive sustainable community development that Common Ground was creating. According to Brawer, "UVic's important role in meshing geography and community-engaged research cannot be understated. This is really what we need more of in order to make our communities resilient, strong, and verdant" (W. Brawer, personal communication, 2011).

To link nationally and globally, Common Ground and many worldwide community mapping efforts work closely with the International Green Map System. Green Map's online tools and international linkages have been a foundation for inspiring and empowering community mapmakers worldwide.

Community Mapping Practice

Dialogue requires an intense faith in human beings; their power to make and remake, to create and recreate; faith that the vocation to be fully human is the birthright of all people, not the privilege of an elite.

– Freire (1986, p. 62)

Community mapping is fun, inclusive and encourages everyone to give free rein to his or her creativity. People realize they don't have to be wonderful cartographers – the most important thing is how they feel about their place.
                                                    – Linda Beare (personal communication, 2001)

Mapping as a pedagogical and planning tool has the potential to conceptualize, create, and use images of place. CBR practitioners recognize that almost anything can be mapped. Examples of mapping projects that community are directly involved in fall under different themes, including:

1 *Personal connections* – sense of place, gifts and assets, values and visions, marketing, outreach tools
2 *Heritage* – community history atlases, heritage trees, sites and Elders stories, walking tours, lost streams, species
3 *Conservation* – greenways and spaces, local farms, habitat and sensitive ecosystems, underground water sources, toxic sites, fruit trees, vacant land for community garden sites
4 *Community planning* – neighbourhood plans, traffic flow, trouble spots, unsafe and high crime areas, housing types, gentrification, income and services, health issues
5 *School curricula* – language arts, social studies, math, information technology, fine arts, physical education, science, personal health, planning
6 *Economic development* – capital flow, resource use, opportunity sites, markets, income, demographics
7 *Sustainability* – alternative energy, food and water systems, resilience, preparedness.

Many examples of community mapping exist. In British Columbia, school children are making walking-to-school maps, and "walking schoolbuses," for personal and ecosystem health, safety, and community building (Kassirer, 2012). In Quebec, the Algonquin First Nation made composite maps to create a local resource management plan, and included spaghetti maps of trap lines and Elders' map biographies. In Montreal, the Eco-Montreal Green Map "Tiotiake" begun at McGill University has expanded into the community and is used by the city ward system to identify local resources and needs (Green Map System, 2009; B. Zuber, Green Map consultant in New York, personal communication, 2003). On BC's Gulf and Coastal Islands, hundreds of local residents and artists participated in the Salish Sea community-mapping project by making artistic community maps and atlases of their local assets and history (Land Trust Alliance of B.C., n.d.). In Yellowknife, a Northern Canadian community, green mappers created 10 Northern "low impact winter activity" icons as part of their Green Map (Canadian Parks and Wilderness Society, n.d.).

These efforts all have two features in common: one is that community mapping is not mapping *for* or *of* a community, it is mapping *by* the community of their values, assets, and visions for the future. The other is that technology, when used, is a tool to accompany the community learning and building process. Hand-drawn maps and community learning opportunities such as workshops, outreach, and walkabouts are the basis of most of the efforts. Online tools provided by the Green Map System (described above) have also proven to be particularly useful.

The following case stories illustrate different community-based and green mapping projects and lessons learned.

The Shelbourne Corridor Project

The Shelbourne Corridor mapping process from 2010 to 2011 was designed to determine existing and desired sustainable housing, transportation, walking and bike routes, and service planning for residents, students, and businesses to guide the next 20 years. The area included 16,000 residents and included the UVic and Camosun College campuses. Maeve Lydon and Ken Josephson facilitated this process to support the local Municipality of Saanich. The foundation of the project was the development of a stakeholder group with local residents, businesses, and NGOs. This step is vital because community-based ownership and leadership development in the planning and/or learning process is the major foundation of community-based mapping. The team worked together to identify their own values and visions for the community, including what personal gifts they brought and what community assets they believe existed.

The second step was to move from the individual and group to the community. The emphasis for the process was to empower the committed local volunteer stakeholders to find and, if necessary, to co-create with the facilitators, the tools, community outreach, and engagement activities necessary to reach as many citizens as possible. As in most community mapping projects related to planning, a community-based survey and interactive print and online maps were created to gather the ideas and data necessary, while sparking the imaginations and interest of the diverse array of people who lived, worked, shopped, owned property, or studied in the area. In this and other similar community mapping processes, students and local leaders were trained as mapping "animators" who then went to local workplaces, meetings, markets, shopping centres, liquor stores, and other community events. In effect they became the community-based researchers. By leveraging existing assets and gifts and connecting people to place from a geographic, economic, and cultural perspective, local citizens participated in unprecedented numbers (according to the Municipality of Saanich) in a municipal planning process. Almost 800 residents filled in the surveys and another 1,000 participated in schools and community workshops, outdoor biking and walkabouts, and natural and human history events. The result was more community relationships and connections, a composite community map with GIS layers that show the existing and desired assets, routes, and changes, as well as a report that expresses the interests, assets, and visions (rather than simply the needs) of the local citizens.

This process created a widespread involvement and enthusiasm for the current (2011–12) stage of implementation and funding that would not have been possible if a small group of planners and mappers had created a plan *for* citizens. Throughout the process there was some push and pull between the stakeholder and senior planners, with the latter expressing concern that managing expectations would become an issue. However, the planners realized that engaging and empowering citizens and employing processes such as community mapping to truly reach out has long-lasting and positive effects. People feel that they have been involved in determining the future of the place they call "home," and not just consulted.

Peninsula Play Spaces Map

Supporting early childhood development through identifying and increasing outdoor recreation opportunities was the goal of this 8-month process. Local citizens – those involved in diverse roles as family and community caregivers, educators, recreation, business owners, and parks planners – were engaged in the creation of this local map and engagement process. Again, as with the Shelbourne Project, a local stakeholder volunteer group worked with the facilitator and university students to create an outreach and survey plan and to find ways to reach citizens creatively.

As with other projects, a particular focus for this and many of the regional mapping projects was to support and challenge the stakeholders to move beyond their own interests and what they wanted to be represented on a map, and instead for them to use mapping as a tool to listen to and mobilize the community. Often, service providers and "representatives" of community "service" the community rather than engage the community in creative change. To break through this divide, an appreciation of the historic and educational significance of the area and, in this particular project, of the need to respect diverse ways of caregiving (particularly in Indigenous communities) was part of the learning and planning process. This was enabled through visiting people's homes, inviting local Indigenous people, parents, local citizens, and schools to meet each other (often for the first time) and to participate in the map and visioning process in fun and creative ways. The result of the process was a beautiful community map distributed widely and illustrated by local artists, children, and Indigenous people, stronger working relationships between caregiver and educator groups, a greater appreciation of the historical and cultural significance of the area and ideas for concrete action to be used by parks, educators, and early childhood advocates to increase access to parks and the outdoors for young children. What also emerged was the recognition that access to green space and recreation opportunities for caregivers and young children was better for the affluent; the project exposed an environmental justice and equity issue, rather than simply one of early childhood development.

From mapping favourite childhood places for personal and group development, mapping excess fruit for food banks, to creating a city-wide land use plan, all these mapping processes are about community connecting and building based on sharing lived experience, values, and visions.

Community Mapping and Academia

For me it is really important that learning not be always a study of what is out there, in other places, all the time. When my [students] were doing the geography of making their own maps, it was their geography, their place. Today I just came from my class and one of my kids said, "We are history." Mapping has been a wonderful way for them to develop that feeling of being a participant.
  – Susan Underwood, schoolteacher (personal communication, 2002)

Over the years, the CBR methods used in community mapping "in the field" have worked their way into innovative methods and approaches that work well in a teaching setting. At the University of Victoria and the University of British Columbia the work of community mapping practitioners, teachers, and scholars offers practical insights into the methods and approaches that work well in a teaching setting.

At the University of Victoria, faculty members and staff are directly involved in a number of community-based and Common Ground/ green mapping initiatives while they share and develop their own mapmaking and research resources and expertise. In turn they receive access to a "living laboratory" in the community when they undertake their research. The UVic Geography Department was closely involved in the development of the Community Green Map of Victoria and Region (2004), and has provided student research support for many neighbourhood, school, and regional projects. Twelve other neighbourhood and regional maps and mapping projects have been supported between 2000 and 2011. The partnerships, projects, and methodologies have had tremendous impact on a number of courses taught and research projects conducted in Geography and Environmental Studies at UVic and have provided myriad opportunities for students and researchers to engage more deeply with communities. (see Figure 5.1) Participatory interactive online community maps are also starting to be used in off-campus, experiential, community-based field schools, particularly in remote, rural, and First Nations communities to document undergraduate student research based on questions posed by and in collaboration with communities.

UVic's cartographer Ken Josephson had worked for over 25 years on mapmaking for government and academic research purposes before he was invited in the late 1990s to take part in the Common Ground mapping project and the world of community-based mapping. Now Josephson works extensively with communities, students, and researchers on many curriculum projects that use mapping for practical hands-on projects for students. Ken often describes his transition from professional cartographer to the world of community mapping as transformative: "I used to make maps for government and academia and did not think about the impact they had on how we look at and relate to land and people. Now my role is more of a mapping facilitator; I see mapping is not neutral and they can truly empower students and community members alike to make significant and lasting changes" (K. Josephson, personal communication, 2011). Josephson now presents on and conducts community mapping workshops in a number of first-, second-, third-, and fourth-year classes in Geography and Environmental Studies and in the University 101 program for those with barriers or challenges to pursuing higher education. (See Figure 5.2.)

Figure 5.1. Creatures of Habitat: Earth Day celebration mapping event with 700 Grade 6 students on Saanich Peninsula (Greater Victoria Region), facilitated by graduate students, faculty, staff, and community volunteers. Photo by Ken Josephson.

Charles Burnett, who specializes in GIS and web mapping applications for community resource development, designed and taught an undergraduate course at the University of Victoria. Burnett has found the best resource for practical community mapping is the challenges that community groups give us – because they are always topical, and the learner can always contribute, even in a small way. The next best resource is learner creativity and initiative. Innovative courses such as Burnett's, based in real-life case studies, and Josephson's cartographic and engagement role are fundamental to the ongoing University–Common Ground community mapping partnership, which is now exploring and expanding the role of the university in supporting on- and off-campus sustainability projects, to be a portal and data repository for geographical and spatial data that communities need, and to facilitate regional, national, and global networking between community mapping projects. Their website – mapping.uvic.ca – has become a useful resource within and between universities and communities alike.

Figure 5.2. Community Planning Game: University 101 program for learners with barriers/challenges to pursuing higher education. Photo by Ken Josephson.

Jon Corbett, co-director the UBC Centre for Social, Spatial and Economic Justice, is an Associate Professor in the Community, Culture, and Global Studies Unit at UBC Okanagan. Jon's community-based research and teaching investigates community mapping processes and tools that are used by communities to help express their relationship to, and knowledge of, their territories and resources. Teaching and supporting undergraduate and graduate students to undertake projects with local and global communities, including many Indigenous communities, is an important focus of Corbett and the Centre. Both theoretical and applied community mapping is taught with action, theory, and research operating in an ongoing cycle. He teaches students how to develop, implement, and evaluate a map and mapping project while understanding and creating an overall and personalized theoretical context. Once the mapping and mapmaking process is complete, he works with the learners to analyse both their experiences and data and to re-theorize it.

In his Geography undergraduate course entitled Cartography and Society, Corbett encourages students to read the subtext of the map from the outset. This is done by asking a series of questions about the map: What is the "story" being told by the map? Whose story is represented? Whose is not? This questioning helps deconstruct the world view of the mapmaker as well as the historic and cultural context. It further lends itself to exploratory discussions related to privileged narratives and cartographic silences and thus echos Kuhn's dominant paradigm, or Haraway's work on the essentializing or totalizing discourse, that sees everything from nowhere instead of the situating narrative or discourse that sees somethings from somewhere. After deconstructing the map, the students are asked what is missing on the map and why?

Wherever possible, Corbett uses problem-based learning (PBL) methods in the classroom. PBL is increasingly used as an alternative to traditional classroom learning and is not reliant on lectures, assignments, or exercises. In PBL, the teacher acts as facilitator and mentor, rather than a source of solutions. Students are presented with, or else identify for themselves, a socially relevant and geographically bounded problem. Because students are not handed "content," the learning process becomes active in the sense that they discover and work with processes, content, and tools that are determined to be necessary to solve the problem, and this solution requires working with some form of community mapping.

In Corbett's Cartography and Society course, students work on a mapping project throughout the semester. The aim of the project is to create a map or mapping related product in any format (paper, electronic, web-based, art form, terrain model, etc.) that directly addresses an issue related to social change and/or community development. This requires choosing a research project that is relevant; in most cases this involves addressing a local issue and working with a local community organization. Three student projects are briefly outlined below.

Fire Mapping: The Facebook of Forest Fires

As climate change makes summers drier, hotter, and more erratic, the Okanagan Valley has seen increasingly severe forest fires as urban development expands into forest fire interface zones. Major forest fires have occurred in 2003 and 2009, affecting many thousands of people. The Okanagan Mountain Park Fire in 2003 was "the most significant interface wildfire event in BC history" (Wildfire Management Branch, 2011), and resulted in the evacuations of over 30,000 people and destroyed 238 homes. In 2009, the Terrace Mountain Fire burnt over 9,000 hectares and led to the evacuation of several communities. Two undergraduate students, Samantha Brennan and Aidan Whiteley, as a part of Corbett's Cartography and Society course, developed a project that provides new insights on the human dimensions of forest fires in the Okanagan through developing a crowd-sourced interactive web-map. Crowd-sourcing is the process of small tasks, in this case short descriptions of experiences and memories, being contributed by large numbers of people to the map. The website, www.firehistory.ok.ubc.ca, serves as an interactive online map that layers images, videos, and text about the fires onto a Google Maps base layer with a scrollable 25-year time line. This Fire Mapping Project contains official data from government and media on fires as far back as 1984 and creates a short history of the subject, organized both spatially and temporally. Users are encouraged to expand the website by posting stories, personal videos, and photos to the map to foster understanding and education regarding forest fire issues.

The website allows users to visualize the scope, scale, and chronology of fires – a different understanding of fire than can be gained from pure text. Students have partnered with the Kelowna Fire Museum, where the website was displayed as an exhibit for the summer of 2011, to gather public knowledge on forest fires and use it for educational, therapeutic, and historical purposes. The resulting database will serve as a spatial, temporal tool with data from governmental, media, and public sources to paint a clearer picture of forest fires in the Okanagan, and to tell "the millions of stories" about the fires that go untold. This partnership, in turn, has helped reorient teaching (not simply research) at the university to be more community service-oriented.

Critical Cartography Curriculum

The BC Ministry of Education website states that elementary students' curricula are guided by principles of learning which entail the active participation of the student in both an individual and a group process. Critical thinking is a core component of the active participation requirements. Working together with the UBC Centre for Teaching and

Learning and local teachers, Kathleen Rhode's project seeks to incorporate a critical cartography component directly into the elementary school curriculum. Basic concepts of cartography such as longitude, latitude, and direction are already integrated into the Social Studies curriculum for the intermediate grades (4 to 7); however, the skills required to critically evaluate the hidden meanings and subtext of the map are lacking. The critical cartography lesson plans and curriculum materials developed in this project will aim to change the children's perception of what a map is and how it is read. The objective of this project is for the children to learn to look at a map critically rather than just using it for a navigation tool. It is important for children to learn to think critically and to judge the information presented to them in a skilful manner. As Rhode moves on to become a teacher, she intends to build a portion of her Master's degree around the concept of developing the potential of building critical cartographic principles into the elementary school curriculum.

Kelowna: A Tale of Two Cities

Gated communities close themselves to the outside social world in the belief that their inhabitants will be more secure. Visually, they are very different from the housing that surrounds them; they have gates most of the time, some always locked while others are not. The average housing price is usually significantly higher within the gates, so one can assume that they contain wealthy residents. To live within the gated communities, there are often restrictions, for example, on family numbers, noise, or visible belongings such as outdoor yard items and vehicles. Kelowna is known for its multiple gated communities. These areas begin to act as areas of social exclusion and in doing so have a profound effect on the surrounding neighbourhoods. Edith Bonnette, an undergraduate student, set out to create a reflective map that combined the locations of the gated communities throughout Kelowna and presented them on a Google Map mashup (a map mashup is a tool that combines web-based media including photos and video hosted on multiple web services and displays them through the interface of an online map, such as Google Maps). Her project involved collaborating with city officials, Remax realtors, and other students from the university newspaper. This map combined her own perspectives on the gated communities with photographs; she tied the separate communities together using selected narrative from the novel A Tale of Two Cities by Charles Dickens.

The use of *A Tale of Two Cities* provided a metaphor for the differences that exist between the Kelowna behind the walls of a gated community and the rest of the city. It draws on the social inequity and exclusivities of Dickensian urban Europe and implies that similar class, gender, and socioeconomic variances remain prevalent today in Canada. The map aims to shock the audience into re-evaluating the Canadian ideals of equality and multiculturalism, and ultimately to "facilitate a spatial understanding of things, concepts, conditions, processes or events in the human world" (Turnbull, 1989, p. xvi).

In each of these cases, the students do not just immerse themselves in the technical endeavour of creating maps; they also have the opportunity to connect directly with a socially relevant issue that in turn often requires a direct connection with local government, a community group, or business. This engagement is not typically a one-way process that results in the student simply "learning more." Rather, it helps them critically engage in the role of activist, inspired and passionate about issues related to social and spatial justice, a core element of the discipline of Geography (Harvey, 1973). Furthermore, because of a map's inherent ability to communicate complex spatial information, the maps created by the students are often used to inform other students in the class and across the university of these social justice related issues, and in so doing, support activists working on campus and in the broader community. In other words, this approach to learning in the classroom can become a tool to activate students, to support them in becoming more socially involved and overall better prepare them to be engaged and vocal citizens in the future.

Another factor is that the map projects undertaken by undergraduate students can also serve to inform university administrators about key issues of relevance within their own communities and influence them to become more engaged. Students are often more socially and environmentally involved than decision makers within the university. Yet, when students begin to generate interest in their mapping work, administrators also often take note and will lend their vocal support for these types of projects. Often, this is not only because of the public relations opportunity, but also because it helps to brand a usually less-than-agile and risk-averse institution as socially relevant to their own immediate geographical constituency. This is well illustrated by level of coverage that the university public relations office has invested in covering and promoting the fire map described above, as well as other socially relevant online maps created by students. This, in turn, has helped students attract internal travel grants and fellowships to further support and promote their community engagement work.

Whether using mapping as a learning process in itself or as part of a wider community project, the following are some guidelines for facilitators lead to the successful Community Mapping projects:

- *Create a positive learning space.* Keep the learning atmosphere focused on listening and making connections between people and their local place. Make sure mapping sessions, inside and outside, are comfortable, friendly, and guided by a skilled facilitator. When working with hand-drawn or topographical maps, have participants gather around a table; four to six per group is ideal and encourages everyone to share.
- *Work for inclusion.* Involve as much as possible a diverse cross-section of the community, particularly children and Elders (seniors and long-term residents). When working with children, remember that they see the world and space in different ways at different ages. With Elders remember that they have plenty of stories and experience to share and may not want to draw or use maps. To encourage cultural diversity try to translate mapping outreach and survey materials and involve local leaders into the learning and design process.
- *Agree on questions and outcomes.* Be clear about why you are mapping and what you need and want to learn with and about the community at various stages and events. Breaking down categories of maps can be helpful for inventory and projects, i.e., tactical (specific purpose and planning oriented) and strategic (social change and vision), or along sustainable development lines, i.e., natural and built environment, economic and socio-cultural features. The Green Map System breaks this down further into mobility, infrastructure, nature (flora and fauna, land and water, toxic hot spots and pollution sites), renewable resources, information, and Economic development.
- *Focus on mapmaking process not product.* Keep the directions simple and encourage people to draw and write directly onto a base map or to make their own personal or collective mental maps. Using icons and numbering special sites linked to sticky it notes with a longer description are easy ways to gather information and not clutter up the map. Forget about technical accuracy when gathering the stories and ideas of local citizens. When working with hand-drawn or topographical maps, have participants gather around a table; four to six per group is ideal and encourages everyone to share.

- *Creativity is vital*. Use a wide range of materials and media: colours, clay, tapestry, photos, written narrative, hand-drawings, when making a community map or atlas. Involve and train locals who have technical interest in putting the stories and inventory on maps if that is necessary. Artists, young and old, weave magic and beauty into the mapping and mapmaking process.

Conclusion: Mapping Our Common Landscape

Love makes you see a place differently, just as you hold differently an object that belongs to someone you love. If you know one landscape well, you will look at all landscapes differently. And if you learn to love one place, sometimes you can also learn to love another.

– Michaels (1996, p. 82)

We need enlightened ways in the world of learning to engage with each other and with the local and global places we call home; community mapping is one such tool that can help facilitate this reconnection, re-enchantment, and, ultimately, love of place. The opportunities and potential for using community mapping as a teaching tool to support CBR, develop community-university partnerships and understanding, and reorient teaching (not simply research) to be more community service-oriented are immense. Not only do community mapping projects support these relationship-oriented objectives within the university, they also have the potential to encourage interdisciplinarity, campus activism, and public engagement, as well as provide students with real-life living laboratory experience that involves the actual experiences of real people in a real place. These experiences directly prepare students to be thoughtful, skilled, and engaged citizens.

From our experience, teaching community mapping empowers the learners and directly connects them to the history and experience of real people in real places (including their own), while recognizing the reality of historical and contemporary social and environmental issues. These personal transformations can become a gateway not only to reinhabit our home places, to echo Aberley, but to alter learning and research to benefit broader society. For example, in Victoria, the late Tsartlip Elder Dave Elliott Sr. (d. 1985) helped create the first First Nations map of the territory; it was designed to be used as a teaching tool, the Saltwater People's Map. His work and the map have inspired many Indigenous and non-Indigenous mapmakers from both within the university and those groups working with the university to affirm the past, however painful it was, and to create a better future. On a global scale, his words resonate with us all:

> We have come through a great disaster and we are like people in shock. We were almost destroyed. We are living in the wreckage of what was once our way of life ... this is a state of shock really – our memories have left us. Many of the young people don't know where they're coming from and where they are going. It's their future. We need to give them their past by telling their history and we need to give them a future. (Elliott, 1983, p. 82)

However, we feel that in many universities the system still largely mirrors the predominant reward system found in the world today. This system is based on capital accumulation. In the case of academia, this "capital" is largely understood in terms of the production, number, and value of peer-reviewed papers and journal articles. This understanding of "value" often finds itself in direct conflict with the CBR movement, where success is contingent on negotiating overlaps of mutual interest, developing and maintaining complex relations and knowledge constructs, while ultimately trying to undertake, reflect on and co-write about relevant and bounded research. This means that academics often feel that they are faced with a disconnect between their research aspirations and expectations, and this in turn can make them feel that they are faced with a binary choice about their research career trajectory. As Edward Said (1996) states:

> I think the major choice faced by the intellectual is whether to be allied with the stability of the victors and rulers or – the more difficult path – to consider that stability as a state of emergency threatening the less fortunate with the danger of extinction, and take into account the experience of subordination itself, as well as the memory of forgotten voices and persons. (p. 35)

As a result, for many academics working in CBR, our role often becomes to mediate the dialogue and expectations between our community partners and university employers.

Despite these tensions, we ultimately conclude that the praxis of community mapping supports new kinds of social innovation as well as teaching and research outcomes that we believe students want and the world needs. Engaging in locally bounded issues through community mapping initiatives makes universities more socially relevant in the eyes of their constituent communities, as well as more broadly within society. We do caution, however, that it is important for community mapping initiatives to remain innovative (as has been demonstrated by the projects profiled in this paper) and for academics working with these tools within a supportive CBR environment to take risks and to experiment with new CBR methods, which often require a non-traditional interdisciplinary framework. It is also important to leverage the resources from within the university to support mapping projects that would otherwise never take form. We are inspired by universities becoming more service-based, with a clear mandate and incentive structure that supports community-engaged teaching and scholarship, as well as the growing recognition by people within the institution of their ability to influence positive social change and to directly support the development and transformation of their constituent communities and society as a whole.

Please see Appendix A for a list of websites and resources for community-based mapping.

6 Facilitating and Teaching Feminist Visual Arts–Based Research

DARLENE E. CLOVER

Prologue

When I reflect back, I realize my first orientation to research, and its links to education and learning, was to those that were participatory, community-based, and oriented to social change. My subsequent – and continued – conviction that these were the most germane forms of enquiry was implanted through my work in the 1980s and 1990s with the International Council for Adult Education (ICAE). The warp and weft of ICAE was a seamless integration of community-based research and adult education as mutually supportive processes of collaborative enquiry, critical questioning, and democratic knowledge creation. Further, the arts – photography, popular theatre, music, poetry, dance, and the like – were valued as powerful instruments of communication engagement that helped enable new understandings and transform lives. This meant that community-based adult educators, researchers, visual artists, poets, musicians, theatre performers, and activists were all mediators of critical social learning and investigation and creators of knowledge. One can therefore, comprehend just how far I was to fall when I made the decisive move during my tenure at ICAE to undertake all three university degrees – undergraduate to Ph.D. – in 9 years. There I was initiated into a world where research was kept "pure" from the real world, education was narrowed to schooling, and the arts were, at best, confined to Fine Arts or English Literature and, at worst, banished to an ontological homelessness of disdain and scorn. Fortunately, I paid this propaedeutic to "higher forms" little mind, not because the teachings were not potent, but because I did not find them particularly useful or interesting. This irreverence did not make my life easy then, and most certainly does not make my life easy as a professor in a traditional Faculty of Education now, but it has kept me sane and my integrity intact.

Introduction

My long-standing identity is a feminist adult educator and community-based researcher. To me, feminism means to acknowledge women's subject status and to believe they – as well as others who and have been systemically marginalized – bring experiences as subjects that can help us to more fully understand, and importantly, change the world. What are newer to me, and my sense of identity, are the visual arts–based approaches I outline in this chapter. I focus on them here, however, because they are now integral to my teaching and research work. Yet, this "aesthetic" identity took longer to cultivate, as I recall all too distinctly an episode in my primary school art class where, when I proudly unfurled my pastel landscape my teacher simply sighed and said: "You will never be an artist." I concur now with Hein (1990), who argues that the credibility of feminist practice is tested in women's experience and it is this experientialism that links feminism fundamentally to the aesthetic, a paradigmatic "of the immediate, multiple and qualitatively diverse" (p. 282) that are women's lives.

This chapter shares my ever-emerging, not an exact science approach to facilitating and teaching feminist visual arts–based methodologies in the community and university classroom. I begin with a discussion of various framings of arts-based research, because, unlike the credence gained by participatory research in the academy, arts-based research and enquiry remain comparatively unfamiliar. My discussion of the characteristics and definitions of arts and research is not intended to be definitive – these emerging practices are by their very nature flexible, adaptive, and contested – but simply to provide the discursive frame from which my own work emerges and builds. Following this and using examples from my own work, I discuss a few elements of arts-based research development, facilitation, and teaching, such as the materials required, the role of the professional community-based artist[1] in the research process, the issue of artistry, knowledge mobilization and dissemination, and data analysis. I also draw particular attention to creativity and imagination and heed Eisner's (2008) warning that making the case for arts-based research is as important as it is daunting. The journey of arts-based research can be an exhilarating ride, filled with celebration, beauty, and wonder. But there are also potholes, merging traffic, and broken pavements with which to contend. I therefore weave into my reflections some of the challenges identified by scholars and exemplified or amplified in my own practice. While I hope this chapter will be useful to researchers already committed to working with and through the aesthetic, it is aimed primarily at those entering the field of arts-based research and enquiry, be they students, professors, researchers, or community members.

Mapping the Scholarly Terrain

In seeking to define or delineate the area of arts[2] and research, there is neither a body of truths nor a central dogma. But like participatory and feminist research in particular, this practice arose as a challenge to the "limitations and oppressive features of traditional scientific research, opening spaces for experimentation of alternative approaches" (Butterwick, 2002, p. 243). In this case, however, researchers weave "aesthetic sensibilities with post-positivistic forms of expression" (p. 243) in a process described by Ball (2002) as "writing outside of the lines, transgressing the rules, while staying within the lines of dominant discursive practices" (p. 2). A number of terms are used to define or characterize the various comings together of the arts and research, including visual methodologies, performance enquiry, image-based research, installation art-as-research, story-work research, or lyric enquiry. Each reflects the use of a different art form or way compiling and analysing data. To my mind, and for the purposes of this chapter, I allocate these under two conceptualizations: "arts-based" and "arts-informed" research or enquiry.

Arts-informed research or enquiry is "influenced by but not based in the arts broadly conceived" (Cole & Knowles, 2008, p. 59). The aim of the study is to acknowledge the "everydayness of knowledge construction and multiple ways of knowing" by creating artistic means, but not necessarily art "objects," to interpret and convey the findings of the study (Cole & McIntyre, 2003, p. 48). Although it is not a steadfast rule, the researcher is often an artist and is central to the process – and I will address this shortly. Essoglou (1995) suggests this independence is because "collaborating aesthetically, compromising around decisions on images, symbols or … fabric and tradition, is always a profound strain on artist-researchers so accustomed to practising individually and developing … ideas independently" (p. 354). Another factor, of course, is the reward system of universities in terms of the exalted – but false – value these institutions place on individual over collaborative works.

An excellent example of arts-informed enquiry is the work of Cole and McIntyre (2003), who created a clothesline (not a traditional art form) of women's undergarments – from diapers, to panties, to thongs, to "sensible" panties, and back to diapers – to metaphorically illustrate the progression of aging, decline, and finally, dementia in the lives of their mothers. Arts-based research or enquiry, the conceptualization I work with and discuss in this chapter, uses "artistic expressions in all the different forms of art as a primary way of understanding and examining experience by both researchers and the people that they involve in their studies" (McNiff, 2008, p. 29). Within this conceptualization the artistic product or medium is equal to any other data gathering method such as interviews and focus groups. The researcher is not necessarily an artist and the final art products, analyses, and interpretations not solely her or his own, although they can be, and she or he always plays an important role(s).

Some forms of arts-based and -informed research and enquiry are closely related to psychology and therapy, their major contribution to develop better understandings of the personal psychological condition. Common methods include hermeneutics, interpretive enquiry, phenomenology, autobiography, quilts, journalling, and narrative. Representational forms such as poetry or dance are also vehicles to share "self-knowledge" and explore one's own personal experiences, journeys, and subjectivities (McNiff, 2008). Of particular relevance here is the emotional aspect, how "the methodological permutation of self-knowledge is used to invite readers or audiences "into places unknown, even though it yields the researcher vulnerable" (Gwyther & Possamai-Inesedy, 2009, p. 107). Peseta (2007) argues that "when you write [or perform, et cetera] vulnerably, others respond vulnerably" and this elicits empathy and opportunities for alternative and multiple interpretations. Indeed, Ellis and Bochner (2003, p. 221) question academics they see as "conditioned to believe that a text is important only to the extent it moves beyond the *merely* personal." Embedded in this stream is often the concept of "self-learning." The art forms are used to explore and interpret dreams, memories, family relationships, health issues, and even professional selves. Leggo (2008) uses poetry to reflect on himself as an educator referring to this "self-practice" as "the fruit of leisure" combined with a "poetic brew" of self-knowledge and discovery (p. 91). But Eisner (2008) also cautions that if a study culminates "in little more than a delightful poetic passage … it is not serving a function" (p. 23). Unless arts-based practices aim towards making some form of pedagogical or social contribution, they can be accused of being simply self-indulgent exercises by a privileged few.

Other scholars who align themselves with less developed but more critically focused arts-based approaches have taken up this challenge. Horsfall and Welsby (2007) describe these as using the arts not to explore one's own ego or dreams, or as a therapeutic tool, but as a different way "to foreground the voices of the women [or other marginalized populations] themselves" (p. 261). It need not be an either/or here, as the arts can be both healing and political. But critical and feminist visual arts–based researchers place more emphasis on the human aesthetic dimension to probe and tackle complex social, cultural, and/or environmental issues – rather than just personal healing. This more politicized work is characterized as collaborative, respectful, and socially or politically transformative (McCormack & Titchen, 2007). The research aims towards women's education and empowerment to speak, name, and re-envision their worlds through aesthetic means. Visual feminist arts–based research is not neutral but seeks to identify and disrupt inequitable knowledge/power patterns and patriarchal assumptions of "truth," and enable criticism to be appreciated as an act of "giving representational form to new thoughts as exegetic to existing discourses" (Carson & Pajaczkowska, 2001, p. 9). In addition – although this is also true of arts-informed enquiry – there is always an element of public interaction through a display, exhibition, or performance of the artwork-data as a means to engage with diverse audiences. It is suggested that artworks allow audiences "to hear silences and see absences and invisibilities" that are not necessarily as apparent in traditional research dissemination practices (Ball, 2002, p. 2). For Strand et al. (2003), community-based research has "three central features: collaboration, democratization of knowledge and social change" (p. 6). From my own experience, I would add critical social learning and skills development (both methods and artistry).

Teaching and Facilitating

I turn now to the process of teaching and facilitating feminist visual arts–based research in the community and the academy. My thoughts are, by the limitations of space, only cursory, and further reading should be done. I have attempted to allocate my thoughts under subcategories but this is an imperfect science and much overlap and interweaving exists. Moreover, what follows is not meant to be a "how to" of feminist visual arts–based methods; contexts, situations, foci, and purposes differ so dramatically as to render that type of exercise ineffectual. I simply share, as stated in the introduction, some ideas, lessons learned, and challenges from my own work.

Material Matters

There were a number of ways I could have framed the discussion in this section, but as my chapter focuses more on the visual arts I felt the best starting point was in the material, to speak both literally and metaphorically. Materials matter in visual arts–based research and they matter in more ways than one. When I leave my office to undertake more traditional, or better said, known feminist qualitative study, I carry a notebook or laptop (or both), pens or pencils, and a voice or video recorder. When I embark on a visual arts–based research venture, I transport pieces of cloth, lace, ribbons, sheets of coloured paper, old magazines, and newspapers, markers, scissors, Post-It notes, tape, glue, paints, glitter, paper mache, plaster cast, clay, thread, fabric stamps and glue, and a variety of other baubles and notions such as feathers, old jewellery, postcards, shells, and even wood chips or bark. I find these items around the house, in parks, and on the beach, at flea markets and bargain shops, and on my international travels, but I also ask the dental and medical office staff to save their old magazines.

You need only provide a few materials; people will be creative with whatever they are presented with, so I am not suggesting otherwise. But I make a case for abundant materials for three reasons. First, the materials thoroughly capture the participants. Time and again I have watched, eyes open in astonishment, smiles of glee and fingers itching to touch when I upend a box and out cascade brightly coloured cloth and the paraphernalia listed above. Second, the materials aid, and I will discuss this in more depth shortly, in helping students or study participants overcome major feelings of artistic inadequacy resulting from persistent aesthetic desocializing processes that have left so many with what Williamson (2004, p. 136) calls an "impoverished sense of the creative possibilities in human life." Finally, an abundance of materials encourages enhanced creative, metaphoric, and symbolic representations as participants or students experiment with form, texture, colour, image, irony, contrast, and juxtaposition.

Time and Space

The amount and diversity of materials also have implications for where the research takes place and the length of time. I have found that what works best is to have a minimum of 3 hours with the participants or students. Equal time should be allotted to the creation of the artwork and reflection, sharing, and questioning. The 1-hour single or small group interview in the coffee shop or pub works if the interviewee has been asked – and has agreed – to create and bring a piece of artwork along. We once held a small group interview with women in a pub in Kelowna, British Columbia. One woman brought a small quilt square of cloth that spoke metaphorically, aesthetically, and enchantingly through its pattern and design of her identity and challenges as a woman politician. The single 1-hour interview in a public space works less well, in addition to the obvious lack of space, if the interviewee must create something on the spot, simply because there is often discomfort around art as noted above, and the researcher can become somewhat impatient waiting for the artwork to emerge as precious time slips away. But more importantly, this hurriedness cheats the value of time: time to consider, time to make connections, time to choose different colours, fabrics, or images. This is a fundamental strength of arts-based research: to both allow and demand deeper reflection and multiple constructions of meaning through a labour-intensive process.

Photography combines space, time, and materials in a somewhat different way. Required are the following: (1) cameras; (2) a laptop or desktop or sometimes, with a group, a bank of computers; and (3) an area diverse and/or interesting enough to make the photography project work, although this, as with every other study, depends on the aims. The research questions guide the art project, but the artmaking – as emergent – encourages other types of questions and opens avenues and spaces of exploration. A hospital setting, for example, will work well for a study involving health care participants, but if the research question aims to move beyond (or challenge) the traditional medical model, the outside world, rife with imagery of well-being and the lack thereof, is equally appropriate. The combinations and locations are endless, but it requires time to travel to and from sites. Another caution is that photography, even digital photography, can be more expensive given printing and/or the need for computers and, like any other artwork, can require technical skill and/or artistry. I will discuss this in more detail shortly.

Imagination and Creativity

Although some suggest the imagination and creativity will lead "think-ers away from the truth ... [and are] too cognitively indeterminate and unstable," I and many others argue differently (Kazemak, 1992; Shakotko & Walker, 1999, pp. 201–4). Symbol, metaphor, and imagery play an important role in reasoning, explaining, and understanding the world, enabling new connections between things concrete, such as earn-ing less than male colleagues, and things abstract, such as the theory of patriarchy. Irony creates the incongruity necessary for enhanced per-ception (Shakotko & Walker, 1999). However eloquent and wide rang-ing the information known methods such as interviews capture, they are only part of how we can represent the complexities and ambiguities involved in experience and ways of knowing (Schuller, 2004). Indeed, humans speak in metaphors and similes, share and describe their worlds through imagery, and it is to these aspects we can become more atten-tive as visual arts–based researchers through the process itself and/or the materials used. The arts also – and this is a critical aspect of femi-nist adult education – provide means for study participants, research-ers, and students to "voice" what often cannot be articulated through mere words. I remember a moment when one woman study participant suggested "the art gave us a way to communicate with each other casu-ally, offhandedly even. As you work to create something together it [the connection] begins to go deeper. These are by far the most powerful conversations I have had with these [a group of homeless] women." What was most fascinating about this comment was during that after-noon of art making almost no words were spoken. Yet something hap-pened through the art making to make her believe something had been spoken, something had connected.

As in all other areas, there are challenges here, too. Eisner (2008) cau-tions against working so imaginatively one simply produces "material that does not communicate" easily or well or connect with others (p. 19). Successful interpretation depends on a passionate engagement with what one sees, and to speak further to this, let me turn to the artists.

Artistry and Community-Based Artists

One need not be an artist to be an arts-based researcher: I am not but I teach and employ the arts all the time. Nor is a focus on the "artistry" of the research product compulsory, nor even a focus on the product itself. Wonderful research results, learning, and community building come from simply making art in response to well-designed research questions. Indeed, some argue it is deeply problematic when aesthetic considerations "trump the need for an epistemic orientation" (Eisner, 2008, p. 21) or the focus is so much on the final art product that one ends up "neglecting the ways in which [the art was] produced and interpreted" (Rose, 2001, p. 37). But there is also the converse, where the product is the primary concern. I come up the middle, favouring neither the process nor the product. What I do is to often use professional community-based artists to assist in the creation of the artworks and invite them as guest speakers into my university classrooms, because I have found that they and their emphasis on artistry and learning can at times, matter. For example, integral to undertaking feminist visual arts–based research is learning how to create or put images (and often with text) together to convey multiple meanings, and this is a strength which professional community-based artists have. Mullin (2003) refers to this as the prowess to attend to both the artistry and the messages. I will use a photography project to illustrate what this looks like.

The focus of the project was to understand and visually capture images of women's power. The final "product" was to be exhibited publicly. A community-based artist was brought in, and she transformed the work from colour film, auto-focus, point-and-shoot to a work of art that directed the gaze, created metaphors through the technicality and artistry, and so forth. So what do I mean by this? First, the artist showed the women how to use chiaroscuro, black and white imaging, explaining how this could enhance what they were capturing and demonstrating how it was done (and the settings). Chiaroscuro in the photos provides a heightened sense of depth, and this attribute greatly enhanced the sense of strength but also the vulnerability of the women captured in the photographs. Second, the format was moulded around feminist theory, oscillating between a single image of a woman for one month – individual power – and a group of women at a political march – the power of the collective. The artist challenged the group to think about the research topic, the theory, but also the artistry, the aesthetics, and how that would work on/for an audience, since the calendar and other photographs created for exhibition were intended for public dissemination. In this sense, she empowered the women to be artists, researchers, interpreters, and creative makers of meaning. To my mind, this reflects the principles of feminist community-based research – to learn, teach, and empower through the research process.

Having said this, let me acknowledge challenges around the concept of "artistry," aligned in many ways with age-old debates in the art world. A well crafted but ambiguous artwork, as Eisner (2008) suggests, may be a work of art, but it runs the risk of being too opaque to be useful. A concrete example of what this looks like comes from a research exhibition of women's quilts in New Zealand. One quilt was a beautifully executed metaphor of the impact of deforestation. Yet, unlike other quilts that combined metaphor, symbol, and realism, it was an abstract constellation of varying colours of green and sizes of material. I watched as audience members glanced at the quilt but immediately walked away. When questioned, one woman said, "It is beautifully crafted but impenetrable and therefore, meaningless." I agree with scholars who suggest that taking the time to learn from artworks (or anything for that matter) that may be difficult or challenging has been lost in our age of instant gratification and learning. It is critical throughout teaching that we instil this as a process and/or means of empowerment. My point as a researcher is to keep in mind your audience and the role you want them to play, an area Guillemin and Drew (2010) refer to as "unexplored yet significant … in visual methodologies" (p. 182). At an exhibition the art piece must often stand and speak alone, perhaps only accompanied by a small caption or a paragraph. The intent and/or imaging of the piece therefore should be to intrigue the audience sufficiently to stop and take the time to "read" or ponder and reflect on the images as the works by the homeless women did, and the work shown in New Zealand did not. But this also brings us to the idea of data analysis. How to "read" images or artworks is an activity in which I engage in both the classroom and the community, and I will return to this shortly.

Knowledge Dissemination and Mobilization

Critical to community-based research is knowledge dissemination, or what is sometimes called mobilization. Knowledge dissemination has to have strategic value, because communications with the public around complex social issues, as addressed in studies by community-based researchers, "must involve more than just transferring information" (Chwe, 1998, p. 48). Art exhibitions are an effective means to disseminate research findings in non-traditional ways to a much broader public. I worked recently on a study with a group of homeless/street-involved women. Over a period of 2 years, we developed artworks ranging from quilts, to collages, to masks around the issue of poverty. This is a critical issue but one that polarizes my community. At the conclusion of the project, we organized three exhibitions in three small art galleries. The aim was to expose the community to the issues in what the women called "a non-threatening" way. More than 300 people attended the gala openings and many more viewed the exhibition over the weeks it remained at the sites. The audience included politicians, artists, university students, and professors, teachers, business owners, homeless men and women, social and community development workers, and a variety of others who were simply intrigued by the idea of the show. The media also attended, as they are "visually oriented" and the arts feed into this. It is unlikely – impossible actually – that this diverse crowd or the media would have attended an academic presentation on women and poverty. For that matter, it is also unlikely – again, impossible – that these very different people from such dissimilar walks of life would mix and communicate so openly without the arts. But as alluded to above, the arts touch people, produce astonishing effects in people, in ways other forms do not. We had of course invited the media to attend the event, as we hoped they would disseminate this activity even further. What emerged the following day in the local daily was perhaps the greatest testament to the arts:

> There is so little opportunity for women in poverty to have their voices heard and their journey openly offered for the public. I normally pride myself on being a particularly sociologically aware teen, but I now see that awareness and up close and personal are vastly different. Judgement is an act that is grotesque and all-consuming, hovering like a festering cloud of smog ... I find myself glad that at least for tonight, there are no barriers. (*Times Colonist*, 3 May 2007, p. C6)

During the gala, we also milled about with attendees asking them if, when they thought of homeless women, they thought of "artists." Our aim was to unsettle assumptions and presumptions and allow the attendees, although we all do this, to reflect on how they have stereotyped and categorized.

Analysing the Data

Textile practices being treated with disregard for so long that it is almost inconceivable ... to acknowledge them as discursive formations from which meaning can emerge.

– Perron (1998, p. 124)

Howells (2003, p. 1) argues we are "surrounded by increasingly sophisticated visual images. But unless we are taught [or learn] how to read them, we run the risk of remaining visually illiterate." We are also overly reliant on texts that "tell" us rather than challenge us (Guillemin & Drew, 2010). These two abstract thoughts became very concrete to me during my first research methods class. None of the students had ever done any real data analysis before, so I developed an exercise that would enable them to engage in the process. The students were given a couple of readings on data analysis, and when they came to class the following week, I divided them into small groups and gave them the transcripts from past interviews, asking them to identify themes, ideas, and anomalies. When the small groups returned, they presented a very sophisticated thematic analysis. I then turned to two quilts and collages I had on the wall. These went with the transcripts, although I did not tell them that at the time. They perused these, and although I could easily see crosscutting themes, symbols, and metaphors, when I asked the groups to identify some of these I was met with silence. When I drew attention to the connection between the transcripts and the images, however, they found it slightly easier but still quite challenging. I concur with Guillemin and Drew (2010), who argue that neither images nor oral data should be privileged, but rather "seen as inextricably linked, requiring simultaneous and not separate analysis ... participant explanations [run] in concert with the images" (p. 184). But this begs the question of how it is so simple to read the texts and identify the themes yet so difficult to "read" the images in the same way? To deal with the situation, I sent the students on a tea break and set about designing questions around content, artistry (how it was put together), metaphor, voice, silences, spacing, symbols, and so forth. I began simply with: What colours stand out the most and what is their aim? How do black and white (or colours) work together (or contrast)? What are the symbols that stand out? Are they reflected in the other collages or the quilts? Are there spaces (like silences), and if so, what do they seem to imply? How are the images or metaphors described in the transcripts illustrated visually? What stands out as an anomaly? By putting these questions to the group, I discovered a key process in visual arts–based research must be to "teach" people how to "see" differently in the text-based oppressiveness of the academy and the world.

Ethics and Purpose

As with all research, there are issues of ethics, and these have their own degrees of complexity. As with all community-based research, feminist visual arts–based researchers suggest it is critical for researchers and participants to develop their own ethical principles and guidelines. This is often done at the beginning of the project by collectively generating guidelines, but it can also emerge during the process. I will use another photography project to illustrate this latter. Some of the participants in the study wanted to illustrate poverty by taking photographs of women pushing their carts in the streets. They argued it would work to just stand across the street, incognito, and take the photograph. After all this was public space, the women were adults, and the photographers had the right as citizens to take photographs of anything unprotected by law. But research is different. What we can do as artists and even citizens and as researchers is quite different, because there are ethical considerations. To simply photograph the women without their permission could contribute to their further exploitation, turning them into objects of study rather than subjects with a story to tell. This why Photovoice appeared; to take the tools of research, the cameras, away from the outside researchers and give them to people so they could tell their own stories. Moreover, by taking the photographs of the homeless women without their knowledge made them part of a study without the respect that would have been shown to other participants, who would have had everything explained to them. Universities have waivers to sign, but the rule here is if you are going to take photographs of human subjects, show respect by speaking with them and sharing what you are doing and why.

Going further, Guillemin and Drew (2010) raise cautions around the arts and emotionality, particularly when dealing with marginalized peoples and difficult social issues such as violence against women or their mental health. They argue "researchers need to expect that asking participants to produce visual material in [these] areas … may result in images that portray emotionally difficult experiences" (p. 185). They go on to say that the researcher must be "pre-emptive of the possibilities of emotional harm," but how is one to do this? First, I would argue that you need to think very carefully about your project if you are not a counsellor, therapist, or accustomed to working with vulnerable populations. As alluded to above, there is something extremely powerful and affective about the visual arts, something freeing in their non-verbal form that can bring out a tide of emotions and sensory responses seldom equalled in an interview or focus groups. People will share things through images that they will not voice, and you may not be prepared to deal with this. Second, I avoid this dilemma by posing research questions in ways that act as a springboard for more empowering and subversive thought, where, for example, women can use their art to become more "irreverent towards the rules set by phallocentric reasoning" or understand their situations as by-products of a masculinist neo-liberal world rather than their own shortcomings (Hein, 1990, p. 283). I use my studies to help women think more politically about their situations, and the world in which they live, to cultivate a stronger sense of rage towards unjust systems and structures. In other words, because I am a researcher and educator I marry arts, research, and education, not arts and therapy. Third, I have the women develop collective pieces of art. Individual pieces can individualize problems and isolate women from one another. Collective pieces such as a quilt encourage collaboration – and yes, struggle and arguments! They take problems from the personal to the political; the individual quilt squares may be the personal stories, but the quilt is not whole and serves no purpose until it comes together as a collective community. My intention is not to imply that art plus therapy is a problem, because this is not the case. But this combination is far easier to find than more politicized processes, so it is those to which I am trying to draw attention.

Final Thoughts

To borrow from Hein (1990), purely because the arts make the world of research much more interesting and energizing should be reason enough to employ them. But they also yield important results in terms of what scholars see as critical to community-based research: democratization of knowledge, collaboration, empowerment, social justice, and change (Strand, Marullo, Cutforth, Stoecker, & Donohue, 2003). In a complex, economically stratified world, rife with anti-feminist backlash and persistent machismo, I believe it is imperative to continue to develop purposeful practice, methodologies that give a different kind of voice to those left silenced and oppressed; that develop innovative ways of communicating knowledge, and employ methods which creatively build new knowledge for change. If we pay attention to the challenges, visual arts–based research will be seen as a positive, critical, and creative addition to the nascent canon of community-based research in this new century.

7 Learning to Listen: Foundations of Teaching and Facilitating Participatory and Community-Based Research

BUDD L. HALL

Poor people do not use money for a weapon.

– Julius K Nyerere

Although I have been doing participatory and community-based research since the early 1970s and teaching it since 1989, I have never systematically reflected on how I teach or facilitate others in their learning about community-based research. This chapter provides some background about to how I first began to learn about doing community-based research in Tanzania in the early 1970s. It also offers my thoughts on important things to keep in mind about teaching or facilitating courses, seminars, or workshops in community-based or participatory research. The key learning objectives in my teaching about CBR are the following: (1) knowing who we are, (2) learning to listen, (3) understanding the centrality of values and commitment, (4) recognizing that there are multiple ways to create and represent knowledge, and (5) understanding the role and meaning of action.

I am a white, heterosexual male in my late 60s. I am of settler origin and give thanks to the privilege of working on Lekwungen traditional territory in Victoria, British Columbia, Canada. I am part of an exclusive and excluding culture. I have lived and worked in Africa, Asia, Latin America, Europe, the United States, and Canada. I see myself as an activist-scholar with many years working in non-governmental organizations (NGOs) before coming to the university world. Within the academic world, I have been a university professor, a departmental chair, a dean, and a founding director of a new community-university research structure. In all my work, whether at the community level or the academic level, I have seen myself as a kind of "social movement plumber," someone who helps fit things together so that the power and flow of the rivers of social change can be enhanced and more effective. I am constantly humbled by my lack of skills and knowledge when confronting a world that I do not like, yet know not how to change. I am also a poet.

We Make the Road by Walking[1]

I'm old school. I mean that quite literally. When I did my doctoral studies at the University of California in Los Angeles between 1968 and 1972, there was no such thing as participatory research or community-based research or any of the other versions of this kind of research. We generated hypotheses as the key activity of our work and then tested them using experimental designs or structured interviews of some kind. The credibility of our work was linked to various approaches to statistical validity and reliability. The only time that I even ventured outside of my classrooms was for a part-time job that I got supervising some field research in the Hispanic neighbourhoods of East Los Angeles. Mostly I read other people's books about other people's theories about how other people lived and learned. My doctorate was done in International and Comparative Education and African Studies. I had been a Peace Corps volunteer, teaching in Nigeria for 2 years before beginning my doctorate. I wanted to continue to study the role of education in Africa as countries across the African continent emerged from the many years of colonial rule.

Much of my journey into participatory research and community-based research has been a kind of lucky accident. The late 1960s were a time of turmoil and changing politics. Young people my age were beginning not only to question the designs of power, but also to organize and act against them. At the University of California at Los Angeles, where I was studying in 1968–70, our formal education was richly augmented by a series of sweeping demonstrations, campus occupations, "teach-ins," and the birth of the alternative school movement. The legendary African American intellectual Angela Davis was teaching Philosophy at UCLA, with nearly 1,000 students in her classes each week. African-American studies were first introduced during these years. The disability movement revolutionized Berkeley, California, by demanding and getting ramps for wheelchairs to move about the city and then into all the buildings of the university.

In Africa, and among people such as me studying African political developments, the ideas of Frantz Fanon of Martinique and Algeria, Amilcar Cabral of Guinea-Bissau, Kwame Nkrumah of Ghana, Augustino Neto of Angola, and Julius Nyerere were being read and discussed in our classrooms, over coffee, and in our homes. Julius Nyerere, in particular, attracted the attention of many of us. A former teacher with a progressive agenda, his leadership of the Tanzanian independence movement was based on ideas and vision of an Africa that could move forward on the basis of Indigenous values, political structures, language, and philosophy. His speeches were thoughtful, tactical, and wonderfully encouraging of engagement in learning about political alternatives. The independence movement of Tanzania of the 1960s was an example of social movement learning, as former colonial subjects transformed themselves into citizens of a new nation. But his ideas were not limited to the achievement of political independence. He brought participatory processes into the national political party of the day, the Tanganyika National Union (TANU), elaborated a new educational philosophy called "Education for Self-Reliance" (Nyerere, 1967b), outlined a national development policy based on traditional ideas of familyhood called in Kiswahili, *Ujamaa* (Nyerere, 1967a). In addition, he led the debates that led to the replacement of English as the language of politics, education, and national trade with Kiswahili. The impact of this adoption was to provide an Indigenous lingua franca that helped to build a sense of national culture and identity.

Nyerere was to many of us a kind of twentieth-century philosopher-king. He was a wily politician to be sure, but a humble, religious, and intellectual leader who was able to articulate new ways forward on behalf of his people. When I had a chance, in May of 1970, to meet Nicholas Kuhanga, I jumped at it. Nicolas Kuhanga was a member of Parliament from Tanzania who was deputy director of the Institute of Adult Education at the University of Dar es Salaam, and was travelling in the United States looking at adult education and outreach structures. I had finished the course work for my doctorate and was looking for a place to do my field research. Nicholas told me that that his Institute of Adult Education was looking for a research fellow, a new post, to work with them in the evaluation of their extensive work all around the country. I told him that I was interested, and within a few months, found myself in Dar es Salaam starting to work.

The course that I taught on research methods as part of the diploma course in adult education was where I learned a lot about new approaches to research. During 1973, the Institute of Adult Education led a national health education campaign involving 75,000 radio study groups all around the nation who met once a week to listen to a radio program called "Mtu Ni Afya" (People Are Health). This was a 13-week campaign that was designed to stimulate participation and discussion about things that ordinary people could do to prevent diseases that were accounting for 80 to 90 per cent of morbidity and mortality for children under the age of 5 years; these included illnesses such as malaria, schistosomiasis or bilharzia, dysentery, and diarrhea. All of these diseases were subject to dramatic reductions in incidence and severity if certain environmental matters were taken into account, such as eliminating standing water near homes, using mosquito nettings, building and using latrines, and not bathing in rivers or streams but instead letting water settle. I was responsible for the evaluation of the campaign (Hall, 1978).

I was teaching the module on research and evaluation to the students who, as it happened, were about to go on home leave during the midpoint of the Mtu Ni Afya campaign. As a last-minute thought, I asked them to go around their villages and ask for stories about the impact of the Mtu Ni Afya campaign. Were people participating? Was it having any results? I had not included them in the evaluation design, which I had previously produced using pre- and post-program knowledge tests and a variety of other measures. When the students returned from their holidays, I asked them to share their stories with me about what was happening in their homes. They had hundreds of fascinating, complex, and compelling stories about the impact that the campaign was already beginning to have. In fact, the stories that my students shared with me brought a great deal of explanatory or illuminative power about the complexities of the way the campaign was working. I realized that my dependence on the basic package of survey research methodology that I had been taught in graduate school was extremely limited. By sitting down informally with friends and family at home, my students had learned more than I had as the formal leader of the campaign evaluation. That moment was the beginning of what was to become several years of disorganized but steady reflections on what might be a better approach to doing research, where the goal was to support learning and action as an integral part of the research process.

By the end of 1974, I was able to pull together a lot of what I had learned in with other researchers in Tanzania and with others in Latin America and elsewhere, and wrote the lead article for the special issue of *Convergence*, the International Journal of Adult Education, on what I called "Participatory Research" (Hall, 1975). I was frankly rather astonished that the framing of research in this way seemed to catch the attention of so many people and was delighted that many years later, this form of research and variations of the approach would become part of most universities' normal offerings in research.

Between 1975 and 1989, the development of the approach to community-based research that I am most associated with, participatory research, grew, developed, and was nourished within civil society and social movement settings. I have written elsewhere about the history of the development of participatory research and how it came "in from the cold" (Hall, 2005, pp. 5–24). In 1989, I was offered the first opportunity to teach a course in participatory research within a graduate program of a university. However, all the teaching and facilitating that I was involved with between 1975, the year I left Tanzania, and 1989, when I was invited to offer my first course in participatory research was within the context of community groups, workshops at international conferences, and network gatherings – all outside of university settings. Since 1989, I have taught graduate courses in participatory or community-based research at York University, the Ontario Institute of Studies in Education at the University of Toronto, and the University of Victoria, with guest talks at universities in Europe, Latin America, and Asia. What follows in this chapter are some of the principles that have emerged over the years about how I have approached the task of sharing these ideas and practices with those who are interested in learning them, particularly with graduate students. For those interested in some of my earlier reflections on the practice of participatory research, I draw your attention to the piece done for the *Handbook of Action Research*, "I Wish This Were a Poem of Practices" (Hall, 2001).

Knowing Who We Are

Indigenous, feminist, anti-racist, queer, differently abled, and anti-colonial theoretical academic discourses have all eloquently made the point that who we are influences how we experience the world, how we see and are seen in the world, how we name the world and how our knowledge or ranges of experiences are taken up or not. If an ethical practice in CBR involves learning to listen, we first need to know who we are or what, as some would say, is our social location. Knowing ourselves allows us to understand the challenges that we face when working with others in our communities and helps to create a respectful openness to hearing in new ways. It supports humility. There may be some who might argue that reflexivity when taken too far becomes navel gazing. Perhaps, but speaking as an older white male who has benefited from society's lack of reflexivity, on balance I feel it is critical to our ability to be effective in the world.

When working with Indigenous peoples in British Columbia, where I now live, when Indigenous scholars, politicians, artists, educators, or Elders introduce themselves, they always begin with their name in their Indigenous language, who they are related to, and where they and their people have come from. This is not done because of having read or heard some academic speak of concepts like "epistemic privilege" (Bat-Ami, 1993), but because relationships are understood to be at the core of all interactions, all learning, all knowledge, and all of life itself. This is a practice of wisdom from which I have learned. It reminds us that at one time in the world in all cultures, people would spend quite a bit of time when first meeting telling each other what they could about their families and locations. Particularly when writing, it is helpful for readers to know more about the author's social location, I believe.

Two of the exercises that I have found quite effective over the years in helping us to understand our individual locations are a variation of what we learned in our anti-racist work in Toronto in the 1980s and 1990s as the "Power Flower" (Arnold et al., 1991) and "Unpacking our invisible knapsacks of privilege" (McIntosh, 1988). The "Power Flower" involves creating a drawing of a daisylike flower with outer petals and inner petals extending out from the centre of the blossom. Collectively, we give names of as many kinds of social locations as we can think of and write them one to each petal, such as gender, race, sexual orientation, age, ethnic origin or heritage, Indigeneity, ability, and so forth. On the outer petal we indicate from a social or political dominance perspective in our community what the dominant social location might be. Generally speaking in dominant society male is dominant over female, non-Indigenous over Indigenous, able-bodied over differently abled, and so forth. On the inner petal, often in pairs, we identify our own location. As I said in the introduction to this chapter, I would write, "white," "male," "straight," and so on. In looking at each of our "Power Flowers," we might even count up the petals where we were holding dominant social locations. Generally speaking, those who have the highest number of dominant social locations are those who have the greatest challenges in learning to listen. Again, generally speaking, those who have the least number of dominant social locations have the most difficulty being seen or heard, or having their knowledge as part of the dominant social awareness. There are many shortcomings to this kind of analysis, because it oversimplifies by creating binary positions or false dichotomies, assumes a fixed rather than fluid and shifting identity, and tends to give all social locators at least graphic equality. Yet, it has proven to be a useful starting point for many of my students. Working with Peggy McIntosh's article on white privilege is a similar awareness-raising exercise that uncovers the hidden privileges of being white or male or whatever that because of the way the dominant society operates, one may not be aware of. The article makes the point that for people who mirror dominant culture social characteristics, we carry an invisible knapsack of privilege. The exercise consists of metaphorically unpacking the knapsack and discussing how privilege works. And although we have many sophisticated and scholarly articles on issues such as white privilege (Rodriguez, 2000) or "othering" (Riggins, 1997), working in groups and in the classroom with some of these exercises can stimulate useful reflection.

The importance of knowing who we are, both our personal locations and our institutional location, is critical to our being able to establish respectful partnership relations in any new context. The heart of all CBR is about relationships. Often, the most productive CBR processes emerge from community, social movement, or organizational settings that we are already a part of. The development of partnerships requires time even when one is already a member; if one has to begin from the outside, it is better sometimes to put aside the idea of doing a CBR project if sufficient time is not available. When I was first invited to teach a CBR course in a university I felt very conflicted. I was not sure that encouraging students to all go out and try doing this type of research within the space of a few months would be at all useful with the community groups and social movements. I still believe this to be the case, but for students coming from an activist location or who are already part of an organizational or movement context whose other group members need research to be done, this is an approach they should use. And for others, they need to be able to deconstruct the weaknesses of other research approaches and give thought to how values and politics are woven into all forms of knowledge creation and representation. As with other kinds of research, we have good examples and bad examples of CBR. Striving for excellence in CBR requires patience, time, openness, knowledge of each other, and sensitivity to the other factors that I refer to in the rest of this chapter.

Learning to Listen: A Role for Poetry

I once asked a friend of mine about his plans for the coming year. He had spent quite a few years in Nicaragua in charge of the logistics for the Nicaraguan Literacy Crusade and had returned to California where he was teaching. I asked him what he had in mind and was taken aback by his reply. He told me that he was going to work for the coming year on "listening well and providing constructive feedback" when people he works with ask for his ideas and suggestions. I had expected him to say that he was working with a new political grouping or taking new challenges to Ottawa or Washington. To me, he was giving "learning to listen" a priority in his life.

I have supported the practices of learning to listen in many ways, from bringing in people from the community to sending students to meetings or events where they would be out of their comfort zones, but I want to share just a few thoughts on a role for poetry as a tool for learning to listen. Poetry, for me, is one of the most powerful means of teaching what learning to listen is all about. Close your eyes to hear or focus on the words on a page and you will find new insights each and every time.

As a poet, over the years I have been interested in the relationship of poetry to learning within the context of social movements. I have taught courses on poetry, adult learning, and social movements over a period of some 15 years, both at the University of Toronto and at the University of Victoria. While I have written before on poetry and social movements (Hall, 2009b), within the context of this chapter on teaching and facilitation of CBR, the role of poetry in allowing us to enter into new world views is worth examining here.

Muriel Rukeheyzer, the US social movement poet, explains in her book, *The Life of Poetry* (1974) that, "in poetry, the exchange is one of energy. Human energy is transferred, and from the poem it reaches the reader. Human energy, which is consciousness, is the capacity to produce change in existing conditions" (p. 23). Poetry among other things is a medium, which is based on the word, the written word, but importantly also the spoken word. The poetic tradition arises from the oral culture. Most poetry is written with the idea that it will be read aloud or listened to. The rhythms and cadences of the lines in poetry and spoken word reflect ancient processes and allow for deep incorporation of the exchanges of meaning. Poetry may have a power to still the rational voice in our heads that tries to interpret things prematurely, which inhibits listening.

In my classes, I have asked students to identify a context or a social movement or an issue of social justice that they are concerned about. I have also asked them to write their own poetry about the issues that concern them. This issue might be or become the focus of their proposal for a community-based research project that they would work on as a class project. I then ask them to find a poem or poems written by persons who are part of that context or location or situation. For example, they may be interested in supporting social action on homelessness or working with women on a project or working on Indigenous identity. They then bring the pieces to class, and in smaller and larger groups we share these by reading the pieces aloud and then discuss what they might mean. From Malika Sengupta (2005), a Bengali activist poet's piece, "Kathamanabi," comes this evocative description of the historic role of women:

> I am "her" voice, recounting her tales.
> From Vedic age to the 21st century.
> The fire that has remained stifled in the ashes of
> History, smothered by time and age,
> I am that woman – I speak of her.
> I read tears, I write fire,
> I live in infamy and consume its ashes
> I endure violence, and still breathe fire.
> I live as long as this fire burns within me.

Read aloud this segment from *My State of War* (2003), Roberta Timothy's piece, a Toronto-based spoken word artist:[2]

> By the age of four
> I knew then
> I was living
> In a State of War.
> Walking out the front door
> Onto the streets
> Headed for kindergarten
> Bag full with
> Caribbean Sweets.
> Greeted by dogs
> Shakin by fear
> Teased, Teared

Black skin Dared.
Neighbours yelling
"Your kind don't belong here!"
Morning
Afternoon
Evening
Running, Screaming, Hiding
Each season
Reason
Black skin treason?
Climbing trees, Jumping fences
Hoping, Wishing, Praying
To Avoid
Viscous, scary
Kanine trenches.
After the age of four
Still living
In a state of war.
Iny Miny Minny moe
On the playground
This war did go.
Ooh! It's a fight
The Piercing lyrics Of
"Nigga Nigga
And a White"
Resound in my head
While images of excrement burning on my lawn
Flash in my eyes
Memories never die.
Childhood's scorn.
Questions, Worries
Unanswered Wrongs
Still Singing
Exploitation songs.
In school
Learning Canadian History
No mention
Of Aboriginal culture, robbery, slavery
Just a mystery!

The Centrality of Values

Paulo Freire (1970) gave us all permission to combine our teaching, learning, and activism when he told us so many years ago that "education is not neutral." He told us that the way that we teach and help others to learn either contributed to the maintenance of dominant systems of privilege, exploitation, power, and exclusion – or did not. I believe that the same can be said of research methodologies. The processes that we engage with in doing research are as much part of the politics of transformation, resistance, or organizing as the content itself. Participatory research emerged in the 1970s as a reaction to the idea that research methods were somehow objective and neutral. It arose, as well, as a challenge to both the orthodox survey research methods of the day and the action research traditions of the late 1940s that had become stuck in the toolkits of organizational development professionals. It is important to note as well that the specific discourse of participatory research, which of course is only one of the streams of what we now know of as community-based research, was a voice coming from Africa, Latin America, and Asia before it had gained widespread visibility in North America and Europe (Brandao, 1985; Fals Borda, 2001; Fals Borda & Rahman, 1991; Tandon, 1988). It is also worth noting that it was developed and refined for nearly 20 years in civil society and social movement organizations before it became more common in academic writing. It was not until the 1980s and 90s, when scholars in the United States such as David Brown (see, e.g., Brown, 1985 or Brown & Tandon, 1983), Peter Park (1993), John Gaventa (1998; 2003), and Randy Stoeker (see e.g., Stoeker & Bonacich, 1992) began to publish and present in academic circles, that the academic world started to take notice.

The question I like to discuss is the following: what is the role or the potential role of research in processes of community transformation and social justice? If we agree with the critique eloquently expressed in Aboriginal communities, for example, that research has been part of the colonial apparatus (Tuhiwai Smith, 1999), a tool of domination and subjugation, how could it be done differently? How can research build organizational capacity with grassroots groups, so that their voices can be heard more clearly where needed? How can research partnerships between universities and communities be set up that respect the communities' capacities to name the issue that they are facing? How do we build long-term relationships, solidarity, allegiances, and friendships that will break the pattern of short-term love affairs between the academy and the community that dissolve when the money runs out?

In teaching the centrality of values, I have most often drawn on early foundational writings to stimulate discussions and debate about the relationships of values and engagement and to provide us with an opportunity to deconstruct or demystify research methods. I have drawn on some of my own early writings, where principles and a rationale for participatory research were first expressed. I have found Patricia McGuire's great book *Doing Participatory Research* (1987), which lays out a feminist critique of the early writings, including my own, to be very helpful to students. Patti Lather's piece on "Research as Praxis" (1986) is a great foundational work as well. In terms of more contemporary pieces, I draw on Strand, Marullo, Cutforth, Stoecker, and Donohue's (2003) work on community-based research, on Ernest Boyer's (1990; 1996) work on engaged scholarship, on Barbara Israel's (1998) definitional piece on CBPR in health, on Meredith Minkler and Nina Wallerstein's (2003) health-based work, on Jeff Corntassel's Indigenous-centred research (Corntassel, Chaw-win-is, & T'lakwadzi, 2009; and chapter in this book), on Maggie Kovach's (2009) Cree epistemology, and on Shawn Wilson's *Research Is Ceremony* (2008). These authors provide a diverse and varied way of linking knowledge creation and use within a process that cherishes values and seeks to extend inclusion and fairness.

Openness to Multiple Ways of Knowing and Representing Knowledge

Knowledge is created in so many extraordinary ways. There is the knowledge of the carvers, who learn from their teacher, add new techniques themselves, and express the knowledge in a welcoming pole or a house pole. There is the knowledge of the poets, representing realities in metaphor and cadence. There is the knowledge of the dancers, who learn to control the body in ways that convey new meanings and understandings. There is the knowledge of the Elders, honed from years of seeking to live in balance with people and the rest of nature, who often share knowledge through stories. There is the knowledge of the writers or the playwrights, creating and representing knowledge through words and images. There are the community organizers, creating knowledge through listening to people's issues and suggesting strategies for collective working together. There are the spiritual leaders, whose source of knowledge is through revelation. There is the knowledge of those without permanent homes who know where food, safety, and health care can be found in the streets.

All of these ways of knowing permeate our lives from birth to death, in families, in communities, in workplaces, in social movements, and in networks that inform or support us. All of these ways of knowing pre-date and still parallel the approaches to knowledge creation that we most often draw on as academics and scholars. What we think of as the scientific method, a way of knowing based on observable phenomena, information that passes through our five senses, is, in the history of humanity, a newcomer to the world of epistemology. It is a product of a particular period of Western European history and is often traced back to Francis Bacon (1626). It can be found in the work of the Arab mathematicians (Abu Ja'fa Muhammed, 630 CE, and Abu l'Hassan al-Uglidisi, 950 CE), of Galileo (1632), of Leonardo da Vinci (1478–1519), and many others whose way of thinking profoundly challenged the prevailing notions of their times that all knowledge was derived from God as interpreted either directly or indirectly, depending on one's religious convictions. During the second half of the twentieth century, the academic community continued to expand its notion of what counts as knowledge, whose knowledge counts, and how to represent knowledge. Community-based research allows, no, *requires* us to remain open to choosing ways of doing research that draw on ways of knowing / doing/being/perceiving that those communities and those people who we are supporting and working with value and respect.

My own thinking on CBR methods has been influenced by the ideas of Paulo Freire and his cultural circles in Brazil (1970), by dian marino's (1988) work on the use of drawing and art for social change, by Augusto Boal's forum theatre (1979), and more recently by many of the authors in this collection, including the work of Darlene Clover on feminist aesthetics and social change (Clover & Craig, 2009; Clover & Stalker, 2007), Catherine Etmanski on teaching participatory research (Etmanski & Pant, 2007), Jo Anne Lee (2006) and Indigenous scholars Williams (Williams & Tanaka, 2007), Corntassel (Corntassel, Chaw-win-is, & T'lakwadzi, 2009), Kovach (2009), and de Finney (Lee & de Finney, 2005). Neither CBR nor participatory research is a research method if one understands research methods as a set of steps or procedures. Rather, they form a set of principles and frameworks that will allow us to engage in knowledge creation and representation within community or movement settings in appropriate ways The point that I hope to make in my teaching is that the research methods that evolve in a CBR or PR project need to fit the context of the situation and need to be understood and to some extent negotiated with or discussed by the partners with whom one is working. Above all, one needs to be very open to making use of knowledge creation strategies, research methods that allow for a broad, engaged, holistic representation of knowledge and which will advance the action agenda of the project or moment.

What about the Action?

Community-based research and the various members of the CBR family are always linked conceptually with the idea of action. As Karl Marx noted in 1845, "philosophers have only interpreted the world ... the point is to change it" (1969, p. 13). There are a variety of ways that this same idea is approached by the CBR community, who note that CBR is meant to be an active process, an engaged process whereby knowledge is created, collective learning occurs, and some forms of action occur. From the field of Health Promotion, "CBPR (in health) begins with an issue of importance to the community with the aim of combining knowledge and action for social change" (WK Kellogg Foundation, in Minkler & Wallerstein, 2003, p. 28). In another description from the health field, Green and colleagues say, "participatory research is a systematic inquiry ... for purposes of taking action or effecting change" (1995, p. 22). From the majority world school of CBR comes the Fals Borda and Rahman understanding that PAR "enables oppressed groups and classes to acquire sufficient creative and transformative leverage as expressed in specific projects, acts and struggles" (1991, p. 4).

In teaching CBR, it is important to allow substantial time to talk through the question of action. We are also always keeping in mind that every single new CBR experience occurs within a different context. There are no cookbook approaches or easy guidelines to follow that will guarantee engagement or positive results. And what passes for action in one context will not be seen as action in another. For me, the fundamental principle that must underscore our work is that the results of a CBR process must be seen to belong to the community. That does not mean that academics cannot write up a study and publish it in an academic journal, but it does mean that the community members need to understand and be comfortable with one's intention to do that prior to getting going with the research itself. The types of action that may emerge from a CBR project are as varied as the contexts themselves, but failure to give some thought to the action component will result in one's research project not falling within the CBR genre – in spite of some authors self-identifying in this way. If I think back over the years about CBR projects that I have been associated with, the "action" has taken many forms. In Tanzanian adult education circles, the action was planning for courses that could be offered in the village adult education programs. Another project in Tanzania involved creating a better type of grain storage silo. In a project with prison guards in a prison that was going to shut down in Ontario, the action component consisted of the development of a portfolio of skills by each of the guards to help them gain entry into the local community college. Indirectly, it resulted in many of the guards gaining a new appreciation and pride in themselves and their accomplishments. In a recent project with the leaders of community-based Indigenous adult education centres in British Columbia, the action was providing visibility for the accomplishments and then gaining recognition by the Ministry of Education of the advantages of the culturally focused and community based adult education provision as a means of helping build the numbers of community members going into postsecondary educational alternatives.

Many of us seek to lead lives where the work that we do is somehow consistent with our values. Many of us seek out academic studies that will give us skills that enable us to contribute more effectively towards making our communities fairer, more equitable, and more inclusive places. Community-based research is an expression by some scholars to align the formal processes of academic worth with these kinds of democratic and inclusive values. Teaching CBR is exceedingly difficult, but at the same time is so important as a path for some of us trying to move forward in a world that we do not like, yet know not how to change.

Part III

Campus beyond the Classroom:
Innovations in CBR Programming

8 Insurgent Education and Indigenous-Centred Research: Opening New Pathways to Community Resurgence

JEFF CORNTASSEL AND ADAM GAUDRY

We are writing this chapter as Cherokee and Métis visitors to Lekwungen homelands and waterways. Awareness of this reality requires us to go beyond a simple acknowledgment. It is a call for justice and the return of stolen lands and waterways to the Indigenous peoples who maintain special relationships to these places. Ultimately, what we are arguing for is a responsibility-based ethic of truth telling: initiating teachable moments where participants identify, discuss, and act on new pathways to Indigenous resurgence and decolonization. According to Mohawk scholar Taiaiake Alfred (2004, p. 95), "to be a real Indigenous intellectual, one must be a warrior of the truth." Truth, in this case, means communicating Indigenous truths: the knowledge and lived experiences of being Indigenous, both in Indigenous communities and in colonial settings. These are experiential truths that go far beyond abstract principles or absolute values – they are grounded in our ongoing relationships and responsibilities to place and the natural world. With this understanding we ask: How do we take our sacred relationships and responsibilities as Indigenous truth-tellers and translate those lived realities into respectful research and teaching relationships?

Responsible research implies deeper collaborations that take place at the community level, undertaken for the benefit of the community. Good pedagogy likewise empowers local people to act, as well as to recognize and confront the oppressive and exploitative relations that affect our everyday lives. We start with the assumption that both research and teaching are more than consumer-driven practices undertaken strictly within the academic-industrial complex. We challenge much of contemporary practice in the university setting – classroom-based, impersonal education, detached research, and university-based academic accountability – and put forward a more human approach to research and education, one that is consistent with Indigenous world views: experiential, community-centred learning grounded in local cosmologies, languages, homelands, and facilitated by people rooted in their land, community, and culture.

What we propose is *insurgent education*, a way of challenging the injustices of colonialism, dispossession, and racist oppression, while reaffirming the world views of our ancestors (Corntassel, 2011). If an insurgency is a state of rebellion or act of rising in revolt against established authority, then insurgent education is an important part of an anti-colonial struggle and pedagogies of decolonization. Insurgent educators seek to initiate discomforting moments of Indigenous truth-telling that challenge the colonial status quo. As part of a larger decolonizing strategy, insurgent education:

- Re-localizes Indigenous struggles
- Counters the politics of distraction by centring Indigenous peoples and their relationships in the discussion
- Occurs in both formal, and, more often, informal settings
- Compels accountability and direct action to counter contemporary colonialism. (Corntassel, 2011)

We begin this chapter by examining a typical approach to academic study, what we call extraction research, and highlight how most research reinforces, rather than destabilizes, existing colonial relationships. Creating a new consciousness regarding the harmful impacts of extractive research practices and contemporary forms of colonialism, we establish a context for discussing current Indigenous struggles and educational strategies. We then examine alternative approaches to research and instruction, those consistent with Indigenous world views and resistance to colonialism. In the final section we look at how these approaches have worked in our experiences, and the success we have had in fostering more responsible relationships in an academic setting.

Teaching the Colonial Context

How does one convey Indigenous realities within the contemporary colonial context? To teach these current realities to settlers, the once invisible struggles of Indigenous peoples must be made visible again. Implementing a "pedagogy of discomfort" (Regan, 2011; Boler & Zembylas, 2003) can be an effective tool for educating those who have become far too comfortable and complacent about living on stolen Indigenous homelands. A pedagogy of discomfort takes both the educator and students beyond their "comfort zones," and is where "testimonial exchange functions as a catalyst for engaging in constructive critical dialogue" (Regan, 2011, p. 52). Putting such a pedagogy into practice might entail informing settler students that they are living on stolen Indigenous homelands and problematizing how they continue to benefit from the colonial status quo to the detriment of the original peoples of the territory.

As an extension of a pedagogy of discomfort, insurgent education opens new pathways for going beyond uncomfortable moments and moving us towards a decolonizing praxis. Settlers are the beneficiaries of colonization processes as they knowingly (and unknowingly) engage in everyday actions that disconnect Indigenous peoples from their land-based and water-based cultural practices. Truth-telling promotes awareness of these colonial realities and creates new accountabilities to Indigenous peoples and their relationships to place, motivating some to make amends and to be responsive to Indigenous struggles for decolonization. However, "extractive" research and teaching relationships often mirror these existing asymmetrical power relationships and can be contextualized accordingly.

More than any other group, Indigenous peoples endure the most exploitative research practices undertaken by both well-meaning and not-so-well-meaning scholars (Tuhiwai Smith, 1999; Schnarch, 2004; Denzin, Lincoln, & Smith, 2008). Similar to the physical "resources" extracted from Indigenous territories by corporations and government entities, one can say that through research, knowledge is also *extracted* from communities for the benefit of outsiders. Exemplifying this process is the extractive research of "Big Pharma." Over 70 per cent of modern plant-based medicines are derived from Indigenous knowledge gained through the extraction of pre-existing medicines from Indigenous communities. Patents taken out on Indigenous medicines allow non-Indigenous individuals and corporations to amass extensive wealth by claiming Indigenous knowledge as their own. The sale of these patents by researchers has fuelled the massive growth of the pharmaceutical industry, which then produces drugs that are priced out of the reach of most Indigenous peoples (A. Smith, 2005, p. 116). Vandana Shiva (2005) writes:

> Patents are supposed to satisfy three criteria: novelty, non-obviousness and utility. "Novelty" requires that the invention not be part of "prior art"

or existing knowledge; "non-obviousness" requires that someone familiar with the art would not take the same step. Most patents based on the appropriation of indigenous knowledge violate these criteria, because they range from direct piracy to minor tinkering involving steps obvious to anyone trained in the techniques and disciplines involved. Since a patent is an exclusive right granted for an invention, patents on life and traditional knowledge are twice as harmful and add insult to injury. Such patents are not based on inventions; they serve as instruments for preventing the poor from satisfying their own needs and using their own biodiversity and their own knowledge. (p. 147)

Similar to those in the physical sciences, social science researchers also engage in "drive-by ethnographies" or extractive methodologies to remove Indigenous knowledge from its community and place-based context, in order to repackage and retransmit it to an audience with little or no involvement with these communities. Social scientific research, then, becomes the tool in which outsiders gather knowledge about Indigenous people, often without the need for involvement with, and responsibility to, the Indigenous peoples participating in the research. Research to educate non-Indigenous people is certainly necessary, but the very process of translating Indigenous knowledges can often distort the original messages in teachings, and can, because of Western interpretations of fundamentally non-Western knowledges, turn the tenets of Indigenous societies into self-referential academic jargon, debating irrelevant issues with no connection to the lived experience of the people involved. In most cases, Indigenous people have little control over what goes on in the process, because the norms of research have become a largely colonial process.

Research is considered extractive when it becomes clear how the researchers benefit from the project – publications, funding, tenure, respect as a knowledgeable person – while the community's gains remain elusive. Unfortunately, most research concerning Indigenous peoples is intended for outside consumption – it is research for settlers and their purposes, not for Indigenous peoples and our national revival. The extractive approach to research, we argue, is as irrelevant to Indigenous peoples as it is unethical. It perpetuates the colonial relationship between researchers and Indigenous communities, and fails to challenge the basic underpinnings of imperialism. Indigenous research, then, must be approached from an Indigenous perspective; it must to challenge oppressive and exploitative relationships; and it is necessary to give something back, in a very concrete and tangible way, to the communities involved in the research project.

Extraction Research

Gaudry (2011) outlines an extraction research model, a process by which Indigenous knowledge is removed from Indigenous communities without following traditional protocol or without establishing a primary commitment to the community "being researched." However, several alternatives to this form of research exist and are regularly put into practice. Documents such as *The Ally Bill of Responsibilities* (Gehl, n.d.) as well as Indigenous community research protocols, such as the *Mi'kmaq Ecological Knowledge Study Protocol* (Assembly of Nova Scotia Mi'kmaq Chiefs, 2009), begin to articulate Indigenous stakes in the struggle against extractive research.

In the extraction model of research, communities rarely participate in the development of research questions or are entitled to determine the validity of research "findings" (Gaudry, 2011, p. 171). The researcher decides what is important enough to be researched and sets about doing it, therefore denying the community meaningful participation in developing the research program from its inception; this is the antithesis of community-based research. The researcher's presence is justified by the notion *freedom of information*, which is based on the idea that all of humanity is entitled to all of human knowledge – that all knowledge is a shared human possession – regardless of whether or not Indigenous communities are interested in sharing it with outsiders. This idea of knowledge sharing, or a freely accessible knowledge commons is itself a Euro-centric assumption. All Indigenous communities have complex protocols and restrictions on the transmission of knowledge, which are intended to protect the integrity of the knowledge and ensure its continuity. These restrictions and protocols have been intensified as the understandable result of the long and ongoing history of intellectual theft by academics and scientists; to put it plainly, Indigenous people are now more cautious about sharing information than they were in the past. As the *Mi'kmaq Ecological Study Protocol* (Assembly of Nova Scotia Mi'kmaq Chiefs, 2009) states, "all research scholars shall assume responsibility to learn the protocols and traditions of the local people with whom they do research and to be knowledgeable and sensitive to cultural practices and issues that ensure respect and accommodation to local norms" (p. 19). Some of these local norms might be to write the results of the study in the language of the participating Indigenous community, as well as providing research training to the participating Indigenous communities.

In terms of output, extraction research is primarily oriented towards a non-Indigenous audience. Because it targets outsiders, researchers almost always translate their research findings into the dominant culture's world view, in order to be most easily understood. Instead of being grounded in an Indigenous world view, the research is grounded in a Euro–North American perspective (Gaudry, 2011, p. 171). It is often accompanied by references to the Western intellectual canon and its great thinkers. The implication of this assumption is that Indigenous thought cannot stand on its own or is otherwise strengthened or justified when grounded in universal values, by which they almost always mean Western values. This runs counter to the most important aspect of community-based research partnerships – the usefulness and accessibility of the research to the community (Strand, Marullo, Cutforth, Stoecker, & Donohue, 2003).

The highest goal of extraction research is thought to be the stimulation of public debate, a process that Linda Tuhiwai Smith (1999, p. 72) describes as:

> "Authorities" and outside experts verify[ing], comment[ing] on, and [giving] judgments about the validity of indigenous claims to cultural beliefs, values, ways of knowing and historical accounts. Such issues are often debated vigorously by the "public" (a category which usually means the dominant group), leading to an endless parading of "nineteenth century" views of race and racial difference.

The result, which Indigenous peoples have seen countless times, is a debate where non-Indigenous researchers position themselves as experts in assessing the relative "value" of Indigenous knowledge. This debate takes many forms, from Widdowson and Howard's (2008) *Disrobing the Aboriginal Industry* (or Thomas Flanagan's *First Nations, Second Thoughts* [2000] that preceded it), where racist and colonial stereotypes are reinscribed and reaffirmed with the intention of provoking outrage by the general population. A more well-meaning (but equally inaccurate) version of this approach is exemplified by John Ralston Saul's discussion of the "Métis" character of Canada in *A Fair Country* (2009). In all of these cases, Indigenous peoples are represented to the dominant culture in inaccurate and distorted ways, rendering us seen but not necessarily heard in our own voices. Just as we seek to represent ourselves on our own terms, we are excluded from the debates where others discuss our lives.

Extraction research, the dominant mode of research today, results in the silencing, fragmentation, and appropriation of Indigenous voices, cultures, ceremonies, and world views. Extraction research undermines Indigenous control of Indigenous knowledges by removing the community, and community protocols and/or world views, from the research process. The challenge becomes to teach within this colonial context, to expose the beneficiaries and framers of an extractive research process and in its place, offer community-centred alternatives, such as OCAP, which emphasizes "ownership, control, access, and possession/protection" for Indigenous peoples (Schnarch, 2004).

Indigenous Approaches to Pedagogy

Despite the predominance of extraction research within the academy, there is a strong tradition among Indigenous scholars who articulate alternative approaches to teaching community-centred research, grounded in Indigenous ways of being. They do this by outlining pivotal Indigenous roles and responsibilities both inside and outside the academy. One of the first people to do this was the late Standing Rock Sioux scholar Vine Deloria, Jr., who challenged Indigenous educators and students to be more like "scouts" by using their "powers of observation" to provide vital information to guide future community decisions (Deloria, 2000, p. 39). For Deloria, if we aspire to act as scouts within the academic context, two fundamental questions must be answered: (1) How does what we receive (or give) in our educational experience impact the preservation and sensible use of our lands? And (2) How does it affect the continuing existence of our nations? (cited in Wilkins, 2005, p. 167).

These questions posed by Deloria integrate community accountability into the process of teaching and research. Maori scholar Linda Tuhiwai Smith in her classic work, *Decolonizing Methodologies*, offers a powerful response. Tuhiwai Smith (1999) urges Indigenous scholars to reclaim the role and responsibility of disseminating their own knowledges:

Indigenous peoples want to tell our own stories, write our own versions, in our own ways, for our own purposes. It is not simply about giving an oral account of a genealogical naming of the land and the events which ranged over it, but a very powerful need to give testimony to and restore a spirit, to bring back into existence a world fragmented and dying. (p. 28)

To put this spirit of resistance and reclamation into practice she outlines "The Indigenous Peoples Project," which has an agenda focused "on the goal of self-determination of indigenous peoples" – more than just a political goal, but "a goal of social justice," meaning that "it necessarily involves the processes of transformation, of decolonization, of healing, and of mobilization as peoples" (Tuhiwai Smith, 1999, p. 116). Tuhiwai Smith advocates not only a research agenda that empowers individuals to reclaim their culture, but one that produces a movement empowering Indigenous communities *as communities* to take control of their knowledge.

Building on this decolonizing approach to research is Anishinaabe scholar Dale Turner's "word warriors" in *This Is Not a Peace Pipe* (2006). Turner defines *word warriors* as those intellectuals and researchers "whose primary function is to engage the legal and political discourses of the state" (p. 72). The task of these word warriors is "representing their communities (and often other indigenous communities) in the intellectual world of the dominant culture" in order to "protect the integrity of indigenous ways of knowing the world even while engaging the dominant intellectual culture in more empowering ways" (pp. 73–4). The word *warrior*, then, has more of an outward orientation when contrasted with Tuhiwai Smith's decolonizing researcher, for the word warrior seeks to engage the dominant discourse in its own arena to have the dominant culture better understand Indigenous knowledges. This approach, however, is based on Turner's (2006, p. 72) assumption that "indigenous forms of knowledge *need to be reconciled with the legal and political discourses of the state*," necessitating a kind of merger or coming together of two disparate knowledges – a hegemonic Western world view with the multitude of Indigenous knowledges, the latter of which have already been the target of 400 years of assimilation attempts by the former. Although some scholars, particularly settlers, may be predisposed to fulfilling the role of a word warrior, attempting to reconcile Indigenous knowledge with the dominant culture's world view is a losing battle, given the intense power imbalance between these two knowledges (Tuhiwai Smith, 1999; Nadasdy, 2003). A word warrior's role as a cultural translator lacks the necessary community grounding of Tuhiwai Smith's decolonizing methodology, yet by engaging the colonial state and challenging its legitimacy in Indigenous communities, word warriors still fulfil an important role – one of challenging the state's colonial hegemony.

It is in Mohawk scholar Taiaiake Alfred's (2004) concept of "warrior scholarship" that we find a way of engaging with colonial institutions that is nonetheless grounded in a thoroughly Indigenous world view, focusing on correcting the power imbalance of the colonial relationship and restoring the power of Indigenous peoples. Taiaiake's idea of warrior scholarship begins with the recognition that "the university is contentious ground" (p. 92). He views the university as the intellectual centre of colonialism that "create the attitudes and beliefs that sustain imperial relations," which "enable injustice by providing innovation on intellectual techniques and training" for "imperial servants in the mechanics of dominion" (p. 96). With an increasing number of Indigenous scholars working in the academy, we face an ever-increasing responsibility to challenge the presumptions of colonial domination and authority. Taiaiake argues that Indigenous scholars have a responsibility "to counter the ongoing production of imperial attitudes and to defy its pretensions" (p. 97). The role of the Indigenous academic is a most important one: to teach "an empowering and truthful sense of the past and who we are, and as visionaries of a dignified alternative to the indignity of our cultural assimilation and political surrender ... The strongest weapon we have against the power of the state to destroy us at the core *is the truth*" (p. 95). Continual contestation of oppression, domination, and colonialism is the way of the warrior-scholar, a powerful voice which reminds us all – Native and non-Native – that "it will be absolutely necessary to redefine and fully reconstruct the governmental and economic relationships between the original peoples and the settlers in this country" (p. 94). The power of the warrior-scholar then is to be an intellectual leader who is firmly bound to his or her community – responsible to them, to speak the truth to the outside and support the meaningful work within the community. This is a voice from the community and the ancestors; it seeks not the validation of hegemonic knowledge, nor to find its place in the false unity of the nation-state, but to achieve the freedom and independence so valued by our ancestors. It is the scholarship, research, and teaching of anticolonial contention, from an Indigenous world view, that makes the warrior-scholar responsible to "the not-so-fortunate and all-too-easily ignored ninety percent of our people who do not get any benefit at all from the new political and economic order" (p. 94). Like Maori scholar Graham Smith's Kaupapa Maori theory, Taiaiake places emphasis on critical pedagogy based on interlocking actions of consciousness raising, resistance, and transformative praxis (Smith, 2003; p. 15).

The warrior-scholar, unlike the word warrior, does not attempt to reconcile differences so much as to work to fundamentally transform the relationship between the settler society and Indigenous peoples. Overall, these projects have different end goals: one is intellectual unification, and an eradication of philosophical contradictions while leaving the nation-state intact; the other is respectful and peaceful coexistence in which Indigenous knowledges are respected in their own right, remaining autonomous and independent from the dominant culture. It is this latter approach to warrior scholarship that we believe holds the most promise for an Indigenous resurgence and the revival of our traditional ways of being.

Grounded in a warrior-scholar ethos, insurgent educators question settler occupation of Indigenous places through direct, honest, and experiential forms of engagement, ultimately demanding accountability and action to address these truths. Insurgent educators act on their responsibilities to defend Indigenous homelands and communities and act on behalf of those being silenced. Insurgent educators exemplify Indigenous forms of "leadership by example" by making their daily struggles for Indigenous resurgence relatable to broader audiences using innovative ways that inspire activism and reclamation of Indigenous histories and homelands and waterways. For Cherokees, leadership usually starts with the individual. An individual has a dream or a vision and then starts living it by incorporating whatever it is that he or she has envisioned into his or her daily life. Then the individual makes it relatable to other people. Only after making these teachings relatable to others can one start organizing people and mobilizing them for change. This is different from a Western kind of model that structures the hierarchical leadership process by organizing everyone at the beginning. Insurgent educators understand that Indigenous struggles must be made relatable to others before mobilization towards change can occur.

According to Shuswap leader George Manuel (1976), "we will steer our own canoe, but we will invite others to help with the paddling" (p. 12). It follows that if one is invited to help with the paddling, then that person's research priorities must be directly relevant and centred on the needs of local Indigenous communities. The following section offers some examples of insurgent education in action as a way to convey the complexities of community-based research.

Indigenous-Centred Case Studies

What does insurgent education look like in practice? One example comes from O'ahu, Hawai'i, which is visited by over 4.5 million people each year. Most of these tourists congregate at the hotels and beaches in Waikīkī, which was once known for its taro fields and natural springs. In 1998, Gaye Chan and Andrea Feeser launched a public art project that challenged tourists to recognize that they are on Kanaka Maoli (Native Hawaiian) homelands. Appealing to the consumerism of Waikīkī tourists, Chan and Feeser packaged small souvenirs for sale and advertised them as an "authentic piece of Waikīkī's past" (Feeser, 2001). In reality, they were selling small chunks of concrete wrapped in plastic accompanied by a historic time line of colonial encroachment and destruction of Waikīkī.

In addition, tourists are invited to take an online tour of historic Waikīkī and enter a website as either Kanaka Maoli (Native Hawaiian), Kama'aina (Native-born), or Haole (White settler). This online anti-colonial reality tour raises awareness of contemporary Kanaka Maoli struggles as well as promoting the idea that "Another Waikīkī is possible." It is an effective insurgent education project for creating discomfort over the idea of being a tourist on Kanaka Maoli homelands and waterways, while also educating them regarding their historic and contemporary impacts as "visitors" to Hawaiian territory.

A second Hawaiian example deals with the role of experiential learning in promoting pathways to Indigenous resurgence. In 2010, the Indigenous Governance (IGOV) Program engaged in an international exchange program with the University of Hawai'i, Mānoa (UHM). This exchange focused on revitalizing Kanaka Maoli land-based and water-based cultural practices as well as strategies for demilitarizing the heavily US-fortified O'ahu. One of our hands-on learning opportunities as students and faculty was to participate in the ongoing rebuilding of the 'auwai (irrigation ditches used by Kanaka Maoli for sustainable wetland taro cultivation) and lo'i kalo (wetland taro field) in 'Aihualama, which is located in the Mānoa Valley. Kanaka Maoli scholar and co-instructor for the UHM-IGOV exchange, Noelani Goodyear-Ka'ōpua discusses the significance of rebuilding of 'auwai and lo'i kalo (wetland taro field) in 'Aihualama as "part of a larger effort to simultaneously rebuild indigenous Hawaiian agricultural and educational systems that allow for the long-term health of Kanaka Maoli and others in Hawai'i" (Goodyear-Ka'ōpua, 2009, p. 48). This community-centred project was not just about viewing 'auwai as a "material technology" but "also as a form of indigenous Hawaiian theory, with its basis in the ancestral, landed practices of Kanaka Maoli" (p. 49).

Kalo (taro) is a sacred plant and is considered an elder sibling to the Kanaka Maoli people. Prior to European invasion, lo'i kalo fields covered at least 20,000 acres (90 square kilometres) over six islands in the Hawaiian archipelago. Today, after more than 100 years of US occupation, less than 400 acres (1.6 sq km) of lo'i kalo remain (Goodyear-Ka'ōpua, 2009, p. 53). Recently, the Hàlau Kû Mäna (HKM) public charter school students and teachers began rebuilding the 'auwai and lo'i at 'Aihulama, which is the first time it had been functioning in more than a century. As Goodyear-Ka'ōpua points out (p. 60), "the project of rebuilding 'auwai and lo'i at 'Aihualama can be seen as part of a larger effort to rebuild indigenous Hawaiian agricultural and educational systems." Since their first taro planting under the full moon in 2006, "students in Papa Lo'i have opened approximately one new field per year, and learned and practised all phases from putting huli in the ground to putting 'ai (food, especially pounded kalo) in people's mouths" (p. 64).

As we were visitors to the lo'i kalo, kumus (teachers) provided IGOV students and faculty with an overview of the strict protocols for planting and caring for the lo'i. While the women planted, the men cleared brush in an effort to open up new ground for future taro cultivation in 'Aihualama. We had several opportunities to speak with the HKM students working at 'Aihualama, and they talked about how much they have learned about their responsibilities to the land and waterways as well as to Kanaka Maoli food security from their semester work in the lo'i kalo. For several of these youth and participants, this was a transformative experience but it was also something deeper. It was the regeneration of sustainable Hawaiian technologies by putting them back into practice. This is where the lines between community-centred teaching and research become blurred. As the preceding examples demonstrate, insurgent education compels action and relocalizes long-standing Indigenous struggles. The latest research on the revitalization of traditional foods and Indigenous technologies, such as the 'auwai, is taught via the mentorship of HKM students using hands-on, community-centred pedagogies.

Another example of insurgent education occurred as a result of new curriculum development of the Indigenous Governance Program. The IGOV mentorship course was developed out of an Indigenous philosophy that "change happens one warrior at a time" (Alfred & Corntassel, 2005, p. 613). After all, it is mentoring and relationship-building that often fosters the most meaningful human development and community solidarity. Based on our previous experience, personal decolonization and regeneration tend to grow from transformations achieved within small group interactions and one-on-one mentoring. In taking this approach to Jeff Corntassel's first mentorship group in 2009–10 (usually no more than five IGOV students), we decided collectively to focus on food security and gardening as key skills to develop. One of the goals of the IGOV mentorship program is to rethink how we learn. Through peer learning and the regeneration of land-based and water-based cultural practices, getting out of the standard classroom environment allows students and instructors to engage with each other in a more substantive, meaningful way. The mentorship tends to focus on the development of traditional skills, whether helping to carve a voyaging canoe in Wsáneć territory with master carver Charles Elliott of the Tsartlip First Nation or managing traditional kwetlal (camas) fields with the removal of invasive species with Cheryl Bryce of the Songhees First Nation. Although such experiences are often de-emphasized within a mainstream university education, these opportunities enable the transmission of Indigenous knowledge and cultural practices to future generations. For IGOV-students, mentorship is research through direct experience and application. These experiences prepare students to work in communities of their choosing for their capstone resesarch project in IGOV, a Community Governance Project under the mentorship and supervision of both community and faculty members. It is no coincidence that this hands-on process of Indigenous learning bears a strong resemblance to the Lil'wat principles of teaching and learning described by Williams, Tanaka, Leik, and Riecken (this volume), because Indigenous pedagogies often share similar philosophies and principles.

An important part of experiential learning in the IGOV mentorship course is establishing a meaningful relationship with the land, as a key part of renewing our responsibilities to defending and protecting Indigenous homelands and waterways. After all, it is this "oppositional, place-based existence, along with the consciousness of being in struggle against the dispossessing and demeaning fact of colonization by foreign peoples, that fundamentally distinguishes Indigenous peoples from other peoples of the world" (Alfred & Corntassel, 2005, p. 597). These land-based and water-based cultural practices – from carving to tanning hides – are what sustain and renew us as peoples, and it becomes our responsibility to protect our homelands against encroachment from colonial entities. The IGOV mentorship is based on the idea that we must continuously renew our ancestral responsibilities by relearning the skills that provide the necessities of life, thus renewing our responsibilities to the natural world. By working with local farmers and Indigenous gardeners, such as Cheryl Bryce from Songhees First Nation, we were able to build up personal skills in terms of growing local plants for seed and composting. We have also organized plant walks to learn more about the native species of plants in the territory and the invasive species that threaten their existence. We have hiked through salmon spawning grounds, which are in a constant struggle against over-exploitation by commercial fisheries and Department of Fisheries and Oceans (DFO) enforcement regimes. We have learned how local Indigenous peoples engage in everyday acts of resistance by working to restore their traditional cultural practices and governance.

The mentorship builds personal, experiential knowledge that ultimately increases the abilities of students to think in terms of sustainability, self-sufficiency, and what being a contemporary warrior entails – learning the skills required to live as our ancestors have. Given the coincidence of the emergence of "guerrilla gardening" at the University of Victoria, as well as other methods of reclaiming space for the regeneration of traditional foods, such as camas, the mentorship is speaking to issues relevant to students, even if the issues are marginalized by traditional university pedagogy.

The 2010–11 IGOV mentorship focused on Cheryl Bryce and her efforts over more than 10 years to regenerate traditional foods, especially camas. Today, much of the camas grows on Victoria's "public" lands, which makes management (including weeding, seeding, harvesting, and burning) of these traditional Lekwungen territories difficult. Our mentorship group this term chose to remove invasive species from the Uplands Park area, and will manage this particular area as part of an IGOV commitment to the health and well-being of the camas in that place. By restoring traditional management practices and revitalizing cultural ceremonies and language around traditional foods, such as pit cooks, it demonstrates that through education and persistence, one can teach future generations to be sustainable again. This has inspired Corntassel to request seeds from his own nation as part of the Cherokee Nation Heirloom Seed Project, including rare types of corn and centuries-old strains of tobacco, to revitalize ceremonies and traditional foods and to produce more seeds for future Tsalagis. The mentorship was also the primary motivation for Gaudry to being an oral history project on his family and traditional Métis knowledge.

An oral history project initiated by Corntassel in partnership with the Tseshaht First Nation in Port Alberni, British Columbia, offers us another example of insurgent education. In October 1975, the Tseshaht First Nation hosted the inaugural meeting of the World Council of Indigenous Peoples (WCIP), which was a global and historic gathering that brought together Indigenous representatives from Sami (Finland), Maori (New Zealand), Inuit (Greenland), Miskitos (Nicaragua), Guaymis (Panama), and several First Nations from Canada and the United States. With goals of establishing an international solidarity network and promoting greater awareness of Indigenous struggles within the United Nations, the WCIP played a pivotal role in initiating the contemporary global Indigenous rights movement, which has now resulted in the ratification of the UN Declaration on the Rights of Indigenous Peoples (2007).

Accounts of the formation of the WCIP are limited to a few written overviews by non-Indigenous scholars and offer little insight into the motivations and legacies of the original participants in this global Indigenous movement. To rectify this, researchers proposed to conduct an oral history of the WCIP by interviewing 20 to 25 of the original participants at this global gathering as well as Indigenous youths who speak about the impact of the WCIP on their community. Rather than having outside researchers conduct the interviews, only people from Tseshaht (youths and Elders) were trained and hired to carry out the conversations with folks in their community. These conversations have provided several unique opportunities to discuss how Indigenous values and knowledges are transmitted to future generations. On completion of this project, the youth and Elder research teams will be teaching their methodologies and findings to future IGOV students in the classroom, as well as to Tseshaht community members in open forums.

For Indigenous peoples, oral histories, such as the one being developed by and for Tseshaht, are vital for reflecting our lived experiences and our responsibilities as individuals, and to re-establish our governance roles within families, clans, and communities. According to Maori scholar Linda Tuhiwai Smith (1999), "on the international scene it is extremely rare and unusual when indigenous accounts are accepted and acknowledged as valid interpretations of what has taken place. And yet, the need to tell our stories remains the powerful imperative of a powerful form of resistance" (p. 35). Overall, oral histories are about honouring our living relationships and are an important way of reasserting Indigenous ways of knowing.

The interviews were fully transcribed in August 2011. They are in the process of being reproduced in oral and written form and will be made available to the participants and wider community. A traditional feast will then be held in Tseshaht to honour the participants and discuss the importance of these oral histories. Naturally, the Tseshaht First Nation will own all of these histories. Researchers will then request a loan of these oral histories for use in an IGOV graduate seminar on research methods. Elders from Tseshaht will be brought into the classroom to discuss the protocols regarding use of oral history in the community, and an oral history assignment on the history of the WCIP will be given to the students. This is where community-based research, insurgent education, and warrior scholarship converge, as students gain experiential knowledge by engaging with these oral histories while also developing their own analysis in order to understand future Indigenous struggles relating to global Indigenous rights.

Overall, these examples help to identify some possibilities for insurgent education as a multipronged strategy for relocalizing Indigenous struggles and recentring Indigenous peoples and their relationships to the land and waterways in the discussion. While several of the examples above were linked to the classroom, we argue that much of the substantive, experiential training took place outside in more informal settings. Finally, these examples demonstrate how accountability to communities and direct action go hand-in-hand in the struggle to reclaim Indigenous homelands and waterways and challenge the colonial status quo. The final section examines some additional strategies for linking insurgent education to community-centred research.

Towards Indigenous Resurgence

If colonization and extraction research are about disconnecting people from community, knowledges, protocols, and homelands, then resurgence is about the reconnection and regeneration of Indigenous land-based and water-based cultural practices. It is about renewing our roles and responsibilities as Indigenous peoples to the sustainable praxis of Indigenous livelihoods, food security, community governance, and relationships to the natural world and ceremonial life that enables the transmission of these cultural practices to future generations (Corntassel, 2008, p. 124). There is great potential for models, such as insurgent education, warrior scholarship, and community-centred research, to work in tandem to offer a transformative and decolonizing praxis for students and faculty. Based on our experiences and findings, several key areas emerge as part of a larger insurgent education pedagogy:

• *Experiential and place-based learning.* For conveying the importance of land-based and water-based cultural practices to learners, there is no substitute for getting hands-on experience. This is especially important for relocalizing our actions on Indigenous struggles nearby while finding one's role in promoting awareness, resistance, and transformative praxis. As Goodyear-Ka'ōpua (2009, p. 69) found with the revitalization of the 'auwi and lo'i in 'Aihualama, "The lo'i teaches us work ethics. The ethics kumu expressed as foundational did not emphasize individual industry but instead focused on collective work that depends on ha'aha'a (humility), shared decision-making, and equal work no matter what one's status."

- *Respecting and regenerating Indigenous protocols.* Whether a community has formalized them or not, it is important to seek out, learn, and follow Indigenous protocols when engaging with Indigenous communities. This creates several opportunities for teachable moments when discussing the differences (or similarities) between the Tri-Council Policy Statement entitled *Ethical Conduct for Research Involving Humans* (Canada, 2010; see esp. chapter 9), Canadian Institutes of Health Research's *CIHR Guidelines for Health Research Involving Aboriginal People* (2007) and local Indigenous protocols, such as the *Mi'kmaq Ecological Knowledge Study Protocol* (Assembly of Nova Scotia Mi'kmaq Chiefs, 2009). Disjunctures between these documents as well as perceptions of them can create useful questions and discussions around formalizing Indigenous research practices, especially when there is an attempt to universalize them or create short-cuts for those with extraction research aims. It may prompt programs to set up their own research protocols to reflect their own practices and relationships with local Indigenous communities, such as those developed by the IGOV program entitled *Protocols and Principles for Conducting Research within an Indigenous Context* (2003).
- *Working for solidarity.* When discussing solidarity within the context of a warrior-scholar model, Alfred (2004, pp. 96–7) describes the pressing need to "develop a sense of accountability to Indigenous values and community in conscious opposition to the imperial accountability enforced in academe (academic disciplines, departmental and university committees, tenure processes, etc.)." This is a continuous process of renewing one's roles and responsibilities to communities when undertaking acts of decolonization and insurgent education. These kinds of discussions can be generated as part of a larger pedagogy of discomfort by drawing on alliance manifestos, such as *The Ally Bill of Responsibilities* developed by Algonquin Anishinaabe scholar Lynn Gehl (n.d.). According to Gehl (n.d.),

being a responsible ally means that researchers "must understand that they are secondary to the Indigenous peoples that they are working for and that they seek to serve. They and their needs must take a back seat" (p. 1). These are the kinds of statements that make settlers uncomfortable but can promote some very practical discussions around the issue of solidarity.

- *One warrior at a time.* The role of mentorships and personal decolonization is crucial to linking critical consciousness with praxis. Just as with the IGOV mentorship program, students thrive in an informal environment that stresses community connections and land-based and/or water-based practices. As Maori scholar Graham Smith (2003, p. 17) states, "the point is that every Maori is in the struggle whether they like it or not, whether the know it or not." Building this awareness takes time and providing opportunities for peer-learning and one-on-one mentorships form the crux of an effective insurgent education strategy. According to Alfred (2004, p. 97), "Power will come from the restoration of connection (among ourselves and to the sources of strength: traditional teachings, land, and community)."

- *Restoring Indigenous community leadership, with non-Indigenous people in supporting roles:* Indigenous people must retain control over teaching and research that directly pertains to our lives. Researchers from outside of Indigenous communities must respect the local knowledge and leadership of the communities they want to engage in research partnerships with, and resign themselves to a supporting role. The quotation from George Manuel referred to the earlier, "we will steer our own canoe, but we will invite others to help with the paddling," underscores this position. Gehl (n.d.) takes this a step further when stating "their [researcher/potential ally] needs must take a back seat" (p. 1). Ultimately, decolonization of Indigenous communities is contingent on the actions of the communities themselves. Non-Indigenous people seeking to act in solidarity with Indigenous peoples must be careful not to re-inscribe colonial relationships. It follows that non-Indigenous peoples and non-community members involved with teaching and researching in Indigenous communities must adopt roles of support without attempting to dictate how decolonization will be pursued. Where non-Indigenous allies can be the most effective is through engaging the dominant discourse and other settlers about their common responsibilities to decolonize, or to remove themselves from a colonial relationship by undermining colonial institutions and privileges.

The thought of Indigenous peoples mobilizing to reclaim their histories and their homelands makes settlers very uncomfortable. Yet, it is through this discomfort that meaningful cross-cultural education, awareness, and action can take place. An insurgent educator calls for new solidarity movements with local Indigenous nations and finds innovative ways to assist in their resurgence efforts. This is a challenge to Indigenous intellectuals and others who want to act in solidarity to become "warriors of the truth," both inside and outside the classroom. When we renew our responsibilities for defending and regenerating Indigenous land-based and water-based cultural practices, we can move from insurgent to resurgent Indigenous peoples.

9 CBR Without Walls: Fostering Learning with Online Collaboration in the Universities Without Walls HIV Health Training Program

CATHERINE WORTHINGTON, FRANCISCO IBÁÑEZ-CARRASCO, SEAN ROURKE, AND JEAN BACON

Universities Without Walls (UWW) is a national, interdisciplinary HIV health research training program that embraces the principles and practices of community-based research (CBR) and uses blended delivery (i.e., a blending of face-to-face, synchronous online, and individualized learning components) to promote learning. UWW is funded by a Strategic Training in Health Research (STIHR) grant from the Canadian Institutes of Health Research (CIHR), and is housed at the Ontario HIV Treatment Network (OHTN) as the training arm of the CIHR Centre for REACH (Research Evidence into Action for Community Health) in HIV/AIDS. UWW is currently funded for a 6-year period to support six cohorts of fellows through the program. As a program that operates outside of traditional university structures, UWW has the ability to work beyond geographical and disciplinary boundaries, and engage a group of fellows who are passionate about a stigmatizing and marginalizing social issue, namely HIV (human immunodeficiency virus, the virus that causes AIDS). Catherine Worthington, for example, is based at the University of Victoria, while Francisco Ibáñez-Carrasco, Sean Rourke, and Jean Bacon are all based in Toronto. CBR and adult learning principles foster co-learning and the development of communities of practice among fellows and mentors. As program developers and mentors, we are cognizant of our own substantial learning about CBR and blended delivery methods as the UWW cohorts grow and the UWW program evolves.

UWW is one of several emerging academic training programs for advanced students and promising researchers in the health field that have only recently begun to be assessed (Kirmayer, Rousseau, Corin, &

Groleau, 2008; Manson 2009). It is important to note that the history of HIV research in Canada is a rich, vibrant one that sets the stage for HIV CBR and learning. Community members from stigmatized communities (including gay/bisexual men, people who use injection drugs, and people who engage in sex work) were among the first to – amid much vocal community action – advocate for research, treatment, prevention, and care programs in the 1980s, and many from these and other affected communities were and continue to be leaders in social, behavioural, and cultural research in this field (Collins et al., 2007; Silversides, 2006). Because of the strong community voice present in the HIV research world, major HIV research funding agencies (such as CIHR and OHTN) have incorporated CBR funding programs and principles into their HIV research funding tools. The UWW program has been structured within this context to build and strengthen the community of active, engaged CBR practitioners across the country.

UWW admits an annual cohort of between 10 to 16 graduate students from a variety of health and social science disciplines as well as community-based researchers active in the HIV field in Canada. Those admitted to the program become UWW fellows. The UWW program components include the following: (1) fortnightly online webinars on topics related to CBR and HIV research; (2) individualized field mentoring placements in community, health policy, and academic settings (largely based on the community service learning model); (3) face-to-face engagement near the beginning of the program at a day-long meeting and at the end of the program during a week-long learning institute held in collaboration with local community (a form of residency); and, (4) a set of self-evaluative and formal pedagogical evaluative tools (described in Appendix B) to measure the increase in short-term knowledge, skills, and experience, and mid- to longer-term impact in terms of involvement in CBR, professional development, and ecological impact on mentors, faculty, and the field of HIV in Canada.

In this chapter, we will first describe the pedagogical foundations of the UWW program, which integrates CBR principles with those of adult education and blended learning approaches. Next, we describe our application of these principles through the UWW training program components. We close with a discussion of a number of lessons learned (from the perspectives of fellows and mentors) in the process of designing, implementing, and evaluating this highly specialized training program that includes a strong online component.

Pedagogical Foundations

CBR Principles

It might be misleading to say that one can "teach CBR," because community-based research is an approach to and philosophy of using traditional research methodological and analytical tools in ways that subvert hierarchical top-down disparities (e.g., the principal investigator as owner or sole authority of the research design implementation, products, and dissemination). Specifically, CBR in HIV in Canada has been defined as "a philosophy of inquiry and not a discrete research framework" (Allman, Myers, & Cockerill, 1997, p. 21). Trussler and Marchand (2005) argue that "the fundamental question underlying the development of CBR in the HIV/AIDS field is not about what knowledge is or is not but about *what knowledge is for*" (p. 45, emphasis added) and suggest that CBR in HIV/AIDS is *for* organizational development, community benefit, best practice improvement, policy development, health promotion, emancipation and empowerment, and rapid assessment.

More broadly, CBR (or CBPR – community-based participatory research) researchers in the larger arena of public health generally endorse Israel and colleagues' (2003) following nine principles of CBPR: (1) CBPR recognizes community as a unit of identity; (2) CBPR builds on strengths and resources within the community; (3) CBPR facilitates equitable partnerships in all phases of the research; (4) CBPR promotes co-learning and capacity building among partners; (5) CBPR integrates and achieves a balance between research and action for the mutual benefit of all partners; (6) CBPR emphasizes local relevance of problems and ecological perspectives; (7) CBPR involves systems development through a cyclical and iterative process; (8) CBPR disseminates knowledge gained to all partners, and involves all partners in the dissemination process; and (9) CBPR involves a long-term process and commitment.

In the Canadian HIV CBR context, we aim to include two pivotal sets of principles, the Greater Involvement of People Living with HIV/AIDS, or GIPA (McClelland & De Pauw, 2010) with a strong social justice and global outlook, and the OCAP principles (Ownership, Control, Access, and Possession) for research with Aboriginal Peoples (First Nations Centre, 2007; Schnarch, 2004) based on historical fiduciary obligations with the original stewards of the land. Both principles assert the rights of the "researched" to be full partners and beneficiaries of research done *with*, *on*, and *for* their communities.

Thus, CBR, GIPA, and OCAP principles applied to our educational venture result in a pedagogical effort where the conventional teaching/learning boundary is blurred. All those who engage with UWW, including staff, subject matter specialists (e.g., academic researchers invited as guest speakers), and even IT personnel are called to be aware of these principles and to apply them to problem-solving and social action. UWW fellows, instructors, and support personnel alike are encouraged to understand how we learn in an interdisciplinary field (e.g., how to navigate the politics of research networks), how we learn in increasingly complex global/technological environments (e.g., how to conduct systematic reviews), and how we unlearn (e.g., how to unpack conventional ways of collecting data). We strive to be self-reflexive, to pay attention to meta-learning, and to share the control over the learning process (e.g., deciding on content, participating in organizing committees for the various components, etc.).

Adult Education, Situated Learning, and a Community of Practice

In addition to the core foundation of CBR principles, congruent principles from adult education form the basis of our pedagogical approach to the UWW training in general, and to the challenge of "learning CBR" online, in particular. We draw on the interrelated principles of adult education and the analytical concept of situated learning to provide the philosophical basis for the UWW team to focus on HIV CBR research.

The principles of adult education, or androgogy, include the involvement of learners in planning and implementing learning activities, drawing on learners' experiences as a resource, cultivating self-direction in learners, creating a climate that encourages and supports learning and fosters a spirit of collaboration in the learning setting, and using small groups. From the vast literature in this field, we favour here the ideas of well-known adult educationists Sharam Merriam (2008) and Malcolm Knowles (e.g., Knowles, Holton, & Swanson, 2005).

We suggest that our UWW blended delivery model facilitates learning for emerging HIV researchers where they are; that is to say, it is a form of situated learning. Situated learning describes a process that begins with *legitimate peripheral participation* (e.g., by newcomers to an academic discipline). These are individuals not yet fully connected to a *trade*, as they change locations, perspectives, and develop identities within social networks and institutional systems (e.g., academic courses and accreditation). This view of learning makes us pay attention to how our trainees move from apprenticeship (e.g., from the mastery of rules and roles in an academic discipline) to situated learning in *communities of practice*, where individual learners gain power over the process, collaborate, and innovate. The purpose is to support apprentice HIV researchers to learn content and skills, to apply content and/or skill in the construction of tangible products (e.g., annotated bibliographies, abstracts, etc.), and also to become well connected and well aware of the very process of connectivity.

Blended Learning: The Right Mix of Connectivity and Logistics

In UWW, two aspects are essential: one is the practical aspect of program delivery and program management that encompass technology and logistics (which on a good day works for the group and the individual), and the other is the relational aspect (connectivity). The UWW team works hard to obtain the right mix of these elements, and we use a number of evaluation measures to feed the results back into the next iteration. Thus, each generation or cohort and each training period look similar, but the program is strategically tweaked to improve the delivery. This allows the program to stay current, attract deeply committed fellows, and provide enough flexibility to individualize the experience (e.g., deadlines, self-directed goals).

Blended learning is a form of learning that mixes face-to-face, synchronous online, and individualized learning components using in-person and technology-mediated interactions (e.g., mentoring over the telephone, Skype, email, PowerPoint presentations over webinar, small group teleconferences), and may include both synchronous (at the same time) and asynchronous (interactions that occur at different times, such as discussion board postings) components. In our design of the online (webinar) components of the program, we have attempted to adhere to the best practices of online learning, which are consistent with CBR and adult learning principles.

The literature on online learning suggests that there are several general practices that promote successful learning in an online environment. Prior to course delivery, it is important to work with a technology specialist who understands the strengths and limitations of various technologies, and can support learner-friendly content that maximizes the use and usefulness of the selected technology (Cook & Dupras, 2004; Fish & Wickersham, 2009). Technical support for learners is also crucial to the successful adoption and use of the online components (Fish & Wickersham, 2009). Because quality learning requires interaction, class sizes should be kept small (i.e., 15 to a maximum of 30, depending on content) (Dykman & Davis, 2008). Content is best developed well prior to delivery, but there is also the need to remain flexible with content (and potentially, deadlines) given the likelihood of technical glitches (Fish & Wickersham, 2009). The online instruction literature stresses that an online *learning community* exists where students feel connected with the instructor and with each other, and interact using a variety of methods (conferences, group projects, blogs, and telephone / Skype) (Dykman & Davis, 2008; Fish & Wickersham, 2009). An active, enthusiastic instructor/mentor presence is seen as being a key to engaging and motivating learners (Lewis & Abdul-Hamid, 2006).

We know that collective dynamic learning can promote communities of practice in online environments (Gagnon-Leary & Fontainha, 2007). Specifically, we approach online learning and the entire UWW training program as the active development of communities of practice and emphasize connectivity through group work, networking (with established and emerging researchers/research networks, and grant funders), and group and individual mentoring.

Blended learning benefits from behaviourist, cognitive, and constructivist theories, and these, as noted earlier, take a co-creation and contextualized approach to learning. An emerging learning perspective that we are currently exploring as a sensitizing concept is *connectivism theory*. Connectivism theory is

> the integration of principles explored by chaos, network, complexity and self-organization theories. Due to the information explosion in the current age, learning is not under the control of the learner. Changing environments, innovations, changes in a discipline and in related disciplines all suggest that learners have to unlearn what they have learned in the past, and learn how to learn and evaluate new information. What must be learned is determined by others and is continually changing. (Ally, 2008, p. 19)

In a digital age, learning involves connecting constantly evolving sets of information and information sources across academic disciplines, sectors (e.g., policy makers, researchers, and other knowledge users), and geographical locations (i.e., global), staying up to date, and staying connected with these networks that act as information resources (Siemens, 2005). Also, it is theorized that a modicum of knowledge resides in the actual appliance used, that is, in learning how to operate the actual gadget and also learning how to use applications for survey building, simultaneous online document editing, website updating, mind mapping, and others for research purposes. Connectivism invites us to think about how learners may be forced to learn some skills and forget others. In learning through CBR, we invite UWW fellows and faculty to step back and think how a new platform will affect their research work (e.g., the data collection or the analysis/interpretation phase of a project) and their interaction with individuals and communities (e.g., telephone qualitative interviews). Anthropologist J.A. Wertsch (1998) reminds us that all technologies, from pills to computers, are "mediational means" often "produced for reasons other than to facilitate mediated action," for example, the typical typing keyboard, as they are also associated with power and authority. Thus, we master these mediational means with intended and some unintended effects, for example, slowing the rate of typing on a keyboard (p. 25).

Many UWW faculty and fellows are trying to effectively incorporate new social media into their CBR, and are reflecting on the ethical challenges this creates (e.g., storytelling with inner city youth operating the video cameras). In tandem with a CBR approach, which often uses grounded theory to generate contextualized theory from the ground up, connectivism emphasizes that learners (in this case, emerging CBR practitioners) not only learn patterns or rules, but they also *learn how to constantly learn new information, patterns, and rules and unlearn others.*

Building Communities of Practice for CBR Learning

The UWW training program allows us to build and support a community of practice and to advance two ambitious and interrelated projects that are harmonious with CBR, one of *community-engaged scholarship* and the other of *interdisciplinarity*. In our design of the UWW program, it is our intention to contribute to the emerging paradigm of community-engaged scholarship. Through community-engaged scholarship, we hope to encourage fellows, and all UWW participants, to think forward to their professional careers, as well as engage with the communities surrounding them, using an engagement that has CBR at its core (Barker, 2004). One of the desired outcomes is to have trainees adopt a

CBR lens and community-relevant approach to the work they are already doing and will do later in their careers – an approach to engaging with the world. Community-engaged scholarship is an approach to scholarly life that values putting the scholar as part of communities, complex networks of interests, motivations, and processes (e.g., political, provoking social change), as well as scholarly outcomes and institutional rewards (e.g., getting an academic or institutional job, promotion, and tenure) (Calleson, 2005).

At the same time, UWW contributes to an evolving paradigm of interdisciplinarity, the process of working well with other academics, policy makers, and community members in a continuum that may include working in teams of different disciplines or amalgamating disciplinarian perspectives, values, and research or evaluation methods (Huutniemi, Klein, Bruun, & Huukkinen, 2010). Thus, as part of the UWW program, promoting the development of a community of learners also means fostering understandings of different disciplines and perspectives.

The UWW Training Program

As a free-standing research training initiative, the UWW program does not grant academic credit. The 9-month program, with individualized and group components, is designed to support academically advanced emerging HIV researchers in Canada in three major interrelated knowledge and skill areas: community-based research, interdisciplinarity/community collaboration, and research ethics. One of the program's unique characteristics is providing academic level training while being based in a non-profit (albeit university-affiliated) environment; we believe this enhances the CBR linkages. Working outside of traditional academic structures provides flexibility in tailoring the UWW components, and also provides the opportunity to bring together resources, and multidisciplinary academic and community mentors from across the country to support and mentor the fellows.

UWW Structure

The structure of the UWW training program determines the characteristics of the delivery of blended learning, and specifically the teaching of CBR online. The Strategic Training Initiative in Health Research (STIHR) grant from the Canadian Institutes of Health Research (CIHR) funds the day-to-day operation of the UWW Training program and provides a training stipend to the selected graduate students from across Canada. Up to three UWW community fellows from the front lines of the HIV sector with a keen interest in CBR are also funded to participate alongside the academic fellows; this provides the program with a unique academic-community interaction, and supports a key principle of CBR – recognition of the strengths of communities and their right to be equals at the table. All academic fellows take part in this training in addition to their home university plan of studies (they are approved by their home university academic supervisor). To date, the UWW fellows have come from epidemiology, public health, the humanities, and the helping professions. Community fellows participate with the support of their organizational supervisors.

The UWW faculty is comprised of directors (authors Rourke and Bacon); a volunteer Education Committee of academic, community, and policy mentors who provide guidance on program design, and review UWW applicants for each cohort (author Worthington is chair); and invited volunteer subject matter specialists in HIV research and related areas. These specialists may be community members, policy players, or academics from a variety of fields. The UWW program manager (author Ibáñez-Carrasco) plays a pivotal role, and supports the communication and collaboration between these partners, the UWW fellows with other research networks and the IT personnel (e.g., web designers), and promotes engagement and enthusiasm.

Ten to 16 fellows with strong community engagement track records are chosen to reflect geographical, disciplinary, and HIV-affected population diversity. As part of the adult-centred/self-directed model, the selected fellows are required to fill out four key evaluative instruments for programmatic purposes and for individual self-direction and self-evaluation: a UWW Application, a Fellowship Plan, a Field Mentoring Plan, and a final Learning Portfolio (see Appendix B). The UWW Fellowship Plan is completed at the start of their tenure. This survey instrument provokes self-reflection and provides information on their baseline comfort with competencies in the knowledge, skills, and lived experience domains (adapted from Brocklehurst & Rowe, 2003). The UWW Fellowship Plan allows fellows to design a self-directed and individualized learning experience in HIV research. Each fellow tailors his or her activities in order to develop in areas they want to strengthen. Group activities, such as the synchronous webinars, field mentoring placements, and learning institute, are incorporated into the learning plan. Survey results from the first two UWW cohorts show statistically significant progress between the baseline (program entry) in knowledge, skills, and experience and their exit points. For example, in the second evaluation report (2010–11 cohort), in the knowledge area of applied ethics in HIV research, 80 per cent of fellows rated themselves as "proficient" at the end of the program, compared with 81 per cent who self-rated as only "competent" or below at baseline; in the skills area, the reported increase in proficiency in "sharing research evidence in the public domain" from 6 per cent to 64 per cent relates directly to our efforts to mentor community engaged scholars (Universities Without Walls [UWW] Evaluation Report, 2011).

At the end of the UWW program, each fellow completes an exit survey, a retrospective posttest (Pratt, McGuigan, & Katzev, 2000) to compare results with the baseline survey, and a Learning Portfolio that includes an online self-assessment on the self-directed learning goals stated in the initial Fellowship Plan, a self-assessment of the field mentoring placement goals and activities, and a number of additional outcome measures required by the funder (traditional measures of academic success, such as number of conference presentations, awards, and publications). These components promote self-reflection, and provide information to refine the program for the next iteration. The most significant contribution of these self-assessments to the formation of CBR researchers in HIV is that they offer a structured opportunity for each fellow to set individual goals regarding new competencies in HIV research at the start. At the end, they are able to measure objectively how closely they met those goals, what emergent benchmarks and experience they will seek in the near future, and the impact of the knowledge, skills, and experience they were seeking on their practice, their outlook on CBR, and their professional development, and even whether those ambitions need reframing and redirection (e.g., it has been the case that, without destabilizing them in terms of their core values and interests, fellows have changed Ph.D. programs, study directions, or even home institutions as they see new opportunities arise as part of their participation in the program).

UWW Components

Within this structure, as previously noted, key components of the UWW training program include fortnightly online synchronous webinars to develop the three target knowledge and skill areas, a field mentoring placement, face-to-face engagement with fellows and mentors at events, most notably the culminating week-long learning institute held in collaboration with community, and individualized follow-up with each fellow (via email, telephone, etc.).

UWW WEBINARS
Online synchronous webinars are held with UWW fellows approximately every 2 weeks. For each online synchronous webinar, UWW fellows are expected to complete readings or assignments and/or activities assigned by the invited mentor. Readings may be a combination of academic texts, public health documents, or grey literature (e.g., reports produced in non-profit organizations that work in HIV). One or two fellows are designated as the respondent to the presenter and start discussion with a set of questions or comments to the mentor. Although attendance is expected, fellows who cannot attend a particular online session may view a recorded version of the presentation and discussion. Skills covered in the online webinars include grant crafting, conference presentation and public speaking, and research peer review skills (e.g., mock reviews of proposals). Other modules include sessions on principles of and tensions in CBR research and CBR ethics. In the UWW training program, the online component has allowed us to augment content knowledge, build skills, review fellows' lived professional and personal experiences in relation to content and skills, and most importantly, to apply contents, skills, and lived experience to enhance their CBR practice.

The online webinars support key program pedagogical principles. In addition to providing a forum for knowledge and skills building in the core content areas (CBR, research ethics, and interdisciplinarity), they also promote the development of a community of learners and communities of practice. The process of completing the modules involves strong collaboration among UWW fellows located in different regions and contexts across Canada. The modules provide opportunities for fellows to become critical friends and allies, encouraging each other in critical inquiry, action, and reflection. Mentors, including people living with HIV, academic, community, and policy mentors, join the webinars to present material, answer questions, and discuss issues with fellows. Webinars are also used as a platform for supporting fellows in their individualized learning components, particularly the community service learning component.

FIELD MENTORING PLACEMENT
During the first months of the UWW tenure, each fellow is presented with options for a field mentoring placement from an existing database

of field mentoring placement profiles maintained by the UWW program manager. In the UWW training program, the field mentoring placement is an unpaid practicum, either in a non-profit, policy, or academic environment, that is individualized, time flexible, and designed in consultation with the home university academic supervisor, the field mentoring placement supervisor, and the program manager. The terms of the field mentoring placement are set out in a Field Mentoring Plan (FMP) online (the FMP detail is described in Appendix B). It is expected that there will be a great deal of strategic professional learning in the negotiating and implementing of the field mentoring placement; hence, the role of the UWW staff as facilitator and not as direct field supervisor. Similar field mentoring placements have been successfully implemented with professional trainees (Dharamsi et al., 2010). In this regard, UWW subscribes to the principles of community service learning advanced by the Canadian Alliance for Community Service Learning:

> Community Service-Learning (CSL) is a powerful vehicle for experiential education that has clear objectives for both the learning that occurs by the involved students and the service being provided in the community organization setting. There is a strong emphasis on inclusive partnerships with non-profit agencies through their direct involvement as co-educators, providing community expertise in all phases of the learning process from planning through to the experiential and evaluation. CSL programs are most effective when including key elements drawn from experiential education theory, especially developing critical thinking skills and implementing intentional reflection components. (Canadian Alliance for Community Service Learning, n.d.)

The field mentoring placement complements the online session and is instrumental in instilling the values and practices of community engaged scholarship. During the online sessions every 2 weeks, after the scheduled speaker and specific topic, UWW Fellows check in and reflect on the progress of their individualized field mentoring placement. This is a technique adopted from classroom teaching of CBR with a central CSL component (Ibáñez-Carrasco & Riaño Alcalá, 2009).

LEARNING INSTITUTE
Where possible, UWW cohorts begin with a face-to-face meeting to introduce the UWW curriculum and to provide a venue for fellows to get to know one another before engaging in the online exchanges and individual field mentoring placements. The other face-to-face engagement

occurs at the completion of the UWW program. Each cohort's tenure ends in a learning institute, a 5-day intensive retreat (or residency) held collaboratively with regional organizations or HIV research related events. The substantial face-to-face contact during the learning institutes with UWW mentors, community, and other UWW fellows fosters a learning community that nurtures, challenges, and supports UWW fellows in their studies as well as their future work. The learning institute also provides an opportunity to augment the online curriculum by offering additional areas of content in HIV research not already covered. As well, during this learning institute, fellows (and mentors) are asked to reflect on their learning processes, and begin to plan ongoing engagement and ways they will choose to maintain their "community(ies) of practice."

Another important component of the learning institute is the collaborative component that the fellows organize in the months preceding the learning institute. The fellows are asked to implement the collaborative component in partnership with local AIDS service organizations to engage the general public. For example, the World Café in Winnipeg (June 2010) was created to discuss the issue of HIV treatment drugs dispensed as a form of HIV prevention (a fairly contentious topic in Canada). The World Café consisted of five thematic tables, each facilitated by two fellows, one advocating the dispensation of HIV drugs as prevention and one opposing this view, from one of the five different perspectives (legal, ethical, organizational, financial, and individual). Guided by a community host, the guests would choose one table and spend about 20 minutes hearing the pros and cons from one perspective (e.g., proposing that the dispensation of HIV drugs as a form of prevention makes financial sense), asking questions and discussing the issue. After this 20-minute period, the guests were invited to join a different table. The event was concluded with a few remarks from the host. A World Café format neutralizes experts' voices by providing the opportunity to discuss a prickly issue with friends and other community members.

The main aim of the collaborative component is to provide a hands-on opportunity to learn the basic skills of HIV research knowledge translation and exchange (KTE) as understood in health care policy and other HIV/AIDS research relevant sources: "the interactive interchange of knowledge between research users and researcher producers to increase the likelihood that research evidence will be used in policy and practice decisions and to enable researchers to identify practice and policy-relevant research questions" (our paraphrase of Mitton, Adair, McKenzie, Patten, Waye Perry, 2007, p. 729).

Lessons Learned: Fellow and Mentor Perspectives

As the UWW program developers and mentors, we have engaged in the learning cycles with the fellows. In addition to strengthening our understanding of the complexities and nuances of CBR, we have learned much about blended delivery methods as the UWW program evolves. In this section, we present some of the fellows' reflections on the blended delivery aspects of the UWW program, as well as our reflections on our learnings about blended and online delivery and the intersections with CBR principles.

Fellows' Assessments of UWW

The results of the evaluation of the first UWW cohort (2009–10; evaluations by the second cohort are currently in progress) show that the training program has met a number of the criteria we set for ourselves, but also has faced some challenges. Key challenges related to the blended delivery have included glitches with, and a lack of trust in, the technology. The fellows have been critical of the inevitable technological issues (e.g., lags, delays, malfunctioning headsets). In addition, the academic disciplinary identity of the cohort participants may at times be a barrier to an untrammeled sense of self required by technology-mediated education. From within their disciplinary perspectives, fellows have at times been critical of specific content that did not fit their individual research interests. Because we do not wish to reveal specific fellows' criticisms, instead we provide a typical critique: within the HIV field, it is often considered that individual level (psychological) behavioural change theoretical models are given prominence over community or structural (e.g., sociological, cultural studies) models and interventions. Related to this disciplinary (hierarchical) lens, there have been instances where students have self-censored (e.g., a Master's student being intimidated in his or her interactions with PhD students online). Challenges to equity at the table may sometimes be enhanced by the online format, which masks reluctance or discomfort.

When reflecting on their collective experience, however, the fellows have identified key benefits from their UWW engagement to their long-term involvement with HIV research (Grace et al., 2010). In particular, the fellows have rated the relational and networking aspect of the program very highly. The online aspect of this relationship development is a core part of the program. We were surprised (although we should not have been) at how quickly the fellows adopted the online communication tools and were able to multitask (e.g., text chat with each other during presentations) and build individual and group relationships through the use of the webinar format. Evidence of this long-term learning outcome is the sustained involvement of most of the fellows with each other on collaborative work and as members of HIV/AIDS local and national research networks. This background/foreground, individual/ collective assessment of the long-term outcomes of UWW training complements the formalistic and specific outcomes (such as completion of the program, number of conference abstracts or peer reviewed publications submitted or accepted, and gaining academic or other sector key paid positions). This type of process evaluation is important in the context of CBR learning, to be able to assess our attainment of CBR and adult learning principles.

Our Reflections on Delivering CBR in a Blended Format

Providing a venue for learning CBR online requires a great deal more than expertise in the subject matter and experience implementing CBR in the field. This type of engagement requires specific attention to developing a teaching and mentoring faculty who have a disposition to using media and who have enough time, energy, and interest to test how they fare with it. This can be a challenge, as potential faculty need to assess how much their personal and professional teaching styles fit or do not fit the requirements imposed by the media, such as the lag time in question and answer period, the absence of verbal and physical cues, and multi-tasking use of chat features. Importantly, faculty must be coached in reformatting materials and subject matter that had been originally intended for classroom workshops or behind-the-podium events. Time permitting, we often try to work through the content ahead of time, provide pointers for best broadcasting, test the technology with our presenters, and instill the sense that they will be immersed quickly in a television-like medium (and potentially one more interactive), unlike the conventional classroom. We have also learned that where invited mentors are not comfortable with the format or technological reliability is suspect, it is best to prerecord presentations, and build discussion around these, rather than have the presentation occur "live."

Another pragmatic challenge for us related to the online delivery has been scheduling. Given that our fellows are in as many as five different Canadian time zones and all have busy academic or community schedules, scheduling conflicts are inevitable. This is also true for invited presenters. Flexibility on the part of the core educational team has been a key ingredient. All online materials are recorded, so fellows may view presentations and discussion at a later date. In addition, set topics and speakers often have to be rearranged and reoriented (e.g., when one speaker did not cover as much as expected of a specific subject matter) and complemented with supplemental material. The Education Committee chair has acted as a "floater" presenter to fill in gaps in content where necessary. This was done initially for pragmatic reasons, but feedback from the fellows has emphasized to us that the personalities and voices of the program manager (Ibáñez-Carrasco) and chair (Worthington) have been important unifying elements for the fellows as guides and principal mentors through the material, and in setting the tone and environment for the development of a community of practice. Through our joint engagement in the online and face-to-face interactions, we have done our best to model true interdisciplinarity and community-engaged collaboration (Ibáñez-Carrasco is a community HIV scholar and CBR practitioner with an educational theory background; Worthington is an academic CBR practitioner with a public health and social work background).

Beyond the pragmatic challenges, there have been several key learnings. CBR is not a set of discrete actions or formulas to follow, but a philosophical approach to research, intervention, and evaluation that is at times highly localized and intimate, that is, developed within a locale and for a specific group (e.g., researching with drug users in the inner city). In this respect, the blended delivery and online teaching of CBR has to develop (and entrust) a number of everyday practical aspects of direct mentoring and teaching (e.g., observing students as they apply conventional data collection methods in specific settings) to people, opportunities, and organizations one step removed from the core faculty for components such as the field mentoring placement (although the program manager tries to provide support and individualized attention via email, video calls, and telephone – as noted previously, this regular contact with students and faculty is crucial to maintaining esprit de corps). We have learned that the UWW faculty members also feel the need for a sense of community of learners and a space of learning for mentors. When possible, we build in a social component for

Education Committee meetings for informal exchange and group co-hesion, and we have also held a separate grant-funded learning day for faculty prior to a fellow learning institute (at which the topic was public pedagogy).

In addition, as the core UWW management team (program manager, Education Committee chair, and directors), we have also learned to work together across disciplinary, geographic, and organizationally dis-parate positions. Although the mission, goals and objectives for UWW were established for the funding application by the UWW directors in collaboration with a large team of academic, community and policy ap-plicants, the program manager was responsible for developing and de-livering the UWW program components under the guidance of the UWW Education Committee. Over time, in addition to quarterly tele-conferences/webinars for the UWW Education Committee, our process has evolved to include a system of frequent informal (sometimes mul-tiple daily email) consultations between the program manager and chair to work out program elements, logistics, and working principles, and regular consultations with the directors. Not surprisingly, attention to key interdisciplinary process skills (respect of diverse viewpoints; role clarity; clear, non-disciplinary specific terminology), not to men-tion humour, mutual support, and face-to-face interaction (e.g., lengthy discussions over lunch), has been crucial to working through UWW program development issues and keeping our practices in line with our vision for the program.

Another key learning in the context of the online/blended learning environment has been the place of power and power differences, given all the different communities and forms of communities (e.g., identity groups differentiated by academic disciplines or profession; practice perspectives; sexual orientation; or ethno-racial community) that are represented in UWW. As noted by the fellows, discomfort over power differentials can be masked by the online communication environment. We attempt to acknowledge the multiple "hats" or positionalities of each member of the UWW community, and keep dialogue on this issue at the forefront in our online conversations about CBR and interdisci-plinarity. This is done through discussion of the fellows' struggles to develop their own research, case examples of mentor/guest presenter research, and discussion of the ethics and tensions related to CBR. Fel-lows are acutely aware of the way views of those in the community change about them as they move further into position as "expert" re-searcher, and the power they are seen to have (and have) shifts. Our team and fellows employ the concept of intersectionality, which examines the relationships among multiple dimensions and modalities of social relationships and subject formations (McCall, 2005), to observe the outside research world and also to see the complexity of the meaning(s) of community and communities, and the differences of power within the UWW group. In our field, we are particularly aware of the intersection of HIV with race, gender, sexual orientation, and other categories of social position. We will continue to grapple with all these differences (including, importantly, self-selection into the UWW application process) as the program continues.

We have also learned to allow fellows to struggle with uncertainties. The design and implementation of the collaborative component for the learning institutes has been an additional way of implementing specific aspects of CBR teaching, particularly the increasingly valued aspect of translating research results into specific products tailored to specific audiences. As noted previously, the collaborative component requires the fellows to prepare an event related to HIV research for a public audience during the culminating learning institute. The fellows are given only a modicum of guidelines to choose: the subject matter (collectively, after consulting with local communities of interest), the format of delivery (e.g., World Café, Speakers' Corner, using social media), and the target audience. The fellows find this process somewhat disorienting, and have initial difficulty working through (multiple) roles and claiming leadership, a process that tends to be more straightforward in classroom settings, where leaders and power disparities may surface faster. Also, because this is an activity that engages players well beyond the UWW group, the fellows are aware that in their professional futures they will likely encounter the same mentors, faculty, and fellows. Some are not sure how to engage, and others worry they will create a bad impression. In order to mediate the anxiety all these factors create, the program manager, in consultation with the Education Committee chair, supports the fellows in decision making and logistics along the way, and often the second portion of the online sessions are used for this purpose. The challenges encountered often have to do with online students not having a sense of place, as they may be gathering and implementing the collaborative component in a geographical and cultural locale unfamiliar to them.

The program manager facilitates connection to local organizations, but the actual discussions and/or negotiations for the event are left to community agency participants and fellows. There is some awkwardness in the negotiations, due to their lack of physical presence in a classroom, the lack of verbal and personality clues (although the audio and video in our particular IT platform helps a great deal), and the students' seeming need for a stronger sense of self-direction (e.g., calling for additional meetings outside the schedule, identifying key helpers on the ground). Learning to deal with the fellows' anxiety and tension before they come to a resolution has been part of our learning as well. We are similarly anxious about the success of the public event (and allow ourselves to remind fellows of timelines), but the responsibility belongs to the fellows to work through the planning and implementation processes. The UWW public events (e.g., the "HIV Test: What's Your Reason?" World Café with a Speakers' Corner in Halifax, Nova Scotia) have been successful in attracting local community audiences and in increasing the fellows' confidence in working with and for community through knowledge translation events.

Because CBR is more of a philosophy of research than a set of discrete actions, we include the "navigation" strategies that fellows use when accessing and working with communities as measurable mid-and long-term evaluation criteria – the starts and stops, the small conversations, the flurry of tactical decisions of who will speak and when – are, indeed, demonstration of CBR principles in action. We have specific questions respecting this in the short-term evaluation (i.e., about their level of preparedness to face other CBR situations) in addition to the pedagogical and technical measures (i.e., how much they learned about specific subject matter, what they learned and how satisfied they are about specific blended delivery aspects). In the long run, we do not lose sight of our alumni, and keep in contact with them to measure long-term involvement in HIV research – asking questions about their level of preparedness to face other CBR situations (i.e., what new projects they have engaged with, who they have stayed in contact with) and to keep them engaged with emerging projects in our partner research networks. One of the mechanisms to track their long-term involvement in CBR is a journalistic set of questions and answers entitled "Where are they now?" The results of these inquiries get edited as newsletter, website news, Twitter, and Facebook written pieces.

Conclusion

Our experience with the UWW program has been a learning journey for all those involved. Similar to other advanced graduate programs in and outside academic walls, we are seeing that fellows, faculty, and mentors learn well from, and like, the blended delivery model. We are also starting to receive positive informal feedback and collect formal measures that CBR, as a philosophy of research, can be understood and applied in virtual space and time if the right combination of online and in-person activities are created, and especially if the students and mentors experience flexibility in the UWW components, a substantial degree of control over its aspects (e.g., when to meet, set their own pace for their goal achievement), and a great degree of social presence (i.e., their online sense of participation).

As the program developers, we are very conscious of how our own depth of understanding of CBR and the complexities of CBR in the HIV arena has shifted as we engage with the fellows. Through the process of developing, implementing, and reflecting on the program, we have also become more aware of our pedagogical foundations, and how our understanding of teaching and learning has changed given the blended delivery context. Adult learning principles, the development of communities of practice, and the notion of connectivity have strongly influenced the program. Because the UWW program is a living entity, we expect to continue to shape and adapt the program as new cohorts enter it. Our aim is to create a cadre of new HIV researchers who will commit to the HIV field. To do this, we provide the fellows with an opportunity to become connected to the HIV communities of (research) practice while completing a degree in their home discipline, or by expanding their ability to work effectively in their community agency. We hope that by bringing graduate and community fellows together to learn, we foster a new generation of HIV researchers who are able to work in an interdisciplinary context, "play well together," and value different perspectives in their work. Rather than viewing HIV research through competing paradigms, we hope that through CBR principles, we assist new HIV scholars to understand the complementarities of different approaches, and the importance of moving from simply studying a problem to developing and acting on solutions with community.

10 Learning and Living Community-Based Research: Graduate Student Collaborations in Aboriginal Communities

E. ANNE MARSHALL, RUBY PETERSON,
JENNIFER COVERDALE, SAMANTHA ETZEL,
AND NANCY McFARLAND

First Nations people seem to be the most researched and the least understood. Knowledge is often "taken" with no benefit derived by the community and at times actual harm is inflicted.
– Lorna Williams, Lil'wat, ACCP Advisory co-chair

Indigenous-centered and decolonized learning is difficult to negotiate and navigate in the western academy. As a group of Aboriginal and non-Aboriginal learners and educators in a graduate counsellor education program, we are challenged to find new spaces to learn, think, and feel that are inclusive and authentic. There are few maps to follow with little time and few opportunities for the type of learning we desire. To simultaneously engage western and Indigenous learning is often traumatic and always challenging. We face a host of dichotomies and apparent contradictions. We must be vigilant and courageous learners or we will be immobilized and discouraged and, amongst ourselves, perhaps end up reproducing the very same conditions that have disrupted our communities. We must also take care in this process to remember the promise to our communities, to our families, and to ourselves.
– Larry Emerson, Dine, ACCP mentor

Envisioning and conducting respectful and authentic Indigenous or Aboriginal research is a particular challenge in the academy. Institutional traditions and procedures are often not consistent with Indigenous values and ways of learning and teaching. There are a number of hurdles: identifying appropriate methodologies; finding support for meaningful research projects; building strong and effective community partnerships;

Figure 10.1. Aboriginal Communities Counselling Program logo.

finding research mentors; enacting ethical practices; navigating the institutional policies and procedures; and finding meaningful ways to evaluate our progress. Our stories highlight how we have faced and addressed these challenges.

In this chapter, we will share our process of weaving together the related strands of authentic community-based research in Aboriginal communities as we learned together in a graduate counsellor education program. In this weaving, the whole is strengthened by the separate and related strands that have blended together. We begin by setting our work within understandings of certain key concepts and within our own cultural context: the Aboriginal Communities Counselling Program (ACCP) at the University of Victoria in British Columbia, Canada. Next, four students' stories illustrate several specific issues, challenges, and solutions experienced: Ruby's story relates her experiences of Indigenous-centred community research; Jennifer gathered adolescent and young adult work-life narratives; Samantha shares her story of community language training as cultural identity development; and Nancy tells of a sharing circle of counsellors describing Indigenous helping methods. Anne shares her story as an instructor and research supervisor. With these stories as a backdrop, we then articulate several key principles of our approach to learning and implementing community-ty-based research (CBR), including the ethical issues involved. We conclude with several lessons we have learned regarding learning and living CBR within Aboriginal contexts.

Key Terms and Understandings

Aboriginal. "Aboriginal" is used in British Columbia and Canadian government documents and refers to First Nations (formerly, "Indian"), Inuit (northern), and Métis peoples. The terms "Native people" and "First peoples" are also used. The intent of the term "Aboriginal" in the ACCP program title was to be inclusive of all three groups and reflected the language used at the University of Victoria when the program was being developed in 2007. For consistency, we have used Aboriginal throughout this chapter, although it is frequently being replaced by the term "Indigenous." It should be noted, however, that Aboriginal people seldom use either term when referring to or introducing themselves – individuals and groups usually use their tribal affiliation, such as Nuu'chal'nulth, Dene, Kwak'wak'kwak, or Cree.

Indigenous. In this chapter, "Indigenous" refers to Aboriginal peoples worldwide.

Culture. We have adopted Chambers' (2000) broad and inclusive definition of culture as "those understandings and ways of understanding that are judged to be characteristic of a discernable group" (p. 852). Culture is nuanced and complex; it includes evolving values, norms, language, traditions, perceived power, role expectations, recognition, priorities, and practices that shape behaviours and ways of understanding (Pedersen, 1991).

Indigenous research lens. Understanding Indigenous research begins with an intense awareness of culturally sensitive issues that include knowledge of the influences of colonialism, residential schools, child apprehensions, living under the paternalistic control of the Indian Act, loss of culture, language, and land base, and how all of these deep losses have affected Indigenous people (Schnarch, 2004; Steinhauer, 2002). Tuhiwai Smith (1999) describes this legacy as a story that needs "rewriting" and "righting" (p. 28).

Community-based research. CBR seeks to answer research questions important to the community or group involved, while engaging in collaboration that focuses on the community's needs. Community partners and researchers work together to identify areas for investigation, gather relevant data for analysis, and disseminate findings that are linked to action in the community (Kemmis & McTaggart, 2000; Sommer, 1999; Whyte, 1991).

The Aboriginal Communities Counselling Program

The name given to our graduate counselling program by Sen̓ćoŧen Elder and language educator John Elliot is *A'tola'nw̱* (pronounced "ah-tol'-ah-nuh"), which means "*a time of hope and respecting one another.*" As learners, we are training to be counsellors and helpers who will return to or take up work in Aboriginal communities. The unique ACCP blended delivery model was created through a collaborative partnership between the Department of Educational Psychology and Leadership Studies and the Office of Indigenous Education (formerly Aboriginal Education) in the Faculty of Education at the University of Victoria – see Marshall et al. (in press) for a detailed description of the A'tola'nw̱ model development and implementation. The vision for the program model was explored at a 2006 retreat of Aboriginal and non-Aboriginal faculty, educators, students, Elders, and community professionals (Marshall, Williams, Emerson, & van Hanuse, 2009). The participants stayed together to form the Advisory and Planning Committee that has continued to guide the ideas, issues, and decisions related to the development and implementation of the program. What makes the ACCP different – unique – is the integration of (Canadian) Aboriginal and global Indigenous values and traditions into all parts of the program. Aboriginal community needs and partnerships are a central focus of every aspect of this initiative – community voices have guided and will continue to guide the direction of the program. The ACCP is specifically designed for adult learners already working in mental health and helping contexts in urban and rural Aboriginal communities.

After the visioning retreat, faculty, Advisory Committee members, community educators, and helping practitioners worked together to establish the seven key values and principles that have guided the program. Dr Larry Emerson recorded them (Emerson, et al., 2007); each is briefly described below:

- *The centrality of the Indigenous paradigm.* Aboriginal and Indigenous world views and practices are incorporated throughout the program in all courses and activities.
- *The sacred and the spiritual dimension.* There is always a spiritual continuum, guided and led by ancestors, in the counselling and healing process.
- *The ancestral dimension.* We are all influenced trans-generationally and multigenerationally. Our stories convey an ancestral reflection. Our ancestors are in the land and sky and are our relatives in the healing process.
- *Stories, ceremony, culture, language, and communal healing.* Traditional counselling always involves our natural world relatives in the healing, survival, recovery, and self-determination process through ceremony, dance, song, and prayer. Food, feasting, and celebrating constitute formal parts of helping, healing, and counselling.
- *The earth and our relatives.* Native people express a "protocol of the land" that is always connected to values of compassionate respect, place, interdependent kinship, and community. Plants, animals, and other life beings of that region are acknowledged and respected and seen as a central part of the healing process.
- *The circle.* We are always the centre of our own healing, and it is simultaneously connected to the family and community circle.
- *The vocation and practice of professional helping.* The counsellor and healer is a witness who understands and appreciates its interconnected and communal sacred dimension.

These values and principles are incorporated into all aspects of the ACCP to make our counselling and research practices more relevant to the needs and traditions of Indigenous communities.

Aboriginal community members and prospective students expressed a desire for graduate counsellor training that would incorporate Aboriginal world views and values, yet also enable graduates to become registered professionals with national and provincial credentialling bodies. Thus, the ACCP is what Duran (2006) terms a "hybrid" program – one that integrates two paradigms, Indigenous and Western, that complement and contrast each other. Indigenous ways of knowing, traditions, practices, and healing methods are used to help students working in Aboriginal contexts, where the dimensions of the spiritual, ancestral, and cultural (stories, ceremony, language and communal healing) play a vital part in how people live. The program follows a "generative model" of curriculum (Ball, 2004) that privileges the voices of students, Elders, and the community. Within the framework of university regulations and counselling professional registration requirements, the program and curriculum have been further shaped by the students and communities involved.

"Walking in two worlds" has been the process in the ACCP. Hatcher et al. (2009) describe this process as "seeing with two eyes ... bringing together Indigenous and western knowledge ... to see from one eye with the Indigenous strengths of knowing and from the other with western strengths of knowing and to use these two eyes together" (p. 3). Shonkoff (2000) maintains that challenges to establishing effective knowledge exchange processes in research reflect the value differences embedded in different cultural world views. Thus, building and sustaining cross-cultural research relationships requires that we identify shared values and assumptions, demonstrate mutual respect, accommodate differences, practise open communication, learn each other's language, and anticipate potential problems. The stories in the next section demonstrate how the blending looked in practice in the ACCP.

Researcher Stories

Ruby's Story

Gilakasla, nugwa'am Pankwa'las. Gayut-an lax Yalis Tsaxis. My traditional name is Pankwalas (Pun-kwa-las), meaning "Filler of belly woman," and my English name is Ruby Peterson, from the Namgis Nation, now in Alert Bay, British Columbia. When our ACCP program began I had a limited understanding of the protocols of academic research. I did know that it was something not well received in our communities, and yet I also knew we needed to be able to give voice to what is effective and relevant in our communities.

In the first year of the ACCP, I spoke to professors, attended research symposia, and joined our local community research group in northern Vancouver Island. It felt very much as if I was fumbling my way through, but I realize now I was actually researching how best to research. I came to understand that community action research could be the way to engage knowledge in our community. At the experiential level, I needed to see how this connected to action. In my community research group, we talked about research and how it could benefit our communities; I brought the voice of our Traditional Knowledge (TKn) to this discussion. In our second year, a group of us attended an Indigenous Research Symposium at the University of British Columbia to represent our cohort with a poster presentation. This was great experience, and in listening to other speakers, I learned yet more about ways to do research in the community.

The next important piece was asking my own community, where I sought guidance from Elders and others. During these discussions, I asked questions about teachings, because the teachings would guide me on how to be with my community. When our program mentor Dr. Larry Emerson came up to our community, we met with invited Elders and leaders to share our intentions of learning our community world view. That day, we received many good guiding teachings about how to be with one another: with *Nok-a* – a good heart, *Ma'yaxila* (My-ya-kya-la) – respect for all things, and *Ikilan* (Ee-key-lan) – walking gently with all things of life.

Our local knowledge has to be central in the research, and the knowledge holders of our life-ways need to be in control of the research, if the answers are to be of benefit to the communities. Shawn Wilson's (2008) point that "research is ceremony" really fit for me. This gave me a way to bridge the need for research and the Elders' teachings of how to be with each other. If the research is based only in Western knowing, it is not in harmony of our world philosophies, and neo-colonial damage is added to an already traumatically colonized people. "When researchers assume that their description of phenomena and their worldview is the only valid means of understanding, it becomes apparent that the purpose of the research is not for community healing" (Duran, 2006, p. 114). To truly connect to community healing we need to take courage and move beyond the confines of Western ideas of research. We need to connect within the relational interconnectedness of research like a spider connects a web – to search again, and find our ability to look through the lens that comes from the depth of our soul. When we see with not just the knowledge of our minds, but through the knowledge of our hearts and spirits – with deep sacred respect for the relationships we have to gain with each other, and with the land, water, and air, with all living things – so we can connect again to the sacred mystery of the spiritual and ancestral realities that are right before us in our research. When we have the courage to go deep within ourselves and connect with life from that deep place, then our research will be centred in the philosophies of Indigenous knowing. Then we will need to analyse our findings from this place as well, rather than trying to tear this knowledge out from its natural place to try to understand it only with our Westernized minds.

Western and Indigenous research methodologies have a dichotomous relationship that I have yet to reconcile. I find it very challenging to express my concerns with the ongoing problem-focused research methodology that is common in Western research, and although many efforts are being made to be more inclusive of Indigenous knowledge, it is still difficult to work with organizations and academics who have excelled in Western research. Finding ways for us to shift our thinking is going to be a challenge. For example, some of you who read this will struggle with my explanation above of taking research beyond the mind. Some may even go as far to say it is "unprofessional." And to answer, I have no words to convince you until you have learned to see beyond your mind. It is this that makes translating my learning into Western language a great challenge. Fortunately, I have recently become part of a local research project in my home community that is guided by the local knowledge of our Elders, called "Local Know-How"; the many lessons within this experience have been a blessing of monumental proportions. With every act, and every question I am researching, I can never assume that I have all the answers, because the wisdom of my grandmother reminds me: "You are never too old to learn" (as my granny told me when she was about 74 years of age).

Jennifer's Story

I come from a mixed family of Métis and Scottish roots – the process of finding balance and walking in two worlds was particularly relevant to the way I engage the world. As an Indigenous student in the ACCP I have had the opportunity to explore and integrate Western and Indigenous counselling practices, with the intent to find a balance that is both respectful of my teachings and relevant to my community. With the support of Elders, professors, mentors, and community, I found this balance by identifying the core values and beliefs that form my world view and aimed to translate both Western and Indigenous teachings through that lens. This practice of interpreting knowledge through my own lens has influenced the way I understood and approached my research.

For my research work, I have been collecting work life narratives of urban Aboriginal youth in order to identify common supports, challenges, and barriers. The goal of the project is to provide this information to those who support young people on their work journey including community mentors, service providers, and policy makers. To make sure that the research process reflected an Indigenous world view and was respectful and relevant to the urban Aboriginal community, several considerations had to be made. At the start, a CBR model was chosen to ensure accountability to the youth participants and their families. Community members were recruited to help guide and inform the research process. Some of the original recommendations from these advisers included: self-identifying as Indigenous researchers for transparency and to help facilitate relationship building, enhancing the community accountability component and dissemination plans, and ensuring that the participants benefited from the experience of sharing their work life narratives. Advisers emphasized that beyond a community-based model, the research must reflect a participant-centred approach. This meant creating questions that used youth friendly language, generating content that was directly relevant to their current work life experience, and, whenever possible, hosting the focus groups within the community. This participant-centred approached was tested during data collection, when one participant said he was unable to answer a question because of cultural protocols. To demonstrate cultural respect, I omitted the question and asked how it might be reworded to address the intent without infringing on protocol. This to me was the epitome of researching with a culturally informed, Indigenous lens that privileged the participants and the community over research outcomes. In another example, a young man requested that the dissemination of results include the youth, so that they might better advocate on their own behalf; I thanked him and assured him that he would be invited to be part of the dissemination plan. These examples demonstrate the accountability of the community-based research process and highlight the commitment to the participants and their futures. This accountability directly reflects my values and beliefs as a Métis person and researcher and demonstrates how the CBR model can help researchers conduct authentic, respectful research.

Samantha's Story

Íy sȼáȼel piȼelánew_ot ŧe ne sná. Ćse lae sen eṯ wsáneć. Good Day, My name is Piȼelánewo_T (pronounced "Pet sa lay'ne whot"), which means "Recognition of the seasons woman." My English name is Samantha Etzel. I am Coast Salish and live on the Wsáneć ("Whsay nech") Territory, in Tsawout Village. I work with the Wsáneć community as a Senćoŧen ("Sen chaw'then") Language Apprentice. I became interested in language revitalization when I participated in the Áleṉeneȼ ("Ay len gu necw") Learning from Homeland program in 2007. While we were learning about our environment we were given the names of plants, trees, animals, sea life, and medicines in the Senćoŧen language and were told the stories that go with the territory. This experience lit a fire inside me to learn my language. I have slowly been taking steps – it has not been an easy journey. I often questioned things within myself and had to work hard to find answers. As I reflect on this journey, it has been the way it needs to be. With all the frustration and disappointments also come triumphs and happiness.

In 2009, the Wsáneć School Board on Vancouver Island established the Sṯá,Sen Tŧe Senćoŧen Department to work towards revitalization and maintenance of the Senćoŧen language. I applied for a position as a language apprentice and was one of seven applicants chosen. The committee that drives this language project includes an Elders' group, three language teachers (Kantenot Helen Jack, Stolȼeł John Elliott, and Ȼosineye Linda Elliott, who teach at Łáu,Wel,New ["Laye wel ngewh"] elementary and high schools), six Senćoŧen Apprentices, the Saanich Adult Education Centre (SAEC) director, and a SAEC Apprentice Program facilitator.

My first step towards collaborative research in an Indigenous community was to inform the Senćoŧen Department at one of our meetings that I wanted to focus on language revitalization for my Master's research project. I said, "I want to write a document that is for our community and something that we could use." I then had to follow protocol and meet with the Elders to make sure they knew what I was doing and would help me with stories or words I needed. I also had to inform the Wsáneć School Board and make a presentation to them. I was in constant contact with the three language teachers to be clear with them about what I was writing. One of the Elders read my project as I wrote and edited. I shared the information freely throughout the community.

My time as a Senćoŧen Apprentice is mostly spent in groups, collaborating among the four Wsáneć communities, Bokećen (Bu cwe' chen), Sŧáutw (Stsay' etwh), Wjołełp (Whjo lelp), and Wsiḵem (Whasiy kem), working on language revitalization. We are working on a Language Authority agreement for the Senćoŧen language, which will include having meetings with other Senćoŧen-speaking communities: Sooke, Semiamhoo, Malahat, and Beecher Bay.

For the Language Apprentices, the most important role is participating in the Elders' sessions, which take place once a week for 3 hours. We serve them tea and coffee, and sometimes lunch. We are creative when it comes to these sessions because we have to accommodate them; two have hearing aids, and one cannot see or hear very well. The Elders have different strengths; we try to learn the most we can from their knowledge. Our discussions include plants, animals, seasons, stories, teachings, history, songs, and creation stories. We do not always know what is in store for us; the time is not always structured. We have to prepare a few different things to work on, in case they get tired of working on the same topic. We never have to worry about running out of work – a number of documents are in development, including a Senćoŧen dictionary.

In our graduate program, we had passionate conversations about the importance of culture and made a commitment to integrate traditional modalities with counselling to clear the path for decolonization. We were reminded of the devastation of colonization and asked to make a promise to our community. I am keeping my promise. I have experienced a positive change with prayer and learning my language – I feel stronger and have hope for our communities. Culture and the traditional teachings that go with the language make a holistic way of learning. My pedagogy involves teaching this way.

Speakers and language champions are key to the successes in our language maintenance and revitalization. Speakers are community members who have been working with the language – developing curriculum and recording and documenting the language. These community members also have expertise in traditional ceremonialism, traditional medicine, and knowledge of plants, animals, arts and crafts, and the land. Language champions are experts in the community who write grant proposals, have language computer skills, share their artistic talents, and teach. There are also allies, such as linguists and others who are passionate about culture and language revitalization.

After I had written my Senćoŧen Journey project draft, I sent it to Elders, mentors, and others in anticipation of feedback and suggestions. One Elder asked me to further develop stories, legends, puppet shows, plays, counselling circles, prayers, protocol, cross-cultural communication, and small community awareness sessions. It seems like an enormous job but I am ready for the work because the outcome will mean that I learn more about the language. I intend to stay in language revitalization, and therefore this will be an ongoing project. I was initially relieved when I completed my project-writing piece for my Master's degree – in actuality, my work will now begin!

As an Indigenous person I am responsible to people who depend on me to pass on traditions and culture to the children. I am a knowledge carrier. I have something to offer the children – a gift I have been given on this journey. I am grateful for the people who have worked more than half their life saving, maintaining, and revitalizing our language.

Nancy's Story

My birth name is Shari Kiyewakan (Key-yay-wa-kahn). I was born to Dakota Sioux and Ojicree parents from the Sioux Valley First Nation and Peguis (Peg-gwiss) First Nation in southern Manitoba. My traditional name is Han Wakan Wacipi Winyan. My English name is Nancy McFarland. I was given up for adoption at birth, adopted at the age of 2, and raised in Montreal, Quebec. At the age of 18, I found my birth family. Soon after, I co-founded and managed an organization named Advocacy for Native Adoptees. I then moved back to Manitoba where I completed a Bachelor of First Nations and Aboriginal Counselling degree, with honours, at Brandon University. I am a mother of five and cherish the family unit. I believe that children are our medicine, our teachers, and the next generation who will take care of us and the world.

When I began my research in the ACCP, it was with the intention to learn more about Aboriginal counselling theory. We had taken many classes that were devoted to discovering what was within our own cultures that related to developing our own counselling styles and interventions, but there was a scarcity of research or theory on Indigenous counselling or therapy from which we could draw (McCabe, 2007; Morrissette, 2008; McCormick, 2009). Results from the First Nations Regional Longitudinal Health Survey in 2005 indicate that 30 per cent of Aboriginal people have experienced a time when they felt sad, blue, or depressed for 2 weeks or more in a row and 31 per cent reported having suicidal thoughts over their lifetime. There are many culturally bound techniques and strategies that are being offered and implemented for Aboriginal clients, but there appear to be no specific counselling theories that have been developed into Aboriginal-based therapy models. At the same time there are a large number of Aboriginal counsellors serving an overload of Aboriginal clients. These issues pointed to a need for an Aboriginal-based counselling theory based on Aboriginal practices and experiences.

I meditated and prayed about what would be a relevant and a significant research project, one that would contribute to the healing process for Aboriginal children, families, and communities. I developed the idea of gathering knowledge from respected, accomplished Aboriginal traditional counsellors and developing a foundation for an Aboriginal counselling theory. I employed a sharing circle, a traditional modality, yet also recognized as a valid (Western) qualitative research method. After gathering counsellors' voices in a sharing circle, I formed a foundational model for counselling called "Inter-relationship-Based Counselling."

Embracing Aboriginal ontology and epistemologies in my research means to work within an Aboriginal paradigm of understanding. This means working from a holistic perspective, incorporating mind, body, and spirit into the research. I listened to all aspects of my being to complete this research and relied on cultural practices to show me what was respectful and how to conduct the research with good intentions. The hardest part of doing the research was being able to integrate the spiritual with the intellectual, amalgamating the logical with the unseen. As suggested by Wilson (2008), the research was conducted as ceremony. Three cultural challenges that arose during the process: First, the number and type of participants were not determined beforehand. Second, family and close community members were involved as participants. Third, identities were honoured by naming the participants. In many mainstream research settings, these three design decisions might be considered instances of bias and would have been addressed differently. However, within Aboriginal culture and philosophy, these decisions actually make the research *more* authentic.

Traditional knowledge, while sacred, belongs to everyone and to no one; it comes through the laws of nature, and will be transmitted through this project if I have adhered to these laws. I was not only asking for approval from a university ethics committee, but also from the

Elders involved and from the Creator. Participants in the sharing circle were highly respected Elders and counsellors who had worked within the Montreal urban Aboriginal community for over 10 years. They possessed knowledge and experience regarding appropriate protocols and process for the transfer of traditional knowledge within this context. They included a family member as well as people with whom I had close relationships – this is not typical in Western studies. However, having a history and relationships with the participants positively affected the quality and quantity of the data collected, because a sense of community and safety was entrenched in the process.

The sharing circle was held at the home of two Elders, because it was recognized as a place of ceremony by the community. Two principles of ceremony are (1) whatever happens in ceremony is meant to happen and (2) no one is excluded. Thus, when two additional participants were invited by the Elders to become a part of the sharing circle, I understood and respected their wishes – the principles of traditional ceremony were privileged over Western expectation of research sampling consistency. In addition, participants' identities were honoured and named because, according to Aboriginal epistemology, knowledge keepers' identities should be known and acknowledged in order for the knowledge to be considered valid and trustworthy. Naming the voices of the informants was an important element in keeping the research culturally authentic and genuine.

The process of developing and conducting my research included visioning, dreaming, prayer, and study. It has revealed to me the importance of structure, protocol, process, and consultation when conducting research within Aboriginal communities. With that understanding is what I find to be the most powerful realization I have made during this research – I have a great responsibility to ensure that my work is done with good intentions. I do this through understanding the appropriate protocols and cultural variables, and by inviting the sacred into my work as well as into my life. Ceremony remained central to this research. It brought me close to the work and to the people involved on a personal and spiritual level, which remains an invaluable gift to me.

Anne's Story: Walking with Graduate Students

I am of Irish and English heritage, and a visitor in Coast Salish territory for more than 30 years. I am a counsellor educator and researcher at the University of Victoria, and co-chair of the ACCP Advisory Committee.

In the Aboriginal Communities Counselling Program, I was particularly aware of my many years in Western academe and how that has shaped my practice. I, too, needed to walk in two worlds and see with two eyes; however, my learning and challenges had a different emphasis – the process of decolonizing a postsecondary graduate program is different for me than for Aboriginal students or for an Aboriginal instructor. In this process, I am grateful to have been guided by wise and patient teachers (including the students), mentors, and colleagues from both cultures. I am also fortunate in that I have been welcomed as a researcher and learner into a number of Native communities for more than a decade. As a research instructor and supervisor in the ACCP, I was always mindful of the question: How do Indigenous knowledge and pedagogy inform the journey as I walk with students, teaching as well as learning how to weave CBR into their practice and process in Aboriginal communities?

**ACCP Principles and Practices
of CBR with Aboriginal Communities**

Our first step when envisioning collaborative research with Aboriginal communities was a serious examination of the historical and political influences that have guided research in these communities up to this point in time (Kenny, 2004). A crucial part of this examination was the acknowledgment that even though residential schools have now all been closed, their impact continues. The history of educational practices forced on Aboriginal people in Canada saw schooling become a tool of cultural destruction and assimilation (Barman, 1997). What was true of educational practice could be generalized to much of the troubled history of research practice in Aboriginal communities.

As Castellano (2004) writes, the ground rules for research and research partnerships in Aboriginal communities and settings need to be made explicit because research has been a "dirty word" in the Indigenous vocabulary. Alien purposes, meanings, impositions, and colonialism have all played a role in the loss of trust Aboriginal peoples have felt towards the non-Aboriginal research process (Schnarch, 2004), regardless of who is doing it. However, recent protocols, principles, and guidelines (e.g., Canadian Institutes of Health Research (CIHR), 2007; Tri Council Policy Statement, 2010; University of Victoria, 2003) indicate a major shift towards more respectful and inclusive research practices. These include:

- Understanding and respecting Aboriginal world views
- Understanding and respecting the community's jurisdiction over how research is conducted
- Emphasizing CBR and participatory models
- Ensuring that research agreements address how the community's cultural, sacred, and traditional knowledge will be used
- Honouring an Aboriginal community's inherent right to retain control of cultural and sacred knowledge, practices, and traditions
- Ensuring that the research will benefit the community as well as the researcher
- Supporting education and training of Aboriginal people in research methods and ethics
- Taking up the obligation to learn and apply relevant Aboriginal protocols
- Ensuring ongoing, accessible, and understandable communication processes
- Recognizing that the Aboriginal community should have a chance to participate in the interpretation of data and be able to review. conclusions drawn.

These principles and practices have been foundational in the teaching and learning of research in the ACCP.

We viewed CBR in Aboriginal communities as an approach that recognizes the importance of collaborating with communities to increase awareness and stimulate change on issues that are important to the people involved. This collaboration ideally happens at every stage of our research. The inclusive relationships common to CBR are characterized by reciprocal influence, where power is shared in an equitable manner among researchers, partners, and participants coming together – a decolonized approach that is critical for Aboriginal communities. In the ACCP, this meant that course topics, research questions, design decisions, and methodology options all needed to be discussed and negotiated with community members from the outset. Concrete tools and strategies used successfully in previous research partnerships were shared and adapted to fit the particular settings and priorities experienced. We continually asked: where are the community and participant voices in what we are doing? The community is the ultimate beneficiary of the research and the site of the research action. As Nyden (2003) observes, "research read by 2000 community residents and used by 5 community agencies to direct their services certainly should be of some comparable value to a journal article read by 200 fellow psychologist or public health professionals" (p. 580).

An Aboriginal ethical world view is not limited to specific rules and guidelines but is an ethic integral to a way of life – it is the ground people stand on (Castellano, 2004). To carry out collaborative research in an Aboriginal community we must be very clear about what we desire from the research, within the guidelines of ownership, control, access, and possession, and we must have a real and genuine commitment to improving Aboriginal representation in key decision-making venues (Schnarch, 2004).

In the ACCP, we began our research preparation early. In every course, instructors and learners critiqued and discussed Western and Indigenous research paradigms, epistemologies, and methodologies. At the beginning of the research project course, we were fortunate to have a workshop with Shawn Wilson, author of *Research Is Ceremony* (2008), in which everyone could share their research ideas, discuss opportunities and potential obstacles, and consider options. Learners then took their ideas to their communities for development, agreement, and collaborative implementation. The assistance from mentors and *community champions* – usually Elders and/or community leaders – was instrumental in supporting these partnerships.

Attention to cultural protocol and practices is essential when partnering with Aboriginal communities (Moewaka Barnes, Henwood, Kerr, McManus, & McCreanor, 2011; Smylie, 2011). A number of scholars have called attention to issues such as exploitation, community damage, inaccurate results, and ethical divergence related to research studies focused on Indigenous populations and communities (Hoare, Levy, & Robinson, 1993; Kirkness & Barnhardt, 1991; McCormick, 1998; Tuhiwai Smith, 1999), and these difficulties have resulted in researchers being mistrusted. In keeping with Aboriginal traditions, ACCP learners were committed to collaborative and community-based research projects that had direct benefits to the Indigenous communities, not only in the present but also for the generations to come.

Power. Attending to power and protocols is particularly important in Aboriginal communities (Castellano, 2004; Hudson & Taylor-Henley, 2001; Piquemal, 2001). In the ACCP we paid particular attention to the effects of power differentials among instructors, learners, researchers, and community partners, and we then used our awareness and experiences as learning and teaching tools. For example, a learner might have related an instance of "top down" decision making, for which classmates generated alternative scenarios and specific language to prevent this occurrence. Power is a central aspect of cross-cultural relationships (Gaventa & Cornwall, 2001; Marshall & Batten, 2004), and perceived and actual power differences present very real barriers to collaborative relationships. Inclusive practices were followed so that the participation of all those who are involved was valued and acknowledged. In classes, supervision, and field experiences, we practised clear and respectful communication of shared goals and expectations that helped address the problems of relationships where power distribution was unequal.

Specific strategies. In our approach to learning CBR, we stressed the importance of personal story and the circle. As Dine scholar Larry Emerson maintains, the circle is held together both literally and figuratively through the telling and hearing of stories: this is how you gain admittance and how the circle is maintained (personal communication, 19 March 2008). In classes, we always sat in a circle, where we could all see one another. We made time for personal sharing and reflection; this allowed us to build relationships and to interact in a climate of trust and acceptance. Respectful and patient listening was highlighted and modelled throughout classes, and we all carried these practices into our CBR projects and partnership building.

The telling of stories was a valuable tool for our learning. Orality is the primary mode of communication in Aboriginal communities; the telling of personal and traditional stories is central (Dei, 2002; Guenette & Marshall, 2008). In the ACCP, stories allowed learning to be authentic and grounded in particular student and community cultural contexts. This often meant hearing the stories of trauma resulting from colonization. We all kept research journals that included artwork, story, and collage as examples of creative, non-textual representations of learning. Our journals fostered an approach to learning that required self-reflection and exploration of walking in two worlds throughout the research process. Discussions related to possible ethical dilemmas were ongoing; there were many challenges to assumptions about cultural affiliations. All were occupying multiple settings and cultural contexts – just because one student was from a particular community did not mean she would be automatically accepted or prepared to carry out research in that setting. Most of us were not working in our home communities; thus, we also had to navigate new and different cultural protocols

Lessons Learned

"Education has now come to be seen as a key arena in which Indigenous peoples can reclaim and revalue their languages and cultures and, in so doing, improve the educational success of Indigenous students" (May & Aikman, 2003, p. 141). Castellano, Davis, & Lahache (2000) maintain that postsecondary education provides entry into professional and vocational roles valued in Canadian society and promises the hope of a better life for Aboriginal people. To integrate Indigenous-centred knowledge into the academy entails the recognition that distinct and different knowledges can co-exist and complement each other (Baskin, 2002). Given their role in expanding knowledge and training educators and other professionals, it is critical that universities begin addressing how to develop an authentic awareness of Indigenous knowledge. The A'tola'nw̲ program provides an example of how this goal can be realized; the experiences shared in this chapter highlight research in particular.

Indigenous knowledge has "epistemic saliency" (Dei, 2002, p. 5), which includes cultural values, belief systems, and a world view that is imparted to the younger generation by community Elders, a knowledge that constitutes a direct experience with nature, place, land, and ensuring relationships with the social world (Castellano et al., 2000; Ermine, 1995). Battiste and Youngblood Henderson (2000) write that the ecologies in which Aboriginal people live are more than mere settings or places, more than homelands: Indigenous people are not surrounded by ecology, but part of an ecology. Because this is true for everyone, we acknowledged how important it was to understand how knowledge is connected to residence in and relationship with place, a particular understanding of the natural world and the mysteries of ecology. This ecological understanding included research knowledge and practices, and thus needed to be addressed in our academic and community research contexts.

Now that our first ACCP cohort has completed the program, students and instructors agree that gaining community-oriented research knowledge and skills is accomplished through multiple and cumulative activities over time – not just within a single research course or project. Through readings, discussions, and experiential activities, we have all learned about relationship building, respectful interactions, community values, and the practice of collaborative methods long before commencing actual research projects. Without this evolving orientation, some of the projects might not have been as successful as they were.

Power is a critical aspect that needed to be addressed early in research relationships and collaborative partnering, particularly in view of the history of oppression and disempowerment in Indigenous communities. Although hierarchical "power-over" issues are perhaps more expected, issues of "lateral violence" and within-community familial conflicts were at least as common in our experience, and sometimes more difficult to resolve. These issues were confronted and addressed through the knowledge and experience of our Aboriginal mentors such as Larry Emerson and Lorna Williams.

Communities often have an expectation that researchers should be involved in the community for extended periods. This necessitates ongoing informed consent (Piquemal, 2001), or "process consenting" throughout the entire process of the project, not just at the outset. This also requires a willingness to negotiate and talk about new issues as they arise. It is vital to have community investment, or the research work and the eventual findings will never be taken up, used, or implemented. We tried to use our own time and the time of the community wisely. Tolerance for ambiguity is also essential – we did not and cannot have all the answers before we start – and at times we found that we might not even have had the right questions!

We were challenged by our diverse and often bicultural backgrounds that meant equally diverse cultural protocols and priorities. As Stewart (2007) observes, there is no "pan-Indigenous" approach that will work for all. Indigenous knowledge is a part of clan, band, community, or even individual experience and resists generalization (Battiste & Youngblood Henderson, 2000). Most of us in the ACCP were no longer living in our home communities; there were both benefits and drawbacks related to this.

As learners and researchers, we have shared our stories of establishing connections with communities, seeking guidance from Elders, adopting an Indigenous-centred research process, respecting traditional knowledge, and walking in two or more worlds. In our experiences, we became empowered within a community context. It is from within the community that we gain the courage and the resources to do this challenging and important work.

Part IV

Promoting Knowledge Democracy: Teaching CBR in University Classrooms

11 Walking Side by Side: Living Indigenous Ways in the Academy

LORNA WILLIAMS, MICHELE TANAKA, VIVIAN LEIK,
AND TED RIECKEN

There is a growing recognition and desire in many sectors to open institutional doors to true mutual collaborations and partnerships with peoples who live and thrive in different cultural worlds. This shift requires all parties to change, adapt and to learn from each other. It necessitates the examination of values, habits, attitudes and practice. It means modifying long-standing protocols, procedures and policies. The story of one university course designed to enact Indigenous ways of teaching and learning in a university environment is told through two studies. The examination of the experience of this course offering in the academy provides a glimpse into some of the considerations vital to the concerns of knowledge exchange and knowledge transformation in the context of community/university relationship evolvement. Learning happens for the students, faculty and community members who learn by experience and participation. Learning also happens for the hundreds of members of the university and Indigenous communities through engaging in negotiating protocols and establishing new rules that guide working and walking together.

Among Western-based intellectual traditions there is a long-standing recognition that both culture and context are central to the acquisition, interpretation, and use of knowledge. Centuries of ethnographic research have established culture as a vital concept within the complex dynamic that allows human groups to thrive and persist through time. More recent work on knowledge acquisition, by individuals such as Cajete (1994), Wenger (1998), and Vella (2002), illustrates how the social environments in which those activities are situated shape cognition and learning.

There is a growing desire in many sectors to open institutional doors to true mutual collaborations and partnerships with peoples who live and thrive in different cultural worlds. This shift requires all parties to change, adapt, and to learn from each other. It necessitates the examination of values, habits, attitudes, and practice, seeking points of resistance. It requires modifying long-standing protocols, procedures, and policies. Corntassel and Gaudry (this volume) call it resurgent action, creating space and place to collaborate responsibly with and be guided by the Indigenous community to tell their own stories in their way, not a way driven by the academy. For institutions to serve a diverse population, there must be a willingness to listen to alternate world views, and a willingness to base decisions on the needs of the people they serve, not on the expediency of organizations that have been built on the assumption of homogeneity.

Despite the long-standing recognition of the importance of culture and context for knowledge acquisition, Western-based universities remain remarkably mono-cultural in their approach to teaching and learning. Knowledge exchange paradigms outside the dominant Western intellectual traditions have made only minimal inroads into the disciplinary bases that constitute the academy. At the same time, the academy makes little concerted effort to include space for other ways of knowing. As a result, non-Western approaches to learning are rarely experienced in university environments. Battiste and Youngblood Henderson (2000) refer to this situation as a kind of cognitive imperialism, and note that because of it, much Indigenous knowledge is not able to find a place for expression or applied within universities or public school systems. In the public schools, for example, studying the histories, cultures, or languages of Aboriginal people has been offered only to Aboriginal students and not to the general public.

In this chapter, we present the story of one university course[1] designed to enact Indigenous ways of teaching and learning in a university environment. Examination of the experience of this course offering in the academy provides a glimpse into some of the considerations vital to the concerns of community/university partnerships and the transformation of institutions to institutionalize alternate forms of teaching and learning. We will draw on two graduate students' research studies – Vivien Leik's Master's thesis, which focuses on learning through community engagement, and Michele Tanaka's doctoral dissertation on student learning and transfer of learning to personal and professional practice; both used the course as the site for their studies.

We will focus on the reciprocal and conversational nature of the interactions that took place around and through the course. We say "around and through" the course because the learning associated with its implementation occurs on a number of levels. Learning certainly happens for the students, but learning also happens at an institutional level. It happens at the level of individual faculty members who participate in the delivery of the course, and it happens for the members of the Indigenous community who participate in the creation and delivery of the course at each step along the way. Learning also happen for the hundreds of members of the university and Indigenous communities when they participate in recognition and acknowledgment ceremonies and a final ceremony celebrating the course at its completion.

In the Indigenous community, ceremony plays a significant role in community affirmation. The ceremony provides an opportunity for the greater public who were not directly involved to witness and partake in the experience. The ceremony is a recognition and acknowledgment of the participants' accomplishments, and their experience becomes a part of the community's collective history. Thus, learning takes place and knowledge is exchanged in a dynamic and fluid way. At this point, it is less a matter of transfer and more a matter of transaction, of knowledge mobilized and flowing into whatever direction it is taken up and used by the course's many participants. The synthesis of what we learn from this experience may be transferred to other situations where multiple worlds come together to streamline, create, blend, change, or dismantle traditional practices to meet the needs of partnerships.

This knowledge exchange is organic and circular, rather than a linear process. Not only does it exist in a temporal context that is different than typical Western notions, it is a dialogue that draws from more than spoken conversation. The experiential nature of the course – for example, working with cedar bark that has been stripped from the surface of ancient trees – provides participants with ways to "listen to" culture through embodied knowledge (Lakoff & Johnson, 1999). In addition, the stories of the Indigenous instructors enable participants to attend to the voices of the ancestors. Gradually over time, the participants learn to listen to the possible lessons embedded in the stories rather than listening to them as "stories" or entertainment. They begin to be more adept at connecting insights from the stories to experiences while working on a task or noting a remark an instructor might have made.

The personal reflection processes of the participants (conversation with ourselves) also come into play. A weekly assignment is to keep a reflective journal, to record experiences, insights, significant learning, and descriptions of activities. A final assignment is to consolidate these reflections into a final essay documenting what was learned and how this learning will be enacted in personal and professional life. A crucial component of knowledge transfer is to be able to see how what has been learned can occur in different contexts. This knowledge exchange model is in keeping with holistic learning theories that "nourish the learning spirit" (Battiste, 2007) and acknowledge the authentic being of the learner (Tisdell, 2003) as opposed to an outside-in model of knowledge transfer.

Within the context of a university-based teacher preparation program, the course is unique in that it represents an Indigenous pedagogy entering the world of the academy, such that the teaching and learning is enacted as it would be within an Indigenous community. The pedagogies are drawn from several Indigenous approaches to teaching and learning, including those of the instructors. In the first offering of the course, one instructor was from the Lekwungen peoples of south Vancouver Island and the other from the Liekwelthout people of the mid-island. The pedagogy of the second offering of the course was drawn from the wisdom keepers from the Wsanc, Lekwungen, Tsouke, Nuuchanulth, Lil'wat, Métis, and Mohawk. The principles of learning for the course were drawn from the Lil'wat culture of Lorna Williams,[2] the course designer and a Canada Research Chair in Indigenous Knowledge and Learning. These Indigenous pedagogies (discussed in depth at a later point) present a much different approach to teaching and learning than what students and university faculty normally encounter in the academic environment, although, faculty members who have been part of the course have remarked that these principles and practices are ones that they themselves strive to include in their instructional practice.

As an authentic enactment of Indigenous pedagogy within the cultural setting of the university, the course is an example of knowledge production that can occur when people of different cultural backgrounds walk "side by side" as part of a process of decolonization (Tuhiwai Smith, 1999). In a similar vein, the president of the Social Sciences and Humanities Research Council of Canada (SSHRCC), Chad Gaffield (2008), refers to this form of knowledge generation as "walking shoulder to shoulder" to connect academics and community members to address problems affecting everyday life. This dimension of the course, which has a co-mingling of people of different backgrounds, ages, cultures, and experience levels, puts it outside normal university practices on a number of levels. The knowledge exchange moves more like a webbed circle or spiral, so that teachers are learning from Elders are learning from students are learning from teachers – and so on. The process moves in this circuitous way throughout the experience.

Description of the Course

Situated within the Faculty of Education at the University of Victoria, the course is designed to immerse educators in Indigenous pedagogy through direct involvement in traditional experiences such as pole carving, weaving, drumming, singing, and storytelling. The goal of the course is to work positively towards modifying individual and societal cultural perceptions and misconceptions. Furthermore, it highlights the value and potential of Indigenous teaching and learning approaches for educational organizations. The course becomes an interactive learning community as it integrates the hands-on practical and creative activities with theoretical and academic objectives. More implicit, but equally important, is the modelling of an Indigenous process of instruction as it is fully placed within the university setting. In this way, the unusual course supports postsecondary curriculum reform by opening an avenue for cross-cultural dialogue between Indigenous and non-Indigenous participants and across knowledge bases.

Within the course, students experience the principles of traditional Indigenous ways of teaching and learning, including: mentorship and apprenticeship learning, learning by doing, learning by observing deeply, learning through listening, learning from stories and singing songs, learning in a community, and learning by sharing and providing service to the community. The pedagogy that underlies the Indigenous course holds a holistic perspective, where educational quality is defined as more than test scores and includes strengthening student learning through varied and diverse approaches. The course enacts the principle that adults can draw from their rich experiences and wisdom to make sense of unfamiliar terrain. Students write in their reflection journals of their discomfort and feelings of resistance to finding their own way to engage in tasks; at first they miss the explicit instructions, guidelines, and readings. The course is offered to student teachers, educators, graduate students, faculty members, and students enrolled in other disciplines, as well as members of the larger community including high school students. This class composition is important to creating a community experience in a university setting that is similar to an Indigenous

Figure 11.1. The pole, called *Schalay'nung Sxwey'ga*. *Schalay'nung* has the double meaning of "teaching of the ancestors" and "to be a true history." *Sxwey'ga* means "man." Photo by Michele Tanaka.

learning community. Inviting the community-at-large to witness, acknowledge, and recognize the work of the class at a midway point and at the end of the class is in keeping with the Indigenous way of measuring accomplishments. The community keeps abreast of what members in the class are experiencing.

In the first offering of the course,[3] the group carved a traditional Lekwungen and Liekwelthout Thunderbird house and welcoming pole (referred to in this writing as the "pole course"). The explicit goal was to witness, experience, carve, learn, and position the pole in the lobby of the MacLaurin Building, which houses the Faculty of Education at the university. The pole would bring a physical and visual presence of Indigenous culture into the heart of the building.

The participants of the pole course divided themselves into five groups at the beginning of the term. The *ceremony group* took leadership in organizing four ceremonies including a blessing for the pole; a ceremony to honour First Nations children in foster care that included replanting trees to replace the cedar tree used for the pole and to plant the trees as a reminder that children need roots; a feast celebration honouring the students who carved the pole; and a final installation ceremony that included traditional dances, speeches by the university and First Nations community members, food, and presentations by the five student teams. The ceremony team made sure that all appropriate First Nations and university protocols were followed in these events. To carry out the ceremonies in a respectful and meaningful manner, it was necessary for the group to understand the purpose and significance of each of the ceremonies to all the parties involved. They negotiated with each party – the Lekwungen on whose territory the ceremony would take place, the Liekwelthout, and the university – every aspect of the ceremony. Each was required to compromise and adjust their traditions without feeling that they were betraying their ancestors.

The *education group* was responsible for organizing visits by school students. The focus of the visits was on the significance of the pole and the promotion of community appreciation and understanding of the pole, and included hands-on participation and involvement with the carvers and the "Old Man" – the name given to the pole. The education group also prepared ways to inform and involve the university community by posting information bulletins and inviting passersby to feel welcome to stop and watch the carving.

The *print group* documented the making of the pole as well as providing research and supporting materials. They developed an interactive information board for the public and wrote an article that was given to guests at the installation ceremony and was published in a peer-reviewed journal (Tanaka, Williams, Benoit, Duggan, Moir, & Scarrow, 2006).

The *video group* documented the entire pole carving process on film (Riecken & Riecken, 2005). The completed video is a historical record of the carving of the pole. The team drew on class discussions, storytelling, scenes from the various stages of the carving process, and interviews with the course leaders, carvers, students, and community members to complete the film.

The *web group* developed a website (Pole Project, 2006) telling the ongoing story of the pole (see http://education2.uvic.ca/Pole). This website serves to inform the university community, First Nations communities, the school community, and the general public. This team used materials developed by the other teams to enhance and complete their website.

Each week, two teams carved the Old Man. On the weeks they were not carving, the teams worked on their small group projects. Each of the projects documented the process of carving the pole, in a different format – website, education, ceremony, print, and film. This enabled the participants to transfer what they had learned from their carving experience and Indigenous instruction into another form. In turn, this gave them an opportunity to reflect on and reconsider their experience and to translate it for another audience.

The second offering[4] of the course revolved around the creation of fabrics and textiles including the media of weaving, buckskin, beadwork, cedar bark, button blankets, and wool (referred to in this chapter as the "earth fibres" course). Again, the participants divided themselves into five groups, and each group worked extensively with one of the described materials. At the end of the course, a mural was created that tells the story of the course through woven pieces. In addition, other pieces created by wisdom keepers located across Canada, the Americas, and Southeast Asia were added to the mural and serve to situate the piece in a global context. Course instructors, community members, and students contributed these pieces. The wampum belt in the mural was made and contributed by Haudensonee students in Ontario because hearing about the course inspired them and they wanted to take part. The mural currently hangs in the Curriculum Library in the education building. In this class, each group worked on projects individually and in family groups, knowing that what they produced would need to fit into the community project in the end. Keeping this in mind was a struggle for many, because as they worked on their individual piece they wanted to claim ownership over that piece, especially when their work was achieved after great effort. The focus in this course is on individual responsibility for the achievement of the community.

The third course focused on drumming and singing, and the fourth on storytelling. We will only draw on the learning from the first two classes in this article.

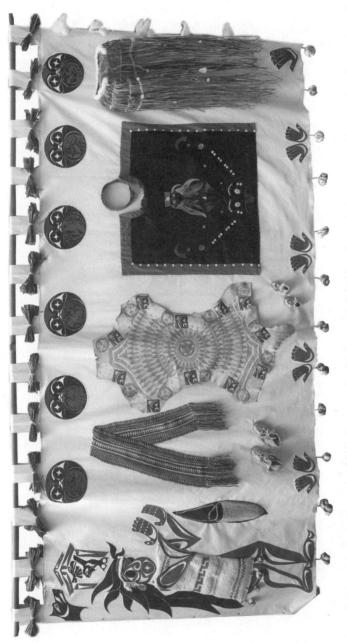

Figure 11.2. The mural, named *Xaxe Siam Seetla*, "Honoured Grandmother of many generations, wise, learned, and respected as Mother Earth" (Side A). Photo by UVic Photo Services.

Figure 11.3. *Xaxe Siam Seetla* (Side B). Photo by UVic Photo Services.

Lil'wat Principles of Teaching and Learning

The course is philosophically based in the following Lil'wat concepts of learning and teaching. In the Indigenous world, knowledge is passed on to the next generation through mentorship learning, indirectly through a complex web of storytelling, as well as through direct instruction, where a more expert other guides learning. Learners integrate knowledge in their own creative way for the benefit of the family and community. Learning and teaching in the Lil'wat community involves an extensive web of storytelling. Stories are used to teach the beliefs and values that guide what it means to be a good human being. Stories are also used to communicate historical passages and changes to the land, families, and community. Expert/novice relationships with rich opportunities for modelling and observation are abundant. From an early age, children and youth work alongside those who are more knowledgeable, skilled, and adept. There are ample opportunities to be involved in creative and innovative practices. They engage in family and community activities that are contextually based and time appropriate. These learning opportunities are relational, interdependent, integrated, and holistic. Much of the work on the land is difficult, intense, monotonous, tedious, and tough, so the work is eased with humour, fun, play, quiet talk, and silence. Maintaining spirit, physical, mental, and emotional balance is important in everyday life. Much of the teaching is designed so that the learner is able to observe and practise with some watchful guidance. They have opportunities to develop their own unique practice. The feedback on accomplishments is usually quiet appreciation. The teaching practice lends itself to habit formation, identity affirmation, and knowledge integration. Learning is purposeful and of benefit to the self, family, and community.

The following are the concepts in Lil'wat that are embedded in the teaching and learning process and were shared at the beginning of the classes and revisited throughout the course at the most optimum times. These concepts come from the Lil'wat First Nation, but they resonate with other Indigenous peoples as sustaining the teaching and learning process:

Cwelelep – being in a place of dissonance, uncertainty in anticipation of new learning, to spin like a dust storm.

Kamucwkalha – the felt energy indicating group attunement and the emergence of a common group purpose; the group is ready to work together, to listen to one another and speak without fear.

Celhcelh – each person is responsible for their learning; it means finding and taking advantage of all opportunities to learn, and maintain openness to learning. Each person must take the initiative to become part of the learning community by finding their place and fitting themselves into the community. It means offering what knowledge and expertise you have to benefit the communal work being carried out.

Emhaka7 – each person does the best they can at whatever the task, and keeps an eye on others to be helpful. This means working respectfully and with good thoughts and good hands.

Responsibility – each person is responsible for helping the team and the learning community to accomplish the task at hand in a good way, entering the work clear of anger and impatience.

Relationship – throughout the course each person will be conscious of developing and maintaining relationships – with the people, the task, the teachers and guides, and the communities beyond the learning community. It also means relating what you are experiencing to your past knowledge and to what you will do with what you are learning.

Watchful listening – oriented to an openness to listening beyond our own personal thoughts and assumptions, being aware and conscious of everything around you as you focus on the task at hand.

A7xekcal – how teachers help us to locate the infinite capacity we all have as learners. Developing one's own personal gifts and expertise in a holistic, respectful, and balanced manner.

Kat'il'a – finding stillness and quietness amidst our busyness and need to know.

Institutional Challenges and Solutions

Integrating the policies and procedures of the university with the traditions and protocols embedded in an Indigenous approach to teaching and learning present a number of interesting challenges. None of these challenges is insurmountable, but addressing them requires a flexibility and a willingness to adapt longstanding ways of doing things to be able to work effectively in the cross-cultural context in which the course is situated. Throughout every step of planning and the ongoing implementation of the course, the two world views of the academy and the Indigenous people need to be discussed and negotiated until appropriate compromises can be found. For example, depending on the pace of the work, the course schedule may need to be extended, or the number of student contact hours expanded beyond those normally stipulated by the university. In the intersecting sets of interests affected by such changes in contact hours, there must be flexibility on the part of the students themselves, on the part of departmental and records offices within the university, and on the part of the Indigenous teachers hired to teach the course.

In the pole course, working within the time schedule that governs university life meant that the carvers needed to have a set carving time each week, rather than their usual working pattern of starting at dawn and ending when the work felt complete for the day. The carver mentors did not have Master's degrees and therefore required special permission to be instructors for the course, which was readily given by the provost and vice president academic. At the same time the instructors, especially the younger carver, visited members of local First Nations communities, letting them know about the project and what was planned. The younger carver also visited First Nations Elders to introduce himself and to describe his task. In this way, he informed all the key people and gave them an opportunity to advise and guide him so that he would be successful.

The course was planned for teacher candidates, but their schedules were tightly filled with courses to meet the requirements of the BC College of Teachers. That would not easily allow them to take the course. Hence, the program supervisor and advisers were obliged to see where there were possible openings in the schedule and to encourage students to register for the course.

Other challenges that the course presents within university environment include the need for an expanded conception of scholarship to include the activities and obligations associated with the development of a non-traditional course offering. The type of off-campus community building, the establishment of partnerships with Indigenous communities, and the appropriate application of Indigenous protocols necessary for successful relationships are time-consuming and labour-intensive activities. In the world of the academy, productivity and academic output is usually measured in the form of publication in peer-reviewed journals. Faculty members who direct their energies towards Indigenous forms of teaching and learning, and away from the traditional metrics of scholarship, are working on the periphery of traditional academic forms of knowledge production. This puts such faculty members at some degree of risk in terms of a typical academic career. To mitigate that risk, recognition is required that scholarship exists in many different forms in cross-cultural settings.

Much as the course presents the academy with a challenge to expanding faculty reward structures beyond conventional forms of scholarly work, assessment of student learning presents a similar challenge. The Indigenous teachers hired from the community were not comfortable with placing each of the students within a graded ranking at the end of term, as is the custom in most university courses. In the Indigenous world learning is to honour the learning spirit of each individual in a community and cannot be judged as a competition. Learning and teaching in an Indigenous world occurs outside of grade-based approaches to feedback, and the mentor carvers did not want to assign marks to the students, each of whom are seen to learn at a rate determined by the students themselves, in a manner that encourages them to take responsibility for their own learning. Throughout the course the mentor teachers worked alongside each individual, modelling, guiding and instructing so each learner achieved competence to carry out the task. As a compromise, and to fit within the university system of course credit and degree requirements, students are credited for the course on a complete/incomplete basis, with feedback taking the form of journals, discussion, and interaction around the individual film, website, writing, or ceremony tasks they were involved in. Many of the students in the course expressed the view that this approach to assessment was beneficial, because it removed some of the competitive ethos that often accompanies graded university courses.

Faculty Participation

For the faculty members who participated in the course, knowledge exchange happened when they stepped aside from their role as instructional leaders, and put themselves in the role of learner instead. This provided them an important opportunity to experience Indigenous ways of teaching and learning as a learner herself would experience it. For faculty members rooted in Western forms of pedagogy and knowledge exchange that are hierarchical and didactic, and based on a separation of teacher and student, their experiences in the course provided an important experiential illustration of alternative ways of knowing. Participating in the course provided faculty with an illustration of how the boundary between teacher and learner can be more fluid than Western pedagogical conceptions, and that the commonly held distinction between teacher and student is not a key feature of every learning environment.

The idea to invite faculty members into the course as participants was a deliberate decision by Lorna Williams in her role as the course designer. She saw including faculty members in the course as one way to achieve one of the objectives within the Faculty of Education's Strategic Plan, which focused on increasing Indigenous ways of teaching and learning throughout the Faculty. Lorna's hope was that those who participated in the course would arrive at a paradigm shift through their experience of being of learner, teacher, and community member all within a single course environment. To be able to provide such an opening, her invitation to faculty members allowed them to be present as either a co-instructor, or as a learner, and within that atmosphere of openness, faculty members settled into whichever role they felt most comfortable in. Several faculty members occupied both spaces as participants, moving back and forth between them, thereby experiencing an Indigenous way of teaching and learning that is situated in the experience itself.

Faculty involvement also played an important role in building community-university relationships. Community members co-participated in learning activities alongside faculty members, who are often seen as holding a remote and esteemed role in a university, and this is part of the relationship building necessary for gaining mutual understanding. Community members need to see that there is openness in the university to their ways of knowing and learning. The course modelled learning through a shared experience, to learn through experiencing the cultural world rather that learning about the culture in a disembodied way and as an object.

In Leik's research study, she documented both Indigenous and non-Indigenous students' and instructors' experiences in the pole course. Butch, one of the Indigenous instructors, expressed the significance of the course as:

> It's very important because [the pre-service teachers] are actually going to go out and share what they've learned and what they've learned about the teachings of First Nation people, and bring that to younger people. So actually, they've brought gifts here, and then they've compiled more gifts. And then they're going to go out in the community and share that, which is really important. So it's a first for the university, and it's probably the best thing that ever could happen to a teacher who's going to be involved with First Nations children. (Butch Dick, DVD)

244 Learning and Teaching Community-Based Research

Butch highlights the implications of this initiative for teachers, students, and the community. He aptly expresses the possibility for positive outcomes through this type of cross-cultural exchange and talked about how course participants had "opened their minds to First Nation culture in a different way" (Butch Dick, DVD).

Rebecca, a non-Indigenous pre-service teacher, said, "I learnt a lot about Indigenous ways. I learnt that sometimes saying that you accept a people was very different than actually experiencing what they are all about." She said that although she thought she was "fairly open and accepting, [she] was also anxious going into the course because [she] didn't understand [First Nations] as a people and didn't understand their culture." As a result, she had not been sure how to interact with Indigenous people and described this as "a boundary, kind of like this hidden wall." Rebecca said: "I feel like the course really broke down that wall and allowed me to feel like we are much more the same than we have previously thought." Jessica, an Indigenous graduate student, said that through these types of educational experiences, she thinks, "there is just so much opportunity to break down the barriers and create respect."

Recognizing and celebrating Indigenous knowledge and practices within the academy demonstrated a new chapter for educational relationship between Indigenous communities and the university. In an interview during the pole course, Lorna expresses how:

> Universities have a long history in their practice, in their values, and their philosophy that, I think, that they guard, you know, very, very carefully. And they are, in a sense, universities are the tradition keepers of the Western world. And to bring Indigenous ways of learning, to bring Indigenous ways of being, to bring Indigenous ways of teaching, to bring Indigenous knowledge into the academy, and to try to construct it being faithful to the Indigenous ways, is the only way I think that people can take, even a tiny step into experiencing another way of being. And, so, for me, to be able to have the Pole Carving course here, it changes, first of all, the space. It changes peoples' sensibilities. It calls people to build a different narrative, finally, into this space, which can only alter people's relationships. People now can't go back. And the people who have been immersed in the project, the students who are will leave the university, but this experience won't leave them. (Lorna Williams, DVD)

Exposure to and engagement with Indigenous knowledge systems and pedagogical practices provided a new frames of reference; expanded individual and institutional awareness; developed understandings that build stronger community connections; and dismantled layers of resistance to learning in different contexts.

The second study was a doctoral dissertation that describes in depth the experience of the pre-service teachers enrolled in Earth Fibres Weaving Stories, the second offering of the course. It brings to the fore the experiences of the pre-service (student) teacher participants by recording their stories and analysing them through the lens of a phenomenological narrative approach (Tanaka, 2007). Just as Leik's study demonstrated the true community partnerships in the course, Tanaka illuminates some of the essential characteristics of the experiences that supported cross-cultural understanding and collaboration. Exploring this study helps us to spiral into a deeper layer of understanding around the course by highlighting the lived experience of some of the cultural concepts. Putting these into action was at the heart of changing inherited perceptions of other cultures. In addition, the experience of these concepts disrupted Western established hierarchies of expertise found in the roles of learner, teacher, and researcher. Instead of a transmissive approach, the course became a cross-cultural pedagogical conversation in which learners, teachers, and researchers thought carefully together about how to make classrooms better places for everyone: in this sense, it was truly community-based research in action.

The Earth Fibres study stemmed from Tanaka's personal experience as a doctoral student enrolled in the pole course as a member of the print group. Through extensive reflection and writing that occurred in conjunction with four pre-service teachers who were also enrolled, Tanaka's study is informed by the insightful and honest writing of these young scholars (Tanaka, Williams, Benoit, Duggan, Moir, & Scarrow, 2007). To enrich our discussion of nourishing CBR, we draw from the voices of these student teachers, and build on them with participant experiences of the Earth Fibres study.

For the non-Indigenous student teachers in both courses, cross-cultural understanding arose through a process that incorporated the Lil'wat principles of cwelelep (dissonance, uncertainty and anticipation), watchful listening (beyond familiar knowing), celhcelh (a sense of personal responsibility for learning), and kamucwkalha (recognizing the emergence of group purpose within an environment of trust). The awareness of and engagement with their personal spirit of learning (as suggested by Battiste), became a critical key to changing perceptions of these emerging teachers, as they went out in the world to "provide the learning contexts in which students can unfold and create their own stories" (Battiste, 2007). The course modelled a way of both unfolding personal stories and co-creating new stories cross-culturally.

Cwelelep. At the outset of the course, participants felt as if they had entered a foreign environment, and many had an overwhelming experience of *cwelelep.* Jill, an undergraduate student in the print group, expresses her fear and hesitation about the process in the context of the pole course.

> Undoubtedly, it is challenging any time, when one "steps out of" their culture and into another. It's like you're suddenly completely naked, without the weight of your own cloak of culture, wrapped around you. In these experiences, your sense of open-mindedness can dissolve easily into a dark cloud of doubt … you experience a moment when it feels like you've stumbled, but a moment to learn from, nonetheless. (Cited in Tanaka et al., 2007, p. 105)

The dissonance of cwelelep manifested in various ways and throughout the course as the participants searched for meaningful learning in the unfamiliarity of another cultural way of knowing. This discomfort was compounded by the complete/incomplete grading structure of the course. The students were used to getting a detailed description of what they need to do to get the grade they hope for. When that structure was removed, they expressed confusion and disorientation. Their sense of certainty was being disrupted, and they were searching for ways of being comfortable in unknowing (Kumashiro, 2008).

Watchful listening. Along with the uncertain experience of cwelelep, the pre-service teachers engaged in a *watchful listening* process to gain deeper understanding of Indigenous ways of learning and teaching. This is a way of attending that went beyond the comfort of personal and familiar knowing, to listen carefully in a way that respected the multilevelled complexities along with the essential spirit of the other (hooks, 1994; Schultz, 2003). It was a listening process that insisted on genuine attention. Becoming watchful listeners was a difficult process, as described by Robyn in the pole course:

> When a question arose for me I would, as usual, take that question to one of our class leaders. Instead of receiving my usual quick and perfunctory answer I often received a story. These stories were enthralling, but often

circular, ending near the beginning and missing an obvious answer to my question. Often when a leader was finished, I would think to myself, "well that's great, but where is my answer?" I grew frustrated and discouraged when I was not handed the answer on a platter. The concept of waiting it out, watching and observing was completely foreign to me. I understood I was learning in a way of a different culture, but I still could not handle how different it was from my own. This led to mounting frustration towards myself. I was unable to comprehend my inability to adapt. I chastised myself for not being able to wait, slow down, and just listen. All I was after was a quick fix, and that fact upset me. (Cited in Tanaka et al., 2007, pp. 103–4)

Robyn's frustration at learning to be a watchful listener reflected her temporary inability to look beyond the familiar and comfortable transmissive model of pedagogy that she grew up with. Robyn expected information to be passed directly to her, and this disrupted her sense of responsibility in the learning process. Robyn's distress temporarily obscured the "anticipation of new learning" that is a basic element of the cwelelep process. The process of watchful listening required taking time in an uncomfortable place before a shift in perspective enabled deeper learning to occur.

Celhcelh. The combined processes of cwelelep and watchful listening, gradually led many of the pre-service teachers to *celhcelh*, a place of personal responsibility for the learning process. Yvonne tells us about her perspective, which has, again, been heavily influenced by a North American transmissive perspective of learning and teaching:

My education has been spoon fed to me. From childhood, I have been told what to know, what to believe, and how to act. When this class began, I opened my mouth to receive my spoonful of knowledge, yet I found no spoon. I found myself confused, not knowing what to do. I asked questions, because that is how I have always been told to find answers. Again, I found nothing. Over time I came to see that while questions would not be automatically answered, answers did exist. This Aboriginal approach to education suggested that finding them was my responsibility. I was suddenly, for the first time, responsible for my own learning in an educational setting. On this recognition, I closed my mouth and opened my eyes and ears. I took advantage of every opportunity to learn. I didn't just watch, I observed. I didn't just listen, I heard. I wanted to learn. I wanted to understand the purpose of all this – I wanted to understand what I was

being told. The potential of discovery of the answers I sought, intrigued
me, motivated me. (Partially cited in Tanaka et al., 2007, p. 103)

Over time, coming into an awareness of their own ability to learn was a
powerful and common experience for students in the course. This gave
them increased confidence in this cross-cultural situation. Through
changing personal experiences as learners, these young teachers began
to translate this into how they would alter the learning environments
within their own classrooms. In her earth fibres reflection assignment,
Jamie explained how a deeper understanding of the internal motivations of celhecelh affected her teaching:

> As a teacher, I want my students to take pride in their work and to be mo-
> tivated by a want to learn rather than by grades. I don't want my students
> to compromise the quality of their work for time, but to instead enjoy the
> process of creating something. Building a community and sense of family
> in my classroom is going to be very important to me as a beginning teacher.
> I want all of my students to feel welcomed, accepted, understood, and re-
> spected. [Our instructor] spoke of an energy one gets when one is poised to
> learn something, but unfortunately we [Westerners] have no word for it.

Cwelelep was the word that Jamie searched for and described her feeling poised towards anticipation of learning. This hints at the "potential
of discovery" that Yvonne referred to earlier. Jamie began to "enjoy the
process," which led to a deeper sense of celhcelh – a responsibility towards learning that transcended external motivators and focused on
the communal work at hand. She continues:

> As a student I can see the benefits of having multiple ways of learning for
> people with different learning styles, and as a teacher I plan to implement
> as many into my daily classroom teaching as I can. I have learned so much
> about myself, about learning, and about teaching along this journey and
> can't wait to pass it on. Our final button blanket was beautiful and I can
> finally say that I am proud to show off something I worked so hard on to
> create with a group of people I can call my family.

Jamie speaks to the experience of the participants' growing awareness
of how they learn as individuals within a different educational environment. Kim articulates how this can extend into her role as a teacher:

Another important principle that I will take away from this course is the appreciation for other ways of learning. Of course, as a future teacher, I have always been aware that every student learns differently. On reflection after this course, however, I realize that it goes beyond the needs of individual learners. As a teacher, I need to be open to ways of learning and teaching that are different from what I have experienced.

There is clearly a desire in these young teachers to carry what they have learned in the Indigenous courses with them, to "pass it on" through changes in their own teaching styles.

Kamucwkalha: In a previous quotation, Jamie refers to her button blanket group as her family. She articulated how she moved from the periphery of a new learning experience to a more central place of practice within this learning community (Lave & Wenger, 1991). For many of the learner-teachers it was a circuitous and sometimes uncomfortable process that led away from familiar and preferred territory. Often, however, participants found themselves in a place of expanded relationships as a new community of learners developed. The importance of community was striking in the data. The pre-service teachers spoke often and with passion about finding a place within community and also about the significance of working together on a common goal.

Kamucwkalha is the act of noticing the point at which the energy of a group moves into an attunement and clarification of group purpose. In the pole course, this became apparent on the day that the pole was moved from the outside workspace to a space inside, more protected from the weather. Because of the considerable weight of the pole, this was no small feat and required the involvement of all the course participants. Swinging sledgehammers, opening doors, moving small logs under the pole to act as rollers, watching the overall direction of the moving mass, each took different but equally important skills to accomplish the goal of relocating the pole.

Individuals had begun to find the jobs that they were drawn to and had increased their skill levels at these jobs. They were nourishing their learning spirit, and finding celhcelh, their place in the group. As this happened, a stronger sense of community emerged and there was the feeling that we could speak freely with each other, knowing that our stories would be respected and listened to by others with open hearts and minds. Developing this community was significant, as Jenni writes in her final reflection assignment from the earth fibres course:

Figure 11.4. Moving the pole into the building. Photo by Michele Tanaka.

> One thing that struck me most in this class was the sense of community among the students and teachers. By bringing the group together in the beginning (of each class session) to say prayers, thanksgivings, thoughts, and ideas, it really opened people up to one another in a way that is not possible in other education classes. I felt I got to know people at a deeper level than otherwise possible. Classmates were supportive and encouraging of other people's work. There was no sense of competition, which is such a relief after three years of competing for grades.

Getting to know people at this deeper, more authentic level became a touchstone for the participants that they could refer back to as they went on in their teaching careers. The course gave them a solid point of reference around the idea of a healthy learning-teaching-researching community. They then took this embodied knowledge forward into their practice.

Jenni's reference to the building of community among students and teachers is also particularly noteworthy, in that it demonstrates how the hierarchy between teacher and learners was disrupted. Many of the participants spoke about how important this was in terms of building relationships and working together in community. This happened, in part, because the course was graded on a complete/incomplete basis. But there was also an underlying philosophy among the course instructors that knowledge was not an object to be transferred; rather, it was the responsibility of each student to seek out and find the learning that was appropriate to them. The acknowledgment of the learning spirit set up a dynamic of power that gave equal respect to the learner and the teacher. This is not to say that the instructors did not hold important knowledge that was unknown to the learner. Rather, it is to highlight that possession of knowledge, or lack thereof, does not change the simple idea that everyone deserves respect equally. From this point of reference, Kamucwkalha is possible.

Overall Implications for Knowledge Exchange in Community-University Partnerships

Our experiences with this course have reinforced our pre-existing belief that coming to know is a cultural process. How one comes to know something, and how one expresses that knowledge, is determined largely by one's language and culture. Looking across the conventions that guide learning and community membership within Lil'wat culture and those within the university, we see there are shared similarities as well as important differences regarding how knowledge is taken up and used. In both, there is a concern with the improvement of the individual, recognition that learning happens over time, and that there is a role for "teachers" in the process. Where there is a difference, it has to do with how one assesses learning, how individuals pursue their goals in learning, and how those doing the teaching interact with those who are learning. As cultural practices, the approaches to teaching and learning used in each of these settings have developed over millennia and have withstood the test of time as effective means of passing knowledge from one generation to another.

It has been our experience that together these approaches enrich one another. We have learned that by standing shoulder to shoulder, and by walking side by side, the pedagogies of Indigenous peoples and those of Western academic institutions can work together to build powerful and worthwhile understandings. This course is an example of ways in which the academy can alter its long-established practices to make space for other ways of teaching and learning. Forging the relationships in the learning community constructed in the courses was a safe way to work through the nuances in building a working relationship between the university and communities. The communities within the various strands of the university also required consideration, and people could see that the changes wrought by the courses did not affect the standards or threaten the overall structure of the university. The experience we share of building relationships between communities of learning can serve as model for those who want to invite the bounty of knowledge and wisdom found in communities into the academy.[5]

12 Making a Difference through Teaching, Learning, and Research: Multidisciplinary Research Internship Courses

JOAQUIN TRAPERO AND AGATA STYPKA

This chapter presents a story of the emergence of an idea and the experience of planning, co-creating, and delivering a series of postgraduate level courses. The idea was to offer Multidisciplinary Research Internship (MRI) courses (also referred to as Interdisciplinary Research Practicum courses) that would provide students a unique educational experience and an opportunity to apply research to policy and practice in the public sector. By conducting research and engaging in experiential praxis together, the value of theory and research are made explicit and result in an increased appreciation of the practical implications of "doing" research (Breunig, 2010).

The University of Victoria's strategic plan outlines the university's commitment to integrating teaching, learning, research, and community engagement across the disciplines (University of Victoria, 2007). As the economic and social environments become increasingly challenging and unpredictable, it is even more important to experiment with innovative course designs that engage both the university and community (Buys & Bursnall, 2007). Strand, Marullo, Cutforth, Stoecker, and Donohue (2003) indicate that the potential of community-based research (CBR) "to unite the three traditional academic missions of teaching, research, and service in innovative ways makes it a potentially revolutionary strategy for achieving long-lasting and fundamental institutional change" (p. 5). Furthermore, the multidisciplinary approach of the MRI course enhances the opportunity to move towards integrative thinking and collaboration (Amey, Brown, & Sandmann, 2002) to address complex world problems. Although academic institutions are traditionally organized in ways that promote strong disciplinary ties, the MRI course transcends the barriers that exist between faculties,

departments, and disciplines. Amey and et al. argue that multidisciplinary opportunities, like the MRI course, allow individuals to overcome deep-seated paradigm conflicts associated with the strong
disciplinary socialization and promote the opportunity to engage in a
more reflective practice, question the assumptions of their own discipline (Adamczyk & Twidale, 2007), and allow for their own disciplinary perspectives to blend together with those of others (Amey, Brown
& Sandmann, 2002). Furthermore, Herman and Willson's experience
(this volume) suggests that "a pedagogy conducive to learning, practising, and teaching key CBR principles must embrace eclectic mixes of
skill-sets that are not part of the traditional repertoire of 'how to do
research' lesson plans." The MRI courses encompass principles of CBR
and aim to address a community-identified need by engaging multiple
stakeholders in the process of learning and research.

The Multidisciplinary Research Internship Course

The Multidisciplinary Research Internship courses were spearheaded
by the UVic Office of Research Services under the Vice President
Research, and emerged from the Knowledge Mobilization (KM)[1] Unit
– a project funded by the Social Sciences and Humanities Research
Council of Canada (SSHRC) and the Canadian Institutes of Health
Research (CIHR). The KM initiative focused on promoting and supporting the use of research evidence by decision makers and practitioners to help solve issues that matter to Canadians. Although the Office
of Research Services was not known for course development, it was
known for managing various research initiatives. Given that UVic was
interested in integrating teaching, learning, research, and community
engagement across the disciplines (University of Victoria, 2007) it was
no surprise that the KM Unit developed a course-based model that
promoted the UVic's priority areas of teaching, learning, research, and
community engagement.

The office envisioned a model encompassing the principles of experiential learning that would encourage collaborations among UVic's
academic units and the greater Vancouver Island community. By focusing "classroom" activities around the research process, the courses aim
to create a platform where UVic has an opportunity to learn from the
community and the community from the university. With clear benefits
to partner agencies and students, the courses facilitate the application
of knowledge in research design and methodology to real-life issues

that organizations face. It is through these non-traditional course offerings that students are given an opportunity to acquire and apply knowledge and skills in an immediate and relevant setting (Cashman & Seifer, 2008).

In an effort to convey a deeper understanding of a Multidisciplinary Research Internship course, each sequence of the course model will be outlined and graphically depicted in the paragraphs to follow.

Course Design

The Multidisciplinary Research Internship course was first offered at UVic in 2007. Since then, eight courses have been co-created and offered with various community organizations, including government ministries. The MRI course is offered through the Faculty of Graduate Studies and, as a result, graduate students from a broad range of disciplines enrol.

Many graduate students interested in taking an MRI course are already taking specialized programs and therefore must receive approval from their thesis or dissertation supervisors to formally enrol. MRI courses are held over 13 consecutive weeks during an academic term (first term, second term, or summer studies). Sessions are held weekly, allotted a 3-hour time slot, and facilitated by one or two course instructors. Generally, students receive 1.5 academic course credits (equivalent to one full-term course) once they successfully complete an MRI course. The physical location of the course varies and is often negotiated with the community partner.

Although most MRI courses are designed to address issues in a particular field (e.g., with an environmental, health, or social science focus) the recruitment efforts span across the disciplines. As discussed, the MRI courses aim to integrate discipline-specific research approaches and theoretical underpinnings and allow for students to engage with other disciplinary perspectives, so that new solutions can emerge (Amey, Brown & Sandmann, 2002).

Partnership and Collaboration

Each partner must trust that the other can be counted on to "do the right thing": exercise good judgment, keep the other's interests in mind, and work for the ongoing success of the partnership. It is also important that each partner share, or work to develop, a faith in the collaborative process itself. This means they have confidence in the partnership: that it is worth developing and sustaining, even as it faces hurdles – and perhaps even failures – along the way (Strand, Marullo, Cutforth, Stoecker & Donohue, 2003, p. 8).

As Figure 12.1 illustrates, the MRI courses are co-created in partnership with community organizations and course instructors. A representative from the KM Unit (MRI Office in Figure 12.1) facilitates the partnership and manages the contracts. Similar to the philosophy expressed above, the MRI team believes that trust, commitment, and shared interest in achieving mutually agreed on goals and objectives are critical to the success of creating and offering the courses. In an effort to design and implement high-quality courses, a significant amount of time is invested in building relationships with potential partners.

In the months preceding the start of a new academic term, a knowledge broker from the university's KM Unit corresponds with several community organizations to gauge their interest in partnering with the university to co-create a course. Broadly speaking, a knowledge broker provides a link between researchers and end users (Dobbins, Robeson, Ciliska, et al., 2009) and facilitates the creation, sharing, and use of knowledge (cited in Meyer, 2010). Traditionally, a knowledge broker bridges the gap between knowledge producers and their results and those who use the results in their practice (Meyer, 2010). Because the MRI course facilitates the co-creation of knowledge, the knowledge produced in a course is made "more robust, more accountable, more usable; knowledge that 'serves locally' at a given time" (p. 123). However, we must acknowledge that the process of knowledge creation is not necessarily representative of the beneficiaries. The condensed academic term (13 weeks) and ethical considerations mean that students participating in the MRI course are predominately working with staff from community agencies. Clients, who may be impacted by the results, are not actively involved in the research and as a result do not have control over the research process. However, we trust that the community groups that UVic collaborates with work in the best interest of the populations they serve. Having said that, the authors acknowledge that evidence-based research does not always have an impact on policy and practice. Herman and Willson (this volume) indicate that the controversy and decision surrounding the needle exchange in Victoria was shaped by the public's opposition to harm reduction and service provision rather than research-based evidence.

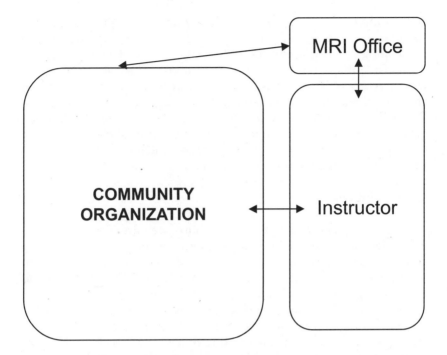

Figure 12.1. MRI partnership and collaboration.

Because the university is responsible for acting in the best interest of its students, the process of identifying and selecting a community partner is rigorous. A representative from the university conducts several face-to-face meetings with potential partners to ensure that organizations are equipped with the resources that facilitate rich learning experiences for all involved. Each student participating in the MRI course is paired with one community mentor and should have access to this person once a week for at least 1 hour. Documents, data, and sources of information that will contribute to the quality of research should also be accessible to students. Finally, if students are required to work onsite, the partner organization is encouraged to provide a workspace for them. It is not only the university that approaches this phase of partnership formation with caution. Community organizations are interested in receiving products that they are able to use inside and outside their organization and as such they are often concerned with the calibre of students.

It is during these initial interactions that both parties present their assumptions, concerns, and strategies for moving forward. Engaging in an ongoing and open dialogue is dependent not only on the development of a mutual agenda, but also on the need for partners to recognize the differences between a university's and community's interests and create mechanisms that will assist in the management of emerging conflicts (Wallerstein & Duran, 2006). It is important to keep in mind that collaborations are cyclical and iterative in nature and partners may need to revisit their goals and objectives (Buys & Bursnall, 2007) to further foster and strengthen the relationship.

Course Content

More often than not, developing new courses requires complying with institutional policies. Depending on its nature, the proposal for a new course needs to be reviewed and approved by a curriculum or program committee; in UVic's case each MRI course was presented at the Faculty of Graduate Studies' Graduate Executive Committee meeting made up of deans, faculty members, and students. By maintaining institutional support throughout the process of course development, both academic rigour is maintained and the meeting of learning objectives and outcomes is ensured. When Cashman and Seifer (2008) developed a service-learning course, they identified areas that should be considered in building institutional support. These include "benefits/risks to the institution and community, how the course can help students achieve specific competencies, and the identification of colleagues or partners who can be helpful" (p. 277). In UVic's, case additional information relating to the course content was required, and often the course director provided additional information in the form of a course syllabus.

Although institutional experts influence the process of design of the course outline, the community organization also plays a vital role in shaping the content of the MRI course. As Figure 12.2 illustrates, the community organization identifies research questions that it would like answered, which then drives the process for course approval. The course is only presented to the Graduate Executive Committee when an organization has identified research questions and has reviewed the course instructor's proposed educational outcomes, preparatory activities, and evaluation techniques. In an effort to ensure that both the community's and the university's expectations are met, the knowledge broker maintains ongoing communication with all parties. A

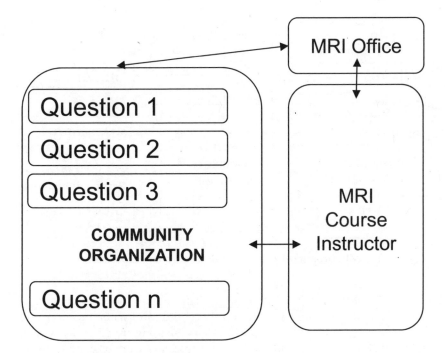

Figure 12.2. MRI course content.

partnership is only solidified when all stakeholders (community and university) have agreed on the terms.

Project Selection and "Classroom" Experience

Project Selection

"Collaborations can be viewed in various forms, from offering general advice to active participation, and may have diverse meanings to different members" (Buys & Bursnall, 2007, p. 73). In this Multidisciplinary Research Internship model, the university and community become engaged in a partnership where elements of teaching, learning, and research are at the core.

Once a course syllabus has been approved, the community organization identifies a group of mentors who will be responsible for assisting students in answering the organization's research questions. As

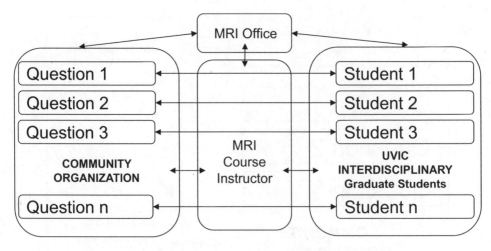

Figure 12.3. MRI project selection and the "classroom" experience.

Figure 12.3 illustrates, each student participating in the MRI will generally be partnered with one community mentor and will be responsible for answering one research question (see also Figure 12.3). However, there have been exceptions where two students were assigned to one research question. The community mentors usually hold senior staff positions at the organization and are assigned the lead for at least one research question. They are vital to the partnership because they bring with them knowledge that is not always found in textbooks or academic publications, along with a community perspective on a particular issue. The mentors share knowledge they have acquired through years of experience and can advise academics on community assets, resources, and norms. More often than not, the local knowledge that is made available to students informs the research process and ensures that questions are addressed with the community's realities in mind. "Community partners are key to helping students expand their frames of reference and understanding so that they are more comfortable and competent working with community members" (Cashman & Seifer, 2008, p. 277).

Students participating in the course are at the graduate level (M.A., Ph.D., etc.) and are enrolled in a broad spectrum of disciplines. Students from different academic disciplines are encouraged to enrol in MRI courses because a set of research questions proposed by the community organization often requires different skill-sets and perspectives. There-fore, it is not uncommon to have an economics student, a student studying environmental studies, and a student from the anthropology department participating in the same course. A "classroom" experience that facilitates multidisciplinary discourse opens students to the ideas and perspectives of others who may be grappling with variations on a similar research area (Peters & Gray, 2007).

Prior to an academic term officially commencing, the university be-gins to facilitate relationships between community mentors and stu-dents. Once a student enrols in an MRI course the knowledge broker connects the student to the course instructor. The course instructor as-sists the student in selecting a research question that is complementary to the student's interests, background, and skill-set. The student then contacts the community mentor who is responsible for assisting the stu-dent in answering that particular research question. Together the two parties begin to define the scope of the project and agree on the out-comes of the project. It is essential to begin this matching process as soon as students begin to enrol in the MRI course, because these rela-tionships require ample time to foster.

"Classroom" Experience

Students enrolled in MRI courses attend a weekly 3-hour meeting that is facilitated by the course instructor. The traditional classroom envi-ronment is transformed and serves as a temporary space for critical reflection on what each student is doing in a particular project (Ibáñez-Carrasco & Riaño-Alcalá, 2011). Learners are encouraged to engage in a process of reflection as students begin to "reflect in different ways on their experiences, and make connections to key concepts and theories and further action" (Taylor & Pettit, 2007, p. 240). These reflective ses-sions are complemented by discussions on themes that are relevant to the research questions the students and community mentors are co-investigating. Examples of topics discussed include: cultural differences between universities, community, governments, and industry; gaps in translation and mobilization of knowledge; building sustainable part-nerships; the importance of research ethics; and the application of re-search to policy and practice. In addition to engaging in self-reflection and focused discussions, students are given ample opportunities to learn from each other. Because students in MRI courses come from dif-ferent disciplines and have a vast set of skills, the exchanges that take place often lead to new solutions and/or broader perspectives. Strand (2000) believes that "the collaborative nature of community-based research also gives it special pedagogical value, as students have many opportunities to learn both from each other and from community partners with whom they work. Students often have different strengths and characteristics that, taken together, help them carry out a project with much greater success than if they were working alone" (p. 88).

"Outside" the classroom environment, students work one-on-one with a community mentor to address a research question. This collaboration results in outcomes that are relevant to the needs of the community and aim to impact local practice and policy. Answers to "real life" questions are not always found in textbooks, and the student and community mentor therefore spend a lot of time discussing the complexity of practice and the scope of their project. As Taylor and Pettit (2007) indicate, "for real learning to be experienced, articulated and shared requires an integration of different theory, disciplines and approaches" (p. 239). Given that students are working with "real life" issues, we must be reminded that finding solutions is seldom a linear process – the reality is that difficulties will surface. Therefore, when facilitating a learning process, it will be important to reconcile chasms, explore assumptions, and discuss unmet expectations (Herman & Willson, this volume).

On average, students who are participating in the MRI course report that they dedicate approximately 10 to 15 hours a week to complete the requirements for this course. Typical projects produced in MRI courses include program evaluation frameworks, literature reviews and critical synthesis, analysis and interpretation of existing data, logic models, and survey instruments. In addition to completing a final product that is submitted to the partner organization, most MRI courses require students to prepare an initial project plan/proposal, an end of term presentation, and a final reflective report that addresses the strengths and challenges of the research approach used within the project.

> Therefore if the partnership is to be worthwhile to the academics involved (i.e. research outputs), it is essential that they educate community agencies about the benefits and limitations of their involvement. Just as important, however, is the need for academics to learn how to turn their research outputs into valuable and useful community tools ... Completion refers to the success of the project in terms of objective and subjective outcomes, and learning outcomes. (Buys & Bursnall, 2007, p. 79)

The Results

For students, community-university partnerships, such as the MRI course, offer substantial benefits. Buys and Bursnall (2007) found in their study of university-community partnerships that "collaborating is the best thing I have even done. I think it allowed us to achieve learning outcomes that we couldn't have reached in other ways. It gave students real experience of working on real projects and with real people and with real conflict of interest, with real difficulties" (p. 80). Because the research questions are driven by the community organization, the research that is produced is intended to be relevant to the partner's needs. Students engaged in MRI courses are, therefore, invigorated by real accountability as they are exposed to realities that reach beyond examples found in textbooks and hypothetical case studies. Arguably, their learning results in a heightened sense of purpose, as their reports are not only submitted to instructors but community organizations evaluate the usefulness of the research that is produced (Strand, 2000).

The completion of a course is marked with a formal knowledge mobilization event. UVic's KM Unit sponsors a forum that is intended to give students an opportunity to share their research results with various stakeholders. The course instructor, the community partner, and knowledge broker work together to develop a list of invitees and the event's agenda. Students and community mentors are encouraged to work together and develop a presentation that resonates with individuals beyond the academic community. The intention is not to isolate the academic community from the process, but to maintain relevance in the messages that are being communicated to the partner community and / or on behalf of the community. Strand, Marullo, Cutforth, Stoecker, & Donohue (2003, p. 7) further elaborate on the idea of data dissemination and the importance of maintaining relevance by stating:

> This means that academics used to thinking in terms of formal jargon-laden research reports and rigid scholarly standards of proof must think first of the need to present results in a form that is comprehensible to neighborhood organizations, politicians, agency personnel, and others who might make use of the research findings. Although this does not preclude formal research reports, it does require that researchers demystify the language of research reporting, present results with clarity and brevity, and consider multiple and even unconventional methods to communicate research findings.

During the final phase of the collaboration, the knowledge broker, responsible for facilitating this partnership, ensures that all parties involved in the process have an opportunity to evaluate their collaborative experience. Representatives from community organizations not only meet with the knowledge broker but also have an opportunity to fill out an anonymous online evaluation. The content of the community evaluation focuses on objective outcomes (i.e., the quality of the projects), satisfaction with the experience of collaboration, and the learning outcomes. Students engage in a debriefing session with their course instructors and are also given an opportunity to fill out an anonymous evaluation. Although each MRI course is different and built on the unique needs of an organization, the feedback generated is valued and used to inform new course proposals. It is only through this systematic evaluation process and open communication that community-university relations are strengthened.

Making a Difference

Collaborations resulting from MRI courses satisfy UVic's commitment to integrate teaching, learning, research, and community engagement. In terms of teaching, students enrolled in an MRI course are exposed to both practical and theoretical knowledge inside and outside the classroom. Students, community mentors, and course instructors benefit from rich learning experiences in which information is not presented to them but, instead, each party engages in a dialogue that facilitates sharing of information. The research that is produced in an MRI course is often co-created with a community mentor and aims to impact social policy and/or practice. Finally, the MRI aims to strengthen existing relationships between the university and the community and form new partnerships with organizations that are interested in engaging in innovative course design by co-creating a course.

13 Creating the Learning Space: Teaching the Arts in CBR

CATHERINE ETMANSKI

Fiction is knowledge. Poetry is knowledge. The arts are ways of knowing. The lingering belief that knowledge is and must be proof, proposition, muscle for prediction and control is bound inextricably with our Western belief in the individual as a separate, autonomous being. It is bound inextricably with our need to tame the earth and its creatures, and it is bound inextricably with our fear of the unknown. We have wanted to accumulate knowledge and to use it as foundation, as fact, as colonialist, neocolonialist, and imperialist commodity, as clout, and as cultural capital. But we are fooling ourselves if we think we can trust knowledge more than we trust fiction to guide us, to teach us. Knowledge, like fiction itself, is liminal space. It never arrives. It is always on the brink.
                                                    – Nielsen (2002, p. 206)

Preamble: A Shift in Perception

I admit that I didn't really get arts-based research at first. Like many graduate students, I had preconceived ideas of what research meant – ideas no doubt formed by the lingering beliefs about knowledge that Nielson points to above. It took time to unlearn my assumptions before I could embrace arts-based research. I clearly recall the "ah-ha" moment when I grasped that theatre and other arts-based methods I had been learning in various facilitators' trainings were not somehow superfluous to the research process; rather, they *could in fact be* my research process.[1] In that moment, I was beginning to "get it" – and the joy of learning in this way continues.

What I understand now, and what I did not understand before, is that there are ways to co-create knowledge, to conduct research, to learn, and to teach one another that involve people as whole human beings. As some of the contributors to this collection have also demonstrated, research can honour and respect our own and our participants' agency and complex identities, and can engage our whole body, all of our senses, our imagination, heart, spirit, *and* our intellect. In this chapter, I focus specifically on how the arts can be employed in community-based research processes and how I have shared in the classroom what I have learned since that pivotal ah-ha moment.

This chapter provides an account of the design and strategies I used for teaching a graduate-level course entitled Cultural Leadership and Social Learning through the Arts. I relate this account by first providing a brief overview of arts-based and arts-informed research practices, accompanied by several resources for the reader to reference for further information. I then outline the course and describe how I endeavoured to create a classroom environment and curriculum conducive to learning about, with, and through the arts. Next, I provide a detailed account of the experiential workshop that participants facilitated as their major assignment in the class, including two key lessons I learned through multiple offerings of this class. I conclude with a few reflections on what this chapter contributes to the teaching of community-based research.

Introduction to the Arts in CBR

Arts-based processes are not (as even I may have previously assumed) fun but somehow unnecessary activities. In a world troubled by complex, interconnected challenges – challenges that knowledge produced through Western science has played a role in creating – the arts are not secondary to the so-called real work of science. They are essential. The seemingly intractable nature of the challenges we currently face means that we can no long rely only on tried and tested strategies and solutions. We need to find new possibilities for collectively co-creating innovative solutions and learning into the future. While all forms of community-based research may have this intent, as will be discussed below, arts-based CBR offers unique ways to build empathy and understanding and tap into our collective creative potential.

Said differently, the process of creating art *is* inquiry and, in that sense, *is* a kind of science. Both art and what has traditionally been conceived as science "involve the use of systematic experimentation with the goal of gaining knowledge about life" (McNiff, 2008, p. 33). In this realm where art is understood as a medium of inquiry, the "epistemological standpoints of artists and social science workers collide, coalesce, and restructure to originate something new and unique among research practices" (Finley, 2008, p. 72). Inquiry through the arts can be understood as a social science which recognizes that we perceive the world through multiple senses, not only through our rational minds. It is a social science that allows us to access other ways of thinking, doing, being, and knowing.

Just as proponents of CBR suggest that research is all around us, art too is a fundamental and universal aspect of human expression. Art transcends time, space, place, culture, and class. Elemental beauty can, of course, be found in nature, but wherever there are humans there is human-made art. Yet, like research, the arts have become relegated to the domain of professionals; that is, they are reserved for people with recognized skills and training and some measure of what has traditionally been called creative genius (see Battersby, 1989, for a critique of this idea). Of course, learning to adeptly utilize specific artistic media does require practice and the refinement of skill – my intention is certainly not to discount the training, the hours of practice, and the level of refinement found in the work of dedicated artists. However, the unfortunate consequence of a division between those seen as possessing artistic talent and those who are not is that many people in this society develop an early aversion to or wound around the arts. Some individuals feel hurt, embarrassed, or inadequate in their ability to express themselves and communicate using an artistic or creative media and therefore avoid it (marino, 1988). Moreover, in our contemporary global capitalist society, art has mostly become a product to consume rather than a natural right of human expression (Diamond, 2004, 2007). For some, this repression of the creative spirit is seen as a form of oppression, which means that reclaiming the arts can lead to sometimes healing, building community, and increasing our innate abilities to communicate using a broader range of strategies. Whether created by professionals or in community settings, the arts can also support us in perceiving, understanding, thinking about, and innovatively addressing the socio-ecological, economic, moral, and intellectual challenges of our times.

For these reasons, many researchers in the methodological traditions associated with community-based research are increasingly calling for "research that more closely follows the imaginary and improvisational processes and practices of artists, poets, and musicians as compared with inquiry that is commonly associated with the logical-rational approaches in the sciences and social sciences" (Garoian, 2011, pp. 157–8). Such arts-based and arts-informed approaches to research have been gaining momentum in the academy over the past few decades.

What distinguishes these approaches from others is that the arts are employed at various stages throughout an inquiry process. For example, just as surveys, interviews, and focus groups may be used as methods for gathering and generating information (traditionally understood as data collection), so too are arts-based methods such as theatre, photography, quilting, and so on. Arts-based methods can also be employed as means for processing and understanding information (data analysis), or as media for presenting information to a wider audience (representation and dissemination of results beyond text-based formats).

It should be noted that the arts are not inherently participatory; in other words, not all arts-informed or arts-based researchers have a predisposition to the action-oriented or participatory approaches to research adopted by CBR practitioners. Individual researchers might collect data through more traditional means and then, in the solitude of a studio, for example, pull out an easel and paintbrush to help them make sense of their data. The research objectives, as well as the researchers' skills and orientation will determine how the arts are employed throughout the research process: which artistic media are best suited to the work and at what point in the process it makes the most sense to introduce them. For the purpose of clarity, in this chapter, as in the course it documents, I am interested in approaches to research that integrate the CBR principles of participation, relationship building, action, and justice, while employing various artistic media as research methods.

In general, it is useful to understand that the arts are not simply tools; rather, they provide a unique epistemological starting point. In other words, the arts provide different ways of knowing as this chapter's opening quotation suggests. What we can come to know through symbolic images – in the theatre, in photographs, in poetry, through story, dance, and so on – may be different from knowledge accessed via direct questions and conversation alone. CBR practitioners who employ the arts recognize "in the creative process the integration of intuitive and rational modes of understanding through engaging the whole of the person (emotions and intellect)" (Simons & McCormack, 2007, p. 297). Employing the arts as research methods can bring to the surface preconscious or previously unarticulated concerns and desires (Davis-Manigaulte, Yorks, & Kasl, 2006), sometimes bypassing the censorship of the brain (Jackson, 2002). Many of the learners in my classrooms

were surprised, as I was, by how powerful, deeply personal, and potentially transformational arts-based research processes could be. Moreover, because symbolism can go straight to the heart, arts-based methods
are powerful in revealing our shared humanity and therefore helpful in
building understanding, empathy, and trust among research participants (necessary in most CBR processes) and also between participants
and audience (useful in CBR work for social change).

Multiple Approaches to the Arts and Research

Just as the practice of CBR draws from various methodological streams
and traditions (see the Introduction to this volume), so too do arts-based
and arts-informed approaches to research. Community-based adult educators in Canada and many other parts of the world have long em-
braced the arts as a means of investigating the human experience and
stimulating learning (e.g., Clover & Stalker, 2007; Harris, 1998; Kidd &
Byram, 1979). In the academy, however, specific methodological traditions have emerged to reflect the various ways the arts are employed in
processes of inquiry. This is particularly true in disciplines related to
education. The Ontario Institute for Studies in Education (OISE) of the
University of Toronto, for example, founded an informal working group
in 1998, which blossomed into the Centre for Arts-Informed Research in
2000. Scholars at the University of British Columbia (UBC) promote another tradition, a/r/tography, which they describe as inquiry through
"an ongoing process of art making in any form and writing not separate
or illustrative of each other but interconnected and woven through each
other to create additional and/or enhanced meanings" (Sinner, Leggo,
Irwin, Gouzouasis, Grauer, 2006, p. 1224). In addition, a key US-based
proponent of the arts in research is the former president of the American
Education Research Association (AERA), Elliot Eisner (e.g., 1981; 1997).
Following a 1993 address to the AERA, "the Arts-Based Educational
Research Special Interest Group of AERA was formed and quickly
grew" (Cole & Knowles, 2008, p. 58). These are but a few examples of
traditions that have influenced the arts in CBR.

   Practitioners of arts-based and arts-informed methodologies are often perceived as "artists-and-teachers-and-researchers" (Springgay,
Irwin, & Kind, 2008, p. 87). In other words, as is the intention with this
book, the methodology and pedagogy are already deeply intertwined.
In teaching this course, I was therefore endeavouring to create a methodological and pedagogical space where research not only intersected

with art, but also with social change – through education, activism, leadership, and community development. The remainder of this chapter will focus on the strategies I used in an effort to create this space. Readers who are interested in gaining more of a background on the arts-based and arts-informed methodological traditions introduced above might consider reading such texts as those by Barndt (2006), Cahnmann-Taylor and Siegesmund (2008), Clover and Stalker (2007), Knowles and Cole (2008), McLean (2010), McLean and Kelly (2011), McNiff (1998), and Sullivan (2005), as well as special issues of the *International Journal of Lifelong Learning, 31:4* (2012); *Action Research, 9:1* (2011); *New Directions for Adult and Continuing Education, 116* (2007); *New Directions for Adult and Continuing Education, 107* (2005); *Convergence, 38:4* (2005); *Journal of Adult and Continuing Education, 16:2* (2010); and the *Alberta Journal of Educational Research, 48:3* (2002), all of which focus on the arts. These are but a few suggestions; the above authors and editors will lead you to many other influential works in this field.

Overview of the Course

Located within the Faculty of Education's Master's of Leadership Studies at the University of Victoria (UVic), this course was informed by theory from leadership, adult education, arts-based methodologies, and CBR. The bulk of classroom learning was comprised of hands-on workshops in a variety of art forms (further described below), but these were directly linked to theoretical debates on the topics of: aesthetic quality and symbolism; individual and collective art-production; methodological issues in research; the inherent values of both process and outcome; the role of the arts in society; the historic division between arts and crafts; communication via artist intention and audience perception; and healing, empowerment, social transformation, and collective resistance through the arts. To engage in this experiential *and* theoretical learning, I asked that all participants, myself included, come to class prepared to learn using our full bodies, all of our senses, our hearts, and our imaginations.

In my three offerings of this course, participants arrived with a range experiences in the arts, some with formal training, others with no training and little experience. Throughout the course we endeavoured to find the ways in which each one of us was *already* an artist (which will be further discussed in the section defining what constitutes art in the context of this class)[2] and encouraged one another to expand the limits of what was possible for our own creative expression by learning and teaching each other.

Creating the Learning Space

Working with the arts can become surprisingly personal, surprisingly quickly, and I have therefore learned to take the time necessary to create a space conducive to light-hearted play and open-hearted communication. I placed a strong emphasis on building community early on, introducing activities in which people could learn one other's names quickly and ensuring people were working with new learning partners on a regular basis to generate more one-on-one connections throughout the group. I asked that people take responsibility for their own well-being and I provided support or intervened where appropriate.

Facilitators and instructors often speak of creating a "safe" environment for learning, whether in community workshop settings or in classrooms. In recent years I have become increasingly wary of this idea – not because I inherently believe learning should be dangerous; rather, because I do not believe we can accurately assert that an environment is safe for another person. We can only name safety for ourselves. Individual personalities and histories of trauma, coupled with latent ideologies of racism, sexism, ableism, classism, and so on, mean that complex dynamics often emerge in group settings. Butterwick and Selman (2006), for example, discussed the politics of feminist coalitions and provided examples of how arts-based processes can support us in listening across differences. Although some facilitators are incredibly skilled at addressing such power inequities in a group setting, others are not, and we all have our own areas of learning or ignorance. In my experience as both a facilitator and participant in countless workshops, I have noticed that even when a facilitator has named an environment as safe, dynamics are often such that people express their concerns more privately, away from the larger group setting. Occasionally, they simply leave without explanation.

Let me be clear that as facilitators I believe that we can – and ought to – do our best to create a safe learning environment, that is, a space where people feel comfortable enough to share both their insights and their concerns, where respectful disagreement is not only tolerated, but encouraged, where mistakes are accepted as part of the learning process, where people feel welcomed for who they are, and secure in being themselves in spite of their and our imperfections and human idiosyncrasies. This ideal is not always possible in practice, however. As facilitators, then, we can remind other learners that simply because they or we feel safe does not mean that everyone does. We can also be mindful that we do not necessarily know the boundaries of one another's comfort zones and we certainly do not know the extent of one another's wounds.

As mentioned above, working with arts-based media can occasionally bring to the surface previously unknown, or unacknowledged insights. Although I – like many other classroom instructors – am not a trained counsellor and it is not my explicit intention to employ the arts as therapy in the classroom setting, at times the experience of working with the arts can nevertheless bring strong emotions into the learning space. This can be unexpected for some participants and particularly unsettling when one's expectation may have been to "have fun" while using the arts. In addition, because many people have been told that they can't sing, can't dance, can't draw, and so on, some (though, of course, not all) people feel quite vulnerable when expressing themselves creatively. For all of these reasons and more, I believe it is my responsibility as a facilitator to alert people to the possibility that strong, unexpected emotions can sometimes arise – although I do not suggest that this must or inevitably will happen in the context of the class. Facilitators who are new to arts-based practices would be well advised to prepare for this possibility (see Zingaro, 2009 for further discussion on this topic). It is useful to know what support services are available, for both participants and facilitators alike.

Somewhere along the way, I picked up three facilitator's guidelines that I find to be quite useful in setting the tone for learning: (1) take care of yourself, (2) respect others, and (3) assume positive intent. I will elaborate on what these mean to me below – and when I speak these in a group setting, I normally ask participants to share their own meanings if they have something to add.

To me, taking care of ourselves acknowledges that we are accountable for our own learning. This is not an effort to shirk responsibility as the instructor; rather, it is a simple reminder that although I have taken the time to design a thoughtful learning process, and will do my best to be flexible and sensitive to the needs and levels of energy in the group, I cannot read minds. Teachers have a certain amount of power in the classroom due to the nature of the position, but we are, after all, only human. If some aspect of the class is not working and I am clearly unaware of it, I need participants to tell me so that I can respond, within reason. Sometimes it is simply not possible to attend to the various interests in a classroom. In asking participants to take care of themselves, I am also clear that although I do encourage everyone to move beyond their own comfort zones, I do not make participation in all activities a *requirement*, nor do I ask people to explain or justify themselves for sitting out – especially when the activity involves physical contact with others, for example, theatre arts (see Cain, 2012, for more on the topic of required participation). This guideline also recognizes that adult learners have the capacity to take initiative to get what they need from the learning environment.

To me, the second guideline of respecting others is not only about common courtesy, but also about the nature of participation. I ask participants to keep in mind that participation does not mean overwhelming each other with all of our observations, questions, and reflections; we can choose which of these to share with others and which to keep to ourselves. Participation also implies a careful balance between listening to, acknowledging, and encouraging others, and likewise respecting when they choose to be silent. Patterns of participation tend to reveal themselves quite early in the class, but this guideline can help participants to develop and demonstrate self-awareness around their contributions to, and presence in, the group setting. This is particularly useful in intercultural settings, where the concept of respect can have multiple and at times contrasting interpretations.

Occasionally the issue of confidentiality arises when we speak of respect. Participants generally ask that people not repeat personal stories or identifying details outside the class, which is a fair request. However, because people will inevitably talk with each other about the activities experienced in class, I also ask that participants choose not to share private details that they would not want repeated elsewhere, which helps to ensure their own privacy.

The third guideline, assuming positive intent, encourages us to try not to take others' comments personally. In group settings, as in the rest of our lives, people occasionally make assumptions, speak from a place of ignorance, and unintentionally cause harm. As facilitators we have a responsibility to unpack such comments and attempt to mitigate the harmful effects, of course. However, rather than self-censor in an effort to avoid saying the wrong thing, working with the first two guidelines of respecting self and others, I encourage us all to seek clarification and approach such moments as opportunities for learning and growth.

In introducing these guidelines to the class, I asked people to spend a little time in pairs or small groups discussing the strategies they found worked well during group learning processes. We then reported these ideas back to the larger group and discussed their implications for the context of our own classroom. Because I often taught educators, people sometimes had their own preferred facilitation strategies. I found that this process of discussion gave people the opportunity to have the expertise they brought to the group heard and validated. Of course, I frequently learned new techniques from the participants as well. We did not record these ideas as formal agreements as some facilitators do, but they did provide a reference point in our collective consciousness as we moved forward.

Finally, because not everyone had been exposed to the participatory learning strategies I employed in these classrooms (particularly in the university context), to help set the tone, I occasionally provided a handout of resources related to stages of group development (Tuckman & Jensen, 1977), a critique of the Banking Model of education (Freire, 2003), an overview of participatory decision making (Kaner, 2001), and the experiential learning cycle (Kolb, 1984).

The points of discussion listed above were intended to help foster a welcoming learning space – one in which people could bump up against their learning edge through play and experimentation. The tone I describe above relates to ways of *being* in the classroom. To better understand ways of *doing* in the classroom, I will turn now to a discussion of the overall curriculum design.

Designing the Experience: The Spiral Model

A balanced relationship between reflection and action is the essence of praxis and central to learning and teaching CBR. It is also essential to what Arnold, Burke, James, Martin, and Thomas (1991) referred to as the "spiral design model" of experiential education: an iterative process for group consciousness-raising and action informed by theory and reflection. Arnold et al.'s spiral design model suggests that learning is an ongoing spiral, similar to Kolb's (1984) experiential learning cycle. This model teaches us that as facilitators of experiential learning processes, we can start by eliciting participants' experiences, look for patterns, then offer new information and theory. We can then support participants in practising new skills, planning for action, and experimenting with this action. The next phase of the spiral begins when we reflect on this collective action, add more theory, plan new actions, and so on through iterative cycles of action and reflection.

This course used the spiral model as its basic design (see Figure 13.1). On the first day of class, we spent significant time getting to know one another, through conversation as well as through theatre-based activities based on David Diamond's (2004, 2007) Theatre for Living techniques. In particular, I elicited participants' experiences with the arts (Step 1), as well as any patterns and themes in the preconceived ideas about what cultural leadership and social learning through the arts meant to them (Step 2). Building on these experiences, over the next 2 days of class, we then moved into an in-depth exploration of the course theory (Step 3). Each learner wrote a summary of one of the assigned readings, and we began teasing out the emerging themes and tensions in the literature. We then linked these emerging themes to people's experiences. With a grounding in the theory, we then moved into a series of arts-based skill-building workshops designed (Step 4) and facilitated (Step 5) by the participants. There was classroom time devoted to collectively reflecting on what we learned from each workshop: what worked well and what we could do differently in other contexts (Step 6). I will discuss these workshops in more depth below, but note that their key purpose was to provide an opportunity for experiential learning and a loop in the spiral of action and reflection.

While these workshops were taking place in the classroom context, learners were also documenting individual lessons learned in the more private context of creative learning journals. The journals supported learners in synthesizing lessons learned and also provided me with a window into their experiences, alerting me to any issues I needed to clarify more publicly and also allowing me to build an individual relationship with each participant. While some learners wrote in standard academic prose, others choose a different creative format for expressing themselves (examples below). When time, energy, and inspiration permitted, I endeavoured to reciprocate in kind by generating my own creative piece in response.

For example,[3] when one student created a snow sculpture as part of her learning journal, I printed off the black and white photograph she submitted and coloured the details in with pastels. She included an artist's statement expressing how it felt as if the sculpture came into

Steps in the Spiral Process

1. ***Start with participants' experience***
2. ***Reflection:*** *Look for patterns in experience and areas for learning*
3. ***Theory:*** *Expand knowledge with assigned readings and link to experience*
4. ***Planning:*** *Design in-class workshops*
5. ***Action:*** *Facilitate and experience workshops*
6. ***Reflection:*** *Discuss workshops in class; independently reflect in learning journals*
7. ***Theory:*** *Independently review literature beyond class materials*
8. ***Planning:*** *Write first draft of a proposal (to be refined in collaboration with supervisor)*
9. ***Action:*** *Conduct research or community-based project once the class ends*
10. ***Reflection:*** *Write final project to complete degree*
11. ***Ongoing learning***

Figure 13.1. Steps in the Spiral Process.

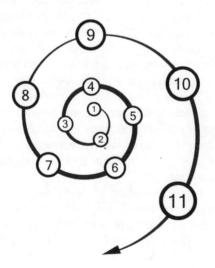

existence through her – she did not plan it in advance; she simply started building. In other conversations, she also revealed to me that she
was pregnant and was coming to terms with her identity as a mother.
Somehow creating the snow sculpture – a reclined, pregnant snow
woman – became a very powerful experience for this student. When I
added colour and form to the details of the pregnant snow-belly, I was
communicating a message (not using the written word) that I perceived
the power of new motherhood in the image she submitted. Her impression is that my circular drawings represented life or energy and
that together we created something even better that now had meaning
for both of us – and potentially for her daughter down the road (V.
Cortés, personal communication, 2 July 2012).

Another student submitted a set of boxes akin to Russian dolls, with
questions on each box asking what was inside us that we *don't know
we don't know* (akin to Joseph Luft and Harrington Ingham's Johari
Window, see, e.g., Luft, 1961) and that working with the arts could sometimes reveal. I returned the box with small trinkets representing a mix
of symbols based on lessons from learning about my own inner workings. I did not explain what they meant using words; I simply offered
the symbols in response to his questions.

A third student submitted two clay sculptures of people, and I returned one wearing glasses and another with a big heart – symbolizing
the dance between emotion and intellect we had been discussing in
class. This student often submitted her journal as a large scrapbook and
began leaving empty spaces where I could respond, in written words or
otherwise.

For me, these creative journals were an invitation to play and to communicate in ways I would not normally have communicated with my
students. If the examples seem vague or unintelligible to an outside
observer, perhaps it is because they were intended as private conversations in response to the students' creative learning journeys. The point
here is that these interactions represented a deeper connection between
the learners and me, using symbolism that was grounded in the moment and based on classroom conversations and whatever simple resources I had on hand during the time I was reading/marking/
engaging with the journals. What was interesting for me to observe was
the very possibility that the students' creative pieces inspired me to reply in kind. This suggests that creativity can be contagious; creativity
begets more creativity. I would normally read (or open) the journals
right after class, and throughout the week an idea would often

spontaneously arise in my mind about how to respond. Not all students submitted creative pieces such as these, but if they were challenging themselves to communicate beyond words, I tried to do so myself.

Aside from the journals, the class concluded with the participants designing a plan for action in their own communities. They drew on the lessons they learned experientially through the in-class workshops, as well as course theory and their own independent research (Step 7), to generate a proposal for a feasible arts-based process that could be implemented in their workplace or other community affiliation (Step 8). Not all learners were able to put this plan into action, but for many, the spiral of action and reflection continued beyond the scope of the classroom when this action plan turned into a proposal for their graduate research projects, which they carried out to complete the requirements of their degrees (Steps 9 and 10).

In-Class Workshop

The spiral design moved the learners through iterative cycles of theory and skills building, in-class practice and reflection. In this section I provide more details on one part of the spiral, the experiential workshops around which this course is built.

The in-class workshop served multiple learning purposes. It:

• Enabled participants to demonstrate their abilities to research and learn about an art form of interest and deepen their knowledge by teaching it to others.
• Provided an opportunity to practise facilitating an arts-based method.
• Encouraged cooperation and social learning through group work.
• Allowed participants to play and experiment with their abilities to communicate complex concepts and theories using a creative format.
• Finally, it enhanced participants' capacities to lead and learn through the arts.

Working in groups, the participants designed a workshop according to their prior skills and learning interests. Although not all participants who registered saw themselves as artists, all of the learners who chose to take this course were willing to experiment with creative, arts-based processes of some kind. The class then became a space where learners became teachers as they practised and honed their arts-based facilitation skills. The assignment criteria asked that they teach the rest of us about the benefits, challenges, history, and practice of the artistic medium the group selected, engage us in a hands-on learning experience using this artistic medium, and creatively communicate the theory and some key points of two required course readings that related to their workshop. This last point was significant, because I asked participants to not only teach us about a particular artistic medium – although that was of course an essential component of the workshop – but also to teach us concepts and theories *through* an artistic medium. I will discuss some examples of the arts-based media below, In the meantime, I will mention that participants have, for example, taken up Foucault's concept of "docile bodies" by bringing awareness to many people's discomfort with dance (drawing from Fremeaux & Ramsden, 2007), or provided insight into transformative learning and the "hero's journey" by creating an experiential journey with theatre (drawing from Dirkx, 1998; Mezirow, 1991; Campbell, 1968).

Different facilitators will use different techniques for teasing out the symbolic connections between the experiential activity and the theory or issue under investigation. The most simple is to organize the discussion according to the questions: "What?" "So what?" "Now what?" David Diamond uses the question "What's inside this for you?" (See Diamond, 2004; 2007; Etmanski, 2007b, for more information.) Other facilitators use the cycle of experience, analyse, generalize, and apply (based on Kolb, 1984). As I introduced the experiential learning model to the participants, I encouraged them – in their roles as facilitators – to move the group through a process of discussing what actually happened in the activity, to what it meant in the context of their lives or the topic under investigation, and, finally, to how this knowledge could inspire action. Experiential learning is closely linked to the spiral design discussed above, and in many ways it also reflects the purpose of action-oriented participatory research: What have we learned from our collective experience? How can we now take action? Just as I gradually began to understand how the arts could enhance processes of inquiry, through this activity, I had the privilege of observing learners come to a similar realization.

In addition, the groups were welcome to move beyond the walls of the classroom if this enhanced the message they were communicating. Several groups chose this option; for instance, one group led us in a circle painting workshop in the centre of campus. Because it was held in a public space, this workshop engaged passers-by, and helped to demonstrate how the arts "can break down resistance" to controversial topics (Branagan, 2005, p. 38) through a non-threatening process. In short, these experiential workshops helped us delve deeper into the theory, while simultaneously teaching hands-on skills for creative activism, facilitation, and community organizing.

Lessons Learned

Over the various iterations of this class, I learned that how I set up this workshop made a difference to its level of success. I will outline two key lessons learned in the sections below.

A Broad Definition of What Constitutes Art

First, I learned it is important that participants have a broad sense of what constitutes art before they begin preparing for this workshop. I recognize that this is a heated topic in some circles, but for the purpose of this workshop, I wanted participants to feel a sense of possibility and permission to play, rather than self-imposed restraint. In the literature related to arts-based and arts-informed methodologies, aesthetic quality or "artistry" is understood to have an impact on the effectiveness of social change processes, particularly when the final product is made publicly available (see Clover, this volume, or Becker, 1994; Clover & Stalker, 2007; Etmanski, 2007a; Marcuse, 1978). This has proven to be a fruitful discussion topic, and different classes have taken the conversation to various depths. I have also encouraged participants to develop their skills beyond this class if they are planning to undertake a larger CBR process in a particular artistic medium. However, in the space of the classroom, since the intention was not to develop in-depth skills in a particular artistic medium per se, but to cultivate our innate abilities to communicate through creative means (i.e., to find our inner artists), I placed priority on generating a range of possibilities.

During the period where we were making specific plans for the workshops, I asked the participants to collectively identify any artistic media with which they were familiar. We brainstormed ideas together, and once we got going, participants often listed dozens, if not hundreds of possibilities. Ideas ranged from the more formal media of painting, sculpture, dance, theatre, music, and literary arts (and all the traditions and variations therein), to practices traditionally understood or perhaps misunderstood as craft (see Carson, 2001; Freeland, 2001; or Lippard,

1984, for more information on the debate around art and craft) such as quilting, knitting, weaving, carving, pottery, and so on. They also listed more contemporary art forms such as zines, beat-boxing, slam poetry, digital arts, culinary arts, ice or sand sculptures, and much, *much* more. Certain individuals told me that they felt most like artists when they were kayaking or fly fishing. In response I told them that there were as many possibilities for this workshop as the participants' imaginations allowed. The only limitation was that they needed to address the assignment criteria listed above and stay within the time limit, which was approximately 1.5 hours, depending on the number of participants. (Although I value flexibility and recognize the Western obsession with time, in this particular instance I framed timing as a skill to develop in preparation for facilitating public workshops where time restrictions are imposed.)

As participants clustered into groups, they could choose one particular medium from this expansive list, or combine several. This assignment elicited an incredible breadth of activities from the learners, including an introduction to: Inuit art, soundscapes, pantomime, theatre, computer animation, photo elicitation, quilting, fabric zines, rhythm and song, instrument making (and the subsequent playing and recording of music made with those instruments), photography, murals and graffiti, poetry, storytelling through narrative Métissage, digital art, mask making, circle painting, and various mixed media creations (painting, collage, sculpture, and more). We recognized that we could only gain a superficial understanding of the chosen creative media within the timeframe, but the workshops always succeeded in moving our thinking in new directions and laying the ground for what was possible in the context of a larger community-based research, learning, development, or activist project. The levels of thoughtfulness and creativity the participants demonstrated, coupled with the fact that they collectively organized all the necessary art supplies, was consistently remarkable. This was especially so given that two of the three class offerings were short, 2-week summer intensives.

Group Work

The second key lesson learned relates to the preference of working in groups. During the first offering of the course, I asked that learners facilitate the workshop on their own, but in later offerings I shifted to a preference for group-based facilitation with an option for individual work. While group and/or individual presentations are common in graduate level classrooms, I noted that the requirement to facilitate *arts-based* content seemed to add a layer of vulnerability, complexity, and even competition that I had not observed in other courses. I have already touched on other measures taken to create a welcoming learning space, but in this particular class I found that group work provided an additional layer of security, where learners could share the risks (and the grades) and could unpack the experience with each other about the overall process of facilitation.

There were several motivations for encouraging participants to work in groups, and one is inherent to the values of participatory, community-based research practice in general: We improve our skill of working together by *practising* working together. Although group work can often be more time consuming, collaboration and teamwork are skills like all others that, of course, transfer to our lives beyond the classroom setting. This classroom provided another venue in which to refine those skills. Working together encouraged cooperation and social learning, which were essential to the topic we were investigating. As many educators already know, small group work also provides an opportunity for people to learn directly from one another's working styles, and quieter members of the class can often express themselves better in small groups than they can in the larger class.[4]

A more technical, but equally important reason to divide the class into groups related to scheduling logistics. With the in-class workshops taking an hour or more of class time, when participants worked in groups this opened up space to go into more depth with the class readings and the theory informing the practice, and also to go on site visits, engage with guest speakers, or watch a film as was appropriate. Additional activities have included a site visit to the *World Upside Down* exhibit (see Art Gallery of Greater Victoria, 2009), followed by a walk around the city to observe how "beauty is all around us." Classes have also included a singing workshop with jazz artist Wendell Clanton, a guest lecture from theatre artist Will Weigler (both of whom are Victoria based), and the screening of Banksy's (2010) film, *Exit through the Gift Shop*. Integrating these opportunities to interact with professional artists or their work added another layer to the conversation about how the arts can promote social change.

Conclusion: Teaching the Arts in CBR as an Act of Love

In this chapter, I have shared a few examples of how I endeavoured to create a space for learning and the primary classroom activity through which I taught the arts in CBR. I have demonstrated that not only did the in-class workshops teach hands-on skills, they also promoted the values of collaborative leadership and social learning. Like Bresler (2009), I offer these examples not as a prescription, but as an invitation for you as readers to take what is useful in generating your own pedagogical approaches. As I attempted to demonstrate in the classroom, there are as many possibilities for teaching the arts in CBR as facilitators' imaginations will allow.

At a 2011 conference on Qualitative Inquiry, I met a scholar and music educator who teaches arts-based research from a different perspective than I do (Bresler, 2007, 2008, 2009, 2013). She draws on an art appreciation approach and encourages prolonged engagement with artwork as a central tenet of her pedagogy. She asks learners to return to one piece of art over a series of sittings, each time considering in greater depth its form, texture, shape, colour, sound, and smell, as well as the interplay of the concrete with the abstract. She asks learners to consider the centrality of context – their own personal responses, the date and time, whether it is the first or second visit, and other contextual details related to who the artists are and the conditions under which they created the work. She asks learners to delve deeper into symbolic meanings, in particular for the works they "don't like" or to which they are not immediately drawn. In other words, she asks them to ponder whether we can learn to love the "other" by learning to love works we do not immediately like. She then asks them to consider: "What are the hindrances to empathy?" and "What don't we know that we don't want to know?" (Liora Bresler, personal communication, 21 May 2011 and 2 June 2012; see also Bresler, 2013).

To me, this last question is fundamental to the process of research. The spirit of inquiry asks that we move beyond our initial preconceived ideas about the world, into the more uncomfortable spaces where we simply don't know. These spaces of unknowing, or – perhaps more daunting – spaces where our current knowing may in fact be wrong, may be uncommon in the context of our everyday lives. Moreover, in this world full of suffering, we – as researchers, educators, and activists – can certainly benefit from strategies for gaining truly novel insights on the complex challenges we seek to address through the practice of community-based research. The arts, I know from my own experience, offer a way into these challenges that can take us out of our habitual ways of thinking, doing, knowing, and being in the world. They offer us ways to not only engage with the "other," but ways to perhaps learn greater empathy, even love.

This book is about learning and teaching community-based research. Other contributors have highlighted the central importance of decolonizing practice and knowledge democracy in the context of teaching CBR (see, e.g., in this volume: Clover, Corntassel & Gaudry, Hall, Marshall et al., Mukwa Musayett et al., or Williams et al.) and this chapter does so as well. In promoting the arts as a way of knowing, this chapter adds an assertion that inquiry through the arts can create a space to honour the whole person and all the senses in the classroom. When facilitated skilfully, learning through the arts in university classrooms can become an act of love in that it helps us to develop greater compassion for one other, as well as deeper self-knowledge. In an academic culture still dominated by dualism, rationality, and competition, this is no small feat.

Part V

Moving Forward:
Productive Tensions and Persistent
Challenges of Learning, Teaching,
and Assessing CBR in Universities

14 "But how do I put this dream catcher into my teaching dossier?" Learnings and Teachings from One Faculty Member's Tenure Experience of Documenting Community-Based Teaching and Learning

EILEEN ANTONE AND TERESA DAWSON

It is widely acknowledged that, for faculty members, one of the most challenging aspects of teaching and learning community-based research is dealing with how their work will be assessed, valued, and rewarded by the established tenure and promotion guidelines of their institution. This is true even in institutions that have adopted the teaching dossier[1] as the main means of assessing teaching, with the intention of broadening the range and scope of teaching and learning activities that will be "counted"; and it is particularly true for Aboriginal faculty members, for whom almost every aspect of the process may be alienating and contrary to their belief systems. In this chapter, we explore the challenge of maintaining an Aboriginal voice and identity while at the same time creating a teaching dossier that complies sufficiently with teaching assessment and tenure guidelines to achieve the crucial goal of retaining Aboriginal faculty, and hence diversifying our institutions of higher education from within. What makes someone qualified to be a teacher in a community context? What "measures" or "data" can we use to determine effective teaching, including the effective teaching and learning of community-based research? What is valued and what is valuable? How is value recognized and appreciated? How do I "translate" my data and their significance? How can others understand the meaning of my "data" on effective teaching? We hope that the lessons learned from these questions will assist other faculty members, both Aboriginal and non-Aboriginal, whose life's work is in their communities to stay in our institutions of higher education and thus to bring about change.

Beginning Together

To begin our work, it is necessary that we share our respective roles as collaborators in this project, which seeks to advocate the valuing of faculty work in a way that is grounded in a holistic – and wholistic – view of that work as not separated from the community in which it takes place. This means, in our particular case, the valuing of the work of Aboriginal faculty members in such a way as to be deeply rooted in the traditions of the Aboriginal people from which they come. As we work together, we try to promote and show in our actions the principle of equality.

In this chapter, which is our story together, we are also attempting to emulate the oral traditions of Aboriginal teachers by trying to capture the experience of the storytelling in a written narrative. It is perhaps easiest to understand how we are speaking if readers imagine us standing before them. Sometimes we each individually speak directly to the reader; sometimes we introduce each other to the reader; and sometimes we speak respectfully about each other while the other person is listening. In this way, we alternate between the first and third person. We have tried to indicate clearly through headings and written cues which circumstance is the case for each section, but the changes in voice are there deliberately to emulate the storytelling process that might typically occur in a teaching circle. In this tradition what the reader hears in the story is not prescribed. The reader should be able to take from the story what he or she needs.

At the start of our journey together, we begin with guiding prayers that reflect our very different contexts but that for both of us bring to bear the meaning and the power of the connection to our history that we need to help us with our work. When we first met, our guiding words were not spoken together. Now they are.

Teresa's Introduction of Eileen

Eileen is a member of the Onyota'a:ka people at Oneida Nation of the Thames and belongs to the Turtle Clan. She is a professor emeritus from the University of Toronto, where she worked for many years as an Aboriginal educator specializing in adult literacy as it concerns Aboriginal people. My understanding of her interest in this project is that she achieved tenure in 2004 at the University of Toronto using a teaching dossier that was *wholistic* in its approach. She has taught me that reflecting on this process is itself a chance for teaching and learning. It is my pleasure to introduce Eileen, who will give us the Thanksgiving Address to help us with our work.

Eileen's Guiding Words for This Work

In keeping with the cultural traditions of the Hotinoshoni, it is important we start with Kanuhelatuksla – words that come before all else. These words are called *Tetwanuhelat'*, the Thanksgiving Address. Our Elders tell us that whenever we meet for any reason we offer prayers of thanksgiving to the Creator and all of creation. And so it will be in our minds.

Before we do anything else we bring our minds together as one and give thanks for one another. Let it be so in our minds.

We give thanks to and for Mother Earth as she brings and sustains life for all of Creation. Let it be so in our minds.

We are thankful for all the fruits that grow on Mother Earth, and especially the strawberry the first fruit of the season referred to as the heart berry. For the medicines from all of plant life that are made from the smallest grasses to the tallest trees. We give thanks for the tobacco we use to send our prayers to the Creator. For all the different trees, and especially the maple that brings to us its sweet juice as the plant world comes to life again in the spring. Let it be so in our minds.

We give thanks to and for all the different kinds of animals that help sustain our lives. We are thankful for the smallest crawlers to the largest four legged that each has a place in the ecosystem. Let it be so in our minds.

We give thanks to and for all the different birds that bring us joy and music. Each has a different song they share with us. We are also thankful for the beauty they bring with their many different colours and for the responsibility they have for spreading seeds to the various areas of the earth. Let it be so in our minds.

We give thanks to and for the waters found in the lakes, rivers, and streams great and small. Without water there would be no life. We also give thanks for the fish that continue to keep the waters clean for us. Let it be so in our minds.

We give thanks that each one of these creations continues to carry out their duties and responsibilities that were given to them by the Creator.

We give thanks for the forces that work together with the earth, our grandfathers the thunders, who bring the rain to renew the earth. For our eldest brother the sun, who gives us light and warmth. For our grandmother moon, who regulates the waters and all of the life cycles on the earth. For the stars that are our relatives, who beautify the sky and continue to guide us in our yearly cycles for hunting, planting, and harvesting. Let it be so in our minds.

We give thanks to and for the four messengers who give us guidance and continue to carry out their duties and responsibilities. Let it be so in our minds.

We give thanks for the messengers who remind us of the way to a wholesome life, by observing our traditions and our ceremonies.

We bring together our minds and give thanks to the Creator of all, for it is the Creator that has brought us together as one. So let it be in our minds. **Ya wa ko.**

Eileen's Introduction of Teresa

Teresa was born in Spain, grew up in England, and immigrated to Ontario in 1989. She has also lived and worked in the United States. In 2000, she returned to Ontario and began working at the University of Toronto, where we met. She now works at the University of Victoria, which is situated in the Coast Salish and Strait Salish territories where she has been a visitor for 6 years. My understanding is that her interest in this project is as an educational developer for over 20 years. In this role, Teresa has supported many faculty members from diverse backgrounds in achieving tenure, using teaching dossiers as an advocacy document to present their integrated scholarly identity. Teresa would you like to add your thoughts here as we start our work?

Teresa's Reflective Words for This Work

The Thanksgiving Prayer from Eileen is the context in which we work together. From my own tradition, I offer the opening lines from William Blake's poem, "Auguries of innocence":

To see a world in a grain of sand
And a heaven in a wild flower,
Hold infinity in the palm of your hand
And eternity in an hour.   – William Blake

For me, this poem evokes and supports a similar wholism with nature and all things to that which is spoken in the Thanksgiving Address. More specifically to this work, it also captures the extraordinary task of trying to portray the intense complexity and enormity of a lifetime of faculty work in a scholarly or teaching dossier "snapshot," which is commonly what we try to do when we make the case for tenure. It also emphasizes the intense meaning that some small, apparently ordinary, daily object may hold for each of us, and, hence, its representational potential in terms of documenting value that others can see and hear.

Now, I would like to ask Eileen to please tell us her story as it relates to this work.

Eileen's Story

In 1999, when I applied for the joint Transitional Year Program (TYP) / Ontario Institute for Studies in Education (OISE) tenure-stream position at the University of Toronto, I had no idea what the tenure process was. In my mind, the TYP hired me and, therefore, I reported to the director of that program, and she was the one that received my Annual Activity Reports. I didn't understand to get a tenure you had to have a home department. Adult Education and Counselling Psychology at OISE was my home department. In 2000, when I was asked by the chair of Adult Education and Counselling Psychology to submit my Annual Activity Report I didn't realize that this was already part of the tenure process and that I was being evaluated to be able to continue my contract in the tenure-stream process. My contract continued, and in the spring of 2003 I was reminded that I needed to get my tenure case together to be submitted in the fall. The director of the Transitional Year Program was an excellent mentor, and so when it was time to be working on my teaching dossier, she asked me if I would be willing to work with the University of Toronto's "expert" on teaching portfolios. Working with an "expert" was a pretty scary idea, because then this expert would find out that I didn't know anything about teaching at a university and that maybe I was doing everything wrong. But I thought if the director thinks this expert will be able to help me develop my teaching portfolio then I am willing to get help.

The director called Teresa, Teresa called me, and we set up an appointment to meet in my TYP office.

Now, Teresa, please tell us your story as it relates to this work.

Teresa's Story

I first met Eileen when she came to give a closing plenary at a teaching and learning for diversity conference we were organizing at the University of Toronto Scarborough campus (UTSC) in 2002. I recall the beautiful words she spoke, drawing on the four directions, laying the foundation for the learning that was to be taken back into each community represented at the conference. I remember the smudge ceremony and its healing powers and the intense dismay of hitting my first of many institutional "walls," as I had to work so hard behind the scenes to convince the health and safety office to allow us to have the ceremony indoors in strong defiance of the fire regulations.

A few months later, I received a call from the director of the Transitional Year Program (TYP) at the "downtown" (main) campus, with whom I had worked in other contexts asking if I could assist one of their faculty members in putting together her teaching dossier for tenure. That faculty member turned out to be Eileen. Imagine my trepidation at this request. Eileen was, and is, an esteemed educator in her community. She was, and is, an extraordinary teacher. What could I possibly contribute? Yet, the more I thought about it, the more I realized that the university guidelines for the putting together of a teaching dossier for tenure, in which I happened to have some expertise, just would not "work" for Eileen's story. A stark reality emerged. There was no question that conceptually Eileen should be granted tenure, with all that that implies in the academy for leadership in teaching and learning. Her wisdom in teaching is far beyond anything many of us can aspire to; her impact on the lives of others was and is transformative. Yet, her story was somehow not fitting into the prescribed boxes of the tenure process, the individualized pieces and laundry lists of items required. I did not have much hope of being able to "help," but I was curious to see how these two worlds might come together.

I made an appointment to go and visit Eileen in her downtown office. I recall being breathless when I had finished climbing the stairs to eaves of the TYP house on St. George Street, where her office was. Eileen ushered me into a chair and waited patiently.

Once I got my breath back, I began naively to talk of the standard methods of creating teaching dossiers. I outlined the classic approaches

I had developed over a number of years for supporting faculty members, including generating claims to teaching effectiveness and how to support these with evidence and data. After some time of this, Eileen showed me something hanging on her wall. It was a beautiful dream catcher made for her by one of her students. What I saw initially was a piece of art. Later I realized this was the most profound evidence of Eileen's teachings, of the learning of the student, and of the impact she had had.

Her disarming question to me that day was: "so how do I put this dream catcher into my teaching dossier?" I missed the meaning of course. I thought she could put a picture of it in to the dossier – problem solved! I totally missed the fact that the reader would not be able to "read" its meaning. This was the highest tribute possible to Eileen's teaching – far more profound than any student evaluation number would ever be.

To this day, I struggle with the answer to that question and others like it. "How do people who do not understand my culture or my communit(ies) *read* (or *hear* in oral traditions) the evidence of my value as a teacher or learner?"

And so began my learning with Eileen. We talked of the nature of learning and teaching, the inseparability of the two, the responsibility to students once a connection is made that never goes away. We talked about the nature of evidence for the impact of teaching. We talked about where learning happens. We talked about how hard it is for any student to learn when they are afraid.

In the end, of course, it was Eileen who found the answers to the intractable "square peg in the round hole" university tenure documentation questions. What she produced was one of the most beautiful pieces of wholistic writing I have ever seen (itself a compromise in an oral tradition) that rose far above the tenure requirements and, I would suggest, in a fascinating inversion of power relations, challenged its assessors. For those of us who read teaching dossier and philosophy statements on a regular basis, her story leaves the usual check boxes far behind. What I realized was that, in her hands, the teaching dossier narrative became an educational tool for modelling or demonstrating teaching and learning in community. The story, and the way of telling it, educated the reader in ways of knowing and learning and teaching so expertly, so clearly, that I was struck with a profound understanding I had previously lacked.

How was this teaching achieved? From my perspective Eileen did what all the best teachers do, she started with the learner and with their current level of understanding. She made compromises on some things. In other places, she challenged the reader to think differently and to understand what was necessary. However, in key areas, I could see there could be no compromise – beginning with the prayer or creation story is one example – and there she held firm.

Overall, I was left with the feeling that Eileen's story offered such important teachings for all of us who struggle to have the teaching and learning of any kind of community work valued by academia, that it should be told (in the Western tradition "it should be published"). Essentially, this is what Eileen has graciously agreed to do in sharing threads of this story with us and allowing me to reflect on our journey together.

Reviewing Current Approaches to Valuing Diverse Ways of Teaching and Learning in the Academy

Teresa's Reflections on the Current Context of Faculty Teaching Assessment

Over the past 25 years, best practices in university teaching assessment have evolved considerably from the "one number derived from course evaluation scores" approach (Shore, Foster, Knapper, Nadeau, Neill, & Sim, 1986; Shulman, 1988; Edgerton, Hutchings, & Quinlan, 1991). Many universities now recognize teaching dossiers, which triangulate multiple sources of information on the teacher's work, as a fairer method of assessment that attempts to acknowledge the diversity of teaching styles and student needs (see, e.g., the University of Victoria's teaching assessment guidelines: Mateer & Dawson, 2009). Peter Seldin's international work has been highly influential in this regard (Seldin 1991, 1993). His work has also been translated into many practical guides and workbooks to assist faculty members in putting together their own teaching dossiers to make the case for tenure (see for example Dawson, 2007) and it has been argued that the use of teaching dossiers, because they allow for much broader definitions of teaching and learning, do promote diversity in the academy (Dawson & Guest, 2003). Yet, perhaps ironically, even these approaches retain many of the inherent assumptions and tensions of the university system that can be so alienating for those from other traditions, such as Aboriginal faculty. For example, the typical approach of creating a teaching dossiers for tenure that suggests colleagues organize their narrative into an argument comprised of: "claims," "data to support those claims," and then "concrete curricular examples to illustrate their depth and breadth" (see, e.g., Dawson, 2007) is inherently fraught with Western assumptions, none the least of which is the separation of the work life into discrete component parts.

Eileen's Reflections on the Current Context of Faculty Teaching Assessment

By contrast, Aboriginal teachings suggest that teaching and learning are not separated into discrete component parts but that teaching and learning are part of the relationships that are part of everyday living. Cajete (1994), an Aboriginal educator from the southwest states:

> By watching, listening, experiencing, and participating everyone learned what it was to be one of the People, and how to survive in community with others. Learning how to care for one's self and others, learning relationship between people and other things, learning the customs, traditions, and values of a community: all of these understandings and more were the daily course of Indigenous education. (p. 176)

Aboriginal people continue to strive for cultural wholeness as they seek ways to carry on their nations with traditional knowledge and values. Archibald (1995) states:

> First Nations people traditionally adopted a holistic approach to education. Principles of spiritual, physical, and emotional growth, as well as economic and physical survival skills, were developed in each individual to ensure eventual family and village survival. Certain learning specialties in these areas were emphasized, including independence, self-reliance, observation, discovery, empirical practicality, and respect for nature. (p. 289)

I found through my thesis work (Antone, 1997) that the Aboriginal voice is lifted up when traditional knowledge and values are incorporated into the education of the Native students. Therefore, I used traditional knowledge and values with the students I worked with at the University of Toronto, and I was able to give voice to this in my teaching dossier.

I found (Antone, 2000) that to be in balance one must have a positive self-identity. The past school system did not promote a positive identity for our people. My work indicates that a positive self-identity is imperative for academic success. At that time I wrote, "as stated earlier my voice had become very muted and silenced during my journey through the elementary and secondary school system. Only in the recent years have I been able to develop and re-establish my voice as an Onyota'a:ka." Although when building the tenure case one has to keep in mind the readers of the file, one also has to be true to oneself in the kind of work that is required of an Aboriginal faculty member.

Documenting the Effectiveness of Learning and Teaching CBR: Examples from a Wholistic Tenure Dossier

I knew what was required in the Western perspective where I received my training, but what about the Aboriginal perspective?
— Antone (2003b, p. 13)

   In this section, we use examples from Eileen's writing of her (previously private and unpublished) tenure dossier narrative to illustrate how she created a wholistic tenure dossier, which succeeded in maintaining her identity and voice while complying with university teaching assessment requirements. We first define wholism and then outline four sets of significant challenges to a holistic approach presented by current faculty teaching assessment methods. These challenges include the apparent need to: be objective; separate out teaching, research, and service; hold narrow definitions of teaching and its methods; and address a lack of understanding around the cultural context of what constitutes evidence of teaching effectiveness. For each, Teresa outlines our analysis of the dilemma that needed to be resolved and then Eileen follows this with a specific example (quoted from her dossier narrative) of how she addressed each issue (all page references in this section refer to Antone, 2003b). While we describe the various dilemmas and the responses in terms of Aboriginal education here, the implications are varied and, we hope, inspiring for anyone who works in community and wants their work to be valued in this light.

Defining Wholism

In Aboriginal teachings, teaching and learning are wholistic. They cannot be separated from community or history, and certainly not from context, and the relationship between teacher and learner is blurred. In working together, we use Eileen's definition of "wholistic" which she described in the following way (Antone, 2003b):

> "Wholistic" describes the Aboriginal philosophy in which "everything is related" by virtue of shared origins. The human being is considered an entire whole mentally, physically, spiritually, and emotionally as an individual, with one's family and extended family, one's people, and with the cosmos in sacred relationships. This is distinct from a "holistic" philosophy in which the term "related" is taken as meaning "all things are interconnected" by virtue of sharing an environment in which action leads to a type of "domino effect" in a secular world. (p. 18)

For example, Eileen explains this definition in the context of Adult Literacy,

> Aboriginal Literacy in its wholistic aspect as distinct from mainstream literacy in that it reflects Aboriginal worldviews in two particular ways. These are: (a) the intergenerational/multigenerational expression of Aboriginal Literacy that includes how it extends to all areas of life; and (b) the process in which teachers become learners and learners become teachers. (p. 20)

Further,

> Being literate in terms of Aboriginal Literacy is more than reading, numeracy and writing towards gaining access to mainstream employment ... Being literate is about resymbolizing and reinterpreting past experience, while at the same time honouring traditional values. Being literate is about living these values in contemporary times. Being literate is about visioning a future in which an Aboriginal way of being will continue to thrive. Meaningful Aboriginal literacy will develop and find expression in everything that is done. (p. 20)

The Issue of Objectivity and the Need to Embed Experience in Context

The first challenge we faced in thinking about the presentation of Eileen's dossier narrative was that the current prescribed methods of presenting a tenure case, with the embedded assumptions around striving for objective analysis, encourage by their very nature a distancing of the writer from her or his own community, a silencing of the context of his or her voice in the pursuit of external validation. Yet, Aboriginal teachings tell us it is often the context itself that provides much of the potential appreciation for the value of a teacher's work. How can the Western assumption (that the writer should distance her/himself from her or his context as much as possible) be challenged, particularly when the power relation is such that much rides on apparently employing the methods the assessment committee expects?

To resolve this issue, Eileen began her tenure case file with an explanation of the alternative method she would be using (storytelling) to write her narrative and with an immediate example to illustrate the value of that methodology. This contextual approach offered readers of the document the opportunity to learn from the beginning of their journey through the text and presented them with a different path (one that valued context) in such a way that they would be enticed to follow it:

Although I have been teaching and researching in my present position for the last four years, I have many years of experience with both of these activities. Throughout this document I will be illustrating my teaching and researching philosophy through the use of story. My earliest memory of having the responsibility of a class was when I was in grade seven. This was the year that Prime Minister Diefenbaker came on an official visit to the Mount Elgin Indian Day School where I attended. We were all excited about this visit, as this was 1960 – the year Aboriginal people finally got the vote in federal elections.

The Oneida Brass Band was always the star attraction at major community events, and now it was going to play for the Prime Minister of Canada. There was one problem, however: the bass sousaphone player had an important school test the same morning as this official visit, and it was to be taken at London Central Collegiate High School. The school principal decided the grade four teacher would make the round trip to London Central Collegiate High School to pick up the bass sousaphone player, but this left the grade four class without a teacher. Imagine my shock when the principal asked for me to be excused from my lesson so that I could cover the grade four class. My assignment was to do the weekly spelling lesson with them. I thoroughly enjoyed the responsibility and the children were very respectful of my presence in the classroom. The day ended well: the teacher got back to take her class to see the Prime Minister; the Oneida Brass Band played beautifully; and I got to shake hands with the Prime Minister of Canada.

At the time I did not realize this would be the beginning of a life-long career journey in the field of education. (pp. 3–4)

The Issue of Separating Teaching, Learning, Research, and Service Duties and the Need to Present Them Wholistically

Tenure guidelines usually ask for documentation of teaching, research, and service to community in separate sections. Yet, teaching, learning, and research are often inseparable in community contexts and cannot be documented separately. Therefore, Aboriginal faculty members frequently find the process of applying for tenure extremely alienating, even to the point of silencing.

How can one's voice be maintained as a faculty member in this situation? We contend that in writing a tenure narrative it is possible to resist "losing one's voice." For example, Eileen stated,

> I have been able to develop and maintain a wholistic philosophy, which enables me to bring together the work I am involved in. Through this work I have come to a better understanding of the Aboriginal way of life and its importance in connecting me to both the Aboriginal and non-Aboriginal worlds. The work that I do has been acknowledged in both the Aboriginal and non-Aboriginal communities and there is great overlap whether it is teaching, research, or community service. This early work has enabled me to practice Aboriginal epistemology in my present position. (p. 8)

Eileen demonstrated this approach in her discussions of the Aboriginal Adult Literacy Project in Ontario. While acknowledging the Western scholarly world of having to publish and obtain grants successfully and documenting these (achievements that assessors within the university are looking for to check off), it was important to express the main focus of the study outcomes in terms of the aspects of wholistic teaching, learning, research, and service that would be valued by the Aboriginal community.

> Data from this project indicate Aboriginal Literacy constitutes a re-expression of Aboriginal knowledge in contemporary terms ... The understanding is that Aboriginal languages reflect and hold the key to maintaining Aboriginal culture and identity in Canadian cultural context. Aboriginal literacy facilitates the development of self-determination, affirmation,

achievement and sense of purpose. In Aboriginal ways, literacy begins with orality and the traditional values found in stories.

As the Aboriginal Peoples recognized Aboriginal literacy as an approach to empowerment, a concerted effort was made to explore and build connections between Aboriginal literacy, healing, community development and self-determination. Aboriginal practitioners who are revitalizing Aboriginal Literacy are effecting a personal transformation from subjugation to self-empowerment and also supporting the achievement of harmonious, reciprocal relationships between Aboriginal and non-Aboriginal peoples and cultures. Aboriginal Literacy is inclusive of English, French and Deaf streams. As we were travelling and speaking at various conferences, French-speaking Aboriginal people approached us asking for the information in the French language. This was an impetus too for us to have a brief summary of the symposium translated and printed in the French language. After many hours of searching we found an Aboriginal translator for the abstracts who could keep the voice of the Aboriginal presenters.

Culture, tradition, language and ways of knowing are all interconnected; in Aboriginal Literacy, where these are described according to the Medicine Wheel, or other cultural symbols, practitioners and learners are able to balance these aspects of their lives when there is harmony. (pp. 17–18)

As one effective resolution of this issue, we would argue for faculty presenting an integrated *tenure* dossier. That is, we suggest *not* presenting the component parts of a tenure file as it is often requested – the teaching dossier, research CV, and so on – but rather explicitly presenting a wholistic tenure dossier that integrates all aspects of a faculty member's work. This was something Eileen explicitly chose to do. For example, she began the *research* section of her dossier by *teaching* her reader about terminology (p. 13), began her *teaching* section by referring to her scholarship, and began her "service" section by referring to contributions to teaching and scholarship (p. 22). In this way it was possible to acknowledge the boxes and boundaries that were in place while at the same time making it clear that they are *mis*placed.

This can result in some important teaching and learning opportunities as shown in the following experience:

One of the highlights of my Wahahi:o participation was at the installation of Robert Birgeneau as the 14th President of the University of Toronto. The music director of this event contacted me to invite the Wahahi:o drumming group to participate in this event. The initial contact asked if we would participate as part of the drumming groups that would be located outside the building when the President came out. During the email exchange I proposed that since "Toronto" meaning "meeting place" was the traditional territory of the Iroquois and Ojibway that both of these drums should be involved in welcoming the President to this territory. The Iroquois Wahahi:o drumming and singing group escorted Robert J. Birgeneau into Convocation Hall up to his seat on the stage and the Ojibway Seventh Fire Youth Spirit Drum Group sang an honour song for the President at the installation ceremony.

The Issue of Defining the Nature of Teaching Work, and Its Methods and the Need to Broaden These Definitions to Be More Inclusive

Teaching is commonly very narrowly defined in university teaching guidelines and assessment policies. It has a directionality (teacher to student), it implies fact transmission devoid of context, it has prescribed methods, and it is assumed to happen in a classroom (or virtual classroom). Yet, much of what is seen as valuable in traditional Aboriginal (and other community based) teaching has little to do with isolated facts, is not acquired by lecturing, begins with the student not the teacher, and does not take place in a classroom. This essentially puts much teaching and learning of community-based research – Aboriginal or otherwise – outside the realm of what higher education institutions value, thereby often being seen as "extra" to their "real" work. This can cause enormous strain on those doing this kind of work, undermining their ability to succeed.

Much of a faculty member's ability to respond to this dilemma pertains to his or her skill in making a strong case for much broader definitions of teaching and learning. For example, Eileen demonstrated her ability to argue for wholistic teaching methods by first connecting to "what is expected," to use the language and phrases of the assessment committee where necessary (serving as a translator between instructional worlds):

This (classroom teaching) work is based on a traditional lecture style using overheads to visualize the Medicine Wheel teachings. The students become involved through the initial activity of brainstorming the concepts of Indian, Native, First Nations, and Aboriginal. (p. 10)

She also pushed the boundaries of her reader's understanding by referring to her use of purely Aboriginal teaching methods such as the use
of sewing circles to instruct in Aboriginal teachings (p. 7).

Finally, she emphasized the utility, indeed the necessity, of bringing
the two views about teaching methodology together by illustrating
how her wholistic methodology can apply and play out in a university
setting.

> In my teaching I base my methodology in Aboriginal epistemology. I
> believe that learning takes place through observing, listening and doing;
> therefore, I encourage all of the students to be involved in a participa-
> tory effort through sharing circles and reflection circles. We begin our
> class time with the traditional Thanksgiving Address to bring our minds
> together as we focus on the issues presented in the class. My philosophy
> is that we are all teachers and we are all learners, and it is for that reason
> that I expect the students to actively contribute to the learning process and
> integrate their learning needs into the course work.
>
> As a faculty advisor at both TYP and Adult Education/OISE, the stu-
> dents come to me seeking both academic and non-academic interaction.
> Listening and reflecting is what I do in many of these situations. In many
> cases both Native and non-Native students come to my office to have a
> smudge, to regroup, and center on the class work that is before them.
> Other times they have many personal issues to deal with before they can
> get on with the academic work. At these times I am able to listen to them
> and then make suggestions based on the oral teachings of the Elders that
> I have encountered in my journey. Other times I might have to contact the
> Aboriginal community to make arrangements for an Elder come in. This
> is why it is extremely important that I continue to be involved with the
> Aboriginal community of Toronto.

The Issue of the Nature of Evidence for Effective Teaching and the Need to Understand Its Cultural Meaning

Often tenure committees will privilege quantitative measures over
qualitative ones when considering evidence of faculty teaching productivity. They may literally equate "teaching accomplished" with "numbers of courses taught" or even "the passage of time"– a certain amount
of "delivered" lecture material in a specified 3-hour block for 12 weeks.
Similarly, there is often a heavy emphasis placed on student ratings of

instruction that are administered directly after the course is over and produce quantitative results. Yet, the most powerful evidence of effective teachings in Aboriginal (and other) community settings is rarely numerical and often not even literally "recognizable" to those conducting assessment at the university, such as the dream catcher in our story. As a result, it is often harder to be successful at getting one's faculty teaching and learning work recognized, rewarded and valued if one participates in community-based teaching and learning.

Eileen employed several effective strategies to deal with this issue. Most involved using historical knowledge of the likely understandings and assumptions the reader might bring and taking the time to explain what might otherwise be unchallenged misconceptions. For example, where tenure requirements asked for the list of courses taught or sample syllabi, Eileen decided it was not sufficient to simply provide a list and say they were taught "wholistically." She was aware enough of her reader to know that he or she might read "wholistic" as "holistic" (or "integrated") and miss the cultural meaning. Instead, she carefully described the courses to show how impossible it is to separate students from their context in the teaching and learning process – not just the immediate context but the long historical one that reaches far back to the ancestors and forward to what may come after:

> A second course that I offered at OISE/UT in the fall of 2003 is called AEC1180F Aboriginal World Views: Implications for Education. In this course, students study some of the philosophical views shared in Aboriginal thought that honours the diversity of identities, culture and language, and geographic locations. Recent literature that highlights culturally appropriate and culturally based Aboriginal education grounded in Aboriginal knowledge and processes gives foundation to this course. Central to understanding Aboriginal World Views is the importance of drawing from and working with traditional wisdom of oral traditions, Elders' knowledge, and cultural symbols that reflect "teachings" (philosophies). Likewise students learn that critical to this process is placing this understanding in the context of Aboriginal Peoples' experiences with colonialism, oppression, and struggles for self-determination, in the past and present. This course promotes an understanding and appreciation of Aboriginal knowings and explores strategies for integrating this knowledge into the work of educators. Students are encouraged to apply relevant knowledge to their own research. (p. 10)

Similarly, when introducing less familiar, but often much more meaningful, pieces of evidence of effective teaching not typically listed in teaching assessment guidelines or lists of criteria and evidence, contextual explanation seemed essential. For example, Eileen offered evidence that, to her, connected directly to Aboriginal teachings:

> To show their appreciation for the work that I do some of the students have given me gifts of symbols that are significant to them (i.e., Candles, Dream catchers, sweetgrass, Tobacco, Sage). (p. 12)

However, given the audience, it was not sufficient to document these items – they had to be explained in terms of their cultural significance, and this can be challenging. For example, "How do I put a dream catcher into my teaching dossier?" is not a simple logistical question, as Teresa had initially thought. The "how" is in the sense of "how in such a way that people who see it understand its meaning(s)" (what it says about me and the impact I have had) and connections? Many traditional items need to be held by community members and touched and shared to be understood. That is very hard to convey or do in a written document, even one with images, because the experience of the item or gift is missing.

With regard to teaching productivity, Eileen tried to educate her readers by encouraging them to ask different questions that lead to broader and much more inclusive concepts of impact. Instead of asking about numbers of students, one might ask instead: What was your connection with your students? How did your stories intersect? Did you walk across the stage with them at graduation, or across campus to take them and show them something they needed? Did you sit and sew with them? What did they teach you? In essence, when do a teacher's duties and responsibilities end – indeed, can they end?

By simply describing the broad continuum of her duties and responsibilities as a teacher, as she sees them, Eileen conveyed this crucial point:

> As part of my TYP mentoring experience I also work with the first year students who have left TYP and are starting their undergraduate work at one of the colleges in Arts and Science. As well as working with these students on their academic work I also help them connect with services and people in their colleges so they will be able to gain comfort in their new place of study. For instance, sometimes I have to go with them to show

them how to access journals or I connect them with the librarian who will then show them how to access information. Other times I remind them that there is a writing lab they can use to help with their papers when I am not immediately available. If they are experiencing funding problems I advise them to contact the registrar who is familiar with funding bodies and how to access them. Many times they just need someone to listen to them and in their own reflection of the situation they find answers they need in order to continue on their path. (p. 11)

Looking to the Future: Keep Moving Forward ...

Eileen's Closing Thoughts

As Art Solomon (1990), a traditional teacher, states, "The traditional way of education was by example and experience and by storytelling" (p. 79), and as I reflect back on this experience of finding voice, I think of the Hotinoshoni Creation story I heard many times as a child.

> This story begins in another world, a sky world. It is a story of a woman who fell from the sky world. As she was falling the beings that lived in the water below marvelled at this strange being that was floating down to their world. On further inspection they determined that she would not be able to survive in their world, as she did not possess the appropriate appendages, body covering or breathing capabilities for water survival. They deliberated among themselves as to the best course of action. They decided that they must help her survive. So as they discussed the situation it became apparent that this being would need a place to land. The giant Turtle offered to let her land on its hard shell back. With this decision, several of the waterfowl flew up to meet her to carry her gently down to the Turtle's back.
>
> The water beings were very curious about this new being in their world. They clamoured around asking her all about herself and where she came from. As she related her story to them she said she would need some land to put on the turtle's back so that it would grow and she would be able to move about. The water beings again congregated to deliberate on how to obtain the earth. As they were discussing one of them remembered hearing that there was earth beneath the water but it was way down very deep under the water. The water animals consisted of many of the animals we know today: Beaver, otter, muskrat as well as the waterfowl: ducks geese, loons, seagulls, etc. They all volunteered to go for the earth. The beaver as

we know builds his house underwater so he decided since he was so big and strong that he should go and get the earth. He tried but was unsuccessful. One by one the water beings tried to get the earth but the earth was too far down. At last it came time for the tiny little muskrat to make his dive for the earth. Would he do it? The others thought not. But this did not stop him. He dove under the water. The beings on the water waited, and they waited. He did not surface. Just as they gave up hope of seeing the little muskrat again he shot up out of the water and in his little paw was a little bit of earth. And the story continues so that we are here today.

Just as Sky Woman had many people to help her adjust to the new world, I also had many people work with me to bring out the traditional knowledge and values at the University of Toronto and was, therefore, able to give voice to this in my teaching dossier.

Teresa's Closing Thoughts

Ten years after we first met, as we discussed this work we were about to undertake together over the computer from either side of the country, I asked Eileen how she coped with this intensely alienating process of tenure with such grace and yet kept her identity and integrity, as well as her hope, intact ("stayed grounded" in my parlance). She talked about the educative journey, that each of us takes steps along the path and that we can endure if, each day, we can see that we "keep moving forward." To do so is a duty and an obligation.

For me, for example, I can see that although teaching dossiers are certainly not a panacea, they do offer somewhat more flexibility for the community-based perspectives on valuing faculty work than do isolated student ratings alone. I can see that in this sense there was enough space in their concept and construct that it was possible, with some considerable effort, for Eileen to maintain her voice. Of course, there is much more work to be done.

As I reflect back on this work and the work of others in this volume, I am reminded of a well-known prayer that has multiple meanings in multiple contexts but that I often use as an ally or advocate. It is brief but I find it works well in academic administration, where "what can be changed" varies from day to day. It says:

God grant me the serenity
to accept the things I cannot change:

courage to change the things I can:
and wisdom to know the difference.

– Reinhold Niebuhr

As I think about working with Eileen, perhaps more than anything her teachings direct us to what unites all of us who contributed to this volume, namely, that we try to live our responsibility to keep the work moving forward. Each of us, in our own way, is engaged in a journey towards teaching and learning community-based research that makes change happen.

Conclusion: Walking on Thin Ice: Tensions and Challenges in CBR

BUDD L. HALL, CATHERINE ETMANSKI,
AND TERESA DAWSON

In the opening chapter of this book, Jessica Ball makes use of an appropriately Canadian story-become-metaphor to talk about her experiences in learning and doing community-based research in Northern Ontario. In her story, the Indigenous community research partners who had invited her to work with them requested that she attend a meeting in a fishing hut on the hard frozen surface of a winter lake. Meeting in a place where they were comfortable sent a message about how they wanted the research to be done. The concern about whether the ice was strong enough served to take her out of her physical and intellectual comfort zones to allow for what Lorna Williams and colleagues refer to in their chapter as a space for "watchful listening."

The powerful stories of engaging in teaching and learning with and about community-based research presented in this book provide evidence of the growing space for critical and transformative approaches to the co-construction of knowledge in collaboration with the academy. But the role of universities as the privileged spaces for colonial, dominant, hierarchical forms of knowledge mean that all of us engaged in this work about contestation and chance have to be aware of the thickness of the ice! Getting to know the strength of our collective ice can be achieved through some reflections on the creative and productive tensions that characterize this work.

Productive Tensions in This Work

The conversations between authors throughout the writing process, and in the lunchtime series that inspired this book, surfaced a number of contradictions and productive tensions inherent to the work of learning and teaching community-based research.[1] We say "productive" because these conversations allowed us to delve into the challenges of teaching CBR in more depth, tease out the nuances of individuals' practices, and understand the specific theories that inform each of us and our work. Simple examples of these tensions included discussion around whether or not to use the word "teaching," in light of its connotations of top-down curriculum delivery, educational practices that – while they may have their specific place – generally undermine the more collaborative co-construction of knowledge we see as fundamental to the scholarship of CBR. They also included discussion around whether to ground our work in the full range of learning experiences, both inside institutions of higher learning and out, or to narrow our scope to the more specific mandate the university is understood to hold in society (compared to, say, the equally essential, but somewhat different mandates of community colleges, poly-technical training institutions, continuing education, and so on). Writing this book has not resolved such tensions. However, by way of summary, we would nevertheless like to make our conversations more public, in order to share important contributions from educators in this area.

In closing, then, we present six areas of unresolved debate and ongoing conversation: from the ideology embedded in teaching CBR, to the complexities and contradictions of institutionally sanctioning CBR and attempting to make change from inside the academy. And from the fluid definitions of learner, teacher, and researcher to a need to re-story the word research and draw from the diversity of knowledges in order to reimagine and understand our place in this world.

One: We Are the World, but Whose World Are We?

Worthington, Ibáñez-Carrasco, Rourke, and Bacon note in their chapter that "it might be misleading to say that one can 'teach CBR,' because it is an approach to and philosophy of using traditional research methodological and analytical tools in ways that subvert hierarchical top-down disparities." So, community-based research has to be understood within a critical understanding of the communities, the spaces, and the worlds that we live in. It has to be understood as linked to an alternative storytelling of the world, a storytelling that exposes inequity, injustice, inequality, dispossession, exclusion, violence, discrimination, colonial appropriation, and more. If our work is not contextualized within an understanding of existing knowledge and power relations, the teaching of methods and processes that make up the artist's palette of community-based research may well have the unintended effect of reinforcing existing relations of power and knowledge. But which critical framework do we share? And where do we start in terms of a critical understanding of the world? How can we find the time in our structured university course schedules to both provide a full critical analysis and offer insights and practices into working in CBR? Admittedly, this is more of a tension in those courses which are offered in a more general manner – CBR approaches for a multiplicity of settings such as the work described by Hall in his chapter or the community mapping courses as described by Corbett and Lydon. By contrast, the Corntassel and Gaudry work on *insurgent education* or the work of Williams, Tanaka, Leik and Riecken, which promotes the Lil'wat concept of Cwelelep, the awareness of dissonance or uncertainty, is working from a recognition of the genocidal colonial past and the continued rendering as invisible of settler-Indigenous power relations for example.

Two: In from the Cold, but Still Chilly Inside

"One might say that participatory research has come 'in from the cold,' that it has come in from the margins to become an accepted member of the academic family" (Hall, 2005, p. 5). Although the teaching and learning of this work is similarly gaining its voice inside the academy, there are nevertheless benefits and dangers of coming in from the cold. It is true that marginal voices are often misunderstood, rebuked, undermined, or blatantly ignored by those who occupy centres of power, and this can be both disheartening and painful. We do not want to romanticize this struggle. Yet, to speak from the margins with an empowered sense of authority is to speak from a position of accountability to one's community first. When one is not seeking approval or acceptance by the mainstream, there is, at least, some freedom in that. To step in from the peripheral cold, then, in one sense entails widening our circle of community to those inside the academy. If one wishes to stay inside, one must, at least in some measure, abide by the rituals herein, often while simultaneously endeavouring to change them. As the teaching of CBR and its related cousins have gradually come in from the cold, its practitioners have had to adapt to the particular institutional context, while endeavouring to maintain a critical edge and integrity in the practice. In this context, Antone and Dawson explore the possibilities for Indigenous resistance and teachings within tenure processes, in their chapter advocating the wholistic representation of a faculty member's teaching, learning, scholarship, and community work in university assessment processes.

Contributors to this book wondered, what has been gained by stepping inside and what has been lost? Has the institutional sanction of the teaching and learning of CBR, for example, through the creation of an Office of CBR, or through grants given out by the Learning and Teaching Centre, created a little more warmth for CBR educators, or has it popularized the terminology to the point where it is no longer used in a meaningful way? Here, we suggest both.

Of course, the idea of margin and centre conjures up a simplistic binary that is much more complex in practice. Margins exist *within* the academy, just as they exist without. The highly gendered and often racialized work of building long-term research relationships continues to hold less value in an institutional culture where publishing is privileged and rewarded through the tenure and promotion process. Likewise, the additional relationship-building work required to teach CBR is equally deterring for some, because not all community service is valued equally. As Strand (2000) suggested, "if we wish to encourage more faculty members to take on the challenges and extra work associated with service-learning [as one form of CBR], then I believe we must make clear the ways that it supports our pedagogical goals and enhances our teaching effectiveness" (p. 95). For historical reasons, some faculties understand and value this work more than others, but in the larger context of academe, CBR is still a marginal practice. When the chairperson of a tenure and promotion committee does not see CBR as "valid science," for example, one's position inside the academy is insecure at best. There may be a sense of synergy around teaching CBR in at the University of Victoria, and perhaps a new warmth for the teaching of CBR in institutions of higher learning in general, but we cannot ignore that it is still a little chilly inside. (See also Hayward, Simpson, & Wood, 2004 for their analogy of being "still left out in the cold" in participatory development.)

Three: The Challenges of Working from an Academic Location

All of the authors in this volume have in some way confronted questions about their positionality and about the impossibility of compartmentalizing research, teaching, and community. Authors have also discussed the reality that this kind of work takes longer and often does not fit into granting cycles, that it brings with it enormous responsibility which cannot simply be terminated at the end of a study, and that there are some aspects of research that students are not always ready or able to do – meaning that we have to balance their enthusiasm with community needs. In an academic climate that rewards short-term projects that have concrete, evidence-based outcomes, the grades, course credits, degrees, certificates, and diplomas associated with CBR begin to serve as currency in the global educational marketplace. As scholars and practitioners, we cannot escape the influence of a neo-liberal ideology that values standardization over diversity and creativity; competition, hierarchy, and individualism over collaboration; and efficiency over generosity. Similarly, in spite of any ontological progress made by qualitative researchers, institutions of higher education are (for the most part, unwittingly) steeped in neo-colonial beliefs around which knowledges are "true," which methods for gathering, producing, and sharing knowledge are "valid," and who is given the authority to determine either of these. In institutions of higher learning, then, people who wish to facilitate the learning of CBR face several constraints. As mentioned above, the structure of a one-semester course does not normally allow for the longer-term relationship that CBR entails, but contributors to this book told us about several other challenges as well. For example, research supervisors struggle with supporting students to finish their programs, while allowing them the time, flexibility, and freedom to respond to community needs. This delicate balance is rendered more difficult – even ethically challenging – when supervisors know that their students are often incurring debt along the way. Student debt, as the *Casseroles* protestors in Quebec and elsewhere have highlighted, has become a major social justice issue of our time. Likewise, students who wish to engage in CBR may not have the institutional support to do so even when they do find a supportive research supervisor. There are limitations to the duration of funding available to students, for instance, and not all students are equipped with the prior knowledge, skills, patience, time, or money to carry a graduate CBR project through to completion (Loiselle, this volume, is a notable exception).

In addition, scholars who have built long-term relationships with members of the community grapple with how to involve students in a meaningful way without harming the community relationship. As Ball (this volume) suggests, the changing conditions of community contexts coupled with the indeterminacy of research processes, outcomes, and the short-term nature of students' average engagement with universities, make it difficult for students with very specific course or research project obligations to fulfil them. For example, community leaders may change the focus of their struggle, causing students to lose interest – or to lose several months' worth of work gaining committee members' (re)approval, ethics approval, course credit approval, and so on.

Four: Who Are the Learners? Who Are the Teachers?
Who Is the Community?

A crucial tension the contributors acknowledged repeatedly in our conversations, relates to the typical relationships that determine who is a teacher or learner, and degrees of insider and outsider in any given community. The practice of CBR has historically called into question notions of "who is the researcher," and promotes a more egalitarian approach to collecting, analysing, and sharing knowledge. Loiselle, Taylor, and Donald in chapter 2, for example, discuss how racialized girls became researchers and writers over the course of the CBR project in which they were involved. Two of the "girls" are, in fact, co-authors of this chapter.

In this book, however, we further call into question who are the teachers and who are the learners. As Antone and Dawson point out, the two may be inseparable and/or the power relation may often be inverted in community contexts. When learning must be assessed with a letter grade, this raises still more challenges of teaching CBR in an academic context. For example, community knowledge keepers or representatives from an organization may be in the best position to assess a student's final product, as Trapero and Stypka suggested, but constraints around the academic credentials needed to teach in a university context often determine who is permitted to be the sanctioned instructor.

Moreover, the idea of what constitutes community is regularly raised in discussions around CBR. Any given campus is, in effect, its own unique community, and people who work on a campus are equally connected to communities outside of their place of work – communities of place, communities of practice, and communities of identity. Students who originally come from a certain community may later be perceived as outsiders as a result of their affiliation with a university, while academics may be perceived as insiders because of the history of their involvement in a specific community. Contributors to this book sought to add complexity to definitions of community, just as they sought to broaden the possibilities around who are learners and who are teachers and how can value be acknowledged in such contexts.

Five: Can We Re-story the Word Research?

Mukwa Musayett, de Finney, Kundouqk, Brown, and McCaffery in their chapter remind us that the word research is one of the dirtiest words in the English language within Indigenous communities (see also, Tuhiwai Smith, 1999). Research has been used by those who seek to control the destinies of Indigenous persons by creating services and programs that respond to some needs while leaving intact the structures of domination and neo-colonialism that have created disparity in the first place. Marshall, Peterson, Coverdale, Etzel, and McFarland in their chapter illustrate one approach to "re-storying" the word *research* through personal storytelling. But the same concerns about the way that research is more generally understood in the community are seen in the context of those who are labelled as (dis)abled, those who are poor, those who are drug involved, those who are old, and all those who simply do not "fit." When we teach workshops and courses in engaged, militant, community-based, or participatory research within university settings, how do we know that we are not domesticating our intentions or co-opting struggles and creating intermediate "experts" who, in fact, reinforce existing relations of power? In his chapter, Hall tells us that when he and his colleagues in Tanzania, India, and Chile first coined the word *participatory research*, they did so in an attempt to create a research word with a completely new story, one that could not be separated from resistance, organizing, and politics. He reports that he was discouraged when, in spite of their best efforts, participatory research as a discourse was picked up by many international development agencies, including the World Bank, and used in ways that those who originally coined the word had not imagined.

Six: Respecting the Diversity of Knowledge Cultures

Knowledge and the creation of stories that explain who we are, who we are not, and how we exist in our worlds are experienced in very different ways in the different places where we live and work. In some ways, the knowledge culture within the academy is one of the most unusual, specialized, and inaccessible forms of knowledge. Even as we acknowledge that knowledge is created in many diverse locations, and that intellectuals and knowledge keepers exist both inside and outside of the academy, we need to also recognize that our cultures of knowledge differ. Knowledge within the context of a harm reduction initiative, as described by Herman and Willson, is directly related to the ability of the organization to prolong the best quality of life for those that they serve. It is also about being able to access public and private funding to sustain the work. Its use is direct and immediate. It seeks knowledge that is sure, clear, and available. Knowledge within some of the First Nations communities in this book serves a different purpose. As Senćoten Elder Dave Elliott Sr. says (cited in the Corbett and Lydon chapter),

> We are living in the wreckage of what was once our way of life ... Many of the young people don't know where they're coming from and where they are going. We need to give them their past by telling their history and we need to give them a future. (Elliott, 1983, p. 82)

Knowledge is about survival, resistance, and a connection to identity, place, and spirituality first and foremost. Both Clover and Etmanski, in their chapters, offer us insights into how the arts not only allow us to know the whole person, but document the importance of recognizing the unique and powerful knowledge cultures of the world of the arts. Trapero and Stypka, in their chapter about creating a course structure to facilitate student involvement in governmental research projects, also illustrate the differences between the research cultures in a policy environment and those within a university setting.

Knowledge within the academic world is commodified and complex. It is the means by which the material rewards and salaries are distributed. Knowledge is increasingly thought of as a private good that may be directly linked to the market through an appropriate recognition of the *intellectual rights* of the scholar. But knowledge structures our workplace into disciplinary units and disciplinary means of sharing our work through specialized journals, conferences, websites, and courses themselves. For partnerships of trust to develop between knowledge workers in academic, Indigenous, and/or community spaces, how do we deepen the understanding of how knowledge works in our quite divergent domains?

Walking Together across the Ice

We hope that the chapters in this book have provided insights into some of the tensions and questions listed above. We also hope it has provided visibility for work that may not have been as well known before. We hope that it will be a platform for deepening your own discussions – discussions among students and discussions among activist intellectuals and knowledge keepers wherever you are. We are so very pleased to be part of the particular feast that this work and this world of radical reimagining represents and of which all who read this work are also part. In closing, we would like to reiterate the words of the late Edward Said, the Palestinian scholar-activist-musician whose penetrating critique of the role of academic knowledge is shaping how we imagined the "other," changed an entire generation of scholars – and is still changing them:

> I think the major choice faced by the intellectual is whether to be allied with the stability of the victors and rulers or – the more difficult path – to consider that stability as a state of emergency threatening the less fortunate with the danger of extinction, and take into account the experience of subordination itself, as well as the memory of forgotten voices and persons. (Said, 1996, p. 35)

Whatever the particular situation in which your community finds itself at the current time, we hope this book will provide the support, the ideas, and perhaps even a sense of community to strengthen you on this more difficult path.

Appendix A
Websites and Resources
for Community Mapping

Websites

Aboriginal Mapping Network
  http://www.nativemaps.org/
  Examples, stories and connections to mapping in over 100 indigenous
  communities. Managed by Eco-Trust Canada.

American Planning Association
  www.planning.org
  Connections to learning resources and participatory projects on planning.

Artistic Community Mapping
  http://ltabc.ca/
  Maps and background information on an extensive community mapping
  initiative undertaken in various islands between Vancouver Island and
  the mainland of British Columbia (including the Gulf Islands).

Canadian Mapping Resources
  www.nrcan.gc.ca
  Extensive information, data, and links to map resources and sustainability
  initiatives for educators, researchers, community developers, and the
  public – coordinated by Natural Resources Canada.

Common Ground UK
  www.commonground.org.uk
  Stories of the parish community mapping in Great Britain including profiles
  of community restoration and art projects.

Community Mapping Network
  http://www.cmnbc.ca/
  Profiles, stories, maps, tools, and links to natural resource conservation
    mapping projects – coordinated by the Department of Fisheries and
    Oceans Canada.

Eco-Trust Canada
  http://ecotrust.ca/
  Information on sustainable community resource management, including
    community mapping.

Integrated Approaches to Participatory Development
  www.iapad.org
  Participatory 3-D mapping and methodologies for local development based
    on case studies in the Philippines.

International Green Map System
  www.greenmap.org
  Profiles of this globally connected, locally adaptable framework for commu-
    nity mapping. Includes online resources, direct examples, and connec-
    tions to green map projects across Canada.

Kids and Community Planning
  www.planning.org/kidsandcommunity
  Information for educators and students to discover and design the local
    community through innovative planning exercises including mapping.

ResilientCity.org
  http://www.resilientcity.org/
  Ten design principles for designing a sustainable urban neighbourhood
    found under the resilience tab.

Resources Zine
  www.planning.org/resourceszine
  Online resources for teaching and involving youth in planning.

UVIC Community Mapping
  www.mapping.uvic.ca
  Stories, photos, videos, links of academic and community-based mapping
    projects

Publishers

Community and Community Economic Development
Centre for Community Enterprise
http://ccednet-rcdec.ca/en/node/3383Community and Global Planning
and Participation

Earthscan Publications from Routledge
http://www.routledge.com/sustainability/*Community and Institutional
Planning and Change*

American Planning Association
www.planning.org

Community and Social Transformation

New Society Publishers
www.newsociety.com

Community Asset Mapping

ACTA Publications
http://www.abcdinstitute.org/

International Planning and Change

Institute of Development Studies
www.ids.ac.uk/ids/publications

Appendix B
Four UWW Evaluative Instruments

The UWW application is a useful instrument not only to select talented students from across the country, but it also allows the UWW Education Committee, reviewers, and core team to spot promising students who have shown accomplishment in the HIV field but need additional learning and networking to succeed and stay in the field. All information is collected online and the centerpiece of the application process is a five-page Career Planning Summary, a self-reflection piece of each applicant's past, present, and future. This summary, in addition to CV and academic transcripts, allows reviewers to assess prior learning, learning styles, and likelihood to succeed and stay in the field of HIV research. In addition, the UWW applications are used collectively to select a group that reflects diversity and is likely to work well together under blended delivery conditions.

The UWW Fellowship Plan is an online form that the student can revisit and revise as many times as necessary. It is used as a learning compass and a point of reference for self-assessment at the end of the formal UWW tenure, and it can continue to be used to support UWW fellows in their academic and professional development. The instrument is adapted from those used in US alternative independent liberal arts colleges. In addition to a baseline survey with pedagogical evaluation questions, the Fellowship Plan requests a brief professional background from the fellow (which enhances the information submitted in the applications); at least three personal learning goals for the UWW tenure; a number of training activities other than those offered by the UWW program (e.g., attendance at specific health related conferences); and a preliminary bibliography (which will be supplemented by the online speaker assigned readings). Finally, the UWW Fellowship Plan asks the fellow to identify expected knowledge transfer and exchange (KTE) products which can range from academic (e.g., abstracts, peer-reviewed papers) to community products (e.g., community presentations, posters, brochures, etc.).

The UWW Field Mentoring Plan (FMP) organizes the interaction between a host/mentor and a fellow in a community, policy, or academic environment. It is created after the "matchmaking" between the site/mentor and the fellow has occurred. Potential mentors and field placements are identified from across the country using an online database of field mentoring profiles that are completed by the potential host/mentor after promotion of UWW activities. The FMP serves as a tool of negotiation of mutual benefit between the parties and a plan for the fellow's activities. Both the mentor and the student are supported through the placement and asked to fill out evaluations at the conclusion. The FMP is filed online by the fellow, and includes general information from the host/mentor; a description of the policy, research, or practice environment (e.g., the general mandate of an AIDS service organization); at least three goals for the particular placement for the host/mentor organization; at least three goals for the fellow; at least three field mentoring activities (e.g., produce a systematic review of literature on HIV prevention); at least three deliverables or KTE products; a description of the roles of the host/mentor and the UWW fellow; an estimate of the time commitment of the fellow and how it will be allocated (e.g., in-person meetings every 3 weeks with the organization's team); and a preliminary timeline.

The fourth UWW instrument, the Learning Portfolio, integrates the pedagogical evaluation questions from the baseline survey in the areas of knowledge, practice (application), and professional/lived experience, a number of indicators of success requested by the CIHR funder, and a number of deliverables that the fellow has produced during, or are directly attributable to, the UWW tenure. These deliverables can be academic (e.g., conference presentations) or community products (e.g., fact sheets).

Notes

Introduction

1 Readers who are interested in the idea of systemwide Change Labs/ Design Labs could look, e.g., to the work of Adam Kahane from Reos Partners, Charles Leadbeater from the UK's Participle, Christian Bason from the Danish Mindlab, Dan Hill Helsinki Design Lab, Ezio Manzini from the DESIS network (Design for Social Innovation and Sustainability), Frances Westley from Social Innovation Generation, or Geoff Mulgan from NESTA.

1. On Thin Ice: Managing Risks in Community-University Research

1 These projects are fully described and documented on the website of Early Childhood Development Cultural Partnerships (ECDIP), University of Victoria, BC, at http://www.ecdip.org/.

2 University-based investigators are referred to variously as faculty in this chapter. The term community-university partnerships is used in this chapter in order to relate specifically to discourse about the particular mission and role of universities in society, which many view as distinctive in terms of their mandate to identify new knowledge sources and generate new knowledge. Other kinds of institutional campuses, such as community and technical colleges, may not depend so heavily on demonstrating their ability to generate knowledge through original research in order to generate revenue and grow.

3 The problems that can arise with networked or multicomponent community-university collaborations that rely heavily on building relationships of trust are addressed elsewhere (Ball & Janyst, 2008).

2. When Girls Talk Back

1 Accessed at http://artemisplace.org/PlaceForGirls
2 Photovoice is a method developed by Wang and Burris (1997) that "entrusts cameras to the hands of people to enable them to act as recorders, and potential catalysts for change, in their own communities. It uses the immediacy of the visual image to furnish evidence and to promote an effective, participatory means of sharing expertise and knowledge" (p. 369). Photovoice can be taken up in different ways, but generally involves community co-researchers using cameras to document their daily realities and collectively analysing each others' photos through the research process to produce deeper understandings of issues in the community, disseminate findings, and generate alternatives, solutions, and actions.
3 I introduced graffiti walls as an activity that would provide a useful entry point to further explore the theme of labels and/or stereotypes that had emerged in our process, and also to further explore girls' skills and strengths. We used two wall-sized pieces of paper where girls' ideas could be captured quickly and graphically while their bodies were free to move around, chat, laugh, and dance and sing to the music in the background. One of our graffiti walls was labelled "Stereotypes" and the other was labelled "Strengths." The juxtaposition of the levity of the atmosphere with the difficult labels girls were writing on the "Stereotypes" wall demonstrates the value of using this method to name and discuss painful experiences and inequities while still breathing fun and humour into the research space.
4 Elicia: In my thesis (Loiselle, 2011; based on Project Artemis) I explore how colonial discourses of charity and care obscure the complicity of white, capitalist structures in (re)producing and benefitting from the socio-material conditions that produce contexts of "risk" and "need" for "others." As Ruth explains ("the article made us seem like helpless victims who wouldn't stand a chance in mainstream society"), these relations of power are acute in the lives of girls in Project Artemis. As colleagues and I have written, "the reproduction of dominant discourses of minoritized girls as only problematic and at risk ignores their agency and limits the infusion of their complex voices into research, policy, and practice" (de Finney, Loiselle, & Dean, 2011, p. 105). Girls' responses to the newspaper article generated an immediate engagement through our research with the tensions between their sense of feeling seen and valued at Artemis Place and the "at-risk" constructions that shape program funding and delivery in complex ways. As an important action that emerged from our research, girls discussed these issues with the Executive Director of Artemis Place and collaborated

on alternative ways to present themselves in the media that would give them more control over how they are seen, and in particular would allow them to contextualize their experiences and highlight their skills and strengths. Later in the school year, the Executive Director asked two Project Artemis co-researchers to be interviewed with her for a newspaper article, which involved the three of them meeting in advance to strategize their messaging. This act of solidarity is an important way to subvert paternalistic notions of individualized "need" within non-profit structures that rely heavily on discourses of charity to survive.

5 We tentatively include race here, although Elicia explores later in the chapter the limited ways in which we interrogated racism and whiteness.

3. Learning CBR through Community Organizing

1 The fixed-site needle exchange was operated by AIDS Vancouver Island and funded by VIHA.

2 Participatory Research, with roots in the social movements and community organizing of nations of the South during the 1970s, is notable for its challenge to the authority, objectivity, and exclusivity of university-based research, and for its central emphasis on making social change. For PR practitioners, "research" was taken up as a critical and legitimizing move, challenging professionalized methods of knowledge gathering and dissemination, on the one hand, and (re)valuing popular knowledges and local social justice projects, on the other (Heaney, 1993, p. 44; Park, 1993, pp. 37–38; Fals-Borda & Rahman, 1991, p. 25). The take-up of Participatory Research within the university, then, completes an odd form of circuit for the language of "research."

3 Several reports calling for improved harm reduction services in Victoria were written years before the needle exchange closed. As early as 2000, e.g., the Centre for Health Evaluation and Outcome Services at the University of British Columbia noted that the "single fixed Needle Exchange site with its limited hours of operation cannot meet the needs of its clients" and recommended more comprehensive harm reduction services in the region (Stajduhar, Poffenroth, & Wong, 2000). In 2003, the City of Victoria, VIHA, and the Victoria Police Department launched the "Downtown Health Initiative Action Plan," which pledged to "provide additional supports to address addiction and mental health problems within the City" (City of Victoria, 2003).

4 As will be further described, these policy-oriented activities were complemented by a range of other tactics.

5 Claire Polster describes the shift in universities towards corporate managerial styles and commitments: "Increasingly, universities – which are public
institutions – are adopting values and practices that are employed in the
private sector. This shift is reflected in the new language being used in
our universities in which our presidents are 'CEOs,' professors are 'human resources' and students are 'clients.' It is reflected in the displacement
of academic criteria by economic criteria in the allocation of institutional
resources. And it is reflected in the many new managerial practices that
are being employed by university administrators – ranging from greater
secrecy in the running of institutional affairs, to various forms of pseudo-
consultation, to the increased use of performance indicators and merit pay
to control and motivate academic workers" (Polster, 2003, p. 1).
6 The number of full-time students who report also being full-time employees has doubled over the past two decades, from 29,500 in 1989 to 71,325 in
2009 (Canadian Association of University Teachers, 2010, p. 40).
7 Average student debt in 2000 was $24,706, double the average student debt
of 1990 (Canadian Council on Learning, 2010, p. 11).

4. Siem Smun'eem (Respected Children): A Community-Based Research Training Story

1 The authors of this chapter are members of the Indigenous Child Welfare
Research Network Steering Committee, which provides leadership in
visioning and capacity building for and with Indigenous communities in
British Columbia. The main tasks include the development, facilitation, and
implementation for Indigenous Child Welfare Research training, which we
refer to as "Fish Soup for the Indigenous Researcher." The committee is a
groupthink and leadership tool in the evolution of the Indigenous Child
Welfare Research Network.
2 Participants sign a consent form giving permission to the Network to
publish comments and content shared during training sessions. To protect
anonymity, we do not specify participant names (unless requested to do so)
or dates and locations of the training sessions. Evaluations are accessible on
our website.

6. Facilitating and Teaching Feminist Visual Arts–Based Research

1 While agreeing fully with the sentiment that we are all artistic, by professional artist I speak not of the exalted genius but, rather, someone
who makes a living through her art and/or is "driven" to do art. A

community-based artist is one who works with community members to create collective artworks. Her work focuses on a combination of education and knowledge construction.

2 When I use the term "art" I speak of the pre-separation of art and craft, of a union of technique and inspiration, innovation and imitation, freedom and utility (Shiner, 2001).

7. Learning to Listen

1 From Antonio Machado, the Spanish poet, who said, "Caminante no hay camino, se hace camino al andar."

2 Unpublished poem by Roberta Timothy, cited with permission.

11. Walking Side by Side: Living Indigenous Ways in the Academy

1 We refer to this as "one course" although each offering of the course has a unique focus (such as carving a Welcoming Pole, drum making, or storytelling) and differing Indigenous Knowledge Keepers/instructors and community involvement; the course continues to evolve in its subsequent offerings and also through its legacy on those involved in each offering.

2 Because of the unusual nature of the course, anonymity is impossible. We consciously include some identifying features of our participants out of respect for the Indigenous ways of acknowledging sources of understanding.

3 Entitled *Thunderbird/Whale Protection and Welcoming Pole: Learning and Teaching in an Indigenous World* (offered Fall 2005).

4 Entitled *Earth Fibres Weaving Stories: Indigenous Ways of Teaching and Learning* (offered Fall 2006).

5 Photos in this chapter are included courtesy of M. Tanaka (Schalay'nung Sxwey'ga and moving the pole into the building) and UVic Photo Services (Xaxe Siam Seetla, Sides A and B).

12. Making a Difference through Teaching, Learning, and Research

1 The concept of knowledge mobilization (KM) is a popular emerging knowledge translation strategy (Dobbins, Robeson, Ciliska, et al., 2009) that promotes the flow of knowledge among multiple agents and aims to have an intellectual, social, and/or economic impact (Social Sciences and Humanities Research Council of Canada). Levesque (2007) defines knowledge mobilization as being the opposite of knowledge exchange which is a push-and-pull strategy that moves data and knowledge between groups

and individuals. Instead, KM is an active process of "creating linkages and exchanges between producers and users of data, information and knowledge to produce value-added outputs" (Levesque, 2007, p. 19).

13. Creating the Learning Space: Teaching the Arts in CBR

1 Many of the insights shared in this chapter were gained through my doctoral study. I would like to acknowledge funding from the Social Sciences and Humanities Research Council of Canada and the Estate of Muriel Beverley Vaio Law.

2 Opening the class with the assumption that everyone is *already* an artist has led to productive conversations in various offerings of the class. Although much popular education work and books like the *Artist's Way* (Cameron, 2002) have promoted everyone's innate capacity for artistry, people continue to have divergent understandings about what being an artist means. Some people are quite adamant that saying that everyone is an artist is akin to saying that everyone is a doctor and is disrespectful of the time and skill artists devote to their work. And yet we all have the capacity to heal. Some people distinguish between "good" artists and amateurs, although the line is blurry to say the least, and the word "good" is always problematic. Some classes have generated a list of criteria for what it might mean to be an artist and then later abandoned the list as insufficient. I use the starting assumption that everyone is an artist to generate productive dialogue and debate and let the students decide for themselves whether or not it is true for them. We are usually able to hold paradox, a sense of unresolved contradiction, and diverging opinions around this assumption throughout the class. All classes have agreed that everyone has the capacity to be creative (which, for some people is a large shift in perception) and that there are differing criteria for aesthetic quality, both of which I discuss in depth later in the chapter.

3 I thank Kathy Bishop, Valeria Cortés, and Marc Labelle for their creative inspiration and permission to use these examples.

4 In her book, *Quiet: The Power of Introverts in a World That Can't Stop Talking* (2012), Susan Cain presents a compelling argument for why we ought to be mindful of how, when, and how often we ask people to work in groups. In arguing that there are times when collaboration can stifle creativity, her work sheds new light on the complexity of teaching CBR and further supports Israel et al.'s (2003) suggestion that not all people should be involved in all parts of the process at all times.

14. "But how do I put this dream catcher into my teaching dossier?"

1 Throughout this chapter we use the terms "teaching portfolio" and "teaching dossier" interchangeably.

Conclusion: Walking on Thin Ice – Tensions and Challenges in Community-Based Research

1 Although the ideas in this section are certainly drawn from all the contributors to this book, we would like to thank and acknowledge in particular the participants of our 21 September 2011 authors' meeting, whose ideas around the tensions in teaching CBR have shaped this section. They are Adam Gaudry, Agata Stypka, Breanna Lawrence, Darlene Clover, Elicia Loiselle, Francisco Ibáñez-Carrasco, Jessica Ball, Joaquin Trapero, Jon Corbett, Leslie Brown, Mark Willson, Michele Tanaka, Sandrina DeFinney, Tamara Hermann, and Ted Riecken.

References

Aberley, D. (1993). *Boundaries of Home: Mapping for Local Empowerment*. Gabriola Island: New Society Publishers.

Aberley, D., & Harrington, S. (1999). *Giving the Land a Voice: Mapping Our Home Places*. Salt Spring Island, BC: Community Services Society.

Aboriginal Mapping Network. (2011). [Website]. Retrieved from www .nativemaps.org

Abu Ja'far Muhammed. (830). *Hisab al-jabr w'al-mugabala* Baghdad, handwritten.

Abu l'Hassan Al-Uqlidisi. (950). *Kitab al-fusul fi-l-hislab al-Hindi*. Baghdad, handwritten.

Adamczyk, P.D., & Twidale, B.M. (2007). Supporting multidisciplinary collaboration: Requirements from novel HCI education. In *Proceedings of CHI*, 1073–1076. http://dx.doi.org/10.1145/1240624.1240787

Alfred, T. (2004). Warrior scholarship: Seeing the university as a ground of contention. In D. Mihesuah & A.C. Wilson (Eds.), *Indigenizing the Academy* (pp. 88–99). Lincoln: University of Nebraska Press.

Alfred, T., & Corntassel, J. (2005). Being indigenous: Resurgences against contemporary colonialism. *Government and Opposition: An International Journal of Comparative Politics*, 40(4), 597–614. http://dx.doi.org/10.1111/j.1477-7053 .2005.00166.x

Allman, D., Myers, T., & Cockerill, R. (1997). *Concepts, Definitions and Models of Community-Based HIV Prevention Research in Canada*. Toronto: University of Toronto HIV Social, Behavioural and Epidemiological Studies Unit.

Ally, M. (2008). Foundations of educational theory for online learning. In T. Anderson (Ed.), *The Theory and Practice of Online Learning* (pp. 15–44). Edmonton: Athabasca University Press.

Amey, J.M., Brown, F.D., & Sandmann, R.L. (2002). A multidisciplinary collaborative approach to a university-community partnership: Lessons learned. *Journal of Higher Education Outreach and Engagement*, 7, 19–26.

Antone, E., Gamlin, P., & Provost-Turchetti, L. (2003). *Literacy and Learning: Acknowledging Holistic Approaches to Learning in Relation to "Best Practice" Literacy Training Program Final Report*. Toronto: Toronto Literary and Learning.

Antone, E.M. (1997). *In Search of Voice: A Collaborative Investigation on Learning. Experiences of All Onyota'a:ka*. Unpublished thesis, University of Toronto.

Antone, E.M. (2000). Empowering Aboriginal voice in Aboriginal education. *Canadian Journal of Native Education, 24*(2), 92–101.

Antone, E.M. (2003a). Aboriginal people: Literacy and learning. *Literacies, 1*(1), 9–12.

Antone, E.M. (2003b). *Case for Tenure and Promotion to the Rank of Associate Professor in the Department of Adult Education and Counselling Psychology*. Unpublished tenure case. Toronto: University of Toronto.

Archibald, J. (1995). Locally developed Native studies curriculum: An historical and philosophical rationale. In M. Battiste & J. Barman (Eds.), *First Nations Education in Canada: The Circle Unfolds* (pp. 288–312). Vancouver: UBC Press.

Arnold, R., Burke, B., James, C., Martin, D., & Thomas, B. (1991). *Educating for Change*. Toronto: Between the Lines & Doris Marshall Institute for Education and Action.

Arnstein, S. (1969). A ladder of citizen participation. *American Institute of Planners Journal, 216*–224.

Art Gallery of Greater Victoria. (2009). *World Upside Down*. [Exhibition]. Retrieved from http://aggv.ca/exhibitions/world-upside-down

Assembly of Nova Scotia Mi'kmaq Chiefs. (2009). *Mi'kmaq Ecological Knowledge Study Protocol*. Retrieved from http://www.aboriginalsustainabilitynetwork .org/wp-content/uploads/2009/01/mikmaq-ecological-knowldege-study-protocol.pdf

Astin, A. (1999). Promoting leadership, service, and democracy: What higher education can do. In R. Bringle, R. Games, & E. Malloy (Eds.), *Colleges and Universities as Citizens* (pp. 31–47). Boston: Allyn & Bacon.

Bacon, F. (1626). *The New Atlantis*. Retrieved from http://oregonstate.edu/ instruct/phl302/texts/bacon/atlantis.html

Ball, H.K. (2002). Subversive materials: Quilts as social text. *Alberta Journal of Educational Research, 60*(3), 1–27.

Ball, H.K. (2008). Quilts. In J. Knowles & A. Cole (Eds.), *Handbook of the Arts in Qualitative Research* (pp. 363–368). Thousand Oaks, CA: Sage.

Ball, J. (2004). As if Indigenous knowledge and communities mattered. *American Indian Quarterly, 28*(3&4), 455–479.

Ball, J. (2005). "Nothing about us without us": Restorative research partnerships with Indigenous communities. In A. Farrell (Ed.), *Ethical Research with Children* (pp. 81–96). Berkshire, UK: Open University Press.

Ball, J., & Bernhardt, B.M. (2008, Aug.). First Nations English dialects in Canada: Implications for speech-language pathology. *Clinical Linguistics & Phonetics, 22*(8), 570–588. http://dx.doi.org/10.1080/02699200802221620 Medline:18645739

Ball, J., & George, R.T. (2007). Policies and practices affecting Aboriginal fathers' involvement with their young children. In J.P. White, P. Maxim, & D. Beavon (Eds.), *Aboriginal Policy Research in Canada* (Vol. 3, pp. 123–144). Toronto: Thompson Educational Press.

Ball, J., & Janyst, P. (2008, June). Enacting research ethics in partnerships with Indigenous communities in Canada: "Do it in a good way." *Journal of Empirical Research on Human Research Ethics, 3*(2), 33–51. http://dx.doi.org / 10.1525/jer.2008.3.2.33 Medline:19385744

Ball, J., & Moselle, K. (1999). Risk-taking behaviours among Singaporean teenagers. In A.C.S. Cheong, S. Gopinathan, & W.K. Ho (Eds.), *Growing Up in Singapore: Research Perspectives on Adolescents* (pp. 43–59). Toronto: Prentice Hall.

Banister, E., Leadbeater, B., & Marshall, A. (2010). *Knowledge Translation in Context: Indigenous, Policy, and Community Settings.* Toronto: University of Toronto Press.

Banister, K. (Ed.). (2005). *Building Healthy Communities: The Role of Community-Based Research.* Proceedings from the University of Victoria Forum held on 23 April 2005. Victoria, BC: Office of Vice-President of Research, University of Victoria.

Banksy. (2010). *Exit through the Gift Shop.* [Motion picture]. http://www .banksyfilm.com/

Barazangi, N.H. (2006). An ethical theory of action research pedagogy. *Action Research, 4*(1), 97–116. http://dx.doi.org/10.1177/1476750306060546

Barber, B. (1992). *An Aristocracy for Everyone: The Politics of Education and the Future of America.* New York: Oxford University Press.

Barker, D. (2004). The scholarship of engagement: A taxonomy of five emerging practices. *Journal of Higher Education Outreach and Engagement, 9*(2), 123–137.

Barman, J. (1997). Schooled for inequality: The education of British Columbia Aboriginal children. In J. Barman, N. Sutherland, & J.D. Wilson (Eds.), *Children, Teachers and Schools in the History of British Columbia* (pp. 57–79). Calgary: Detselig.

Barndt, D. (Ed.). (2006). *Wild Fire: Art as Activism.* Toronto: Sumach Press.

Barnes, T., & Duncan, J. (1992). *Writing Worlds: Discourse, Text and Metaphor in the Representation of Landscape.* London: Routledge.

Baskin, C. (2002). Re-generating knowledge: Inclusive education and research. Paper Presented at the Annual Conference of the Canadian Indigenous and Native Studies Association, Toronto.

Bat-Ami, B.O. (1993). Marginality and epistemic privilege. In L. Alcoff & E. Potter (Eds.), *Feminist Epistemologies* (pp. 83–100). London: Routledge.

Battersby, C. (1989). *Gender and Genius: Towards a Feminist Aesthetics.* Bloomington: Indiana University Press.

Battiste, M. (2007, May). Nourishing the learning spirit. Paper presented at the Canadian Society for the Study of Education 2007 Conference, Saskatoon.

Battiste, M., & Youngblood Henderson, J. (Sa'ke'j). (2000). *Protecting Indigenous Knowledge and Heritage: A Global Challenge.* Saskatoon: Purich.

Baumgardner, J., & Richards, A. (2000). *Manifesta: Young Women, Feminism and the Future.* New York: Farrar, Straus & Giroux.

Becker, C. (1994). Herbert Marcuse and the subversive potential of art. In C. Becker (Ed.), *The Subversive Imagination: Artists, Society, and Responsibility* (pp. 113–129). New York: Routledge.

Becker, H.S. (1967). Whose side are we on? *Social Problems, 14*(3), 239–247. http://dx.doi.org/10.2307/799147

Bender, B. (1996). *Mapping Alternative Worlds in from Place to Place-Maps and Parish Maps.* London: Common Ground.

Berman, M. (1989). *Coming to Our Senses: Body and Spirit in the History of the West.* New York: Bantam Books.

Boal, A. (1979). *Theatre of the Oppressed.* London: Pluto.

Boler, M., & Zembylas, M. (2003). Discomforting truths: The emotional terrain of understanding difference. In P.P. Trifonas (Ed.), *Pedagogies of Difference* (pp. 110–136). New York: Routledge/Falmer.

Boyer, E.L. (1990). *Scholarship Reconsidered: Priorities of the Professoriate.* San Francisco: Jossey-Bass.

Boyer, E.L. (1996). The scholarship of engagement. *Journal of Public Service and Outreach, 1,* 11–20.

Boyte, H., & Kari, N. (2000). Renewing the democratic spirit in American colleges and universities. In T. Ehrlich (Ed.), *Civic Responsibility and Higher Education* (pp. 37–61). Phoenix, AZ: American Council on Education and Oryx Press.

Bradbury Huang, H., … (n.d.). Action Research: Transforming the Generation and Application of Knowledge. Manifesto published by the Action Research journal. Retrieved from http://arj.sagepub.com/site/author_resources/Action_Research_manifesto.pdf.

Branagan, M. (2005). Environmental education, activism, and the arts. *Convergence (Toronto), 38*(4), 33–50.

Brandao, C.R. (1985). *Repensando a Pequisa Participante.* Sao Paulo: Fonte.

Bray, J.N., Lee, J., Smith, L.L., & Yorks, L. (2000). *Collaborative Inquiry in Practice.* Thousand Oaks, CA: Sage.

Bresler, L. (2008). The music lesson. In J.G. Knowles & A. Cole (Eds.), *Handbook of the Arts in Qualitative Inquiry: Perspectives, Methodologies, Examples, and Issues* (pp. 226–237). Thousand Oaks, CA: Sage. http://dx.doi.org/10.4135 / 9781452226545.n19

Bresler, L. (2009). Research education shaped by musical sensibilities. *British Journal of Music Education, 26*(1), 7–25. http://dx.doi.org/10.1017/ S0265051708008243

Bresler, L. (2013). The spectrum of distance: Empathic understanding and the pedagogical power of the arts. In B. White & T. Constantino (Eds.), *Aesthetics, Empathy and Education* (pp. 9–28). New York: Peter Lang.

Bresler, L. (Ed.). (2007). *International Handbook of Research in Arts Education.* Dordrecht, The Netherlands: Springer. http://dx.doi.org/10.1007 / 978-1-4020-3052-9

Breunig, M. (2010). SEER 2009 opening address: Research as experiential praxis. *Journal of Experiential Education, 32,* 257–260.

Bridge, R. (2009). The law governing advocacy by charitable organizations: The case for change. *Philanthropist, 17*(2), 2–33.

British Columbia Ministry of Health. (2005). *Harm Reduction: A British Columbia Community Guide.* http://www.health.gov.bc.ca/library/publications/year / 2005/hrcommunityguide.pdf

Brocklehurst, N.J., & Rowe, A. (2003, May). The development and application of a public health skills assessment tool for use in primary care organisations. *Public Health, 117*(3), 165–172. http://dx.doi.org/10.1016/S0033-3506(03) 00079-9 Medline:12825466

Brody, H. (1988). *Maps and Dreams: Indians and the British Columbia Frontier.* Toronto: Douglas & McIntyre.

Brown, D., & Tandon, R. (1983). Ideology and political economy in inquiry: Action research and participatory research. *Journal of Applied Behavioral Science, 19*(3), 277–294. http://dx.doi.org/10.1177/002188638301900306

Brown, L., & Reitsma-Street, M. (2003). The values of community action research. *Canadian Social Work Review, 20*(1), 61–78.

Brown, L.D. (1985). People-centered development and participatory research. *Harvard Educational Review, 55*(1), 69–75.

Brunner, I., & Guzman, A. (1989). Participatory evaluation: A tool to assess projects and empower people. In R.F. Conner & M. Hendricks (Eds.), *International Innovations in Evaluation Methodology: New Directions for Program Evaluation* (pp. 9–18). San Francisco: Jossey-Bass. http://dx.doi .org/10.1002/ev.1509

Buchanan, D., Shaw, S., Ford, A., & Singer, M. (2003). Empirical science meets moral panic: An analysis of the politics of needle exchange. *Journal of Public*

Health Policy, 24(3/4), 427–444. http://dx.doi.org/10.2307/3343386 Medline:15015873

Buechler, S.M. (2000). *Social Movements in Advanced Capitalism: The Political Economy and Cultural Construction of Social Activism.* New York: Oxford University Press.

Burke, W.W., Lake, D.G., & Paine, J.W. (2009). *Organizational Change: A Comprehensive Reader.* San Francisco, CA: Jossey-Bass.

Burman, E. (2003). From difference to intersectionality: Challenges and resources. *European Journal of Psychotherapy, Counselling and Health, 6*(4), 293–308. http://dx.doi.org/10.1080/3642530410001665904

Butterwick, S. (2002). Your story/my story/our story: Performing interpretation in participatory theatre. *Alberta Journal of Educational Research, 60*(3), 240–253.

Butterwick, S., & Selman, J. (2006). Embodied metaphors: Telling feminist coalition stories through popular theatre. *New Zealand Journal of Adult Learning, 34* (2), 42–58.

Buys, N., & Bursnall, S. (2007). Establishing university-community partnerships: Processes and benefits. *Journal of Higher Education Policy and Management, 29*(1), 73–86. http://dx.doi.org/10.1080/13600800601175797

Cahill, C. (2007). Repositioning ethical commitments: Participatory action research as relational praxis of social change. *ACME: An International E-Journal for Critical Geographies, 6*(3), 360–373.

Cahill, C., Rios-Moore, I., & Threatts, T. (2008). Different eyes/open eyes: Community-based participatory action research. In J. Cammarota & M. Fine (Eds.), *Revolutionizing Education: Youth Participatory Action Research in Motion* (pp. 89–124). New York: Routledge.

Cahnmann-Taylor, M., & Siegesmund, R. (Eds.). (2008). *Arts-Based Research in Education: Foundations for Practice.* New York: Routledge.

Cain, S. (2012). *Quiet: The Power of Introverts in a World That Can't Stop Talking.* New York: Crown.

Cajete, G. (1994). *Look to the Mountain: An Ecology of Indigenous Education.* Durango, CO: Kivakí Press.

Calleson, D.C., Jordan, C., & Seifer, S.D. (2005, Apr.). Community-engaged scholarship: Is faculty work in communities a true academic enterprise? *Academic Medicine, 80*(4), 317–321. http://dx.doi.org/10.1097/00001888-200504000-00002 Medline:15793012

Calliou, S. (1995). Peacekeeping actions at home: A medicine wheel model for a peacekeeping pedagogy. In M. Battiste & J. Barman (Eds.), *First Nations Education in Canada: The Circle Unfolds.* Vancouver: UBC Press.

Cameron, J. (2002). *The Artist's Way: A Spiritual Path to Higher Creativity*. New York: Tarcher/Penguin Putnam.

Cammarota, J., & Fine, M. (2008). Youth participatory action research: A pedagogy for transformational resistance. In J. Cammarota & M. Fine (Eds.), *Revolutionizing Education: Youth Participatory Action Research in Motion* (pp. 1–11). New York: Routledge.

Campbell, J. (1968). *The Hero with a Thousand Faces*. (2nd ed.). Princeton, NJ: Princeton University Press.

Campbell, J. (2002). A critical appraisal of participatory methods in development research. *International Journal of Social Research Methodology, 5*(1), 19–29. http://dx.doi.org/10.1080/13645570110098046

Canada. (2008). Indian residential schools statement of apology. Retrieved from http://www.aadnc-aandc.gc.ca/eng/1100100015677/1100100015680

Canada. (2010). *Tri-Council Policy Statement: Ethical Conduct for Research Involving Humans*. Retrieved from http://www.pre.ethics.gc.ca/pdf/eng/tcps2/TCPS_2_FINAL_Web.pdf

Canadian Alliance for Community Service Learning. (n.d.). *Glossary of terms and definitions*. Retrieved from http://www.communityservicelearning.ca /en/welcome_glossary.htm

Canadian Association of University Teachers. (2010). *CAUT Almanac of Post-Secondary Education in Canada, 2010–2011*. Ottawa: Author.

Canadian Council on Learning. (2010). *Tallying the Costs of Post-Secondary Education: The Challenge of Managing Student Debt and Loan Repayment in Canada*. Ottawa: Author.

Canadian Institutes of Health Research. (2007). *CIHR Guidelines for Health Research Involving Aboriginal People*. Retrieved from http://www.cihr-irsc.gc.ca/e/29134.html

Canadian Parks and Wilderness Society. (n.d.) Retrieved from http://www.cpaws.org/

Carson, F. (2001). Feminist debate and fine art practices. In F. Carson & C. Pajaczkowska (Eds.), *Feminist Visual Culture* (pp. 25–36). New York: Routledge.

Carson, F., & Pajaczkowska, C. (Eds.). (2001). *Feminist Visual Culture*. New York: Routledge.

Cashman, S.B., & Seifer, S.D. (2008, Sept.). Service-learning: An integral part of undergraduate public health. *American Journal of Preventive Medicine, 35*(3), 273–278. http://dx.doi.org/10.1016/j.amepre.2008.06.012 Medline:18692742

Castellano, M.B. (2004). Ethics in Aboriginal research. *Journal of Aboriginal Health*, 98–114.

Castellano, M.B., Davis, L., & Lahache, L. (2000). Introduction to Part 4: Postsecondary education: Negotiating the promise. In M.B. Castellano, L. Davis, & L. Lahache (Eds.), *Aboriginal Education: Fulfilling the Promise* (pp. 171–175). Vancouver: UBC Press.

Chambers, D.E., Wedel, K.R., & Rodwell, M.K. (1992). *Evaluating Social Programs.* Needham Heights, MA: Allyn & Bacon.

Chambers, E. (2000). Applied ethnography. In N.K. Denzin & Y.S. Lincoln (Eds.), *The Handbook of Qualitative Research* (2nd ed., pp. 851–869). Thousand Oaks, CA: Sage.

Chambers, R. (1994). Participatory rural appraisal (PRA): Challenges, potentials and paradigm. *World Development, 22*(10), 1437–1454. http://dx.doi.org/10.1016/0305-750X(94)90030-2

Chambers, R. (1997). *Whose Reality Counts?: Putting the Last First.* London: Intermediate Technology Publications.

Chambers, R., & Blackburn, J. (1996). The power of participation: PRA and policy. Falmer: Institute of Development Studies, University of Sussex.

Chandler, D., & Torbert, B. (2003). Transforming inquiry and action: Interweaving 27 flavors of action research. *Action Research, 1*(2), 133–152. http://dx.doi.org/10.1177/14767503030012002

Cheney, J. (1989). Postmodern environmental ethics: Ethics as bioregional narrative. *Environmental Ethics, 11*(2), 117–134. http://dx.doi.org/10.5840/enviroethics198911231

Chwe, M.S.Y. (1998). Culture, circles and commercials: Publicity, common knowledge and social coordination. *Rationality and Society, 10*(1), 47–75. http://dx.doi.org/10.1177/104346398010001002

City of Victoria. (2007). *Executive Summary, Mayor's Task Force on Breaking the Cycle of Mental Illness, Addictions and Homelessness: A Victoria Model.* Victoria, BC: Author.

City of Victoria, VIHA and the Victoria Police Department. (2003). *The Downtown Health Initiative Action Plan.*

Clover, D.E., & Craig, C. (2009). Street-life's creative turn: An exploration of arts-based adult education and knowledge mobilization with homeless / street-involved women in Victoria. *Canadian Journal for the Study of Adult Education, 21*(2), 21–36.

Clover, D.E., & Stalker, J. (Eds.). (2007). *The Arts and Social Justice: Re-crafting Adult Education and Community Cultural Leadership.* Leicester, UK: NIACE (National Institute of Adult Continuing Education).

Coghlan, D., & Brannick, T. (2010). *Doing Action Research in Your Own Organization.* (3rd ed.). Los Angeles, CA: Sage.

Coghlan, D., & Coughlan, P. (2010). Notes toward a philosophy of action learning research. *Action Learning Research and Practice, 7*(2), 193–203. http://dx.doi.org/10.1080/14767333.2010.488330

Cole, A.L., & Knowles, J.G. (2008). Arts-informed research. In J.G. Knowles & A.L. Cole (Eds.), *Handbook of the Arts in Qualitative Research* (pp. 55–70). Thousand Oaks, CA: Sage.

Cole, A., & M. McIntyre. (2003). Arts-informed research for public education: The Alzheimer's Project. In P. Cranton (Ed.), Charting the Learning Society: Twenty-Second National Conference of the Canadian Association for the Study of Adult Education Proceedings (pp. 45–50). Halifax: Dalhousie University.

Collins, E., Cain, R., Bereket, T., Chen, Y.Y., Cleverly, S., George, C., ..., & Travers, R. (2007). *Living & Serving II: 10 Years Later – The Involvement of People Living with HIV/AIDS in the Community AIDS Movement in Ontario.* Toronto: Ontario HIV Treatment Network.

Conlon, M. (2000). Betrayal of the public trust: Corporate governance of Canadian universities. In J. Turk (Ed.), *The Corporate Campus: Commercialization and the Dangers to Canada's Colleges and Universities.* Toronto: Lorimer.

Cook, D.A., & Dupras, D.M. (2004). A practical guide to developing effective web-based learning. *Journal of General Internal Medicine, 19*(6), 698–707. http://dx.doi.org/10.1111/j.1525-1497.2004.30029.x Medline:15209610

Corbiere, A.J. (2000). Reconciling epistemological orientations: Towards a wholistic Nishnaabe (Ojibwe/Odawa/Potowatomi) education. *Canadian Journal of Native Education, 24*(2), 113–119.

Corntassel, J. (2008). Towards sustainable self-determination: Rethinking the contemporary Indigenous rights discourse. *Alternatives: Global, Local, Political, 33*(1), 105–132. http://dx.doi.org/10.1177/030437540803300106

Corntassel, J., Chaw-win-is, & T'lakwadzi. (2009). Indigenous story telling, truth telling and community approaches to reconciliation. *English Studies in Canada, 35*(1), 137–159. http://dx.doi.org/10.1353/esc.0.0163

Corntassel, J. (2011, 12 Jan.). Indigenizing the academy: Insurgent education and the roles of Indigenous intellectuals. [Web log post]. Canadian Federation for the Humanities and Social Sciences. Retrieved from http://www.congres2013.ca/blog/indigenizing-academy-insurgent-education-and-roles-indigenous-intellectualsx

Creese, G., & Frisby, W. (2011). *Feminist Community Research.* Vancouver: UBC Press.

Creswell, J.W., & Miller, D.L. (2000). Determining validity in qualitative inquiry. *Theory into Practice, 39*(3), 124–130. http://dx.doi.org/10.1207/s15430421tip3903_2

Davies, B. (2000). *A Body of Writing: 1990–1999*. New York: AltaMira Press.

Davis-Manigaulte, J., Yorks, L., & Kasl, E. (2006). Expressive ways of knowing and transformative learning. *New Directions for Adult and Continuing Education*, (109), 27–35. http://dx.doi.org/10.1002/ace.205

Dawson, T. (2007). *Creating a Teaching Dossier: A Guide for Faculty, Lecturers, Librarians and Graduate Students*. Victoria, BC: Learning and Teaching Centre, University of Victoria.

Dawson, T., & Guest, K. (Eds.). (2003). *Teaching and Learning for Diversity: Reflections from a Conference*. Scarborough, ON: Teaching and Learning Services, University of Toronto at Scarborough.

de Finney, S., Loiselle, E., & Dean, M. (2011). Bottom of the food chain: The minoritization of girls in child and youth care. In A. Pence & J. White (Eds.), *Child and Youth Care: Critical Perspectives on Pedagogy, Practice, and Policy* (pp. 70–94). Vancouver: UBC Press.

DeBlieu, J. (2000, May–June). Sacred cartography: Mapping your most intimate terrain. *Utne Reader*. (Minneapolis, MN).

DeFilippis, J., Fisher, R., & Schragge, E. (2010). *Contesting Community: The Limits and Potentials of Local Organizing*. New Brunswick, NJ: Rutgers University Press.

Dei, G.J. (2002). Rethinking the role of Indigenous knowledge in the academy. *NALL Working paper*, *58*, 1–25.

Deloria, V. (2000). *Red Earth, White Lies*. Golden, CO: Fulcrum.

Denzin, N.K., Lincoln, Y., & Smith, L.T. (Eds.). (2008). *Handbook of Critical and Indigenous Methodologies*. New York: Sage.

Desmond, M. (2004). Methodological challenges posed in studying an elite in the field. *Area*, *36*(3), 262–269. http://dx.doi.org/10.1111/j.0004-0894.2004.00223.x

Dharamsi, S., Espinoza, N., Cramer, C., Amin, M., Bainbridge, L., & Poole, G. (2010). Nurturing social responsibility through community service-learning: Lessons learned from a pilot project. *Medical Teacher*, *32*(11), 905–911. http://dx.doi.org/10.3109/01421590903434169 Medline:21039101

Diamond, D. (2004). *A Joker's Guide to Theatre for Living* (Rev ed.). Vancouver: Headlines Theatre.

Diamond, D. (2007). *Theatre for Living: The Art and Science of Community-Based Dialogue*. Victoria, BC: Trafford.

Dirkx, J.M. (1998). *Knowing the Self Through Fantasy: Toward a Mytho-poetic View of Transformative Learning*. [Conference Proceedings]. Retrieved from http://www.adulterc.org/Proceedings/1998/98dirkx.htm

Dobbins, M., Robeson, P., Ciliska, D., Hanna, S., Cameron, R., O'Mara, L., …, & Mercer, S. (2009). A description of a knowledge broker role implemented as part of a randomized controlled trial evaluating three knowledge translation strategies. *Implementation Science, 4*(1), 23–31. http://dx.doi .org/10.1186/1748-5908-4-23 Medline:19397820

Driver, S. (2007). Beyond "straight" interpretations: Researching queer youth digital video. In A.L. Best (Ed.), *Representing Youth: Methodological Issues in Critical Youth Studies* (pp. 304–324). New York: New York University Press.

Duncan, J., & David, L. (1993). *Place/Culture/Representation*. London: Routledge.

Duran, E. (2006). *Healing the Soul Wound: Counseling with American Indians and Native People.* New York: Teachers College Press.

Dyer, R. (2002). The matter of whiteness. In P.S. Rothenberg (Ed.), *White Privilege: Essential Readings on the Other Side of Racism* (pp. 9–14). New York: Worth.

Dykman, C.A., & Davis, C.K. (2008). Online education forum: Part two – Teaching online versus teaching conventionally. *Journal of Information Systems Education, 19*(2), 157–164.

EcoTrust Canada. (2011). [Website]. Retrieved from http://www.nativemaps.org

Edgerton, R., Hutchings, P., & Quinlan, K. (1991). *The Teaching Portfolio: Capturing the Scholarship in Teaching. AAHE Teaching Initiative.* Washington, DC: AAHE (American Association for Higher Education).

Eisner, E. (2008). Persistent tensions in arts-based research. In M. Cahnmann-Taylor & R. Siegesmund (Eds.), *Arts-Based Research In Education* (pp.16–27). New York: Routledge.

Eisner, E.W. (1981). On the differences between scientific and artistic approaches to qualitative research. *Educational Researcher, 10*(4), 5–9. http://dx.doi.org / 10.3102/0013189X010004005

Eisner, E.W. (1997). The promise and perils of alternative forms of data representation. *Educational Researcher, 26*(6), 4–10. http://dx.doi.org/10.3102 / 0013189X026006004

Elliott, D., Sr. (1983). *Saltwater People.* Saanich: Dave Elliott Sr. and School District 63.

Ellis, C., & Bochner, A. (2003). Autoethnography, personal narrative, reflexivity: Researcher as subject. In N.K. Denzin & Y.S. Lincoln (Eds.), *Collecting and Interpreting Qualitative Materials* (2nd ed., pp. 199–258). Thousand Oaks, CA: Sage.

Emerson, L.E., et al. (2007). *Emerging Values and Principles.* University of Victoria. Unpublished document created for the Aboriginal Communities Advisory Board.

Ermine, W. (1995). Aboriginal epistemology. In M. Battiste & J. Barman (Eds.), *First Nations Education in Canada: The Circle Unfolds* (pp. 101–112). Vancouver: UBC Press.

Ermine, W. (2006). The space between two knowledge systems. Lecture delivered at the University of Alberta. Retrieved from http://www.folio. ualberta.ca/43/14/11.html /

Essoglou, T.A. (1995). Louder than words: A WAC chronicle. In N. Felshin (Ed.), *But Is It Art?: The Spirit of Art as Activism* (pp. 333–372). Seattle: Bay Press.

Etmanski, C. (2007a). Opportunities and challenges of using legislative theatre to "practise" democracy. In D.E. Clover & J. Stalker (Eds.), *The Art of Social Justice: Re-crafting Activist Adult Education and Community Leadership* (pp. 105–124). Leicester, UK: NIACE.

Etmanski, C. (2007b). *UNSETTLED Embodying Transformative Learning and Intersectionality in Higher Education: Popular Theatre as Research with International Graduate Students.* Unpublished doctoral dissertation, Victoria, BC, University of Victoria. Retrieved from https://dspace.library.uvic. ca:8443/handle/1828/233

Etmanski, C., & Pant, M. (2007). Teaching participatory research through reflexivity and relationship: Reflections on an international collaborative curriculum project between the Society for Participatory Research in Asia (PRIA) and the University of Victoria (UVic). *Journal of Action Research, 5*(3), 275–292. http://dx.doi.org/10.1177/1476750307081018

Evans, D.M., Fox, M., & Fine, M. (2010). Producing selves and knowledges: Reflections on participatory youth inquiry. In N. Ares (Ed.), *Youth-Full Productions: Cultural Practices and Constructions of Content and Social Spaces* (pp. 97–124). New York: Peter Lang.

Eyler, J., & Giles, D.E. (1999). *Where's the Learning in Service-Learning?* San Francisco: Jossey- Bass.

Fals Borda, O. (2001). Participatory (action) research in social theory: Origins and challenges. In P. Reason & H. Bradbury (Eds.), *Handbook on Action Research* (pp. 27–37). London: Sage.

Fals Borda, O., & Rahman, M.A. (1991). *Action and Knowledge: Breaking the Monopoly with Participatory Action Research.* New York: Apex.

Feeser, A. (2001). Real-time and digital communication in and about contested Hawai'i: The public art project historic waikiki. *Jouvert, 5*(3). Retrieved from http://english.chass.ncsu.edu/jouvert/v5i3/feeser.htm

Fine, M. (1994). Working the hyphens: Reinventing the self and other in qualitative research. In N.K. Denzin & Y.S. Lincoln (Eds.), *Handbook of Qualitative Research* (pp. 70–82). Newbury Park, CA: Sage.

Fine, M. (2009). Postcards from metro America: Reflections on youth participatory action research for urban justice. *Urban Review, 41*(1), 1–6. http://dx.doi .org/10.1007/s11256-008-0099-5

Fine, M., & Rosenberg, P. (1983). Dropping out of high school: The ideology of school and work. *Journal of Education, 165*(3), 257–272.

Fine, M., & Torre, M.E. (2004). Re-membering exclusions: Participatory action research in public institutions. *Qualitative Research in Psychology, 1*(1), 15–37.

Fine, M., Weis, L., Weseen, S., & Wong, L. (2000). For whom: Qualitative research, representations, and social responsibilities. In N.K. Denzin & Y.S. Lincoln (Eds.), *Handbook of Qualitative Research* (2nd ed., pp. 107–132). Thousand Oaks, CA: Sage.

Finley, S. (2008). Arts-based research. In J.G. Knowles & A.L. Cole (Eds.), *Handbook of the Arts in Qualitative Research* (pp. 71–81). Thousand Oaks, CA: Sage.

First Nations Centre. (2007). *OCAP: Ownership, Control, Access and Possession.* Sanctioned by the First Nations Information Governance Committee, Assembly of First Nations. Ottawa: National Aboriginal Health Organization.

Fish, W.W., & Wickersham, L.E. (2009). Best practices for online instructors: Reminders. *Quarterly Review of Distance Education, 10*(3), 279–284.

Fitzgerald, H.E., Burack, C., & Seifer, S.D. (2010). *Handbook of Engaged Scholarship: Contemporary Landscapes, Future Directions.* East Lansing: Michigan State University Press.

Flanagan, T. (2000). *First Nations, Second Thoughts.* Montreal and Kingston: McGill-Queen's University Press.

Flavelle, A. (1996). *Community Mapping Handbook: A Guide to Making Your Own Maps of Communities & Traditional Lands.* Auburn, WA: Endangered Peoples Project Society & Lone Pine Foundation.

Flicker, S. (2008, Feb.). Who benefits from community-based participatory research? A case study of the Positive Youth Project. *Health Education & Behavior, 35*(1), 70–86. http://dx.doi.org/10.1177/1090198105285927 Medline:16740514

Flicker, S., Guta, A., Larkin, J., Flynn, S., Fridkin, A., Travers, R., …, & Layne, C. (2010). Survey Design from the Ground-Up: Collaboratively creating the Toronto Teen Survey. *Health Promotion Practice, 11*(1), 112–122. http://dx.doi .org/10.1177/1524839907309868 Medline:18367639

Flicker, S., Savan, B., McGrath, M., Kolenda, B., & Mildenberger, M. (2007). "If you could change one thing ..." What community-based researchers wish they could have done differently. *Community Development Journal, 43*(2), 239–253. http://dx.doi.org/10.1093/cdj/bsm009

Forster, D. (1998). *Capturing a Sense of Place: A Personal View of an Innovative Experiment in Community Mapping.* Vancouver, BC: Social Change Institute.

Frankenberg, R. (1997). Introduction: Local whitenesses, localizing whiteness. In R. Frankenberg (Ed.), *Displacing Whiteness: Essays in Social and Cultural Criticism* (pp. 1–33). Durham, NC: Duke University Press.

Freeland, C. (2001). *But Is It Art? An Introduction to Art Theory.* New York: Oxford University Press.

Freire, P. (1970). *Pedagogy of the Oppressed*. New York: Continuum Press.

Freire, P. (1986). *Pedagogy of the Oppressed*. New York: Continuum Press.

Freire, P. (2003). *Pedagogy of the Oppressed* (Rev ed.). New York: Continuum Press.

Fremeaux, I., & Ramsden, H. (2007). We disobey to love: Rebel clowning for social justice. In D.E. Clover & J. Stalker (Eds.), *The Arts and Social Justice: Re-crafting Adult Education and Community Cultural Leadership* (pp. 21–37). Leicester, UK: NIACE.

Frisby, W., Maguire, P., & Reid, C. (2009). The "f" word has everything to do with it: How feminist theories inform action research. *Action Research, 7*(1), 13–29. http://dx.doi.org/10.1177/1476750308099595

Gaffield, C. (2008, 29 Sept.). Speech to the Canadian Club of Toronto.

Gagnon-Leary, P., & Fontainha, E. (2007, Sept.). Communities of Practice and Virtual Learning Communities: Benefits, Barriers and Success Factors. In *eLearning Papers*, No 5. Retrieved from http://www.elearningpapers.eu / index.php?page=home&vol=5

Galileo. (1632). *Dialogue Concerning the Two Chief World Systems*. (1957). (S. Drake, Trans.). Berkeley: University of California Press.

Gare, A.E. (1995). *Post-Modernism and the Environmental Crisis*. London: Routledge.

Garoian, C.R. (2011). The exquisite corpse of arts-based research. In N.K. Denzin & M.D. Giardina (Eds.), *Qualitative Inquiry And Global Crises* (pp. 155–177). Walnut Creek, CA: Left Coast Press.

Gaudry, A. (2011). Insurgent research. *Wicazo Sa Review, 26*(1), 113–136. http:// dx.doi.org/10.1353/wic.2011.0006

Gaventa, J. (1998). Poverty, power and social exclusion in north and south. IDS Bulletin, 29(1), 50–57.

Gaventa, J., & Cornwall, A. (2001). Power and knowledge. In P.W. Reason & H. Bradbury (Eds.), *The Sage Handbook of Action Research* (pp. 70–80). London: Sage.

Gaventa, J., & Merrifield, J. (2003). Participatory Research in North America and India. In R. Tandon (Ed.), *Participatory Research: Revisiting the Roots* (pp. 122–137). New Delhi, India: Mosaic Books.

Gehl, L. (n.d.). *The Ally Bill of Responsibilities*. Retrieved from http://www .lynngehl.com/uploads/5/0/0/4/5004954/ally_bill_of_responsibilities_ poster.pdf

Gibson, C.M. (2006). New times demand new scholarship: Research universities and civic engagement, a conference report. Tufts University and Campus Compact. Retrieved from http://www.compact.org/wp-content/ uploads/initiatives/research_universities/conference_report.pdf

Goodman, S. (2003). *Teaching Youth Media: A Critical Guider to Literacy, Video Production, and Social Change.* New York: Teachers College Press.

Goodyear-Ka'ōpua, N. (2009). Rebuilding the 'auwai: Connecting ecology, economy and education in Hawaiian schools. *AlterNative: An International Journal of Indigenous Scholarship, 5*(2), 46–77.

Grace, D., Pickard, A., Gilbert, H., Oliver, B., Baidoobonso, S., & Greenspan, N. (2010, Nov.). From online to the frontlines: Reflections on community research and learning by Universities Without Walls fellows. Oral presentation at *Research at the Front Lines: Targeting the Complexities of HIV*, OHTN Annual Conference, Toronto.

Grant, S. (2007). Learning through being and doing. *Journal of Action Research, 5*(3), 265–274. http://dx.doi.org/10.1177/1476750307081017

Graveline, F.J. (1998). *Circle Works: Transforming Eurocentric Consciousness.* Halifax, NS: Fernwood.

Graveline, F.J. (2002). Teaching tradition teaches us. *Canadian Journal of Native Education, 26*(1), 11–29.

Green, L.W., George, M.A., Daniel, M., Frankish, C.J., Herbert, C.P., Bowie, W.R., & O'Neill, M. (1995). *Study of Participatory Research in Health Promotion.* Ottawa: Royal Society of Canada.

Green Map System. (2009). [Website]. Retrieved from www.greenmap.org

Greenwood, D.J. (2007). Teaching/learning action research requires fundamental reforms in public higher education. *Journal of Action Research, 5*(3), 249–264. http://dx.doi.org/10.1177/1476750307081016

Griffin, C. (2004). Good girls, bad girls: Anglocentrism and diversity in the constitution of contemporary girlhood. In A. Harris (Ed.), *All about the Girl: Culture, Power and Identity* (pp. 29–44). New York: Routledge.

Guenette, F., & Marshall, E.A. (2008). Indigenizing counsellor education: Implementing post-secondary curriculum change. *Canadian Journal of Native Education, 31*(1), 107–122.

Guillemin, M., & Drew, S. (2010). Questions of process in participant-generated visual methodologies. *Visual Studies, 25*(2), 175–188. http://dx.doi.org/10.1080/1472586X.2010.502676

Guishard, M. (2009). "The false paths, the endless labors, the turns now this way and now that": Participatory action research, mutual vulnerability, and the politics of inquiry. *Urban Review: Issues and Ideas in Public Education, 41*(1), 85–105.

Gwa'sala-Nakwaxda'xw. (2010). *History and vision.* Retrieved from http://www.gwanak.info/about-us/history-vision

Gwyther, G., & Possamai-Inesedy, A. (2009). Methodologies à la carte: An examination of emerging qualitative methodologies in social research.

International Journal of Social Research Methodology, 12(2), 99–115. http://dx
.doi.org/10.1080/13645570902727680

Hall, B.L. (1975). Participatory Research: An approach for change. *Convergence*
(Toronto), *8*(2), 24–31.

Hall, B.L. (1978). *Mtu ni Afya: Tanzania's Health Campaign*. Information Bulletin
No 9. Washington, DC: Clearinghouse on Development Communications.

Hall, B.L. (1992). From margins to center? The development and purpose of
participatory research. *American Sociologist, 23*(4), 15–28. http://dx.doi.org/
10.1007/BF02691928

Hall, B.L. (2001). I wish this were a poem of practices of participatory research.
In P. Reason & H. Bradbury (Eds.), *Handbook of Action Research: Participative
Inquiry and Practice* (pp. 171–178). London: Sage.

Hall, B.L. (2005). In from the Cold? Reflections on Participatory Research
1970–2005. *Convergence (Toronto), 38*(1), 5–24.

Hall, B.L. (2009a). Higher education, community engagement and the public
good: Building the future of continuing education in Canada. *Canadian
Journal of University Continuing Education, 95*(1), 11–23.

Hall, B.L. (2009b). Lyrics of the dawn: Poetry and social movements. *Conducive
Magazine*. http://www.conducivemag.com/2009/06/lyrics-of-
the-dawn-poetry-and-social-movements/

Haraway, D. (1988). Situated knowledges: The science question in feminism
and the privilege of partial perspective. *Feminist Studies, 14*(3), 575–599.
http://dx.doi.org/10.2307/3178066

Harley, J.B. (1989). Deconstructing the map. *Cartographica, 26*(2), 1–20. http://
dx.doi.org/10.3138/E635-7827-1757-9T53

Harm Reduction Victoria. (2009, 8 Sept.). Harm Reduction Victoria releases
Guerrilla Needle Exchange distribution and recovery results, plans
for community forum [Press Release]. Retrieved from http://www
.harmreductionvictoria.ca/?q=node/12

Harm Reduction Victoria. (2010). *Harm Reduction Principles*. [Website].
Retrieved from http://harmreductionvictoria.ca/?q=node/80

Harm Reduction Victoria. (2011). *Our Demands* Retrieved from http://www
.harmreductionvictoria.ca/?q=node/79

Harris, C.E. (1998). *A Sense of Themselves: Elizabeth Murray's Leadership in School
and Community*. Black Point, NS: Fernwood.

Hart, S. (1995). Action in reflection. *Educational Action Research, 3*(2), 211–232.
http://dx.doi.org/10.1080/0965079950030207

Harvey, D. (1973). *Social Justice and the City*. Baltimore, MD: Johns Hopkins
University Press.

Hatcher, A., Bartlett, C., Marshall, M., & Marshall, A. (2009). Two-eyed seeing.
Green Teacher, Fall (86), 3–6. Retrieved from http://www.integrativescience.

ca/uploads/files/2009-GREEN-TEACHER-Integrative-Science-Two-Eyed-Seeing(all).pdf

Hayward, C., Simpson, L., & Wood, L. (2004). Still left out in the cold: Problematising participatory research and development. *Sociologia Ruralis*, *44*(1), 95–108. http://dx.doi.org/10.1111/j.1467-9523.2004.00264.x

Heaney, T.W. (1993). If you can't beat 'em, join 'em: The professionalization of participatory research. In P. Park, M. Brydon-Miller, B. Hall, & T. Jackson (Eds.), *Voices of Change: Participatory Research in the United States and Canada* (pp. 41–46). Westport, CT: Bergin & Garvey.

Hein, H. (1990). The role of feminist aesthetics in feminist theory. *Journal of Aesthetics and Art Criticism*, *48*(4), 281–291. http://dx.doi.org/10.2307/431566

Heron, J. (1996). *Co-operative Inquiry: Research into the Human Condition.* Thousand Oaks, CA: Sage.

Hoare, T., Levy, C., & Robinson, M.P. (1993). Participatory action research in Native communities: Cultural opportunities and legal implications. *Canadian Journal of Native Studies*, *8*(1), 43–68.

Holmen, R. (2009, 11 Nov.). Princess Avenue needle exchange axed. *Victoria News.*

hooks, b. (1989). *Talking Back: Thinking Feminist, Thinking Black.* Cambridge, MA: South End Press.

hooks, b. (1994). *Teaching to Transgress: Education as the Practice of Freedom.* London: Routledge.

Horsfall, D., & Welsby, J. (2007). If someone actually asked us, you'd find we have a lot to say: Arts-based inquiry with women who have an intellectual disability. In J. Higgs, A. Titchen, D. Horsfall, & H. Armstrong (Eds.), *Being Critical and Creative in Qualitative Research* (pp. 260–271). Sydney: Hampden.

Horton, A.I. (1989). *The Highlander Folk School: A History of Its Major Programs, 1932–1961.* Brooklyn, NY: Carlson.

Howells, R. (2003). *Visual Culture.* Cambridge, UK: Polity.

Hudson, P., & Taylor-Henley, S. (2001). Beyond the rhetoric: Implementing culturally appropriate research projects in First Nations communities. *American Indian Culture and Research Journal*, *25*(2), 93–105.

Huutniemi, K., Klein, J., Bruun, H., & Hukkinen, J. (2010). Analyzing interdisciplinarity: Typology and indicators. *Research Policy*, *39*(1), 79–88. http://dx .doi.org/10.1016/j.respol.2009.09.011

Ibáñez-Carrasco, F., & Riaño-Alcalá, P. (2011). Organizing community-based research knowledge between universities and communities: Lessons learned. *Community Development Journal*, *46*(1), 72–88. http://dx.doi.org / 10.1093/cdj/bsp041

Ignagni, E., & Church, K. (2008). Disability studies and the ties and tensions with arts-informed inquiry: One more reason to look away? In J. Knowles &

A. Cole (Eds.), *Handbook of the Arts in Qualitative Research* (pp. 625–639). Thousand Oaks, CA: Sage. http://dx.doi.org/10.4135/9781452226545.n52

Ilcan, S., & Basok, T. (2004). Community government: Voluntary agencies, social justice, and the responsibilization of citizens. *Citizenship Studies, 8*(2), 129–144. http://dx.doi.org/10.1080/1362102042000214714

Indian and Northern Affairs Canada. (1996). *Report of the Royal Commission on Aboriginal Peoples.* Retrieved from http://www.collectionscanada.gc.ca/webarchives/20071115053257/http://www.ainc-inac.gc.ca/ch/rcap/sg/sgmm_e.html

Institute for Community Research. (2007). Case studies in community-based collaborative research. Hartford, CT: Author. http://www.incommunity research.org/documents/CaseStudiesinCBCRFinal12.17.08.pdf

Israel, B., Schultz, A., Parker, E., Becker, A., Allen, A., & Guzman, J.R. (2003). Critical issues in developing and following community-based participatory research principles. In M. Minkler & N. Wallerstein (Eds.), *Community-Based Participatory Research for Health* (pp. 53–76). San Francisco: Jossey-Bass.

Israel, B.A., Schulz, A.J., Parker, E.A., & Becker, A.B. (1998). Review of community-based research: Assessing partnership approaches to improve public health. *Annual Review of Public Health, 19*(1), 173–202. http://dx.doi.org/10.1146/annurev.publhealth.19.1.173 Medline:9611617

Israel, R., Eng, E., Schulz, A.J., & Parker, E.A. (2005). Introduction to methods in Community-Based Participatory Research for health. In B. Israel, E. Eng, A.J. Schulz, & E.A. Parker (Eds.), *Methods in Community-Based Participatory Research for Health* (pp. 3–26) San Francisco: Jossey-Bass.

Israel, R., Eng, E., Schulz, A.J., & Parker, E.A. (Eds.). (2005). *Methods in Community-Based Participatory Research for Health.* San Francisco: Jossey-Bass.

Ivsins, A., Chow, C., Marsh, D., Macdonald, S., Stockwell, T., & Vallance, K. (2010). *Drug Use Trends in Victoria and Vancouver, and Changes in Injection Drug Use after the Closure of Victoria's Fixed Site Needle Exchange.* (CARBC Statistical Bulletin). Victoria, BC: University of Victoria. Retrieved from http://carbc.ca/Portals/0/PropertyAgent/558/Files/1/CARBC_Bulletin6.pdf

Jackson, A. (2002). Translator's introduction. In A. Boal (Ed.), *Games for Actors and Non-actors* (pp. xxii–xxix). (A. Jackson, Trans.). New York: Routledge.

Jackson, E.T., & Kassam, Y. (1998). *Knowledge Shared: Participatory Evaluation in Development Cooperation.* West Hartford, CT: Kumarian.

Jansson, S.M., Benoit, C., Casey, L., Phillips, R., & Burns, D. (2010, Jan.). In for the long haul: Knowledge translation between academic and nonprofit organizations. *Qualitative Health Research, 20*(1), 131–143. http://dx.doi.org/10.1177/1049732309349808 Medline:19801416

Johnson, S. (2011). Wrap a star blanket around each one: Learning from the educational experiences of Indigenous former children in care on Coast Salish territory. In K. Kufeldt & B. McKenzie (Eds.), *Child Welfare: Connecting Research, Policy and Practice* (2nd ed., pp. 339–352). Waterloo, ON: Wilfrid Laurier University Press.

Johnson, W.B. (2007). *On Being a Mentor: A Guide for Higher Education Faculty.* New York: Lawrence Erlbaum.

Kahne, J., & Westheimer, J. (1996). In the service of what? *Phi Delta Kappan, 77,* 592–600.

Kaner, S. (2001). The dynamics of group decision-making. In *Facilitator's Guide to Participatory Decision-Making* (pp. 18–21). Gabriola Island, BC: New Society. [Originally Published in 1996].

Kanu, Y. (2005). Teachers' perceptions of the integration of Aboriginal culture into high school curriculum. *Journal of Educational Research, 51*(1), 50–68.

Kassirer, J. (2012). British Columbia's way to go! program. *Tools of Change. Proven methods for promoting health, safety, and environmental citizenship.* Retrieved from http://www.toolsofchange.com/en/case-studies/detail/135

Kazemak, F. (1992). Looking at adult literacy obliquely: Poetry, stories, imagination, metaphor and gossip. *Adult Basic Education, 2*(3), 144–160.

Kemm, J. (2006). The limitations of "evidence-based" public health. *Journal of Evaluation in Clinical Practice, 12*(3), pp. 319–324.

Kemmis, S., & McTaggart, R. (2000). Participatory action research. In N.K. Denzin & Y.S. Lincoln (Eds.), *Handbook of Qualitative Research* (2nd ed., pp. 567–605). Thousand Oaks, CA: Sage.

Kenny, C. (2004). *A holistic framework for Aboriginal policy research.* Ottawa: Status of Women Canada. Retrieved from http://www.turtleisland.org/resources/hresearch.pdf

Kidd, R., & Byram, M. (1979). *Popular Theatre: A Technique for Participatory Research. Participatory Research Project.* Working Paper no. 5. Toronto: International Council for Adult Education.

Kindon, S., & Elwood, S. (2009). Introduction: More than methods – Reflections on participatory action research in geographic teaching, learning and research. *Journal of Geography in Higher Education, 33*(1), 19–32. http://dx.doi.org/10.1080/03098260802276474

King, T. (2003). *The Truth about Stories: A Native Narrative.* Toronto: Anansi.

Kinsler, K. (2010). The utility of educational action research for emancipatory change. *Action Research, 8*(2), 171–189. http://dx.doi.org/10.1177/1476750309351357

Kirby, S.L., Greaves, L., & Reid, C. (2006). *Experience Research Social Change: Methods beyond the Mainstream* (2nd ed.). Peterborough: Broadview.

Kirkness, V.J., & Barnhardt, R. (1991). The four R's: Respect, relevance, reciprocity, responsibility. *Journal of American Indian Education, 30*(3), 1–15.

Kirmayer, L.J., Rousseau, C., Corin, E., & Groleau, D. (2008, July–Aug.). Training researchers in cultural psychiatry: The McGill-CIHR Strategic Training Program. *Academic Psychiatry, 32*(4), 320–326. http://dx.doi .org/10.1176/appi.ap.32.4.320 Medline:18695034

Knowles, J.G., & Cole, A.L. (Eds.). (2008). *Handbook of the Arts in Qualitative Inquiry: Perspectives, Methodologies, Examples, and Issues.* Los Angeles: Sage.

Knowles, M., Holton, E. F., III, Swanson, R. A. (2005). The Adult Learner: The Definitive Classic in Adult Education and Human Resource Development (6th ed.). Burlington, MA: Elsevier.

Kolb, D.A. (1984). *Experiential Learning: Experience as the Source of Learning and Development.* New Brunswick, NJ: Prentice-Hall.

Korzybski, A. (1941). *Science and Sanity.* (2nd ed.). Lancaster, PA: International Non-Aristotelian Library Publishing.

Kothari, U. (2001). Power, knowledge and social control in participatory development. In B. Cooke & U. Kothari (Eds.), *Participation: The New Tyranny?* (pp. 139–151). London: Zed Books.

Kovach, M. (2009). *Indigenous Methodologies: Characteristics, Conversations, and Contexts.* Toronto: University of Toronto Press.

Kuhn, T. (1970). *The Structure of Scientific Revolutions.* (2nd ed.). Chicago: University of Chicago Press.

Kumashiro, K.K. (2008). Partial movements toward teacher quality and their potential for advancing social justice. In M. Cochran-Smith, S. Feiman-Nemser, D.J. McIntyre, & K.E. Demers (Eds.), *Handbook of Research on Teacher Education: Enduring Questions in Changing Contexts* (3rd ed., pp. 238–242). New York: Routledge.

Kur, E., DePorres, D., & Westrup, N. (2008). Teaching and learning action research: Transforming students, faculty and university in Mexico. *Action Research, 6*(3), 327–349. http://dx.doi.org/10.1177/1476750308094648

Ladson-Billings, G. (2000). Racialized discourses and ethnic epistemologies. In N. Denzin & Y. Lincoln (Eds.), *Handbook of Qualitative Research* (2nd ed., pp. 398–432). Thousand Oaks, CA: Sage.

Lakoff, G., & Johnson, M. (1999). *Philosophy in the Flesh: The Embodied Mind and Its Challenge to Western Thought.* New York: Basic Books.

Land Trust Alliance of BC. (n.d.). Retrieved from http://ltabc.ca/

Lather, P. (1986). Research as praxis. *Harvard Educational Review, 56*(3), 257–277.

Lave, J., & Wenger, E. (1991). *Situated learning: Legitimate peripheral participation.* Cambridge: Cambridge University Press. http://dx.doi.org/10.1017/ CBO9780511815355

Leadbeater, B. (Ed.). (2006). *Research Ethics in Community-Based and Participatory Action Research with Children, Adolescents, and Youth.* Toronto: University of Toronto Press.

Lee, J.-A. (2006). Locality, participatory action research, and racialized girls struggle for citizenship. In Y. Jiwani, C. Mitchell, & C. Steenbergen (Eds.), *Girlhood: Redefining the Limits* (pp. 89–108). Montreal: Black Rose Books.

Lee, J.-A., & de Finney, S. (2005). Using popular theatre for engaging racialized minority girls in exploring questions of identity and belonging. *Child and Youth Services, 26*(2), 95–118. http://dx.doi.org/10.1300/J024v26n02_06

Leggo, C. (2008). The ecology of personal and professional experience: A poet's view. In M. Cahnmann-Taylor & R. Siegesmund (Eds.), *Arts-Based Research in Education* (pp. 89–98). New York: Routledge.

Leik, V. (2009). *Bringing Indigenous Perspectives into Education: A Case Study of "Thunderbird/Whale Protection and Welcoming Pole: Learning and Teaching in an Indigenous World."* Unpublished Master's thesis, University of Victoria, Victoria, BC.

Levesque, N.P. (2007). *Network: The Key to Acting on Knowledge.* Unpublished discussion paper on a pan-Canadian network of community-engaged research and learning partnerships. Victoria, BC: University of Victoria.

Levin, B. (2008). *Thinking about Knowledge Mobilization.* A discussion paper prepared at the request of the Canadian Council on Learning and the Social Sciences and Humanities Research Council. Toronto: Ontario Institute for Studies in Education. Retrieved from http://www.ccl-cca.ca/pdfs/OtherReports/LevinDiscussionPaperEN.pdf

Levin, M., & Martin, A. (2007). The praxis of educating action researchers: The possibilities and obstacles in higher education. *Action Research, 5*(3), 219–229. http://dx.doi.org/10.1177/1476750307081014

Lewin, K. (1948). *Resolving Social Conflicts.* New York: Harper & Bros.

Lewis, C., & Abdul-Hamid, H. (2006). Implementing effective online teaching practices: Voices of exemplary faculty. *Innovative Higher Education, 31*(2), 83–98. http://dx.doi.org/10.1007/s10755-006-9010-z

Lewis, M. (1987). The origins of cartography. In D. Turnbull (Ed.), *Maps Are Territories, Science Is an Atlas* (pp. 51–52). Chicago: University of Chicago Press.

Lincoln, Y.S., Lynham, S.A., & Guba, E.G. (2011). Paradigmatic controversies, contradictions, and emerging confluences, revisited. In N.K. Denzin & Y.S. Lincoln (Eds.), *The Sage Handbook of Qualitative Research* (4th ed., pp. 97–126). Thousand Oaks, CA: Sage.

Lippard, L.R. (1984). *Get the Message? A Decade of Art for Social Change.* New York: E.P. Dutton.

Living Knowledge: The International Science Shop Network. (n.d.). E.U. Science & Society. [Website of Resources]. Retrieved from http://www .livingknowledge.org/livingknowledge/

Loiselle, E. (2011). *Resistance as Desire: Reconfiguring the "At-Risk Girl" through Critical, Girl-Centred Participatory Action Research.* Unpublished Master's thesis, University of Victoria, Victoria, BC.

Luft, J. (1961). The Johari Window: A graphic model of awareness in interpersonal relations. *Human Relations Training News, 5*(1), 6–7.

Lydon, M. (2000). Finding our way home. *Alternatives Magazine, 26*(4), 26–29.

Lydon, M. (2000, Jan.). *Mapping: The Recovery of Natural Knowledge and the Creation of Sustainable Communities. Discussion Series D.* Victoria, BC: University of Victoria Eco-Research Chair.

Lydon, M. (2002). *(Re)Presenting the Living Landscape: Community Mapping as a Tool for Transformative Learning and Planning.* Unpublished Master's thesis, University of Victoria, Victoria, BC.

Lydon, M. (2007). *Mapping Our Common Ground: A Community and Green Mapping Resource Guide.* Victoria: Common Ground.

Lyon-Callo, V. (2001). Making sense of NIMBY: Poverty, power, and community opposition to homeless shelters. *City & Society, 13*(2), 183–209. http:// dx.doi.org/10.1525/city.2001.13.2.183

Machado, A. (1912). *Proverbios y cantaras: Campos de Castilla.* Madrid: Renacimiento.

Macintyre, S. (2007). Universities. In C. Hamilton & S. Maddison (Eds.), *Silencing Dissent: How the Australian Government Is Controlling Public Opinion and Stifling Debate* (pp. 41–59). Sydney: Allen & Unwin.

MacNeil, J., & Pauly, B. (2008). *Reaching Out: Evaluation of the Needle Exchange on Vancouver Island Island.* Victoria, BC: School of Nursing, University of Victoria.

MacNeil, J., & Pauly, B. (2011, Jan.). Needle exchange as a safe haven in an unsafe world. *Drug and Alcohol Review, 30*(1), 26–32. Retrieved from http:// onlinelibrary.wiley.com/doi/10.1111/j.1465-3362.2010.00188.x/abstract. http://dx.doi.org/10.1111/j.1465-3362.2010.00188.x Medline:21219494

Maguire, P. (2001). Uneven ground: Feminisms and action research. In P. Reason & H. Bradbury (Eds.), *Handbook of Action Research: Participative Inquiry and Practice* (pp. 59–69). London: Sage.

Manson, S.M. (2009, Apr.). Personal journeys, professional paths: Persistence in navigating the crossroads of a research career. *American Journal of Public Health, 99* (S1 Suppl 1), S20–S25. http://dx.doi.org/10.2105/ AJPH.2007.133603 Medline:19246673

Manuel, G. (1976). The rights of the Indians of Canada as the Aboriginal people of North America. In C. Linklater (Ed.), *Speeches by George Manuel:*

President of National Indian Brotherhood, 1970–1976 (Part 1, pp. 1–12). Vancouver, BC: National Indian Brotherhood.

Marcuse, H. (1978). *The Aesthetic Dimension: Toward a Critique of Marxist Aesthetics*. (Rev. ed.). Toronto: Fitzhenry & Whiteside.

marino, d. (1988). *Wild Garden: Art, Education and the Culture of Resistance* Toronto: Between the Lines.

Marshall, E.A., Emerson, L., Williams, L.B., Antoine, A., MacDougall, C., Peterson, R. with the Aboriginal Communities Counselling Program Students. (in press). A'tola'nw: Indigenous-centred learning in a counselling graduate program. In S. Stewart, R. Moodley, & T. Beaulieu (Eds.), *Indigenous Mental Health and Healing on Turtle Island: A Multifaceted Approach*. Thousand Oaks, CA: Sage.

Marshall, E.A., & Batten, S. (2004). Researching across cultures: Issues of ethics and power. *Forum Qualitative Sozialforschung / Forum: Qualitative Social Research, 5*(3). Retrieved from http://www.qualitative-research.net/index .php/fqs/article/view/572/1241

Marshall, E.A., Shepard, B., & Leadbeater, B. (2006). Interdisciplinary research: Charting new directions collaboratively. *International Journal of the Humanities, 2*(2), 953–960.

Marshall, E.A., Williams, L., Emerson, L., & van Hanuse, A. (2009, Sept.). *A'tol'now: A graduate counselling program for Aboriginal communities*. Paper presented at the annual NMHAC Conference. London, Ontario.

Marullo, S. (1996). The service-learning movement in higher education: An academic response to troubled times. *Sociological Imagination, 33*(2), 117–137.

Marx, K. (1969). *Selected Works of Marx and Engels*, vol. 1 (pp. 13–15). Moscow: Progress.

Mateer, K., & Dawson, T. (2009). *University of Victoria Teaching Assessment Guidelines: Assessment of Teaching Effectiveness and Teaching Excellence for Decisions Concerning Reappointment, Tenure and Promotion*. Victoria: University of Victoria. Retrieved from http://www.ltc.uvic.ca/servicesprograms / documents/UVic_teaching_guidelines_Final_Oct_8_09.pdf

May, S., & Aikman, S. (2003). Indigenous education: Addressing current issues and developments. *Comparative Education, 39*(2), 139–145. http://dx.doi .org/10.1080/03050060302549

McCabe, G. (2007). The healing path: A culture and community derived Indigenous therapy model. *Psychotherapy: Theory, Research, Training and Practice, 44*(2), 148–160. http://dx.doi.org/10.1037/0033-3204.44.2.148

McCall, L. (2005). The complexity of intersectionality. *Signs* [Chicago, IL], *30*(3), 1771–1800. http://dx.doi.org/10.1086/426800

McClelland, A., & De Pauw, L. (2010). *Good Practice Guide: Greater Involvement of People Living with HIV (GIPA)*. Hove, UK, and Amsterdam: International

HIV/AIDS Alliance and the Global Network of People Living with HIV (GNP+).

McClelland, S.I., & Fine, M. (2008). Writing *on* cellophane: Studying teen women's sexual desires, inventing methodological release points. In K. Gallagher (Ed.), *The Methodological Dilemma: Creative, Critical and Collaborative Approaches to Qualitative Research* (pp. 232–260). New York: Routledge.

McCormack, B., & Titchen, A. (2007). Critical creativity: Melding, exploding, blending. In J. Higgs, A. Titchen, D. Horsfall, & H. Armstrong (Eds.), *Being Critical and Creative in Qualitative Research* (pp. 43–55). Sydney: Hampden.

McCormick, R. (1998). Ethical considerations in First Nations counselling. *Canadian Journal of Counselling, 32*(4), 284–297.

McCormick R. (2009). Aboriginal approaches to counselling. In L.J. Kirmayer & G.G. Valaskakis (Eds.), *Healing Traditions: The Mental Health of Aboriginal Peoples in Canada* (pp. 337–354). Vancouver: UBC Press.

McGuire, P. (1987). *Doing Participatory Research: A Feminist Approach* Amherst, MA: Center for Non-Formal Education, University of Massachusetts.

McIntosh, P. (1988). *White Privilege: Unpacking the Invisible Knapsack Paper Wellesley*. Wellesley, MA: Wellesley College Center for Research on Women.

McLean, C. (2010). *Creative Arts in Interdisciplinary Practice, Inquiries for Hope and Change*. Calgary: Detselig.

McLean, C., & Kelly, R. (Eds.). (2011). *Creative Arts in Research for Community and Cultural Change*. Calgary: Detselig.

McNiff, S. (1998). *Art-Based Research*. London: Jessical Kingsley.

McNiff, S. (2008). Art-Based Research. In J.G. Knowles & A.L. Cole (Eds.), *Handbook of the Arts in Qualitative Research* (pp. 29–40). Thousand Oaks, CA: Sage.

Merriam, S. (2008). *Third Update in Adult Learning Theory: New Directions for Adult and Continuing Education, Number 119*. San Francisco: Jossey-Bass.

Meyer, M. (2010). The rise of the knowledge broker. *Science Communication, 32*(1), 118–127. http://dx.doi.org/10.1177/1075547009359797

Mezirow, J. (1991). *Transformative Dimensions of Adult Learning*. San Francisco: Jossey-Bass.

Michaels, A. (1996). *Fugitive Pieces*. Toronto: McLelland & Stewart.

Mikel-Brown, L. (2005). In the bad or good of girlhood: Social class, schooling, and white femininities. In L. Weis & M. Fine (Eds.), *Beyond Silenced Voices: Class, Race, and Gender in the United States Schools* (pp. 147–162). Albany, NY: State University of New York Press.

Minkler, M., & Wallerstein, N. (Eds.). (2003). *Community-Based Participatory Research for Health*. San Francisco: Jossey-Bass.

Minkler, M., & Wallerstein, N. (2008). Introduction to CPBR: New issues and emphases. In M. Minkler & N. Wallerstein (Eds.), *Community-Based*

Participatory Research for Health: From Process to Outcomes (2nd ed., pp. 5–24). San Francisco: Jossey-Bass.

Mitton, C., Adair, C.E., McKenzie, E., Patten, S.B., & Waye Perry, B. (2007, Dec.). Knowledge transfer and exchange: Review and synthesis of the literature. *Milbank Quarterly, 85*(4), 729–768. http://dx.doi.org/10.1111 / j.1468-0009.2007.00506.x Medline:18070335

Moewaka Barnes, H., Henwood, W., Kerr, S., McManus, V., & McCreanor, T. (2011). Knowledge translation and Indigenous research. In E.M. Banister, B.J. Leadbeater, & E.A. Marshall (Eds.), *Knowledge Translation in Context: Indigenous, Policy, and Community Setting* (pp. 161–180). Toronto: University of Toronto Press.

Mohanty, C.T. (2003). *Feminism without Borders: Decolonizing Theory, Practicing Solidarity*. Durham, NC: Duke University Press.

Mooney, L.A., & Edwards, B. (2001). Experiential learning in sociology: Service-learning and other community-based learning. *Teaching Sociology, 29*(2), 181–194. http://dx.doi.org/10.2307/1318716

Moraga, C. & Anzaldua, G. (Eds.). (1983). *This Bridge Called My Back: Writings of Radical Women of Color*. (2nd ed.). New York: Kitchen Table Press.

Morrissette, P.J. (2008). Clinical engagement of Canadian First Nations couples. *Journal of Family Therapy, 30*(1), 60–77. http://dx.doi.org/10.1111 / j.1467-6427.2008.00416.x

Mullin, A. (2003). Feminist art and the political imagination. *Hypatia, 18*(4), 189–213. http://dx.doi.org/10.1111/j.1527-2001.2003.tb01418.x

Nadasdy, P. (2003). *Hunters and Bureaucrats: Power, Knowledge, and Aboriginal-State Relations in the Southwest Yukon*. Vancouver: UBC Press.

Neilsen, L. (2002). Learning from the liminal: Fiction as knowledge. *Alberta Journal of Educational Research, 48*(3), 206–214.

Nutley, S., Walter, I., & Davies, H. (2007). *Using Evidence: How Research Can Inform Public Services*. Bristol: Policy Press.

Nyden, P. (2003, July). Academic incentives for faculty participation in community-based participatory research. *Journal of General Internal Medicine, 18*(7), 576–585. http://dx.doi.org/10.1046/j.1525-1497.2003.20350.x Medline:12848841

Nyerere, J.K. (1967a). *The Arusha Declaration*. Dar es Salaam: Tanganyika African National Union.

Nyerere, J.K. (1967b). *Education for Self-Reliance*. Dar es Salaam: Government Printers.

O'Connor, A. (2001). *Poverty Knowledge: Social Science, Social Policy, and the Poor in 20th Century US History*. Princeton, NJ: Princeton University Press.

O'Looney, J. (1998). Mapping communities: Place-based stories and participatory planning. *Journal of the Community Development Society, 29*(2), 201–236.

Oakley, P. (1991). *Projects with People: The Practice of Participation in Rural Development*. Geneva: International Labour Office.

Pain, R. (2009). Commentary: Working across distant spaces: Connecting participatory action research and teaching. *Journal of Geography in Higher Education, 33*(1), 81–87. http://dx.doi.org/10.1080/03098260802276599

Palloff, R., & Pratt, K. (2001). *Lessons from the Cyberspace Classroom: The Realities of Online Teaching*. San Francisco: Jossey-Bass.

Park, P. (1993). What is participatory research? A theoretical and methodological perspective. In P. Park, M. Brydon-Miller, B. Hall, & T. Jackson (Eds.), *Voices of Change: Participatory Research in the United States and Canada* (pp. 1–19). Westport, CT: Bergin & Garvey.

Park, P., Brydon-Miller, M., Hall, B., & Jackson, T. (Eds.). (1993). *Voices of Change: Participatory Research in the United States and Canada*. Toronto: Ontario Institute for Studies in Education Press.

Pauly, B. (2008, Feb.). Harm reduction through a social justice lens. *International Journal on Drug Policy, 19*(1), 4–10. http://dx.doi.org/10.1016/j.drugpo.2007.11.005 Medline:18226520

Pauly, B., Reist, D., Schactman, C., & Belle-Isle, L. (2011, 31 Jan.). *Housing and Harm Reduction: A Policy Framework for Greater Victoria*. The Greater Victoria Coalition to End Homelessness. Retrieved from http://www.homelesshub.ca/(S(cbktsc45bmzvmjn31tluzrqw))/ResourceFiles/GVCEHPolicyFramework_Jan_31_2011.pdf

Pedersen, P.B. (1991). Multiculturalism as a generic approach to counseling. *Journal of Counseling and Development, 70*(1), 6–12. http://dx.doi.org/10.1002/j.1556-6676.1991.tb01555.x

Perron, M. (1998). Common threads: Local strategies for inappropriated artists. In I. Bachmann & R. Scheuing (Eds.), *Materials Matters: The Art and Culture of Contemporary Textiles* (pp. 121–136). Toronto: YYZ Books.

Peseta, T. (2007). Troubling our desires for research and writing within the academic development project. *International Journal for Academic Development, 12*(1), 15–23. http://dx.doi.org/10.1080/13601440701217253

Peters, J.M., & Gray, A. (2007). Teaching and learning in a model-based action research course. *Action Research, 5*(3), 319–331. http://dx.doi.org/10.1177/1476750307081021

Phillips, D.C. (1995). Art as research, research as art. *Educational Theory, 45*(1), 71–84. http://dx.doi.org/10.1111/j.1741-5446.1995.00071.x

Phillips, S., & Levasseur, K. (2004). The snakes and ladders of accountability: Contradictions between contracting and collaboration for Canada's voluntary sector. *Canadian Public Administration, 47*(4), 451–474. http://dx.doi.org/10.1111/j.1754-7121.2004.tb01188.x

Piquemal, N. (2001). Free and informed consent in research involving Native American communities. *American Indian Culture and Research Journal*, 25(1), 65–79.

Place, A. (n.d.). [Website]. Retrieved from http://www.artemisplace.org/ Artemisplace.org/Artemis%20Place.html

Pole Project. (2006). Retrieved from http://education2.uvic.ca/Pole //

Polster, C. (2003). The privatization of our public universities. *Saskatchewan Notes*, 2(7), 1–4. Saskatoon: Canadian Centre for Policy Alternatives. Retrieved from http://www.policyalternatives.ca/sites/default/files/ uploads/publications/Saskatchewan_Pubs/sasknotes2_7.pdf

Poole, R. (1972). *Towards Deep Subjectivity*. London: Harper & Row.

Pratt, C.C., McGuigan, W.M., & Katzev, A.R. (2000). Measuring program outcomes: Using retrospective pretest methodology. *American Journal of Evaluation*, 21(3), 341–349.

Rabinovitch, J. (2004). *Transforming Community Practice: [Re]Moving the Margins*. Doctoral dissertation, School of Interdisciplinary Arts and Sciences, Union Institute and University, Cincinnati, Ohio.

Reason, P., & Bradbury, H. (Eds.). (2001). *Handbook of Action Research: Participative Inquiry and Practice*. London: Sage.

Regan, P. (2011). *Unsettling the Settler Within: Indian Residential Schools, Truth Telling, and Reconciliation in Canada*. Vancouver: UBC Press.

Reitsma-Street, M. (2002, Spring-Fall). Processes of community action research: Putting poverty on the policy agenda of a rich region. *Canadian Review of Social Policy*, 49–50, 69–92. Retrieved from http://web.uvic.ca/spp/ documents/processcommaction.pdf

Riecken, T., & Riecken, J. (2005). *Schalay'nung Sxwey'ga: A Transformational Story*. [DVD].

Riggins, S.H. (1997). The rhetoric of Othering. In S.H. Riggins (Ed.), *The Language and Politics of Exclusion: Others in Discourse* (pp. 1–30). Thousand Oaks, CA: Sage.

Ristock, J.L., & Pennell, J. (1996). *Community Research as Empowerment: Feminist Links, Postmodern Interruptions*. Toronto: Oxford University Press.

Rodriguez, N. (2000). *Dismantling White Privilege: Pedagogy, Politics and Whiteness*. New York: Peter Lang.

Rose, G. (2001). *Visual Methodologies*. London: Sage.

Rose, N. (1996). The death of the social? Re-figuring the territory of government. *Economy and Society*, 25(3), 327–356. http://dx.doi.org/10.1080/ 03085149600000018

Rose, N. (2000). Community, citizenship and the Third Way. *American Behavioral Scientist*, 43(9), 1395–1411. http://dx.doi.org/10.1177/00027640021955955

Rosenstock, L., & Jackson Lee, L. (2002). Attacks on science: The risks to evidence-based policy. *American Journal of Public Health, 92*(1), 14–18.

Rosenthal, M.S., Lucas, G.I., Tinney, B., Mangione, C., Schuster, M.A., Wells, K., & Heisler, M. (2009, Apr.). Teaching community-based participatory research principles to physicians enrolled in a health services research fellowship. *Academic Medicine, 84*(4), 478–484. http://dx.doi.org/10.1097/ACM.0b013e31819a89e8 Medline:19318782

Rukehezer, M. (1974). *The Life of Poetry*. New York: Morrow.

Sá, C.M., Li, S.X., & Faubert, B. (2011). Faculties of Education and institutional strategies for knowledge mobilization: An exploratory study. *Higher Education, 61*(5), 501–512. http://dx.doi.org/10.1007/s10734-010-9344-4

Sabo Flores, K. (2008). *Youth Participatory Evaluation: Strategies for Engaging Young People*. San Francisco: Jossey-Bass.

Said, E. (1996). *Culture and Imperialism*. New York: Knopf/Random House.

Saks, D.L. (2009). Education at a distance: Best practices and considerations for leadership educators. *Journal of Leadership Education, 8*(1), 137–147.

Sandmann, L.R., Thornton, C.H., & Jaeger, A.J. (2009). Editors' notes. *New Directions for Higher Education*, (147), 1–4. http://dx.doi.org/10.1002/he.352

Santos, Boaventura de Sousa. (Ed.). (2007). *Cognitive Justice in a Global World: Prudent Knowledges for a Decent Life*. Lanham: Lexington.

Santos, Boaventura de Sousa. (2012). The university at a crossroads. *Human Architecture: Journal of the Sociology of Self-Knowledge, 10*(1), 7–16.

Saul, J. (2009). *A Fair Country: Telling Truths about Canada*. Toronto: Penguin Canada.

Schnarch, B. (2004). Ownership, control, access and possession (OCAP) or self-determination applied to research. *Journal of Aboriginal Health, 1*(1), 1–37. http://www.research.utoronto.ca/ethics/pdf/human/nonspecific/OCAP%20principles.pdf

Schragge, E. (2003). *Activism and Social Change: Lessons for Community and Local Organizing*. Guelph, ON: Broadview Press.

Schuller, T. (2004). Visual imagery, lifecourse structure and lifelong learning. *Studies in the Education of Adults, 36*(1), 72–85.

Schultz, K. (2003). *Listening: A Framework for Teaching across Differences*. New York: Teachers College Press.

Secwepemc Cultural Education Society. (2010). *Our Story*. Retrieved from http://www.secwepemc.org/about/ourstory

Seldin, P. (1991). *The Teaching Portfolio: A Practical Guide to Improved Performance and Promotion/Tenure Decisions*. Bolton, MA: Anker.

Seldin, P. (1993). *Successful Use of Teaching Portfolios*. Bolton, MA: Anker.

Selener, D. (1997). *Participatory Action Research and Social Change*. Ithaca, NY: Cornell Participatory Action Research Network.

Senguptha, M. (2005). *Kathamarabi, Her Voice and Other Poems*. Kolkata, India: Bhashanagar.

Shakotko, D., & Walker, K. (1999). Poietic leadership. In P. Begley & P. Leonard (Eds.), *The Values of Educational Administration* (pp. 201–222). London: Falmer.

Shefner, J., & Cobb, D. (2002). Hierarchy and partnership in New Orleans. *Qualitative Sociology, 25*(2), 273–297. http://dx.doi.org/10.1023/A:1015422902692

Shiner, L. (2001). *The Invention of Art: A Cultural History*. Chicago: University of Chicago Press. http://dx.doi.org/10.7208/chicago/9780226753416.001.0001

Shiva, V. (2005). *Earth Democracy: Justice, Sustainability, and Peace*. Cambridge, MA: South End Press.

Shonkoff, J.P. (2000, Jan.–Feb.). Science, policy, and practice: Three cultures in search of a shared mission. *Child Development, 71*(1), 181–187. http://dx.doi.org/10.1111/1467-8624.00132 Medline:10836572

Shore, B.M., Foster, S.F., Knapper, C.K., Nadeau, G.G., Neill, N., & Sim, V. (with L. Caron, translator). (1986). *The Teaching Dossier: A Guide to Its Preparation and Use*. Ottawa: Canadian Association of University Teachers.

Shulman, L.S. (1988). A union of insufficiencies: Strategies for teacher assessment in a period of educational reform. *Educational Leadership, 46*(3), 36–41.

Sibley, D. (1995). *Geographies of Exclusion*. London: Routledge. http://dx.doi.org/10.4324/9780203430545

Siem Smun'eem. (n.d.). [Website]. Retrieved from http://web.uvic.ca/icwr/

Siemens, G. (2005). Connectivism: A learning theory for the digital age. *International Journal of Instructional Technology and Distance Learning, 2*(1). Retrieved from http://itdl.org/Journal/Jan_05/article01.htm

Silversides, A. (2006). *Collaboration and Advocacy: The Canadian Association for HIV Research – the First 15 Years*. Toronto: Canadian Association for HIV Research.

Simons, H., & McCormack, B. (2007). Integrating arts-based inquiry in evaluation methodology: Opportunities and challenges. *Qualitative Inquiry, 13*(2), 292–311. http://dx.doi.org/10.1177/1077800406295622

Sinner, A., Leggo, C., Irwin, R.L., Gouzouasis, P., & Grauer, K. (2006). Arts-based educational research dissertations: Reviewing the practices of new scholars. *Canadian Journal of Education, 29*(4), 1223–1270. http://dx.doi.org/10.2307/20054216

Skott-Myhre, H. (2008). *Youth and Subculture as Creative Force: Creating New Spaces for Radical Youth Work*. Toronto: University of Toronto Press.

Slaughter, S., & Rhoades, G. (2008). The academic capitalist knowledge/learning regime. In A.S. Chan & D. Fisher (Eds.), *The Exchange University: Corporatization of Academic Culture* (pp. 19–47). Vancouver: UBC Press.

Smith, A. (2005). *Conquest: Sexual Violence and American Indian Genocide.* Cambridge, MA: South End Press.

Smith, D.E. (2005). *Institutional Ethnography: A Sociology for People.* Toronto: AltaMira Press.

Smith, D.E. (2006). Incorporating texts into ethnographic practice. In D.E. Smith (Ed.), *Institutional Ethnography as Practice* (pp. 65–88). Toronto: Roman & Littlefield.

Smith, G.H. (2003). *Indigenous struggle for the transformation of education and schooling.* Keynote Address to the Alaskan Federation of Natives (AFN) Convention, Anchorage, Alaska. Retrieved from http://www.kaupapamaori.com/assets/indigenous_struggle.pdf

Smith, K. (2010, Mar.). Research, policy and funding – academic treadmills and the squeeze on intellectual spaces. *British Journal of Sociology, 61*(1), 176–195. http://dx.doi.org/10.1111/j.1468-4446.2009.01307.x Medline: 20377602

Smylie, J. (2011). Knowledge translation and Indigenous communities: A decolonizing perspective. In E.M. Banister, B.J. Leadbeater, & E.A. Marshall (Eds.), *Knowledge Translation in Context: Indigenous. Policy, and Community Settings* (pp. 181–200). Toronto: University of Toronto Press.

Sobel, D. (1998). *Map-Making and Childhood: Sense of Place Education for Elementary Years.* Newmarket, ON: Heinemann.

Social Sciences and Humanities Research Council of Canada. (2009–11). *SSHRC's knowledge mobilization strategy.* Retrieved from http://www.sshrc-crsh.gc.ca/about-au_sujet/publications/KMbPI_FinalE.pdf

Solomon, A. (1990). Education. In M. Posluns (Ed.), *Songs for the People: Teaching on the Natural Way* (p. 79). Toronto: NC Press.

Sommer, R. (1999). Action research: From mental hospital reform in Saskatchewan to community building in California. *Canadian Psychology, 40*(1), 47–55. http://dx.doi.org/10.1037/h0092490

Springgay, S., Irwin, R.L., & Kind, S. (2008). A/r/tographers and living inquiry. In J.G. Knowles & A.L. Cole (Eds.), *Handbook of the Arts in Qualitative Research* (pp. 83–91). Thousand Oaks, CA: Sage.

Stajduhar, K., Poffenrothb, L., & Wong, E. (2000). *Missed Opportunities: Putting a Face on Injection Drug Use and HIV/AIDS in the Capital Health Region.* Final report for Health Canada, BC Centre for Disease Control and the Capital Health Region. Victoria, BC: Capital Health Region. Retrieved from http://web.uvic.ca/~senage/documents/research_reports/Stajduhar-RARE_report-Drug_CRD.pdf

Stall, S., & Stoecker, R. (1998). Community organizing or organizing community? Gender and the crafts of empowerment. *Gender & Society, 12*(6), 729–756.

http://www.jstor.org/stable/190515. http://dx.doi.org/10.1177/
089124398012006008

Steinhauer, E. (2002). Thoughts on an Indigenous research methodology. *Canadian Journal of Native Education*, 26(2), 69–81.

Stephenson, J. (Ed.). (2001). *Teaching and Learning Online: Pedagogies for New Technologies*. London: Kogan Page.

Stewart, S. (2007). *Curriculum change: Through the lens of Indigenous pedagogy.* Unpublished manuscript, University of Victoria.

Stoeker, R., & Bonacich, E. (1992). Why participatory research? Guest editors' introduction. *American Sociologist*, 23(4), 5–14. http://dx.doi.org/10.1007/BF02691927

Stoecker, R. (1999). Are academics irrelevant? Roles for scholars in participatory research. *American Behavioral Scientist*, 42(5), 840–854. http://dx.doi.org/10.1177/00027649921954561

Strand, K.J. (2000). Community-based research as pedagogy. *Michigan Journal of Community Service Learning*, 7, 85–96.

Strand, K., Marullo, S., Cutforth, N., Stoecker, R., & Donohue, P. (2003). Principles of best practice for community-based research. *Michigan Journal of Community Service Learning*, 9(3), 5–15.

Stringer, E. (2007). *Action Research.* (3rd ed.). Thousand Oaks, CA: Sage.

Sullivan, G. (2005). *Art Practice as Research: Inquiry in the Visual Arts.* Thousand Oaks, CA: Sage.

Tanaka, M. (2007). *Transforming Perspectives: The Immersion of Student Teachers in Indigenous Ways of Knowing.* Doctoral dissertation, University of Victoria, Victoria, BC.

Tanaka, M., Williams, L., Benoit, Y., Duggan, R., Moir, L., & Scarrow, J. (2007). Transforming pedagogies: Pre-service reflections on learning and teaching in an Indigenous world. *Teacher Development*, 11(1), 99–109. http://dx.doi.org/10.1080/13664530701194728

Tandon, R. (1988). Social transformation and participatory research. *Convergence (Toronto)*, 21(2–3), 5–18.

Tandon, R. (Ed.). (2002). *Participatory Research: Revisiting the Roots.* (Revised ed.). New Delhi, India: Mosaic Books.

Taylor, P., & Pettit, J. (2007). Learning and teaching participation through action research: Experiences from an innovative master's programme. *Action Research*, 5(3), 231–247. http://dx.doi.org/10.1177/1476750307081015

Tempalski, B., Friedman, R., Keem, M., Cooper, H., & Friedman, S.R. (2007, Nov.). NIMBY localism and national inequitable exclusion alliances: The case of syringe exchange programs in the United States. *Geoforum*, 38(6), 1250–1263. http://dx.doi.org/10.1016/j.geoforum.2007.03.012 Medline:18978931

Thomas, L. (2002). Student retention in higher education: The role of institutional habitus. *Journal of Education Policy*, *17*(4), 423–442. http://dx.doi.org/10.1080/02680930210140257

Timothy, R. (2003). Poem read at the ICAE World Assembly of Adult Education in Ocho Rios, Jamaica.

Tipa, G., Panelli, R., & Moeraki Stream Team. (2009). Beyond "someone else's agenda": An example of Indigenous/academic research collaboration. *New Zealand Geographer*, *65*(2), 95–106. http://dx.doi.org/10.1111/j.1745-7939.2009.01152.x

Tisdell, E. (2003). *Exploring Spirituality and Culture in Adult Higher Education*. San Francisco: Josey- Bass.

Torre, M.E. (2009). Participatory action research and critical race theory: Fueling spaces for *nos-otras* to research. *Urban Review*, *41*(1), 106–120. http://dx.doi.org/10.1007/s11256-008-0097-7

Torre, M.E., & Fine, M. (2008). Participatory action research in the contact zone. In J. Cammarota & M. Fine (Eds.), *Revolutionizing Education: Youth Participatory Action Research in Motion* (pp. 23–44). New York: Routledge.

Torre, M.E., Fine, M., Stoudt, B.G., & Fox, M. (2012). Critical participatory action research as public science. In H. Cooper & P. Camic (Eds.), *APA Handbook of Research Methods in Psychology* (pp. 171–184). Washington, DC: American Psychological Association. http://dx.doi.org/10.1037/13620-011

Tri-Council Policy Statement. (2010). Ethical Conduct for Research Involving Humans. Retrieved from http://www.pre.ethics.gc.ca/eng/policy-politique/initiatives/tcps2-eptc2/Default/

Trussler, T., & Marchand, R. (2005). HIV/AIDS community-based research. *New Directions for Adult and Continuing Education*, (105), 43–54. http://dx.doi.org/10.1002/ace.168

Tuck, E. (2009a). Re-visioning action: Participatory action research and Indigenous theories of change. *Urban Review*, *41*(1), 47–65. http://dx.doi.org/10.1007/s11256-008-0094-x

Tuck, E. (2009b). Suspending damage: A letter to communities. *Harvard Educational Review*, *79*(3), 409–427.

Tuck, E., Allen, J., Bacha, M., Morales, A., Quinter, S., Thompson, J., … (2008). PAR praxes for now and future change: The collective of researchers on educational disappointment and desire. In J. Cammarota & M. Fine (Eds.), *Revolutionizing Education: Youth Participatory Action Research in Motion* (pp. 49–83). New York: Routledge.

Tuckman, B.W., & Jensen, M.A.C. (1977). Stages of small group development revisited. *Group & Organization Management*, *2*(4), 419–427. http://dx.doi.org/10.1177/105960117700200404

Tuhiwai Smith, L. (1999). *Decolonizing Methodologies: Research and Indigenous Peoples*. London: Zed Books/University of Otago Press.

Turnbull, D. (1989). *Maps Are Territories: Science Is an Atlas*. Chicago: University of Chicago Press.

Turner, D. (2006). *This Is Not a Peace Pipe: Toward a Critical Indigenous Philosophy*. Toronto: University of Toronto Press.

Turner, N., with C. Bryce & B. Beckwith. (2002). Home place. *Torch: The University of Victoria Alumni Magazine*. Victoria, BC: University of Victoria. Retrieved from http://web.uvic.ca/torch/torch2002f/feature_vox.html

Universities Without Walls. *UWW Training Evaluation Report (2010–2011)*. (2011) Unpublished report. Retrieved from http://www.centreforreach.ca:82/uww_public/Pages/UWWResources.aspx

University of Victoria. (2003). *Protocols & Principles for Conducting Research in an Indigenous Context*. Faculty of Human & Social Development. Retrieved from http://web.uvic.ca/igov/index.php/forms

University of Victoria. (2007). *A Vision for the Future – Building on Strength. A Strategic Plan for the University of Victoria. Planning and Priorities Committee*. Planning and Priorities Committee.

Vancouver Island Health Authority. (2006). *Closing the Gap: Integrated HIV/AIDS and Hepatitis C Strategic Directions for Vancouver Island Health Authority*. Retrieved from http://www.viha.ca/NR/rdonlyres/90755627-1758-4A5C-A446-16D26CB680C7/0/ClosingtheGapJuly252006.pdf

Vancouver Island Health Authority. (2009, 16 Nov.). *VIHA to Increase Island-wide Needle Exchange Services*. [Press Release].

Vancouver Island Health Authority. (2010). Mobile Needle Exchange and "No Service" Areas in Victoria. Retrieved from http://www.viha.ca/NR/rdonlyres/6A664518-55C1-4D8F-B690-23A38EDBCFCF/0/fs_Mobile_Needle_Exchange_and_No_Service_Areas_Victoria.pdf

Vella, J. (2002). *Learning to Listen, Learning to Teach: The Power of Dialogue in Educating Adults*. San Francisco: Jossey-Bass.

Vio Grossi, F. (1981). *Investigación participativa y praxis rural: Nuevas conceptos en educación y desarrollo comunal*. Lima: Mosca Azul.

Vogelgesang, L.J., Denson, N., & Jayakumar, U.M. (2010). What determines faculty-engaged scholarship? *Review of Higher Education, 33*(4), 437–472. http://dx.doi.org/10.1353/rhe.0.0175

Wallace, B., & Willson, M. (2008/2010). *A Review of the Evidence Supporting Supervised Consumption Sites (SCS) and Comprehensive Harm Reduction Services in Victoria BC*. Prepared for Harm Reduction Victoria. Retrieved from http://www.harmreductionvictoria.ca/?q=node/77

Wallerstein, N. (1999, July). Power between evaluator and community: Research relationships within New Mexico's healthier communities. *Social Science & Medicine, 49*(1), 39–53. http://dx.doi.org/10.1016/S0277-9536(99)00073-8 Medline:10414839

Wallerstein, N., & Duran, B. (2006, July). Using community-based participatory research to address health disparities. *Health Promotion Practice, 7*(3), 312–323. http://dx.doi.org/10.1177/1524839906289376 Medline:16760238

Wallerstein, N., & Duran, B. (2008). The conceptual, historical and practical roots of community-based participatory research and related participatory traditions. In M. Minkler & N. Wallerstein (Eds.), *Community Based Participatory Research for Health* (pp. 27–52). San Francisco: Jossey-Bass.

Walsh, C.A., Rutherford, G.E., & Sears, A.E. (2010). Fostering inclusivity through teaching and learning action research. *Action Research, 8*(2), 191–209. http://dx.doi.org/10.1177/1476750309351360

Wang, C.C., & Burris, M.A. (1997, June). Photovoice: Concept, methodology, and use for participatory needs assessment. *Health Education & Behavior, 24*(3), 369–387. http://dx.doi.org/10.1177/109019819702400309 Medline:9158980

Warhus, M. (1997). *Another America: Native American Maps and the History of Our Land.* New York: St Martin's Press.

Way-To-Go Schools Program. (2003). [Website]. Retrieved from: http://www.toolsofchange.com/en/case-studies/detail/135

Welton, M. (2001). *Little Mosie from the Margaree: A Biography of Moses Michael Coady.* Toronto: Thompson Educational.

Wenger, E. (1998). *Communities of practice.* Cambridge: Cambridge University Press.

Wertsch, J.A. (1998). *Mind as Action.* New York: Oxford University Press.

Westley, F., Geobay, S., & Robinson, K. (2012). Change lab/design lab for social innovation. Waterloo, ON: Waterloo Institute of Social Innovation. Retrieved from http://sigeneration.ca/documents/Paper_FINAL_LabforSocialInnovation.pdf

Whyte, W.F. (Ed.). (1991). *Participatory Action Research.* Newbury Park, CA: Sage.

Widdowson, F., & Howard. A. (2008). *Disrobing the Aboriginal Industry: The Deception Behind Indigenous Cultural Preservation.* Montreal and Kingston: McGill-Queen's University Press.

Wildfire Management Branch. (2011). *Summary of Previous Fire Seasons.* Retrieved from http://bcwildfire.ca/History/SummaryArchive.htm#2003

Wilkins, D.E. (2005). Keynote address. *Wicazo Sa Review, 20*(1), 163–168. http://dx.doi.org/10.1353/wic.2005.0017

Williams, A., Labonte, R., Randall, J.E., & Muhajarine, N. (2005). Establishing and sustaining community-university partnerships: A case study of quality of life research. *Critical Public Health, 15*(3), 291–302. http://dx.doi.org/10.1080/09581590500372451

Williams, L., & Tanaka, M. (2007). Schalay'nung sxwey'ga: Emerging cross-cultural pedagogy in the academy. *Educational Insights, 11*(3). Retrieved from http://ccfi.educ.ubc.ca/publication/insights/v11n03/articles/williams/williams.html

Williamson, B. (2004). *Lifeworlds and Learning.* Leicester: NIACE.

Wilson, S. (2008). *Research Is Ceremony: Indigenous Research Methods.* Black Point, NS: Fernwood.

Wood, D. (1994). Memory, love, distortion, power: What is a map? *Orion Magazine, 13*(2), 24–33.

Wright, R. (1991). *Stolen Continents: The New World through Indian Eyes since 1492.* Toronto: Viking.

Zangger, C. (2011). *Distribute, recover, educate & refer: A qualitative study examining the impact of the fixed site needle exchange closure on service delivery.* [Draft Report]. Prepared in partnership with AIDS Vancouver Island, with funding from the Vancouver Public Interest Research Group (VIPIRG).

Zingaro, L. (2009). *Speaking Out: Storytelling for Social Change.* Walnut Creek, CA: Left Coast Press.

Zuber-Skerritt, O. (2002). The concept of action learning. *Learning Organization, 9*(3), 114–124. http://dx.doi.org/10.1108/09696470210428831

Contributors

Eileen Antone is a member of the Oneida of the Thames First Nation–Turtle Clan. She is professor emeritus from the University of Toronto. Dr. Antone has many years of experience advocating for Aboriginal perspectives. Her research, professional writing, teaching, and field development has been focused on Aboriginal knowledge and traditional ways of being.

Jean Bacon has worked in HIV/AIDS since 1985. Her focus is on using research as well as front-line experience to identify and analyse trends and to influence policy and practice. She is the senior director of the Ontario HIV Treatment Network's Policy and Knowledge Translation and Exchange and a co-principal investigator in Universities Without Walls.

Jessica Ball, M.P.H., Ph.D., is a professor in the School of Child and Youth Care at the University of Victoria. Dr. Ball is the principal investigator of an interdisciplinary, grant-funded program of community-engaged research on the cultural nature of child and family development (www.ecdip.org). She is the author or co-author of over 100 journal articles and book chapters and three books.

Leslie Brown, Ph.D., is a professor in the School of Social Work and Director of the Institute for Studies and Innovation in Community-University Engagement at the University of Victoria. She is the co-editor of *Research as Resistance: Critical, Indigenous and Anti-Oppressive Approaches*.

Darlene E. Clover, Ph.D., is a professor in the Faculty of Education at the University of Victoria. Her areas of focus include community and cultural leadership and feminist and arts-based adult education and research. Her most recent book is entitled *Lifelong Learning, The Arts and Community Engagement in Contemporary Universities: International Perspectives.*

Jon Corbett, Ph.D., is an associate professor of Geography in Community Culture and Global Studies at the University of British Columbia–Okanagan. His areas of research interest include participatory mapping and the facilitation and promotion of community and ecosystem-based models of land and resource use in communities in Australia, Indonesia, the Philippines, and British Columbia, Canada.

Jeff Corntassel, Cherokee Nation, Ph.D., is an associate professor in Indigenous Governance at the University of Victoria. Dr. Corntassel's research interests include sustainable self-determination and insurgent education. His forthcoming book is a co-edited volume (with Tom Holm) entitled *The Power of Peoplehood: Regenerating Indigenous Nations.*

Jennifer Coverdale was a student in the University of Victoria's Aboriginal Communities Counselling Program.

Teresa Dawson is the director of the Learning and Teaching Centre and senior instructor in Geography at the University of Victoria. Her areas of interest include effective teaching assessment, faculty and graduate student professional development, supporting and enhancing diversity in the academy, and achieving teaching and learning-related institutional change, particularly regarding curricular reform and community-based scholarship.

Sandrina de Finney, Ph.D., is an associate professor in the School of Child and Youth Care at the University of Victoria and research adviser with the Siem Smun'eem Indigenous Child Welfare Research Network.

Elizabeth Donald currently lives in Campbell River. She wants to get into politics, and more specifically, to be prime minister. She finds joy in making the world a better place.

Catherine Etmanski, Ph.D., is an assistant professor in the School of Leadership Studies at Royal Roads University (RRU). She is also the first year Program Head for the Master's of Arts in Leadership. She taught various courses at the University of Victoria (UVic) between 2005 and 2011 and was awarded for excellence in her pedagogical approach. Dr. Etmanski also worked closely with UVic's Office of Community-Based Research and Learning and Teaching Centre to organize the workshop series that generated this book.

Samantha Etzel (Pi̱telá005_T) was a student in the University of Victoria's Aboriginal Communities Counselling Program who worked with the Wsáneć community as a Senćoṯen language apprentice.

Adam Gaudry is Métis and an assistant professor in the Department of Native Studies at the University of Saskatchewan. His doctoral work in Indigenous Governance at the University of Victoria (UVic) focused on the historical development of Métis governance and political thought in the nineteenth-century North-West. During 2012–2013, he was the Henry Roe Cloud Fellow at Yale University.

Jacquie Green (traditional name, Kundouqk), from the Haisla territories, is a Ph.D. candidate and associate professor at the School of Social Work, University of Victoria, and project manager for the Indigenous Child Welfare Research Network.

Budd L. Hall, Ph.D., is a professor in the School of Public Administration at the University of Victoria (UVic), secretary of the Global Alliance for Community Engaged Research, UNESCO co-chair in Community-Based Research together with Dr. Rajesh Tandon, and the founding director of the Office of Community-Based Research at UVic. He is also a poet.

Tamara Herman is a community organizer, independent journalist, and researcher who has been active for over 10 years with a diverse range of groups and collectives working for justice, dignity, and self-determination. She is the research coordinator at the Vancouver Island Public Interest Research Group (VIPIRG) and recently completed a Master's degree in Studies in Policy and Practice at the University of Victoria.

Francisco Ibáñez-Carrasco is the director of Education and Training at the Ontario HIV Treatment Network. He is the driving force behind Universities Without Walls, a Strategic Training Health Research

Initiative funded by the Canadian Institutes of Health Research. He writes on sexuality and gay men living with HIV.

Shelly Johnson (traditional Saulteaux name, Mukwa Musayett), Ed.D. is an assistant professor at the School of Social Work, University of British Columbia (UBC-Vancouver). Her Indigenist research interests include international work to Indigenize the academy, national First Nations court (justice), Indigenous women in political leadership, Indigenous child health, well-being and educational issues.

Vivian Leik, M.A., is a co-op coordinator at the University of Victoria, where she collaborates with community partners to develop experiential learning opportunities for students both locally and internationally. Her interests include Indigenous knowledge and pedagogy from global contexts and developing cultural understandings to deepen intercultural connections.

Elicia Loiselle is an activist/youth worker/researcher who has worked over the past 12 years in the fields of sexual health, women's and queer rights/health, counselling, youth work, and sexualized violence prevention. She is committed to participatory, action-oriented approaches to research that mobilize the knowledge and resistance of marginalized communities and incite social change.

Maeve Lydon is the associate director of the Institute for Studies and Innovation in Community-University Engagement at the University of Victoria where she focuses on partnership development between campuses and multisector groups. She has worked with local and national NGOs for 30 years in the areas of human rights, community development, participatory learning, and sustainability. She is on the International Advisory for Green Map.

E. Anne Marshall, Ph.D., R.Psych., is a professor of Counselling Psychology and the director of the Centre for Youth and Society at the University of Victoria. Her research interests include emerging adulthood transitions and identity, mental health in cultural and Indigenous contexts, counselling interventions, life-career development, qualitative methodologies, and knowledge exchange.

Shanne McCaffrey, M.A., is from the Métis Nation and senior instructor in the School of Child and Youth Care at the University of Victoria.

Nancy McFarland is Dakota/Ojicree from Sioux Valley, Manitoba, and a clinical counsellor. She has 8 years' experience working with urban Aboriginal families in the helping field. She is currently a family development worker for Hulitan Family and Community Services Society. Her areas of interest include applying a family-centred approach to counselling Aboriginal communities.

Ruby Peterson (Pankwalas) was a student in the Aboriginal Communities Counselling Program at the University of Victoria.

Ted Riecken, Ph.D., is dean of the Faculty of Education and an associate professor in the Department of Curriculum and Instruction at the University of Victoria. His current research project, Traditional Pathways to Health, involves a collaborative partnership working with First Nations students and their teachers to produce short educational videos on health and wellness.

Sean B. Rourke received his Ph.D. in Clinical Neuropsychology from the University of California–San Diego. He is currently the scientific and executive director of the Ontario HIV Treatment Network; director of the Canadian Institutes of Health Research Centre for REACH in HIV/AIDS and of Universities Without Walls; scientist at St. Michael's Hospital in Toronto; and professor of Psychiatry at the University of Toronto. He is internationally recognized for his work in neuro-AIDS.

Agata Stypka recently completed a Master of Arts degree in the Department of Educational Psychology and Leadership at the University of Victoria (UVic). While at UVic, she worked for the Knowledge Mobilization Unit and supported the development of the Multidisciplinary Research Internship courses. She is currently a consultant and research associate in higher education.

Michele Tanaka, Ph.D., has been an educator for over 30 years in a variety of contexts across the life span. She currently works with pre-service teachers at the University of Victoria. Her research interests include Indigenous education, learning and teaching in cross-cultural settings, transformative learning communities, and Transformative Inquiry.

Ruth Taylor was one of the first girls to attend Artemis Place and, in June 2009, became the first to graduate from Grade 12 in the program. As a co-researcher in Project Artemis, she co-directed the film

The Artemis Effect: When Girls Talk Back. She is pursuing higher education in Toronto.

Joaquin Trapero, Ph.D., is the Knowledge Mobilization manager in the Office of Research Services at the University of Victoria (UVic). Dr. Trapero spearheaded the Multidisciplinary Research Internship (MDRI) initiative, which originally blossomed as a joint undertaking with York University. As the coordinator, his vision is to share the UVic's research with the community and have UVic learn from the community's needs.

Lorna Williams, Ed.D., is Lil'wat from the St'at'yem'c First Nation. She holds the Canada Research Chair in Indigenous Knowledge and Learning at the University of Victoria, and and is the current chair of the board of directors for First Peoples Culture Council. She is the former director of Aboriginal Teacher Education and the previous director of the Aboriginal Education Enhancement Branch at the BC Ministry of Education. She also served as a First Nations Education Specialist with the Vancouver School Board.

Mark Willson is a Ph.D. student in Political Science at the University of Victoria, and interim research coordinator at the Vancouver Island Public Interest Research Group (VIPIRG) where he is currently working with grassroots community organizations to investigate and address the implementation of harm reduction services, the policing of poverty, and the neo-liberalization of postsecondary education.

Catherine Worthington, Ph.D., is associate professor in the School of Public Health and Social Policy, University of Victoria. She partners with communities vulnerable to HIV in Canada to conduct community-based research to improve community health and social services. She is chair of the Universities Without Walls HIV health training program.

Index

A7xekcal (developing one's gifts), 240. *See also* Lil'wat pedagogy

Aboriginal, use of term, 208. *See also* Indigenous

Aboriginal Adult Literacy Project, 299–300

Aboriginal Communities Counselling Program (ACCP), 206, *207*, 208. *See also* counsellor education in Indigenous communities

action research (AR), 6, 7, 14, 160

adult education principles, 189–90

AIDS. *See* HIV/AIDS research and training

Alfred, Taiaiake, 167, 175–6, 183, 184

The Ally Bill of Responsibilities, 171, 183–4

alternative education PAR. *See* girl-centred PAR

Antone, Eileen, 21, 287–307

AR. *See* action research (AR)

The Artemis Effect (film), 46, 52, 59, 60–1, 66–8

Artemis Place, Victoria, 18–19, 52. *See also* girl-centred PAR

arts-based research: art appreciation, 283; art communities and map-ping, 120–1; artistry and artists, 142–4, 282, 326n1; art materials, 140; arts-based processes, 265–70; arts-based vs. arts-informed research, 137–8; "everyone is an artist," 328n2; in girl-centred PAR, 48–9, 60–1, 324nn2–3; and Indigenous insurgent education, 177; knowledge dissemination, 144–5; multiple ways of knowing, 161–3; overview, 136–9, 265–70; social change/justice issues, 145; terminology and traditions, 7. *See also* feminist visual arts–based research

arts-based teaching and learning, 265–84; arts vs. crafts, 280–1, 327n2; community building, 271–4, 281–2; course, 266, 270–1; curriculum model (spiral), 274–9, 276f; emotional power, 268–9, 272, 282; evaluation of programs, 280–2; "everyone is an artist," 328n2; facilitator's guidelines, 272–4; group work, 274, 278, 281–2, 328n4; journals, 275, 277–8; knowledge dissemination, 268,

279–80, 282; overview, 265–70, 282–4; power relations, 271, 272–3; skill sets, 278–9, 280–1; social change/justice issues, 270, 280, 282–4; student-led workshops, 275, 278–81; students, 270–1, 280

assessment of learners: health training with online collaboration, 194–5, 321–2; Indigenous teaching and learning, 242, 246, 250–1; personal skills, 15. See also evaluation of programs

A'tola'nw program, 209, 224

at-risk youth. See youth at risk

"Auguries of Innocence" (Blake), 290–1

Bacon, Jean, 20, 186–205

Ball, Jessica, 18, 25–44

Barnhardt, R., 103

Blake, William, 290–1

blended course delivery. See health training with online collaboration

Bonnette, Edith, 129–30

Brawer, Wendy, 118–19

Brennan, Samantha, 128

Brown, Leslie, 19, 93–112

Bryce, Cheryl, 17, 179, 180

Burnett, Charles, 125

Canadian Institutes of Health Research, 183, 186, 193, 220, 254

Cartesan, Monique, 49, 60–1

CBPR. See community-based participatory research

CBR. See community-based research

celhcelh (responsibility for learning). See Lil'wat pedagogy

Centre. See Learning and Teaching Centre (UVic)

Change Labs, 323n1

Chekonen. See Lekwungen

Cherokees, 176, 180

children. See early childhood development; education (K–12)

child welfare training in Indigenous communities, 93–112; evaluation of programs, 103–10; funding, 103; historical background, 98, 100–2; in local communities, 95–9, 103–5; and non-Indigenous research, 105–10, 314; overview, 93–8, 110–12; participants, 97–8, 103–4, 108–9; power relations, 107–8; principles of ICBR, 96; principles of Indigenous research (4R), 103–4; respect for protocols, 95, 97, 98, 99–102; sense of place, 17, 93, 95–9, 103–5; social change/justice issues, 111–12; storytelling, 111; traditional symbols and research metaphors, 99–102, 109–10; training content, 97–8, 105–12; training resources, 94–5, 97, 110–11

class and critical PAR. See critical PAR

Clover, Darlene, 19, 135–49

Coast Salish: basket weaving as research metaphor, 99–100, 102; language revitalization, 215–17

Common Ground mapping project, 114, 118, 119, 125

community and university research partnerships, 25–44; community benefits, 31–4, 39–40; comparison of university and community, 29–30; ethical space, 28, 41; funding, 35–6, 40–1; guiding principles, 26, 37; ice fishing metaphor, 25–6, 43, 308; knowledge dissemination,